MOSCOW MONUMENTAL

MOSCOW MONUMENTAL

Soviet Skyscrapers and Urban Life in Stalin's Capital

KATHERINE ZUBOVICH

PRINCETON UNIVERSITY PRESS
PRINCETON AND OXFORD

Published by Princeton University Press
41 William Street, Princeton, New Jersey 08540
6 Oxford Street, Woodstock, Oxfordshire OX20 1TR

press.princeton.edu

All Rights Reserved

Library of Congress Cataloging-in-Publication Data
Names: Zubovich, Katherine, author.
Title: Moscow monumental : Soviet skyscrapers and urban life in Stalin's capital / Katherine Zubovich.
Description: Princeton, New Jersey : Princeton University Press, 2020. | Includes bibliographical references and index.
Identifiers: LCCN 2020011491 (print) | LCCN 2020011492 (ebook) | ISBN 9780691178905 (hardcover) | ISBN 9780691205298 (ebook)
Subjects: LCSH: Stalinskie Vysotki (Moscow, Russia) | Skyscrapers—Russia (Federation)—Moscow. | Architecture—Composition, proportion, etc. | Communism and architecture—Russia (Federation)—Moscow. | Architecture and society—Russia (Federation)—Moscow. | Moscow (Russian Federation)—Buildings, structures, etc.
Classification: LCC NA6234.R82 M679 2020 (print) | LCC NA6234.R82 (ebook) | DDC 720/.483094731—dc23
LC record available at https://lccn.loc.gov/2020011491
LC ebook record available at https://lccn.loc.gov/2020011492

British Library Cataloging-in-Publication Data is available

Editorial: Priya Nelson, Thalia Leaf
Production Editorial: Terri O'Prey
Text Design: Carmina Alvarez
Jacket/Cover Design: Monograph/Matt Avery
Production: Danielle Amatucci
Publicity: James Schneider, Kate Farquhar-Thomson

Jacket/Cover Credit: Construction of Moscow State University, 1951. From the Collection of the Moscow City Archive GBU

This book has been composed in Charis SIL

Printed on acid-free paper. ∞

Printed in the United States of America

1 3 5 7 9 10 8 6 4 2

FOR GENE

Contents

Acknowledgments

This book would not have been possible without the support of advisors, colleagues, family, and friends and I am glad to have this opportunity to express my thanks. Above all, I am grateful to Yuri Slezkine, Victoria Frede, and Greg Castillo. This book began through conversations with them at Berkeley a decade ago and their continued support has sustained me in this project. I also thank the two reviewers of the book, Steven Harris and Richard Anderson. Their generous comments on the manuscript improved it in innumerable ways.

I am grateful to the many librarians and archivists who assisted me as I worked in collections in Russia and the US. Thank you to Liladhar Pendse for advice on Berkeley's collection and to the archivists at the Hoover Institute at Stanford University. I also thank the archivists and staff at the Russian State Archive of the Economy, the State Archive of the Russian Federation, the Main Archival Administration of the City of Moscow, the Memorial Society Archive in Moscow, the Russian State Archive of Literature and Art, the Russian State Archive of Social-Political History, the Russian State Archive of Contemporary History, and the A. V. Shchusev State Museum of Architecture. I am also grateful to Mueser Rutledge Consulting Engineers for allowing me access to archived files relating to the firm's work in the 1930s on the Palace of Soviets. I am thankful also to the archivists, librarians, and experts who curate and maintain a growing collection of digital resources, including Prozhito, the Memorial Society Archive digital maps, and the Wilson Center digital archive.

This book benefitted from the generosity, collegiality, advice, and commentary of many individuals, including Anna Alekseyeva, Alan Barenberg, Stephen Bittner, David Boyk, Andra Chastain, Jean-Louis Cohen, Kathleen Conti, Christina Crawford, Tom Cubbin, Heather DeHaan, Jeff Hardy, James Heinzen, Anna Ivanova, Tatiana Klepikova, Nancy Kwak, Katherine Lebow, Nicholas Levy, Michał Murawski, Mila Oiva, Anatoly Pinsky, Cynthia Ruder, Deirdre Ruscitti Harshman, Sarah Selvidge, Andrew Shanken, Iuliia Skubytska, Danilo Udovički-Selb, Lynne Viola, Milya Zakirova, and those involved in the Second World Urbanity network. I am also grateful for feedback I received from members of the University of Toronto Russian history reading group and U of T's Slavic Languages and Literatures seminar series. I also thank Art Blake, Jenny Carson, and Rob Teigrob at Ryerson University. I am grateful for the research assistance of Hareda Fakhrudin and Mira Golubeva. Thank you also to Margaret Boittin, Emily Nacol, Tameka Grimes, Alea Holman, and Cassondra Marshall for their support and encouragement.

Very special thanks go to my cohort of Russianists at Berkeley and to cohorts above ours who consistently offer their mentorship and support. For their comments on the earliest drafts of these chapters, I am grateful to David Beecher, Michael Coates, Rhiannon Dowling, Bathsheba Demuth, Clarissa Ibarra, Eric Johnson, Joseph Kellner, Emiliana Kissova, Thomas Lowish, Hilary Lynd, Jason Morton, Joy Neumeyer, Brandon Schechter, Charles Shaw, Yana Skorobogatov, and Mirjam Voerkelius. Thank you also to Nicole Eaton, Christine Evans, Eleonory Gilburd, Alexis Peri, Erik Scott, and Victoria Smolkin. I am also thankful for the support I have received from mentors, colleagues, and friends Seth Bernstein, Courtney Doucette, Orysia Kulick, Angelina Lucento, Tracy McDonald, Natalie Mendoza, Megan Swift, Lilia Topouzova, Joseph Torigian, and Serhy Yekelchyk. In Moscow, I thank Svetlana Frantsevna Pokrovskaia for her kindness and hospitality and Aleksandr and Natallia Koshmar for their friendship. I am especially grateful to Natalia Melikova for her permission to use two of her photographs in this book. Natalia's photography of Moscow over the last decade will be an invaluable source for generations of historians to come.

I would like to thank the editors of *Kritika* for permission to use parts of a previously published article in chapter 5 of this book (from "The Fall of the Zariad'e: Monumentalism and Displacement in Late Stalinist Moscow," *Kritika: Explorations in Russian and Eurasian History* 21, no. 1 [2020]: 73–95). I am delighted to express my gratitude to Brigitta van Rheinberg, Eric Crahan, Thalia Leaf, and the staff at Princeton University Press. I thank Amanda Peery for her incisive comments on the manuscript. I acknowledge financial support received from the Social Sciences and Humanities Research Council of Canada and from the Institute of Slavic, East European, and Eurasian Studies at Berkeley. I am thankful to Edward Walker, Jeffrey Pennington, Zachary Kelly, and Louanna Curley at ISEEES for their support. The publication of this book was also supported by a grant provided by the Office of the Dean of Arts, Ryerson University.

Finally, I thank my family. I am grateful to Mary, Jonathan, Michael, Jen, Steve, Anne, Faina, Mikhail, Dave, Andrea, Margaret, and Adrianne for their support and love. I am grateful also for the support of Janet and Roman, both of whom I deeply miss. To Gene, my husband and intellectual partner, I dedicate this book to you.

Note on Transliteration

Russian words are transliterated in accordance with the simplified Library of Congress system. An exception is made for those words or names with a commonly accepted English transliteration, such as "Mayakovsky" rather than "Maiakovskii."

ABBREVIATIONS

Amtorg:	Amtorg Trading Corporation (*Amerikanskoe aktsionernoe obshchestvo*)
Glavpromstroi:	Main Office of Industrial Construction of the MVD
Gosplan:	State Planning Committee of the Council of Ministers of the USSR (*Gosudarstvennyi planovyi komitet soveta ministrov SSSR*)
Gosstroi:	State Construction Committee (*Gosudarstvennyi komitet SSSR po delam stroitel'stva*) Exists from 1950–1991
Gulag:	Main Administration of Camps (*Glavnoe upravlenie lagerei*)
Komsomol:	All-Union Leninist Young Communist League (*Vsesoiuznyi Leninskii kommunisticheskii soiuz molodezhi*)
Oblast':	province or administrative subdivision of a Union Republic
MGU:	Moscow State University (*Moskovskii gosudarstvennyi universitet*)
MID:	Ministry of Foreign Affairs of the USSR (*Ministerstvo inostrannikh del SSSR*)
Minaviaprom:	Ministry of Aviation Industries of the USSR (*Ministerstvo aviatsionnoi promyshlennosti SSSR*)
Mingorstroi:	Ministry of Urban Construction of the USSR (*Ministerstvo gorodskogo stroitel'stva SSSR*) Replaces State Architecture Committee, exists from 1949–1951, offices transferred to Gosstroi in 1951
Mintiazhstroi:	Ministry of Construction of Heavy Industry of the USSR (*Ministerstvo stroitel'stva predpriatii tiazheloi industrii SSSR*)
Minvoenmorstroi:	Ministry of Construction of Army and Navy Industries of the USSR (*Ministerstvo stroitel'stva voennykh i voenno-morskikh predpriatii SSSR*)

MPS: Ministry of Railways of the USSR (*Ministerstvo putei soobshcheniia SSSR*)

MVD: Ministry of Internal Affairs of the USSR (*Ministerstvo vnutrennikh del SSSR*)

Narkompros: People's Commissariat of Education (*Narodnyi komissariat prosveshcheniia*)

NCASF: National Council of American-Soviet Friendship

RSFSR: Russian Soviet Federative Socialist Republic (*Rossiiskaia sovetskaia federativnaia sotsialisticheskaia respublika*)

Sovmin: USSR Council of Ministers (*Sovet ministrov SSSR*)

State Architecture   Committee on the Affairs of Architecture of the Sovnarkom/
Committee: Sovmin SSSR (*Komitet po delam arkhitektury pri Sovnarkome SSSR*) Existed from 1943–1949, replaced by Mingorstroi

UIA: International Union of Architects

USDS: Administration for the Construction of the Palace of Soviets (*Upravlenie stroitel'stva dvortsa sovetov*)

VOKS: All-Union Society for Cultural Ties Abroad (*Vsesoiuznoe obshchestvo kul'turnoi sviazi s zagranitsei*)

ZhKO: Communal housing office (*zhilishchno-kommunal'nyi otdel*)

MOSCOW MONUMENTAL

INTRODUCTION

In 1947, Soviet architects and engineers embarked on a project to transform the cityscape of the Soviet capital through the construction of eight skyscrapers. When seven of these monumental buildings were completed in the 1950s, they would serve as elite apartment complexes, as luxury hotels, and as the headquarters of Moscow State University, the Ministry of Railways, and the Ministry of Foreign Affairs. Yet, in 1947, the function of Moscow's skyscrapers was secondary to the role these structures were to play collectively on the cityscape. These buildings stood as monuments to Soviet victory in the Great Patriotic War, as pillars of Russian cultural achievement, and as evidence of the USSR's emergence as a world superpower in the postwar era. The skyscrapers were designed with the express purpose of transforming Moscow into a world-class capital city—as Stalin put it, "the capital of all capitals."[1] Monumental by design, Moscow's skyscraper project had far-reaching consequences for the urban fabric of the Soviet capital and its inhabitants alike.

This book is a study of monumentalism and its consequences. It is a history of efforts during the Stalin era to transform Moscow from a provincial and run-down former Russian capital into *the* showcase socialist city. In the 1930s, Soviet officials and leading architects began to implement large-scale building projects in Moscow, including the Moscow-Volga Canal and the first lines of the Moscow metro. Construction of the Palace of Soviets also got underway during the 1930s. This enormous structure would have been the tallest building in the world had it been completed as planned. While in the interwar period Muscovites celebrated the construction of the large underground palaces of the metro, they would have to wait until the postwar years to witness the emergence of tall towers on their cityscape.

Moscow's postwar skyscraper project built upon the work begun in the interwar years with an even more ambitious program. The vision for the capital that emerged in 1947 placed the still-unbuilt Palace of Soviets at the center of a citywide skyscraper ensemble. With the Palace in the middle, there were to be nine skyscrapers in all. And although in the end only seven of these structures were completed, the desired effect was achieved. Each building is positioned at some distance from the next, elevating the cityscape with staccato peaks that gaze toward one another across the city below. The similarities between these tiered, ornate structures serve to unite the cityscape, creating a sense of continuity and repetition along the horizon. Moscow's skyscrapers continue to stand today as the quintessential architectural works of the Stalin era. Collectively, they are known, in English, as the "seven sisters." In Russian, they are known as Stalin's "*vysotki*." Together, they made, and make, Moscow monumental.

■ ■ ■

There is nothing new about architectural monumentalism. In fact, many who study this phenomenon are experts in the history of the ancient world. As archaeologist Bruce Trigger explains, architecture is monumental when its scale exceeds the practical function that the building is intended to perform.[2] Whether it is a residential structure or a public building, that which exists in excess of pure necessity is, by this definition, part of what makes the building "monumental." This is not to say that monumentalism is without function. Monumental structures do more than simply contain and shelter people and things; they also guard and convey meaning and memory. From palaces to temples to tombs, monumental architecture throughout history has served the purpose of honoring one's connection to the sacred and communicating the right to rule. Building monumentally typically serves an official purpose, tied as it is to the desire to project power or make a statement. Whether it is a pyramid or a ziggurat, a Gothic cathedral or a skyscraper, monumentality has proven useful to many societies throughout history. The Soviet Union was no exception.

The Soviet Union under Stalin was, among twentieth-century societies, one of the most enamored with architectural monumentalism. In Moscow in the 1930s, the question of architectural monumentality was brought to the fore by the Palace of Soviets. This building project prompted not just architects and engineers, but ordinary Soviet citizens as well, to reflect on monumentalism. What was the purpose of monumental structures in a "proletarian" state? What symbols and values should they communicate? While the Palace of Soviets was to stand as a monument to an individual—Lenin—it was also a structure that would bring together the collective. As Henri Lefebvre put it when commenting on the long global history of building monumentally, "monumental space offered each member of a society an image of that membership, an image of his or her social visage. It thus constituted a collective mirror more faithful than any personal one."[3] That Soviet citizens might look up at the Palace of Soviets and see themselves was precisely the point.

But the Palace of Soviets was never finished. Instead, in 1947 work began in Moscow on eight other structures, seven of which were completed. The Palace of Soviets would remain an important icon through the Stalin years, but only its progeny—a ring of skyscrapers—would take real form. While historians have typically focused on the idealized visions for Moscow's iconic structures, this book looks at what happened when monumental plan met material reality during the final years of the Stalin era. From the displacement of residents to the downfall of architectural and political elites, Moscow's skyscrapers changed the course of political, social, and cultural life in the Soviet capital. Insofar as they served as mirrors in which each individual could understand their place in the collective (to borrow Lefebvre's phrase), Moscow's skyscrapers reflected different images to different people. This book explores what those diverse groups, from architects to workers to residents, saw in these buildings.

■ ■ ■

The enormous energy dedicated to making Moscow monumental brought with it a number of consequences specific to the Soviet, and Stalinist, context: it fostered internationalism, reshaped the city of Moscow in unintended ways, and served as an opportunity to connect the Soviet capital to the pre-revolutionary Russian past. First, Soviet architectural monumentalism compelled Moscow's architects to engage with the wider world beyond socialist borders. In their work on the Palace of Soviets in the 1930s, Moscow's architects went abroad, seeking technical knowledge that would enable them to build ever higher. In 1934, Palace of Soviets architect Boris Iofan led a group of his colleagues on a study tour of major building sites across the United States. On this trip, Iofan and his team hired a New York-based engineering firm to assist with work on the Palace of Soviets in Moscow. And when they were in Manhattan, the Soviet group toured the Rockefeller Center construction site, where they made lasting connections to the American building industry. The relationship between Soviet internationalism and monumentalism changed in the postwar years, when the focus shifted from the dream of the Palace of Soviets to the construction of eight other skyscrapers. Moscow's postwar skyscrapers, in contrast to the never-realized Palace of Soviets, transformed Soviet monumentalism from socialist realist projection to built reality with long-lasting consequences.

Built in the first years of the Cold War, Moscow's skyscrapers signaled a shift in the way the Soviet Union positioned itself globally. Gone were the days when Soviet architects would go abroad—least of all to America—for assistance. Now, architects from the expanding socialist world would flock to Moscow to study the capital city's new buildings. There was newfound irony in transforming the icon of capitalist triumph, the skyscraper, into a symbol of communism. And the message about Soviet supremacy that Moscow's architects sought to convey with their buildings was one that refused to translate beyond socialist borders. Nonetheless, Moscow's skyscrapers played an important role in the shifting dynamics of Soviet internationalism. By examining the 1930s through the 1950s, this book traces the long build-up to the *Zhdanovshchina*: the xenophobic and anti-Western ideological campaigns that dominated Soviet culture in the postwar Stalin period.

Second, this book argues that Stalin-era monumentalism had much larger consequences than its planners and architects originally intended—consequences that affected both the shape of the Soviet capital and the lives of its inhabitants. Moscow's postwar skyscrapers symbolized the stability and longevity of the Stalinist regime in the wake of Soviet victory in 1945. Yet in the day-to-day life of the capital these buildings were destabilizing structures that rose only to create new chasms in late-Stalinist society. In 1952, I. G. Kartashov wrote a letter to Lavrentii Beria, the Soviet official who oversaw the construction of Moscow's eight skyscrapers until his arrest in 1953. Kartashov had worked on the skyscraper at the Red Gates. "I took part in the construction," Kartashov wrote, "and the whole time I cherished a dream that I might be lucky enough to live out my old age in that building."[4] Kartashov dreamed of escaping the damp room he lived in with his family in a communal apartment in Moscow. His hopes, like those of so many others, would not and could not be satisfied by Stalinist monumentalism. While the Soviet state granted apartments in the residential skyscrapers to a number of elites, far more Soviet citizens were left to carry on dreaming.

In addition to creating disillusionment among Muscovites like Kartashov, Moscow's postwar skyscrapers led to disappointment among another group: the tens of thousands of people evicted from their homes and displaced to the outskirts of the city. Monumentalism propelled the urban expansion of Moscow outward, all while solidifying and making ever more visible the social hierarchies of late Stalinism. The project also required the influx of large numbers of construction workers—both free and incarcerated—brought into Moscow from the hinterland. In order to build the skyscrapers, construction managers found themselves tasked with hastily building housing and other amenities for uprooted Muscovites and incoming workers. In tracing how the skyscraper project pushed Moscow's expansion into the forested suburbs, villages, and collective farms around the capital, this book examines how, in requiring so much other construction, the project to build skyscrapers in Moscow was in the end far grander and more all-encompassing than its architects ever imagined.

Finally, this book argues that Moscow's skyscrapers tied the Stalin era to the Russian past in ways that both bolstered and undermined the Soviet state's claims to legitimacy. Designed in stylistic reference to the Kremlin towers, Moscow's monumental new buildings harmonized with the existing cityscape. But these structures also stood as evidence of the tension between history and revolution. The skyscraper project was publicly unveiled in September 1947 during Moscow's 800th anniversary celebrations, an occasion that threatened to overshadow the upcoming thirtieth anniversary of the Bolshevik Revolution. In the lead-up to this new municipal holiday, city officials and residents alike struggled to draw a straight line between the long pre-revolutionary past and the comparatively short Soviet present. Moscow's skyscraper architects faced a similar challenge in early design discussions held in that autumn of 1947. Which past Moscow's skyscrapers should represent—which heritage they should build upon—was a vexing question with no clear answer.

When time came to break ground and build, skyscraper construction managers were confronted by the past in yet another way. In 1949, workers digging the foundation pit for the skyscraper in the *Zariad'e* district unearthed the remains of a settlement more than eight hundred years old. Upturned in the soil lay earthenware vessels, glass bracelets, and other remnants of the distant past. While these objects may well have been ignored in earlier decades, the feverish historicism of the late-Stalin years made them valuable. Construction work on the Zariad'e skyscraper would be delayed while archaeological digs were carried out on the site in 1949 and 1950. Ultimately, the backward glance of late Stalinism both shaped and complicated Moscow's postwar urban transformation. Today, the historical symbolism of the skyscrapers is less complex: they stand out on the Moscow cityscape simply as indelible symbols of Stalinism.

■ ■ ■

Moscow Monumental develops its tripartite argument about international engagement, urban restructuring, and historical ties in eight chapters. The book begins by examining how Moscow was seen and imagined in the late 1920s, in the years immediately following its designation as the Soviet capital and in the period immediately before the city's so-called "socialist reconstruction." The tensions that flared up in this moment between destruction and preservation and between the old and the new would remain alive throughout the subsequent Stalin era.

When Soviet officials began to take charge of the redevelopment of their new capital city in the 1930s, they embarked on a series of iconic projects, including the Palace of Soviets. Although it was never completed, the Palace was the cornerstone of interwar debates about urban monumentalism, and any history of Stalin's post-war skyscrapers is incomplete without it. This book builds on the established narrative of the Palace's design to also consider its attempted construction. Not only did this gargantuan structure provide a stylistic precedent for the city's postwar monumental development, its construction established important institutional structures and international ties. Moscow's, and the Soviet Union's, experience at war starting in 1941 also served as a crucial step on the path to postwar monumentalism. Before turning to the postwar period, the third chapter of this book explores Muscovites' wartime ordeals, including the flight of the Palace of Soviets architects to the Urals in 1941.

With the fourth chapter, the book turns to Moscow's postwar skyscraper project by analyzing the design and planning process that led up to construction. Top Soviet leaders and architects were influenced in their discussions in 1947 by the broader political and cultural context of the postwar Stalin era. The postwar ideological campaign, known as the *Zhdanovshchina*, and the Cold War more generally, influenced the planning process in fundamental ways, ensuring that Moscow's skyscrapers would be conceived as examples of both Soviet world supremacy and Russian national achievement. When the skyscraper project got underway, however, idealized plans had unintended consequences on the ground. The fifth chapter of this book focuses on Moscow's Zariad'e, the district chosen for skyscraper development closest to the Kremlin. This chapter examines the buildings, people, and pasts that existed already on the plots chosen for skyscraper development. It describes how social differentiation was embedded in Moscow's urban terrain as tens of thousands of Muscovites were moved away from the skyscraper plots to new housing built for them on the outskirts of the capital.

The book moves in its final chapters to the histories of those who built and those who lived in Moscow's skyscrapers. These chapters explore how skyscraper building served as a means through which both the state and the self could be rebuilt after the war. Chapter 6 follows the experiences of builders, both regular workers and Gulag laborers, who came mainly from regions beyond Moscow. This chapter weighs the idealized skyscraper builder—the "*vysotnik*"—against the reality of life on these construction sites. Chapter 7 turns to investigate the lives of Soviet elites who requested apartments in the residential skyscrapers. This elect group sought to escape Moscow's housing crisis by appealing to top officials for apartments in one of the city's new towers. Drawing on letters of request written to Beria and other Soviet leaders, Chapter 7 explores the hope and disappointment that Moscow's skyscrapers represented in the popular and elite imaginations. Those who created and those who benefited from the skyscrapers, like those displaced for them, were compelled to engage directly with the Soviet state. As Chapters 5 through 7 show, architectural monumentalism served not only to reshape the skyline of the Soviet capital, but also to reframe relations between state and society in the final years of the Stalin era.

At the very moment Moscow's skyscrapers were completed in the mid-1950s, they became symbols of Stalinist "excess." The final chapter of *Moscow Monumental* charts Nikita Khrushchev's attack at the Builders' Conference in December 1954 on these structures and on the architects who built them. Moscow's monumental buildings were swiftly cast as villains in the battle against uneconomical design. Yet the capital's new skyscrapers, as useful as they were monumental, continued to dominate the cityscape. During the Khrushchev era, Moscow State University, in particular, served as a key site of the Thaw. And when identical buildings were given as "gifts" to Eastern European capitals in the 1950s, the Stalinist skyscraper cast its long shadow from Moscow to Warsaw, Riga, Prague, Bucharest, and Kiev.

■   ■   ■

In the trajectory of Stalinist construction projects, Moscow's skyscrapers were late arrivals. The smokestacks of Magnitogorsk had been billowing for two decades by the time the skyscrapers made their debut in the Soviet capital. Through the 1930s, industrialization drove urban development across the Soviet Union.[5] Moscow's postwar refashioning was different. The buildings that made Stalinism legible on the skyline of the Soviet capital appeared at the moment that the Stalinist regime was coming to an end. This timing has had an effect on how the skyscrapers are seen—or, often, not seen—by historians.

It was Nikita Khrushchev who first provided the script still used to interrogate Moscow's skyscrapers today. In his speech at the Builders' Conference in 1954, Khrushchev denigrated Moscow's new buildings, casting them aside as remnants of an earlier, illegitimate past. That Moscow's skyscrapers were so closely associated with Stalin himself made them particularly good targets in 1954. In his speech, Khrushchev characterized Moscow's skyscrapers as frivolous, wasteful buildings that epitomized Stalinist "excess." The rising Soviet leader provided the template by which historians have understood these buildings ever since. This book looks beyond Khrushchev's template to tell a more complicated story about how these buildings were designed and constructed—and what they reveal about life in the Soviet capital during late Stalinism. We may well agree with Khrushchev's characterization of Moscow's skyscrapers, but in order to understand these buildings historically, we must view them through the lens of late-Stalinism, not through the script of de-Stalinization.

Historians have also overlooked Moscow's skyscrapers, even though they loom so prominently on the city's horizon, because much of the scholarly literature on Stalinist architecture in Moscow focuses on the Palace of Soviets. This unbuilt structure is often seen as the most significant and symbolic architectural monument of the Stalin era, while also serving as a central metaphor for the grand ambitions and real-world failures of Stalinism. The Palace of Soviets lends itself well to moralizing narratives of the Soviet Union's foolishness and hubris: the failure to build the Palace of Soviets is equated with the failure of the Soviet project more broadly.

As monumental structures that were actually built, Moscow's skyscrapers have much to tell us about the eight or so years that make up the late-Stalin period. The skyscrapers embody the contradictions of their era: they are ornate, monumental structures built at a time of deep physical and economic devastation. Moscow's skyscrapers represented both the hope of a grand Soviet capital and the disillusionment of displaced populations and workers who would never be allowed to live in the buildings they constructed. In her foundational work on the postwar period, Elena Zubkova shows how hope gave way to disillusionment in a restless postwar society. She observes that this disillusionment was kept in check in the final years of the Stalin era by an increasingly repressive state.[6] As this book shows, architectural monumentalism served to encapsulate and intensify many of the continuities and changes that characterized postwar life in the Soviet capital.

In numerous ways, late Stalinism saw a return to patterns of the 1930s. The *Zhdanovshchina*, the Leningrad Affair, and the "Doctors' Plot" were all reminiscent of the purges of the pre-war years. But less repressive measures of state control carried into the postwar period as well. The social and cultural "embourgeoisement" that characterized Soviet society in the 1930s returned as the Stalinist state continued after the war to reward its most loyal citizens with the promise of "middle-class" lifestyles. The good life might take the form of a holiday on the Black Sea coast or a skyscraper apartment, both of which were part of an agreement between the postwar state and society that Vera Dunham has labeled the "Big Deal."[7] The war itself also served to prolong and intensify pre-war initiatives. Official efforts to elevate Russian national sentiment and shore up the cult of Stalin gained added strength from Soviet victory in 1945.[8] The Gulag system that swelled in the years of the Great Terror continued to expand during the war and into the postwar period, when forced labor became a crucial instrument for the country's reconstruction.[9] In rebuilding Soviet cities after the war, planners and officials turned to the prewar past for inspiration. But they also faced concerns and challenges that were unique to the postwar years.[10]

The late-Stalin era saw a return to the past, but this period also ushered in new developments, some of which bring these years more in line with what was to come during the Khrushchev era. Juliane Fürst argues that late Stalinism was a time of contradiction and flux. This "Janus-faced" period, she writes, was "as much about reinvention as it was about reconstruction."[11] Fürst and others have questioned the break typically seen in 1953, stressing continuities from the late-Stalinist into the Khrushchev and Brezhnev eras.[12] In cutting across four historical moments—the Stalinist 1930s, the war, the postwar Stalin era, and the Khrushchev period—this book engages with questions of continuity and discontinuity. The skyscrapers that stand at the center of this book echoed the architecture of the planned Palace of Soviets and drew inspiration from other ambitious urban projects of the 1930s. At the same time, they reflected the Soviet Union's efforts to reposition itself internationally after 1945.

This is the first book about Moscow's Stalinist skyscrapers that is grounded in archival sources. Earlier studies have relied mainly on the extensive record of published materials relating to these buildings, while often foregrounding aesthetic questions.[13] This book, by contrast, draws on archival material from both Russian and American collections. Documents from the Russian State Archive of the Economy, the State Archive of the Russian Federation, and the Moscow City Archives form the archival basis of the book. Archival sources address questions about how and why these buildings were built while also bringing new voices into this history. From residents who watched the skyscrapers emerge on the horizon of their city, to construction workers who built Moscow's skyscrapers, and on to those who were permitted to live in these structures—the archives are full of their stories.

■ ■ ■

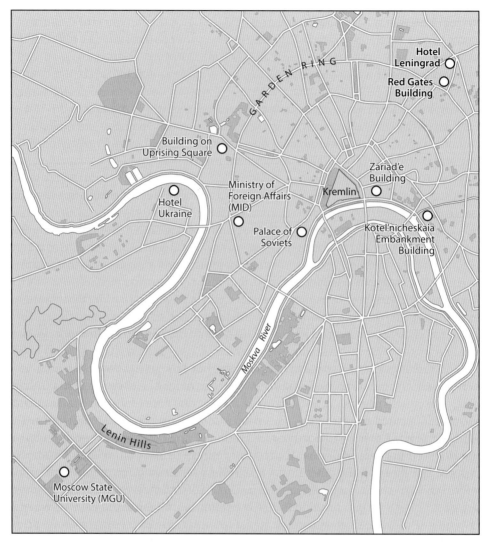

Figure I.1: Map of Moscow c. 1950s with Stalinist skyscrapers marked.
Map by Cox Cartographic Ltd.

Anyone who has spent time in Moscow knows the buildings discussed in this book well. Today, nearly seventy years after their completion, Moscow's Stalin-era skyscrapers continue to serve in their original roles as key residential, institutional, and tourist sites in the city. Built at key junctions throughout the capital—on hilltops, at river bends, and next to railway terminals—these structures mark the horizon even now, in a city that has tripled its 1947 population.

Following the Moscow River as it winds its way into the city from the northwest, we come first to the Hotel Ukraine. This building, which stands on the southern bank of the river near the Kiev Train Station, was the last of the skyscrapers to be completed in 1957. For many decades to come, it would host foreign dignitaries and tourists in its opulent interiors. Across the river to the north stands the residential skyscraper on Uprising Square. Completed in 1954, this building faces toward the

Garden Ring Road, then the largest of Moscow's circular arteries. To the south and across the Garden Ring stands the headquarters of the Ministry of Foreign Affairs (MID), a building completed in 1953. Just as the hotel is still a hotel, and the residential skyscraper still contains apartments, this last building remains the headquarters of MID in Moscow today.

Heading back along the river from the MID skyscraper we arrive at the showpiece structure of the lot: Moscow State University (MGU). This thirty-six-story building stands tall above the riverbank below, overlooking the city from its place atop the Sparrow Hills, or Lenin Hills as they were called in the 1940s. When it was under construction, the MGU skyscraper was on the outskirts of town. But by the time the first class of students graduated, the southwestern region of Moscow was better connected to the center of the city.

Continuing back along the river, we pass under the bridge along the Garden Ring Road and into central Moscow. Here, not far from the Kremlin, we arrive at the site selected in 1931 for the Palace of Soviets. Still following the river, passing the Kremlin on our left, we see the plot chosen for the skyscraper on the Zariad'e. Neither of these centermost skyscrapers was built to completion, but plans for their construction nonetheless changed the shape of central Moscow. The Zariad'e neighborhood was cleared in the late 1940s and early 1950s to make way for this structure. A handful of churches were left standing on the site and they remain there to this day.

As the river makes its way southward, we come to the Kotel'nicheskaia embankment tower not far from the Zariad'e plot. From the time it was completed in late 1952, Moscow's cultural, scientific, and bureaucratic elites lived in this residential skyscraper, located closest to the city center, not far from the eastern side of the Garden Ring Road. As we head north up this road, we come to the last two skyscrapers. The Hotel Leningrad, built next to a trio of railway terminals, welcomes visitors to Moscow. Not far from the hotel is the skyscraper at the Red Gates, home to the Ministry of Railways and to residents housed in one, two, and three-bedroom apartments.

Moscow's skyscrapers, positioned at key points throughout the capital, were designed to speak loudly, to impress the viewer with the constructive power of the Soviet state. In lifting the Soviet capital skyward, these buildings changed the face of Moscow and altered the course of the city's history.

1

RED MOSCOW

In 1928, the Moscow-based art historian Aleksei A. Sidorov published an album in Berlin of photographs recently taken in New Economic Policy (NEP)-era Moscow (figs 1.1–1.5). In arranging these photographs of the Soviet capital for a German audience, Sidorov drew the reader's attention to the contrasts and "contradictory feelings" that Moscow—the centuries-old "heart of Russia"—elicited in the viewer.[1] Moscow was founded in the twelfth century, and it stood as the center of Russian Tsardom until Peter the Great moved the Russian capital north to St. Petersburg in 1712. When Moscow became a capital city again in 1918, it was of the new Russian Soviet Federative Socialist Republic (the RSFSR), and then of the Union of Soviet Socialist Republics (the USSR) as a whole when the federation was created in 1922. Moscow was an important battleground in the struggles of 1917 and in subsequent years the city served as a stage for the Bolsheviks' new revolutionary politics. Still, a decade after the Bolshevik Revolution many observers and visitors still saw evidence of a former provincialism in Moscow's urban terrain. In 1928, when Sidorov published the 200 photographs that made up his Moscow album, the "socialist reconstruction" of the Soviet capital had scarcely begun.

In the late 1920s, more than mere traces of pre-revolutionary life remained on the cityscape of the Soviet capital. The very structure of the city itself, with its medieval fortress, circular plan, winding lanes, and old stone walls, served as a constant reminder of Moscow's pre-modern, and pre-Petrine, origins. The Kremlin's tall cathedrals still marked the city as sacred ground. In the fifteenth and sixteenth centuries, Muscovite rulers replaced the wooden buildings of the Kremlin with these ornate and durable stone structures, marking Moscow as the symbolic center of their domain. Russia's early rulers communicated their right to rule in monumental cathedrals that drew on varied stylistic influences, from the Italian Renaissance to the architecture of nearby regions newly brought into the realm, like Novgorod and Pskov.[2] Moscow also retained elements in the 1920s of its more recent Imperial-era development. Starting in the 1770s, Catherine II sought to transform Moscow into a modern European city, recasting it in light of her newly enlightened politics. She oversaw infrastructure reforms that brought Moscow up to broader European standards, but the city was largely neglected by her successors.[3]

In the decades prior to 1917, Moscow was shaken by rapid and chaotic urban growth. Like other Russian cities of the late-Imperial period, Moscow suffered under the strains of industrialization, a process that began timidly in Russia in the 1860s, only to take off in the last decade of the nineteenth century before ebbing and flowing in the years of war and revolt that preceded 1917. As a result, Moscow gained a large population of transient, casually employed, and poorly housed industrial workers who maintained close ties to the countryside. Late-imperial Moscow was a merchant city and, as such, its pre-revolutionary urban growth was mainly the product of private economic investment rather than state-led or publicly funded development. The city's social services and public transportation networks were inadequate. Its municipal leaders, beholden to Petersburg, lacked both funding and legitimacy. And at the turn of the twentieth century, Moscow had the distinction of being the unhealthiest large city in all of Europe.[4]

The first decade of Soviet rule saw little improvement. The population of Moscow in 1928 was only slightly higher, at just over 2 million, than it was in early 1917. During the harsh years of the Civil War, the city's population had dipped to just over 1 million. But little by little Moscow grew again, as the Bolshevik approach to governance began to shift in 1921 from the punishing edicts of War Communism to the brief reprieve of NEP. By 1939, when Moscow's "socialist reconstruction" was well underway, the city would boast a population of over 4 million.[5] Rapid and continuous population growth would become a persistent problem in Red Moscow, ensuring that the city's new leaders faced many of the same challenges as their pre-revolutionary counterparts. The Bolsheviks swiftly abolished private property, but this did not solve the problems caused by uncoordinated construction and the rapid influx of new residents from the countryside.[6] Moscow's city planners soon found that whatever advantage they gained in state control of land and buildings they lost in the chaos of daily urban life. In its early decades, Red Moscow was a challenging city to plan and to govern.

PORTRAIT OF A CITY

As the art historian Aleksei Sidorov saw it in the late 1920s, Moscow was "dirty and provincial."[7] In his photo album published in Berlin in 1928, Sidorov worked to make the city legible to foreign eyes. He showed Moscow as a city in the making caught between two worlds, one old and the other new. As Sidorov wrote in the introduction to his album, Moscow was "the liveliest spot in a wide, awakening Russia."[8] "Located at the border between Europe and Asia is Moscow," Sidorov explained,

> Once the City of the Tsars, the heiress of Byzantium, the winner of the fantastic idea of the "Third Rome." Under the emperors of the eighteenth and nineteenth centuries, it was a beautiful provincial town—baroque, lost in thought, and a little lazy. Before the revolution, it was the city of big industrialists, a liberal center of the intelligentsia, of the merchant opposition, and of art collections in which Picasso and Matisse mingled with Russian icons. Then, revolutionary Moscow in the first terrible years of upheaval was starved and neglected, nearing death. And today, Red Moscow, the Soviet capital . . . Of all the cities in the world Moscow may trigger the most contradictory feelings.[9]

In Sidorov's album, Moscow is pictured as a city just beginning to show signs of its vanguard position in world history. New buildings and monuments had begun to appear in the capital and as early as 1918 the new architectural studio established at the Moscow City Council (Mossovet) began work on a general plan that drew on

Figure 1.1: Lenin Mausoleum. Alexys A. Sidorow, *Moskau*, Berlin: Albertus-Verlag, 1928.

elements of British garden-city design.[10] Ivan V. Zholtovskii and Aleksei V. Shchusev, both former members of the Imperial Academy of Arts, headed this studio.[11] Zholtovskii and Shchusev would maintain powerful positions in the Moscow architectural establishment well into the late 1940s, but their initial plan for the new Soviet capital was never implemented; in fact, the city did not adopt the first General Plan for the Reconstruction of Moscow until 1935. In Sidorov's album, the small handful of buildings heralding the emergence of Red Moscow include a mixture of modernist and classicist structures from the experimental 1920s. The new Lenin Institute, boxy and modernist, was one such building.[12] It stood opposite the new Obelisk to the Constitution on Soviet (formerly Tverskaia) Square. The Lenin Mausoleum on Red Square, designed by Shchusev and captured by Sidorov in multiple shots (one of which was reprinted in a 1929 issue of the *New York Times*), was still in its wooden incarnation (fig. 1.1).[13] This temporary structure would soon be replaced by a final version made of granite and marble.

Sidorov also included in his album shots of Moscow's new constructivist architecture, including the tall headquarters of Mossel'prom, the Soviet retail trust that was at the forefront of constructivist-inspired developments in advertising (fig. 1.2). Mossel'prom's portable street kiosks tempted passersby with the slogan "Nowhere else but Mossel'prom" ("*Nigde krome kak v mossel'prome*")—nowhere else could Muscovites find macaroni, sausage, and Red Star caramels with agitational wrappers designed by the futurist poet Vladimir Mayakovsky.[14] Avant-garde buildings, billboards, and kiosks like these made good foils when photographed alongside an older Moscow. A billboard for Avtopromtorg, the Soviet state's new transportation company, is framed in Sidorov's album in juxtaposition to the cobblestone street below,

Figure 1.2: Mossel'prom Building. Alexys A. Sidorow, *Moskau*, Berlin: Albertus-Verlag, 1928.

where horse-drawn cart remained the more common form of transportation (fig. 1.3). As Walter Benjamin observed in 1926, having been in the Soviet capital for about a month, "Moscow is the most silent of great cities, and doubly so when there is snow. The principal instrument in the orchestra of the streets, the automobile horn, is rarely played here; there are few cars."[15]

Other photographs in Sidorov's Moscow album drew on the conventions of documentary urban photography of the kind established by American social reformer Jacob Riis in the late nineteenth century. Washerwomen are shown cleaning linens in the Moscow River (fig. 1.4) and workmen are seen mending the riverbank by the Kremlin after a still-routine bout of flooding in the city center. In Moscow's bustling

Figure 1.3: Tverskaia-Iamskaia Street. Alexys A. Sidorow, *Moskau*, Berlin: Albertus-Verlag, 1928.

Figure 1.4: Washerwomen along the Moscow River. Alexys A. Sidorow, *Moskau*, Berlin:
Albertus-Verlag, 1928.

open-air marketplace at the foot of the seventeenth-century Sukharevskii tower, where countryside and city collided among the rows of stalls, Sidorov found a bygone era in the economic concessions and partial capitalism of NEP (fig. 1.5).[16] Yet Sidorov did not publish his Moscow album merely to document contradictions and depravations. As a sympathetic observer of the revolution, he narrated the city through images that showed the beginnings of revolutionary progress. In part, this narrative was achieved through "before and after" comparisons. A photograph of

Figure 1.5: Market at the foot of Sukharevskii tower. Alexys A. Sidorow, *Moskau*, Berlin: Albertus-Verlag, 1928.

homeless children from 1920–21, carefully titled to indicate the earlier period, is placed in the album adjacent to an image of a meeting of bright-eyed Young Pioneers. Red Moscow, as seen in images of the city's new buildings and new people, was gradually coming into view.

Few in Red Moscow appreciated the power of images more than Aleksei Sidorov. Born in 1891 in the Ukrainian region of the Russian empire, Sidorov enrolled in 1909 as a student in the Historical-Philological Faculty at Moscow University, where he would specialize in art history and archaeology. Like so many young Russian scholars of the period before the First World War, Sidorov studied abroad, making his way westward in 1913 to Italy, Austria, and Germany—places to which he would return as a representative of the Soviet state after the revolution. Sidorov hailed the arrival of the Bolsheviks in 1917.[17] As Russia moved that year from one revolution to the next, he was busily preparing his first art historical work: an article on Albrecht Dürer's sixteenth-century painting of the four apostles. Sidorov used the German master's monumental Reformation-era diptych to argue that images must be interpreted in relation to the ideas and creative practices that informed their production. Art, in other words, is the product of its unique historical moment.[18]

As the Bolsheviks established power in his city, Sidorov railed against the apolitical "formalism" of his mentors and peers. Realism was his preferred artistic style, but Sidorov found common ground with many modernists of the period in his determination to uncover the vital link between art and politics. Just as Dürer, in Sidorov's reading, was shaped by the Reformation, so too must Russian artists respond to the revolutionary events underway around them. In 1918, Sidorov published a pamphlet called "Revolution and Art" in which he aimed to shore up artistic support for the Bolshevik path. "Where is our Marseillaise?" Sidorov demanded to know. "It is as if art has fallen silent . . . where is the artist who could depict the unending grandeur of experiencing this moment? Why are there no statues glorifying battles and victories? Perhaps it is because the revolution is still continuing, because she has not uttered her last word?"[19] Sidorov would soon move from pamphleteer to public servant when he began working for Narkompros (the USSR People's Commissariat of Education). From there, Sidorov worked to nurture artistic production during the first Soviet decade. It was on a trip in 1927 to Austria and Germany that he connected with the German publisher of his Moscow photographic album. Sidorov, who would soon be named head of the Department of Prints and Drawings at Moscow's Museum of Fine Arts, had been dispatched by Narkompros to Central Europe to forge ties with foreign museum workers.[20] Back at home in 1928 as his Moscow album was being published abroad, Sidorov was curating an exhibit that would introduce Dürer to a Soviet audience.[21] For Sidorov, there was still much to be learned from the past. Questions about the usefulness of history would be raised repeatedly in the coming years in debates about the urban planning of Red Moscow.

Despite Sidorov's unimpeachable revolutionary and artistic bona fides, the photographs that make up his Moscow album of 1928 were not in the mode favored by the new Stalinist state for official depictions of the capital. While "before and after" sets of images would occasionally be used to narrate Moscow's socialist transformation, on the whole documentary-style photography had little place in the burgeoning visual culture of Stalinist socialist realism. But beyond this issue were the types of monuments that appeared on the album's pages. In addition to the street scenes in Sidorov's album depicting ordinary life in early Soviet Moscow, dozens upon dozens of photographs showed the city's churches and aristocratic estates. The style in which these images were taken was at odds with the latest trends in Soviet image-making. In the late 1920s, Alexander Rodchenko and other members of the avant-garde experimented with photography, creating dynamic posters and photomontages that drew on the conventions of Dadaism and served as propaganda for the revolutionary state. Sidorov's album, by contrast, featured images taken by photographers Yuri Yeremin, Petr Klepikov, and Aleksandr Grinberg—all members of the more traditional Russian Photographic Society, established before 1917.[22] Sidorov's photographers were Pictorialists or "art photographers," dedicated to a photographic style that mimicked the emotion and beauty of impressionist painting. Their soft lenses and painterly angles gave Moscow a moody, melancholy feel. The uncertainty of the early Soviet period and a nostalgia for the past dripped from the page.

Mass visual culture during the coming era of socialist realism would strive instead to show Moscow not as it currently was or had been before but as it would be, in architectural drawings and photographs that were heavily doctored.[23] The socialist realist aesthetic, officially adopted in the 1930s, relied principally on the imagination. Soviet citizens would be aided in their daydreaming by images of a future Moscow that were widely printed in the Soviet press and showcased within the city itself. Moscow's Gorky Street, newly expanded into a model socialist realist boulevard, featured storefront exhibitions displaying the latest architectural drawings and

Figure 1.6: Gorky Street Exhibition Window. *Arkhitektura SSSR*, 1934, no. 1.

plans (fig. 1.6).[24] Sidorov's album served instead to document Moscow for a foreign audience in the period immediately before the city's "socialist reconstruction." And yet, while new visual conventions would soon dictate that Moscow be cast in a new light, the contrasts and contradictions spotted by Sidorov were part of the urban reality that Soviet leaders continued to reckon with on a daily basis.[25]

In 1920s Moscow Komsomol meetings, May Day parades, and electric light displays took place largely within the cultural spaces of pre-revolutionary Russia. Aside from a handful of new buildings, most Soviet institutions were housed in former palaces and merchant estates. The art nouveau Moscow Merchants Club, built in 1907–1909, had become by 1927 the Theater of Young Workers. A late-nineteenth-century mansion once belonging to a member of the wealthy Morozovs (the great industrialist and art-collecting family) had been taken over by a Moscow branch of *Proletkul't*. This building, with its Moorish-revival style, was now known as the "House of Proletarian Culture."[26] An eighteenth-century mansion once home to the Assembly of the Nobility had been transformed into the House of Unions (fig. 1.7). Its grand pillared hall now hosted Communist Party Congresses rather than gentry assemblies.[27] In the 1930s this same building would be the site of the Moscow Show Trials. Other buildings simply maintained their earlier purposes. The conservatory was still the conservatory, the university was still located in its building across from the Kremlin, and the Kremlin was still the seat of power. The guiding idea in Moscow's reconstruction, shared by architects and artists of the period as well as by Soviet leaders, was that a new material reality would help to bring about a new world. But for practical purposes, the fabric of the old world would have to serve, for now, as the backdrop for the new.

Figure 1.7: The House of Unions decorated for the May 1 holiday. Alexys A. Sidorow,
Moskau, Berlin: Albertus-Verlag, 1928.

THE OLD AND THE NEW

That material culture proved to be so obstinate and enduring was not necessarily an
unwelcome realization to the Bolsheviks. They understood early on that the symbolic spaces of Imperial and Muscovite Russia could be made useful in ways beyond
mere expediency. In returning the capital to Moscow, Bolshevik leaders connected
their vision of the future with a historical narrative of the deep Russian past, gaining for themselves a legitimacy and prestige that they may not otherwise have at-
tained. Seated in Petrograd in February 1918 these leaders, in need of a more central and better-fortified capital, secretly agreed to move their government to Moscow.
The following month, two trainloads of personnel and their families arrived in the
new capital. Many of them would soon take up residence in the Kremlin, while others
moved into Moscow's five-star hotels.[28]

The Bolsheviks' early festivals helped to smooth the transition to Moscow by in-
corporating older city spaces into the pantheon of the revolution. In 1918, during
the first anniversary celebrations of the October Revolution, Moscow was ablaze with
red garlands and firework displays. The official ceremonies were held on Red Square,
and Lenin himself unveiled a new statue of Marx and Engels outside the Bolshoi Theater on what was now called Revolutionary Square.[29] While new monuments and
new names encouraged Muscovites to associate familiar places with the new regime,
older symbols could also be used, albeit selectively, to depict the seamless and pre-
destined transition from past to present. During the period of the Civil War, Bolshevik propaganda began to draw increasingly on the rhetoric of historical progress.[30]
Early festivals helped to make Moscow the "sacred center of the Russian Revolution,"

as Richard Stites writes.[31] This was achieved not just by adding new content to city spaces but also by adapting and reinterpreting existing structures and symbols.

The Bolsheviks nonetheless inherited in Moscow a capital that was run-down and badly in need of modernization, however rich the city was in symbolism and gravitas. As Sidorov fixed his gaze on the Moscow of the 1920s, debates raged among different groups of architects and planners about how best to transform the capital. Large-scale planning would take a level of coordination and centralization not yet achieved in the 1920s. The first decade after 1917 saw instead an outpouring of utopian visions put forth by individuals and collectives ranging in their approaches from the academic to the anti-academic, the classicist to the modernist. Moisei Ginzburg and other members of the Organization of Contemporary Architects (OSA) experimented with house-communes (*doma-kommuny*).[32] El' (Lazar) Lisitskii proposed a series of eight "horizontal skyscrapers" for Moscow's Boulevard Ring.[33] And a number of foreign modernists also took part in architectural competitions and debates of this early period. The adoption in 1928 of the First Five-Year Plan provided new opportunities for foreign specialists to work in the USSR. Le Corbusier, Hannes Meyer, Ernst May, and Albert Kahn all passed through Moscow in the late 1920s, when the city was still a hub for the international avant-garde. That the Five-Year Plan, which sought to rapidly collectivize and industrialize the country, happened to coincide with the collapse of the global economy worked in the Soviet Union's favor.

In 1930, Soviet leaders began to take charge. Responding to "the absence of well-planned urban services, the poor integration of industrial services with industrial construction, and inattention to the rising expectations of the capital's population," the Politburo appointed a special commission of inquiry in December 1930 that would lead in time to the creation of the Moscow General Plan.[34] To ensure firmer local control over decision-making, Moscow's territorial autonomy was reinstated; the city of Moscow was formally separated from Moscow *oblast'* (province) in February 1931. Moscow now had its own executive, bureaucratic, and budgetary offices that reported directly to the RSFSR and USSR levels of the state administration. But while the city's autonomy was henceforth guaranteed in state institutions, the Communist Party's Moscow oblast' and city-level offices remained closely linked until 1949. The men who headed Moscow's Communist Party institutions played leading roles in the city's redevelopment. In 1930, Lazar M. Kaganovich was cross-appointed as First Secretary of the Moscow oblast' party committee (obkom) and the Moscow city party committee (gorkom), posts that he held until 1935, when his protege Nikita Khrushchev took over these positions.

In 1931, the Communist Party Central Committee continued the work begun by the Politburo's commission of inquiry of one year earlier, passing a resolution at its June 1931 plenum titled "On Moscow's Urban Services and the Development of Urban Services in the USSR." Based on a report compiled by Kaganovich, the June resolution set the path away from the mere "restoration" of urban services toward the "socialist reconstruction" of Moscow as a whole.[35] Kaganovich planned to build housing for half a million people and to solve serious problems in the city's fuel and water supplies.[36] He wanted to develop the local Moscow Coal Basin (since, as Kaganovich put it, "we cannot rely indefinitely on the Donetz Basin") and to replace Moscow's cobblestone streets with asphalt.[37] "In Moscow" the city's party boss proclaimed, "it is high time to build like cultured people. That is not a matter of luxury. Asphalt, granite setts and clinker are a matter of hygiene and of protecting our automobile transport."[38] Although the Moscow General Plan was not adopted until 1935, Kaganovich's June resolution of four years prior initiated many of the large building projects that would form the basis of the later plan. These included the Moscow-Volga canal and the Moscow metro.[39] The centerpiece in the city's redevelopment would be the new government headquarters known as the Palace of Soviets. Begun in 1931, Moscow's "proletarian tower" (*proletarskaia vyshka*) was to stand as the "center of social and political life in the socialist country."[40]

The idea to build a new headquarters for congresses and meetings held in the capital was first proposed in 1922, but planning for the Palace of Soviets began in earnest only in the late 1920s.[41] By 1931, the site of the Byzantine-style Cathedral of Christ the Savior had been chosen as the most suitable location for the new Palace. The cathedral, completed in 1883 and photographed for Sidorov's Moscow album in the 1920s (fig. 1.8), was built in commemoration of the Russian victory over Napoleon in 1812.[42] The new Palace would instead symbolize Bolshevik victory in the October Revolution of 1917 and in the First Five-Year Plan that was, at the time, nearing completion. According to the description printed for the open design competition announced in 1931, although the idea for the Palace had been proposed back in 1922, it was "only in the current time . . . only as we are approaching the completion of the Five-Year Plan . . . that all the necessary preconditions exist for . . . the creation in Moscow of the Palace of Soviets of the USSR."[43] The First Five-Year Plan had, indeed, created more favorable conditions for large-scale urban construction projects. By the early 1930s, Soviet planners had gained greater access to the materials, equipment, and know-how that flowed into the country alongside visiting German and American experts. Yet the ability to build on a mass scale raised new questions about what in the built environment should be saved and what should be discarded. Underlying planning discussions of the 1930s were two contradictory instincts: the desire to destroy and the impulse to preserve.

On December 5, 1931, years before a final design for the Palace was selected, the Cathedral of Christ the Savior was demolished and the plot was cleared for the new building. The site of the cathedral was not the first location considered for the Palace, but it was the most sensible, from the Bolshevik perspective. Whereas the other plots considered would have required the destruction of valuable residential and institutional structures, the demolition of the now-defunct and centrally-located cathedral not only dealt a symbolic blow to Tsardom and to Orthodoxy, but it was also by the Bolsheviks' calculation cheaper.[44] Nevertheless, there were some items of value that would have to be salvaged from the sacred center of the former empire. Before the cathedral's demolition, large sculptural friezes and medallions were removed from the structure's façade for safekeeping. Deemed by the managers of the Palace project to be "of artistic value," these pieces were sent to the Tret'iakov Gallery where, to the dismay of the gallery's curators, there was scant room to house them and they languished out in the open air. As one curator put it in a letter in 1932, even though these pieces were "among the best examples of Russian monumental sculpture of the nineteenth century" they "clutter up the entire yard" and "create a negative impression on the many Russian and foreign visitors to the gallery."[45] State officials re-

Figure 1.8: View from Ivan the Great Bell Tower (within the Kremlin) looking West. The Cathedral of Christ the Savior stands in the distance. Alexys A. Sidorow, *Moskau*, Berlin: Albertus-Verlag, 1928.

sponded by approving funds for a canopy of sorts to protect these artifacts from the elements.

While some involved in the Palace of Soviets pursued their preservationist impulses, others indulged their zeal for destruction. After the cathedral had been blown up in December 1931, Viacheslav Molotov and Avel' S. Enukidze received a report from the excited manager at Vzryvprom, the Office of Demolition Industries.[46] The demolition manager reported that the cathedral's destruction had gone according to plan and he made a pitch for the importance of demolition work for the continuing revolution. Despite freezing temperatures and other difficult working conditions, this manager reported that "with heroic expressions of enthusiasm and Bolshevik persistence" the *vzryvniki* had managed to destroy the cathedral in a single month, instead of the year-and-a-half it was estimated to take had they pulled the building apart by hand.[47] The speed with which the cathedral was destroyed was clearly exciting for some, but it was not followed by the speedy adoption of a plan for future construction. While there was agreement among Soviet leaders in 1931 that the monuments of old could swiftly and unceremoniously be cleared to make way for the new, a coherent vision for the Palace of Soviets—and for the future of Red Moscow— had yet to emerge.

In his short story "The Day," written not long after the Cathedral of Christ the Savior's destruction, Soviet writer Yuri K. Olesha mused on the complex relationship between history and revolution in the Soviet Union. "Perhaps the entire cathedral could be moved to a museum," one character suggests. "To hell with the old!" replies a young man wearing a blue undershirt. Later, the youth recants: "But you've just said that all that is old must be wiped away," says an older man. "All except that which holds historical value," replies the young man in blue.[48] As Moscow's socialist reconstruction and the Palace of Soviets competition both got underway, the city's architects and higher-ups were coming to a similar conclusion about the value of history. Iconoclasts though they were, the Bolsheviks were also ardent iconophiles. They were some of the twentieth century's most brazen image-makers and boldest city planners. The 1930s would see the replacement of sepia-toned images of an aging provincial city, like those in Sidorov's Moscow album, with new and colorful visions of a bright, happy, and monumental future.

PLANNING RED MOSCOW

The demolition in late 1931 of Moscow's—and Russia's—largest Orthodox cathedral was a powerful symbolic act, but it would take more than this to convincingly assert Soviet power over this old and complex urban space. While Soviet officials would always struggle to control the growth of Moscow, this task was especially challenging in the first decades of Bolshevik power. In part, the capital city's unruliness was the result of its explosive population growth. The First Five-Year Plan pushed growing numbers of peasants into cities, which grew at an unprecedented pace. During the span of those years alone, Moscow's population increased by 60 percent. In 1930, the city's train stations were overflowing with newcomers whose arrival seemed to catch officials by surprise. And unlike in earlier moments of peasant in-migration, many of these new arrivals would settle in the city for good, finding year-round employment in the booming industrial and construction industries.[49] Severing ties with the villages they had left behind, these peasants became urbanites, joining the ranks of New Soviet Men and Women—or so Soviet officials hoped.

Beyond the need to find solutions to what was quickly becoming an urban crisis was the Bolsheviks' faith in the revolutionary power of cities. City planning was a central plank of the Bolsheviks' revolutionary vision. The Soviet Union was an urban project and Stalinist officials clearly and unabashedly favored the city over the countryside. They also favored architectural monumentalism as the means through which to convey and shore up power and ideology. As the state's primary architectural journal, *Arkhitektura SSSR (Architecture of the USSR)*, put it in 1935, "the monumental architecture of the new Moscow will be majestic and simple. It will give birth to new joyful feelings between the individual and the collective."[50] In the 1930s, Stalinist officials and architects alike increasingly discussed urban space as a tool that could be used to inspire, transform, and even bring happiness to Soviet citizens.[51] And in the great and growing constellation of Soviet cities, Red Moscow played the leading role in this reformation. Rebuilding the Soviet capital became a priority—and a metaphor—for revolutionary progress in the country as a whole. As the capital was rebuilt in reality, it was also reconstructed in texts, images, films, and paper plans that circulated far beyond Moscow and became currency in the Bolshevik bid for the future.

The Stalinist state's vision for Red Moscow would take its most concrete form in the city's first General Plan. The plan came to life in July 1935 when the Council of

People's Commissars and the Central Committee of the Communist Party issued a joint decree titled "On the General Plan for the Reconstruction of the City of Moscow." The decree began by diagnosing the problem: "The spontaneous expansion of Moscow over the course of many centuries," read the opening line, "reflects even in the best years of its development the character of barbarous Russian capitalism."[52] The fabric of the city itself—the "narrow and curving streets, the irregularity of the neighborhoods with dozens of lanes and dead-ends, the unevenness of construction in center and periphery, the cluttered center with warehouses and petty enterprises, the low height and decrepitude of houses overcrowded to the extreme, the disorderly distribution of industrial enterprises, rail transport" and so on—all of this disrupted the rhythms of normal, everyday life in this rapidly expanding metropolis.[53] Over the course of ten years, the General Plan was to guide planners and architects as they straightened and expanded city streets, decluttered the city center, and built new housing to ease overcrowding in Moscow. The plan was to furnish the city a sense of coherence and unity that could only be achieved, its authors believed, by a Communist state.

The General Plan of 1935 introduced into Moscow a comprehensive program for urban development that coordinated planning across a range of construction projects, a number of which were already underway in the city. Sergei E. Chernyshev and Vladimir N. Semenov, who served as Moscow's first Chief Architect from 1932 to 1934, created the plan. In addition to bringing into the General Plan existing projects already underway, such as the Moscow metro and the Moscow-Volga canal, these architects also brought new ideas and international influences to the table.[54] They extended city limits to an area double Moscow's existing size, bringing the surrounding countryside into the fold and making room for future growth. For a projected population of 5 million residents, the General Plan aimed to provide all necessary services and cultural amenities while also lowering population density in the center and building new residential districts on the periphery. Residential construction would be undertaken throughout the city, with the southwestern region in particular receiving 1 million square meters of planned housing construction. While the city's population would be evenly distributed, the city center would remain distinct. Not far from the Kremlin, a new government headquarters, the Palace of Soviets, was to stand at the center of the new Moscow.

In addition to building up Moscow's center and periphery, the General Plan also worked to improve and build upon the city's existing amenities. Former aristocratic estates would be transformed into vast public green spaces. Waterways would be developed and the villages newly brought into the city's boundaries would be built up. Moscow's transportation networks would be expanded to regions beyond the city center. And to incorporate the updated water system supplied by the new Moscow-Volga canal, waterways would be carved into the fabric of the city, winding their way through open parkland and underground tunnels. The Moscow River would be lined with granite embankments and newly paved streets; tall new buildings would run alongside them, creating novel architectural ensembles and revivifying urban vistas. The Moscow General Plan aimed to raise the living standards of Muscovites by providing new and improved urban amenities, but it also sought to beautify the city and to create a sense of aesthetic coherence.

The increased centralization and coordination of city planning from the early years of the Stalin era was matched by concurrent moves to bring urban experts more firmly under the state's control. In April 1932 the Communist Party Central Committee ordered that all independent cultural organizations in the USSR be abolished. New artistic unions were established for each branch of the arts. Two months later, the USSR Union of Soviet Architects was created. Based in Moscow, the Union would oversee discussions and developments in the architectural profession across the country. Republic-level branches of the union were also created (at the RSFSR level, for example), and at the municipal level a Moscow section of the Union was established to coordinate local affairs. In July 1933, the USSR Union of Architects began publishing its monthly journal, *Arkhitektura SSSR.* The journal remained an important source of information for the Soviet architectural profession, communicating debates and ideas from Moscow to the periphery, but also containing information about developments outside the capital and in the international arena.

Architectural pedagogy was also brought more directly under state control when in 1934 the USSR Academy of Architecture was established in Moscow as the central state institution for higher architectural education and research. The academy's students were drawn mainly from Moscow and other large Soviet cities. Studios led by master architects trained students in a curriculum that emphasized an appreciation of the past. In their first year, students studied examples of classical architecture from ancient Greece, Rome, and the Renaissance. Second year students moved on to Russian classical models. Supporting this curriculum were dozens of new Russian translations of texts by Palladio, Alberti, Vitruvius, and Viollet-le-Duc.

The newfound importance of models from the classical past prompted the founding in 1934 of a Museum of Architecture, created initially as a branch of the Academy and housed on the grounds of one of Moscow's many Orthodox sites, the Donskoi Monastery. Despite the Soviet state's hostility to religion, the monastery itself became an object for display and historical study during its life as a museum. Exhibitions were held in the monastery's five-domed Grand Cathedral, built in the seventeenth century, and additional buildings in the Donskoi complex were used to store objects rescued from other churches threatened with destruction. While the museum's curators aimed early on to build a collection of items from world architecture, their first permanent exhibit in 1936 was on the theme of Russian classicism. The second exhibit, on the Russian baroque, opened a year later, and in 1938 the museum displayed images and objects of Russian architecture from the eleventh to seventeenth centuries. It was only in 1939 that the exhibition theme at the Museum of Architecture was "Soviet Architecture."[55]

The institutional and ideological changes of the 1930s marked the end of the pluralism that characterized the 1920s. But these changes did not lead to the creation of a streamlined and simplified urban planning apparatus. Soviet bureaucratic structures were complex, and the tangled lines of competing jurisdictions all crossed in Moscow. The capital's new artistic unions and academies took shape alongside a wide range of new state planning institutions. For example, the State Institute for the Design of Cities (Giprogor) was created in 1929 as the city planning arm of the central State Planning Agency (Gosplan), the main agency in charge of economic planning and the Five-Year Plans. Then there were the local institutions that managed specific elements of Moscow's design and construction. Metrostroi, created in 1931, oversaw the construction and maintenance of the Moscow metro. In 1933, twenty design studios were established by Mossovet. Headed by the city's master architects, these studios were tasked initially with working on the completion of the General Plan. The People's Commissariats (in 1946 renamed "Ministries"), based in Moscow, also ran their own construction offices, each of which commissioned architects to work on plans for new administrative and residential construction in the capital. It was through large-scale urban planning documents, like the Moscow General Plan of 1935, that these many players were brought together in a single unified planning effort—at least in theory.

By the time the General Plan was unveiled, the Soviet Union had become an institutionally complex, but also a more closed and controlled space. An internal passport regime was introduced in 1932 in order to control population movement. Soviet nationalities policy shifted that same year from an approach that sought to foster nation building in the non-Russian SSRs to a policy encouraging the rehabilitation of Russian national culture and the forging of a new set of relations between Soviet nationalities based on the notion of the "Friendship of the Peoples." These changes in Soviet policy reverberated in the urban development of Moscow. Architects built palatial new workers' clubs for the city's growing proletariat, drawing inspiration from Moscow's historic landmarks and Russian styles.[56] Thanks to the adoption of internal passports, the capital's urban planners also stood to benefit from the state's increased ability to monitor population movement.

The Moscow General Plan of 1935 would have a lasting influence on subsequent visions for the capital, and on planners outside the city who looked to Moscow as a model. This influential planning document struck a delicate balance between old and new. The plan called for the modernization of Moscow's amenities and infrastructures while also instilling in the city's future a commitment to the past. While modernist architects active in the 1920s might happily have done away with Moscow's Kremlin and the radial network of streets that emanated from it, these features of the eight-hundred-year-old city became crucial components of Moscow's "socialist reconstruction." Moscow's pre-revolutionary past would, according to the plan, guide planners toward the communist future.

In part, the General Plan's historicism was the result of one of its creators, Vladimir Semenov. The architect was inspired by British Garden City design, as well as the American "City Beautiful" movement that, at the turn of the century, had sought to inculcate citizens with progressivist values through the creation of monumental and beautiful city spaces.[57] Beyond Semenov's own influence, this historicism resulted from the ongoing debates of the time about socialist realism, the new and official artistic doctrine of the Soviet Union. First elaborated in 1934 at the conference of the Soviet Union's new Writers' Union, socialist realism was a malleable and poorly-defined doctrine that emphasized thinking (or writing, painting, acting, and so on) in multiple times—both present and future—at once. The socialist realist maxim calling for art to be "national in form, socialist in content" promised the doctrine's relevance across a diverse Soviet geography as well. Initially, socialist realism was most clearly developed in literature. Socialist realist literature charted the progress of a hero from "spontaneity" to "consciousness."[58] Socialist realist art, in turn, depicted real life but in its most ideal form, or as it would be experienced in the "bright communist future." In architecture, the doctrine opened the door both to historicism and monumentality.

What the doctrine of socialist realism should mean for architecture would be the subject of debate for the rest of the Soviet period. But it became clear very quickly in the 1930s that socialist realism during the Stalin era would be tied to the valuing and influence of the past. In a radical departure from the doctrine of modernism that had earlier been influential in Moscow's architectural circles, architects of the 1930s described the need to build on past forms in their pursuit of solutions for the new socialist city. This approach made its way directly into the Moscow General Plan. As Jean-Louis Cohen writes, the plan "'assimilated' an 'inheritance' that was now conceived in different terms. Once considered as a legacy of the feudal or capitalist past, the concentric, radial shape of Moscow—dismissed by Le Corbusier as 'the old carcass of an Asiatic village'—became a treasure, something to be not only preserved but further developed."[59] This did not mean that Moscow's architects and planners of the 1930s were firm preservationists. As the fate of the Cathedral of Christ the Savior showed, there was ample opportunity in the new plan for destruction.

In 1938, a full decade after Aleksei Sidorov published his Moscow album of photographs, the city's General Plan had been adopted and Moscow's socialist reconstruction including work on the symbolic center—the Palace of Soviets—was underway. That year, the Moscow party office published a special issue about the Palace of Soviets in its printed series *Answers to the Questions of Workers and Collective Farmers.* In response to the question "What will the Palace of Soviets be like and how is its construction going?" party officials delivered a lengthy reply that guided curious workers and farmers through the Palace project, from the initial idea for its creation in 1922 to the design competitions of the early 1930s and on to the tower's construction in the present. But this official account of the Palace of Soviets did not stop there. It pressed forward, vacillating between present and future tenses, to describe the Palace in such vivid detail that the reader had the feeling of actually having visited. "On this round earth," the description began, "there is no building that will be taller and larger than the Palace of Soviets."[60] The Cathedral of Christ the Savior would have fit within the Palace's main hall, the account noted as it moved from future to present tense. Approaching the monumental building from the widened boulevard below, visitors ascend the gigantic front staircase and, once inside, they find themselves in a sublime interior space built for up to thirty thousand people. The Palace—with its 148 elevators and 62 escalators, its library of half a million books, and its domed amphitheater surmounted by a skyscraper with a 100-meter tall statue of Lenin at its crown—was a marvel.

The scale of the Palace of Soviets, with its magnificent exterior and opulent interior, exceeded what most Muscovites had ever seen. But it was the more mundane elements of the building, as described in 1938, that signaled the unreality of the monumental structure being conjured on the page. The solution that had reportedly been implemented for the cloakroom was especially surreal. As *Answers to the Questions of Workers and Collective Farmers* explained, one of the greatest challenges a person would face when arriving at the Palace of Soviets was the problem of where to hang one's coat amidst the throng of thirty thousand people. The building's clever planners had thought of everything, the *Answers* explained:

> On the first floor of the Palace there will be two thousand chambers. In each chamber—16 cabinets that move along a vertical conveyor belt. An illuminated signal shows the visitor which chamber is free.
>
> Visitors hang their clothes in a cabinet and, taking the special tag off the hook, the cabinet swings upward on the conveyor belt.
>
> In order to pick up their belongings when exiting, it suffices to lower the tag back onto the same hook. And just like that the conveyor belt moves, stopping at just the right point . . . and the door of the cabinet automatically opens . . . The visitor is free to go.[61]

This automated cloakroom at the Palace of Soviet verged on fantasy, not least because it would require the elimination of the powerful figure of the cloakroom attendant. But the description may not have raised too many eyebrows among the readers of *Answers to the Questions of Workers and Collective Farmers*. By the late 1930s, Soviet citizens had grown accustomed to both the fantastic quality of socialist realist narratives and the empty commitments of state and party officials. Unfulfilled promises about the Palace had been made before.

According to the construction schedule published in the autumn of 1931 in *Sovetskoe iskusstvo (Soviet Art)*, the Palace of Soviets was to be completed by 1933. The projected timeline stated that in the winter of 1931–32, the foundation of the new Palace would be laid and by February 1932 the design would be ready. Designs were being commissioned, *Soviet Art* explained in 1931, from architects in America and from Le Corbusier and Auguste Perret in France. Preliminary construction of the building would be finished in 1932, the interior would be completed in 1933, and by the end of that year the monumental edifice would open.[62] Work on the Palace of Soviets began during the period of the First Five-Year Plan, a time of outsized pronouncements and oversized ambitions. If new Soviet industrial cities like Magnitogorsk could be built seemingly overnight, why should the Palace of Soviets in Moscow be any different? As it turned out, the timeline described in *Soviet Art* was impossible to achieve. As the following chapter will discuss, the design competition for the Palace of Soviets would be held across four stages between 1931 and 1933, and the final design was approved only in early 1934. In the years that followed, the empty pit of Moscow's former Cathedral would lay open for much longer than planned.

2

THE PALACE

The Palace of Soviets was never built to completion, but in the 1930s it existed nevertheless in texts and images, not to mention on candy wrappers and stationery. This building was to be the centerpiece of Moscow's "socialist reconstruction," and the design that was chosen for it in 1934 was a testament to the Stalinist state's desire to build monumentally. According to the description published in *Pravda* in 1934, the Palace of Soviets would have enough room at its base to hold state proceedings and official gatherings of up to 20,000 people in the grand amphitheater, and gatherings of up to 6,000 in a smaller hall. Perched atop the main amphitheater's dome a skyscraper would be built, forming a nearly 100-story pedestal for an 80-meter-high statue of Lenin placed on top (fig. 2.1).[1] Had it been completed as planned, this structure would have been the tallest building in the world at that time. Construction began in the mid-1930s, but in the end this monumental structure was never built. The Palace of Soviets would, however, have an outsized influence on the course of Soviet architecture—an influence that stretched through the interwar years and into the postwar period. In 1947, the office in charge of building the Palace of Soviets would be assigned to build two of Moscow's postwar skyscrapers. While the Palace of Soviets was never completed, its design studios and staff oversaw the construction of Moscow State University, which opened its doors in 1953.

The Palace of Soviets project created institutions necessary for Moscow's postwar development, but it also served to reshape the Soviet Union's cultural relations with the outside world in the 1930s. Since its inception, the ambitious Palace of Soviets construction project attracted international attention as well as consternation. The building stood at the heart of how the Soviet Union imagined itself in the 1930s, but it also shaped how the country was seen abroad. The series of design competitions held for the Palace served as important moments of contact between Soviet and foreign architects. In the scholarly literature on the Palace of Soviets, historians have tended to focus on these design competitions, held between 1931 and 1934, concentrating mainly on the aesthetics of the Palace's design, to the exclusion of the building's later construction.[2] The final design chosen for the Palace was indeed consequential. The building was seen in the 1930s, as it is now, as marking a turning point in Soviet architecture. In the 1930s, a decade in which Moscow's architects were searching for a distinctly "Soviet" approach to architecture and urban design, the Palace provided the model. Following this building's example, "monumentality, wholeness, [and] simplicity" was the mantra for a "new era" in Soviet architecture.[3]

In addition to the Palace's role in charting a new course for Soviet architecture, this building project seemed to mark a different type of break as well: a break between

Figure 2.1: Palace of Soviets, with the Kremlin turrets in the foreground. Engraving on wood by P. Riabov. *Moskva*, Moscow: Izd. gazety "Rabochaia Moskva," 1935.

Moscow and the West. The design chosen for Moscow's premiere structure in 1934 signaled a rejection of the international modernist movement and a turning away in Moscow from the Soviet avant-garde that flourished in the 1920s. Soviet architecture under Stalin would move instead toward a more conservative, neoclassical, and reactionary monumentalism. Indeed, the very monumentality of Stalin-era architecture has led historians to classify it, alongside Nazi and Italian fascist architecture, as "totalitarian" design. This is a category that is carefully cordoned off from global design trends, viewed as a case *sui generis*.[4] This chapter, by contrast, argues that Stalinist architectural monumentalism did not spell the end of Soviet architectural ties with the outside world; rather, Stalinist monumentalism generated new forms of Soviet international engagement, in particular with the United States.

The Palace of Soviets, and the concurrent adoption of socialist realism in Soviet architecture, certainly caused a number of foreign architects, not least Le Corbusier, to turn their backs on the Soviet Union. And yet, this large-scale building project also required Soviet architects and engineers to travel abroad in search of foreign technical assistance. In shifting the focus, as this chapter does, from design to construction, it is not Soviet insularity that is striking, but rather the desire on the part of the architects, engineers, and party leaders involved in the project to engage with foreign technology and ideas. The search for monumentality in Stalin-era architecture demanded that projects like the Palace of Soviets be carried out through transnational networks of expertise and with foreign assistance. Far from being a symptom of cultural backwardness and isolation from global trends, the monumentalism of Stalinist architecture, in effect, tied Soviet architecture and urban planning to the outside world, in particular to the United States. This ensured that the Soviet Union's relationship to "the West" was perpetually on the minds of those architects and engineers engaged in making Moscow monumental.

THE SEARCH FOR MONUMENTALITY

The stakes were high for those involved in the design competitions for the Palace of Soviets. As many participants would come to realize, the four rounds of competitions held between 1931 and 1934 were about much more than just the Palace. This architectural competition was different from the dozens of other design contests held in the Soviet Union's first decade-and-a-half. The competition for the Palace of Soviets was the stage upon which the many possibilities open before Stalinist architecture were publicly reigned in. And at the end of it all, in the place of the many paths once available, architectural monumentalism and neoclassicism rose to preeminence.

While there were four rounds of competitions held for the Palace of Soviets, the second "open" contest was by far the most exciting. The international Open Design Competition for the Palace was officially announced in July 1931. The officials in charge of finding a design for the Palace of Soviets had decided from the start that there would be four rounds, and that the first, third, and fourth rounds would be by invitation only.[5] By contrast, the second competition was open to all who wished to enter it. Out of a total of 160 entries in the Open Competition, 24 were from foreign architects, some of whom had been encouraged by Soviet officials to participate and were later awarded prize money in foreign currency for their entries.[6] The participation of a number of famous foreigners guaranteed the Palace of Soviets project an added level of prestige and international attention, while also promising a considerable degree of drama.

Many of the foreign architects who took part in the Open Competition were connected to the modernist movement. When neoclassical designs were chosen among the three grand-prize winners in the Open Competition, the modernists were outraged. In April 1932, writing on behalf of the *Congrès internationaux d'architecture moderne* (CIAM), Le Corbusier, who had himself participated in the competition, sent an angry telegram directly to Stalin. Le Corbusier saw the competition results as "a direct affront to the spirit of the revolution and the fulfillment of the Five-Year Plan." He decried the fact that, as he put it, "the Palace of Soviets will embody the old regimes and manifest complete disdain for the enormous cultural effort of Modern Times." Le Corbusier summed up the whole affair as a "dramatic betrayal!" before threatening to find a new location for the fourth meeting of CIAM, scheduled to take place in Moscow the following year.[7] In the end, CIAM met elsewhere for its fourth congress (on an ocean-liner traveling from Marseilles to Athens), and a firm break was established between the spokesmen of the modernist movement and the revolutionary state that they had once seen as their "promised land."[8] When asked two years later why Le Corbusier left the USSR, Boris Iofan, Chief Architect of the Palace of Soviets, explained that "Soviet architecture has already passed through the era of constructivism and functionalism."[9] Iofan's prickly response, suggesting that the Soviet Union had evolved beyond Le Corbusier's approach to design, may have been partly personal—the state architect had little in common with the modernist master, who only "passed through Moscow periodically,"[10] as Iofan put it—but it also reflected the changing fate of modernism in the USSR.

In April 1932, the same month that Le Corbusier sent his telegram to Stalin, all independent cultural organizations in the USSR were disbanded and Soviet artists of all stripes were organized into new artistic unions. As architects debated the role of history and the legacy of modernism in the new Union of Soviet Architects and at Moscow's new Academy of Architecture, "constructivism" and "functionalism" were increasingly used as pejorative terms associated with an earlier, chaotic, and impractical period in revolutionary development. Although many still advanced the position that modernism held a number of useful lessons for Soviet architecture, the 1930s saw most architects turning instead to historical models and neoclassical forms.[11] In the search for the tenets of the new socialist realist approach to design, Soviet architects also began to see beauty and happiness as values that should be captured in architectural form.[12] This value-driven approach to design was officially encouraged. In a 1933 speech, Kaganovich stated that

> some people think that simplification and crude design [*gruboe oformlenie*] is the style of proletarian architecture. Excuse me, but the proletariat does not only want housing, does not only want to have a place that is comfortable to live in, but also to have housing that is beautiful. And he will make sure that his cities, his houses, his architecture are more beautiful than that in other cities in Europe and America.[13]

In Moscow's architectural studios, master architects and their students articulated the new approach to their craft: "the new architecture should be truly humane [*chelovechnyi*], with a concern for the person, in the best way satisfying his needs and wants, including his aesthetic wants."[14] Architects warned against the blind copying of past forms, but asserted that by building on the best examples from the past they would find their new architecture.

The Open Competition for the Palace of Soviets served as an experimental venue for these architectural discussions.[15] All 160 entries to the competition were publicly on display in the spring of 1932 at the Museum of Fine Arts in Moscow, a location chosen for its proximity to the construction site of the future Palace of Soviets (fig. 2.2).[16] The popular Soviet writer Aleksei N. Tolstoi attended the exhibition and wrote an article describing the works on display for the main state newspaper, *Izvestiia,* in late February 1932. "Searches for Monumentality," as this article was titled, described the exhibition as "exceptionally important and meaningful, in particular in the formulation of an important question: the proletariat, having taken hold of history, must put forth its own monumental forms in architecture."[17] Guiding the reader on a tour of the development of architectural styles throughout history, Tolstoi arrived at the present and asked, "along which path will creative new forms be found? And what from past heritage will be assimilated and reworked, and what will be cast aside as foreign [*chuzhoe*] and unexpressive?"[18] The path would not be found, Tolstoi argued, in the Gothic, in American skyscrapers, or in "*Korbiuzionizm*." The

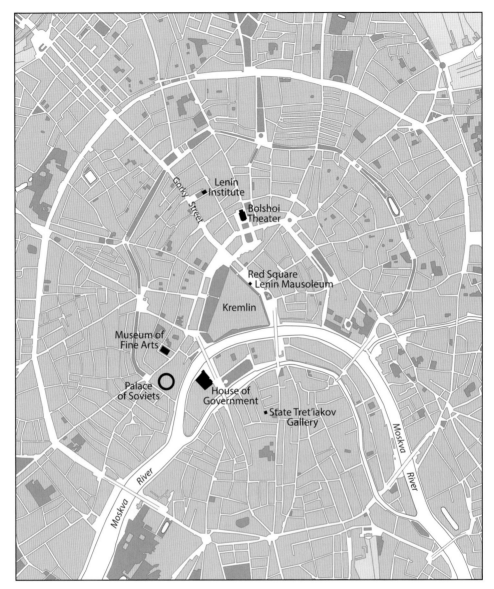

Figure 2.2: Map of central Moscow in the 1930s. Map by Cox Cartographic Ltd.

classical architecture of Rome was the closest of all, with its openness and its functionality.[19] "Borrowing does not mean imitating," Tolstoi asserted. "Borrowing is the creative process of jumping from the height of culture to an even higher pinnacle of achievement."[20] Did the exhibition of competition entries contain any designs that fully satisfied the demands of a building as important as the Palace of Soviets? No, Tolstoi thought. But it marked the first step in a new direction.

Not all visitors to the exhibition were as enthusiastic as Tolstoi about the new direction in architecture found among the competition entries. In early February 1932, a note on the letterhead of the Arts Division of Narkompros (the People's Commissariat of Education) written by one of the country's leading avant-garde sculptors and theorists reached the office of Bolshevik leader Avel' Enukidze, who sat on the state's special Council for the Construction of the Palace of Soviets. "Dear Avel' Safronovich, Comrade Enukidze," Vladimir Tatlin, then head of Arts at Narkompros, began: "regarding the works on display from the competition for the Palace of Soviets, I must tell you, with regret, that my impression was very poor." The proposals, Tatlin lamented, "contain only Western forms, and because of this they turn out to be agitators for bourgeois ideology." Moreover, Tatlin explained, "our Soviet forms are nowhere to be seen" (nashei sovetskoi formy net). Busy with other work, Tatlin had been unable to participate himself in the competition for the Palace, a building that "must characterize the Soviet way of thinking." But Tatlin, who had designed the famed Monument to the Third International one decade earlier, was willing to prepare within a month and a half a large model along with sketches for a new design for the building, one that would be based on "entirely new constructive material-forms."[21] By way of resume, Tatlin instructed Enukidze to look him up in volume 8 of the Small Soviet Encyclopedia. Tatlin's letter was sent down through the bureaucratic chain to Vasilii M. Mikhailov, who had just taken over as Palace of Soviets Head of Construction, but Mikhailov never followed up.[22]

A number of prizes were awarded in 1932 for the Open Competition, but the three projects that were tied for grand prize showed a clear preference among the jury for classical design. Ivan V. Zholtovskii had submitted a grand-prize entry that was explicitly Renaissance-inspired. Boris M. Iofan's grand-prize-winning design had all the monumental elements of his later Palace but in deconstructed, and more Italianate, form. Both Zholtovskii and Iofan were Soviet architects of high esteem. The third grand-prize winner of the Open Competition was the 27-year-old British-born American architect Hector Hamilton, from East Orange, New Jersey. Hamilton's design, for which he was awarded $6,000 (or 12,000 rubles), was a low and long symmetrical building faced with white and black granite (fig. 2.3).

The American journal Architectural Forum was told about Hamilton's success ahead of time so that they could prepare a special supplement to their March 1932 issue. Hamilton, the journal noted, had only secondary school education plus two years at New York's Cooper Union, but he was "far from being the novice he was represented to be in the newspapers."[23] Hamilton had followed the parameters set in the Soviet government's competition brief, which stated that "the Palace of Soviets must be a monumental structure, outstanding in its architectural features, and fitting in artistically with the general architectural scheme of Moscow."[24] In applying these precepts, Hamilton, who had never been to Moscow, said that he had attempted to "abolish any style similar to that which is in error called 'modernistic.' I felt that Russia did not want carved festoons or friezes, either, but a sensible, straightforward expression of practicability."[25]

Hamilton was somewhat confused about what it meant to win the Open Competition—the second round of four—in 1932. Upon learning of his successful entry, Hamilton entered into negotiations with the USSR via the Amtorg Trading Corporation (Amtorg), an American joint-stock company based in New York City that functioned as the Soviet Union's representative in business within the US. Assuming that he would begin work immediately in Moscow on his new building, Hamilton requested that the Soviet state pay for his travel expenses to and from the Soviet

Figure 2.3: Hector Hamilton, Palace of Soviets open competition entry, 1932. Collection of the Shchusev State Museum of Architecture.

capital, that they cover his hotel costs during his stay, and that they pay him an additional 1,000 ruble living allowance.[26] Hamilton's request received a swift response, via telegram, from Moscow. Vasilii Mikhailov, Head of Construction for the Palace of Soviets, deemed the architect's conditions unacceptable and instructed Amtorg to break off negotiations entirely with Hamilton. But the staff at Amtorg would do no such thing. From their offices in New York, Amtorg agents were more familiar with America and Americans and they decided to ask Mikhailov, on behalf of Hamilton, for a more modest sum of 500 rubles for living expenses. Fearing a scandal, Amtorg strongly advised that Moscow agree to Hamilton's terms, since "the invitation of Hamilton to visit the USSR has been widely reported in the American press."[27] In the end, none of this back-and-forth mattered, for Hamilton was already on his way to Moscow. As the *New York Times* reported in its Business Opportunities section in mid-April 1932,

> Mr. Hamilton was honored at a farewell reception at the American Russian Institute . . . prior to his sailing on Friday for Russia, where he will act as architect-in-chief in working out final plans for the huge structure. Mr. Hamilton said he would be assisted by two Russian architects, I. V. Zholtoffsky and B.M. Yofan, who also won first prizes of $6,000, in the work of adapting several features from the other designs submitted, but the final word will rest with the young American architect.[28]

This account in the *New York Times* of events relating to Hector Hamilton and the Palace of Soviets would have surprised Soviet officials back in Moscow.

Where Hamilton got the idea that he would be leading a design team of senior Soviet architects is unclear. As a prize-winner in the second round of Palace of Soviets competitions, Hamilton *had* earned the honor of advancing to the third, closed competition held in the summer months of 1932.[29] But Hamilton was adamant that he was the architect of Moscow's Palace of Soviets. As he told the American press before leaving for Moscow, the major change to his original design would be the addition of a 400-foot tower "of the American skyscraper type, a modern adaptation of the upflowing lines of Gothic architecture," which would provide "more space for governmental executive offices."[30] This vision for Moscow's new palace was indeed similar to the final design that would be selected in the end but, in truth, Hamilton was not the Chief Architect of the Palace of Soviets and the final word did not rest with him.[31] The position of Chief Architect had, in fact, been held since 1931—before the design competitions had even begun—by Soviet architect Boris Iofan. Occupying what was initially an administrative position, "Chief Architect" Iofan had, like Hamilton, won a grand prize in the Open Competition of 1932. As he advanced in the following months through the third and fourth rounds of the competition, Iofan's administrative post would come to coincide neatly with his status as architect of the final design for the Palace of Soviets.

THE ADMINISTRATION FOR THE CONSTRUCTION OF THE PALACE OF SOVIETS

From the project's early stages, the patrons and main decision-makers working on the Palace of Soviets were high-ranking members of the Soviet state and Communist Party, a number of whom would be swept up in the Great Terror just as construction work on the Palace was beginning in the late 1930s. A special Council for the Construction of the Palace of Soviets had been created in 1928 within the Presidium of the Central Executive Committee (TsIK) of the USSR. Headed by Viacheslav M. Molotov, this Council was made up mainly of Old Bolsheviks, including Lazar Kaganovich, Kliment E. Voroshilov, Konstantin V. Ukhanov, and Avel' Enukidze. Stalin also took part in decisions relating to the Palace project. In August 1932, he wrote a letter to Kaganovich, Voroshilov, and Molotov expressing his disapproval of the design proposed by Zholtovskii, which "smacks of 'Noah's Ark'," as Stalin saw it.[32] Nor did he like a proposal submitted by leading Soviet architect Aleksei Shchusev. "Shchusev's is just another 'Cathedral of Christ the Savior,' but without the cross," wrote Stalin, who was convinced that Shchusev planned to "add on" the cross at a later date.[33] Iofan's design, by contrast, was one that Stalin could live with, so long as a few changes were made. The building should be extended upward, he wrote, by hoisting, if possible, a column on top of the Palace. Atop the column should be placed "a hammer and sickle that will be electrically lit from within."[34] As Stalin envisioned it in 1932, statues of Marx, Engels, and Lenin would stand in front of the Palace.

The high level of patronage for the Palace of Soviets project was also reflected in the managers and architects brought in to work on the building early on. The Palace of Soviets construction office, called the Administration for the Construction of the Palace of Soviets (*Upravlenie stroitel'stva dvortsa sovetov*, or USDS), was created in

Figure 2.4: Palace of Soviets architects Vladimir G. Gel'freikh, Vladimir A. Shchuko, and Chief Architect Boris M. Iofan with a model of their building, 1934. Collection of the State Central Museum of Contemporary Russian History.

1931. Boris Iofan was officially made Chief Architect at the USDS and in this post Iofan himself was in charge of organizing the design competitions.[35] In 1934, when his own design entry won the fourth and final round of competitions for the Palace, Iofan carried on in the position of Chief Architect, now assisted on the project by two architects from Leningrad, Vladimir Gel'freikh and Vladimir Shchuko. While Iofan would remain the primary architect on the project, all three would contribute to the building's final design (fig. 2.4).

Iofan would be a permanent fixture at the USDS, right up to the organization's dissolution after Stalin's death in 1953. Yet, holding the position of Chief Architect at the USDS did not make Iofan the ultimate head of this organization. From its creation in 1931, the USDS would be headed by a succession of managers holding the title of Head of Construction. The first Head of Construction was an architect, Mikhail V. Kriukov, who found Iofan so impossible to work with that he left within months of his appointment.[36] The second and longer-lasting appointee was Vasilii Mikhailov, who took over from Kriukov in the autumn of 1931. Mikhailov was a party man. He had worked as Secretary of the Moscow Committee of the Communist Party and as head of the Moscow Trade Union Council, before being sent away from the city, by way of demotion, to work as deputy head of construction of the Dniepr Hydroelectric Dam. Mikhailov was soon brought back to Moscow to head up construction of the House of Government, also known as the House on the Embankment. Completed in 1933, this large residential complex for top Soviet officials, also designed by Iofan, was located directly across the river from both the Kremlin and from the site of the future Palace of Soviets. Mikhailov and Iofan, then, knew each other well. While the design competitions for the Palace of Soviets were underway in the early 1930s, the pair finished their work on the House on the Embankment. When this first building was completed, both men moved with their families into new apartments in that residential complex that they had jointly built.[37]

By 1934, Mikhailov and Iofan turned their attention to the Palace of Soviets. As Head of Construction at the USDS, Mikhailov oversaw the three branches of the organization in charge of building the Palace: the administrative-financial office, the architectural-planning department headed by Iofan, and the construction office.[38] As Chief Architect at the USDS, Iofan presided over discussions to determine the requirements for a building such as the Palace. Back in February 1931, Iofan met with two engineers and three architects to draw up a plan for managing the project.[39] Iofan also oversaw the production of blueprints for the potential building sites chosen for the Palace. An earlier location considered was between Okhotnyi riad, Tverskaia Street, Georgievskii Lane, and Bol'shaia Dmitrovka. The site that was selected—the location of the Cathedral of Christ the Savior—was proposed only in late 1931.[40] Iofan's duties as Chief Architect also included reworking the final design for the structure; hiring and firing workers; site development and the construction of new housing, if necessary, for anyone who might have to be evicted from the construction site; and the creation of all production schedules and work plans for the financing and supply of construction, as approved by the Head of Construction.[41]

When the fourth and final design competition for the Palace of Soviets concluded in May 1933, a "working basis" for the building was established. Iofan's submission had won in the last round and in June 1933 he was joined by Gel'freikh and Shchuko to work out the final project. Through this process, Iofan's design was extended upward to a height beyond what the architect had initially proposed. The result was a tall, tiered structure topped by a giant statue of Lenin with right arm outstretched. The final design, co-authored by Iofan, Gel'freikh, and Shchuko, was officially approved on February 19, 1934, and a perspectival drawing of the project was printed for all to see in *Pravda* the following day (fig. 2.5). All told, the Palace of Soviets was to be 415 meters tall, making it at the time the tallest building in the world.[42]

In the months immediately after the announcement of the final Palace of Soviets design, models and drawings of the future building were put on display for public viewing at Moscow's Museum of Fine Arts. Encouraged to leave comments at the

Figure 2.5: Perspectival Drawing of the Palace of Soviets by Boris Iofan, Vladimir Gel'freikh, and Vladimir Shchuko. Printed in *Pravda* on February 20, 1934 and in *Arkhitektura SSSR*, 1935, no. 6.

exhibition, a number of visitors offered suggestions for how to improve the Palace's design.[43] Some fixated in their comments on the crowning statue of Lenin. One visitor, a sculptor, was concerned that Lenin would not be visible from the ground.[44] Others had the opposite impression: "The figure of Lenin is somewhat rough for such an elegant building," wrote one commenter. "In my opinion," they continued, "a somewhat reduced figure would make it sleeker."[45] Another visitor chimed in, writing that while he did like the overall design, he wondered if Lenin "wasn't a little too big for that dome?"[46]

In addition to their concerns about Lenin, museumgoers worried about the landscaping around the Palace. A worker from Metrostroi asked why there were no parks or gardens as part of the design. A steelworker engineer asked if the early-nineteenth-century Manege building located nearby could be moved in order to fully integrate the new Palace square with the new Lenin Avenue that was to extend outward from it. Someone else suggested that the Manege simply be demolished to make way for the new architectural ensemble. Another commenter wondered about the Palace's location on the Moscow River. Could something not be done about the water level, he asked, which was too low "even after the construction of the Moscow-Volga Canal" to create a nice effect alongside the Palace?[47] For many who visited the Museum of Fine Arts to see the long-anticipated design for the Palace of Soviets, the monumentality of the proposed new building was clearly at odds with the city around it. How to reconcile the scale of the structure with the city and its people below presented a serious challenge. One visitor addressed a comment on this point to the Palace's Chief Architect himself. "Comrade Iofan, make space for your colossus," this visitor wrote. As he explained, the small plot on which the Palace would be built was "far too cramped for it."[48]

There were, of course, many others who left complimentary comments when visiting the Palace of Soviets exhibition in 1934. A student from a construction technical college wrote that he was "sure that you will be victorious and create a monument worthy of our time and the great Lenin."[49] An agronomist from Central Asia, who had read about the building many times but never seen an image of it, "admired the beauty, grandeur, and yet seeming lightness of the Palace."[50] Another visitor expressed their enthusiasm for the project and their impatience at the time it was taking to build the structure: "a fleeting glance at the model leaves an unforgettable impression. I want to see it sooner in reality."[51] The Palace of Soviets generated a level of excitement similar to the interest and enthusiasm popularly expressed during the construction of the great industrial sites of the First Five-Year Plan. Some visitors to the exhibition in 1934 worked to strengthen that connection between the country's recent feats in industrialization and Moscow's ongoing "socialist reconstruction." A shock worker wrote in his comment that the exhibition was "exceptional" and asked if the model and drawings of the Palace could go on tour to the country's many factories.[52] Similarly, an artist suggested that there be a "Palace of Soviets" construction magazine and that regular reports be broadcast on the radio to inform the country about the project, but also to ensure that work was progressing at the proper tempo.

The notion that public supervision was necessary was surely based on what visitors had seen—or not seen—on their way to the Palace of Soviets exhibition. Across the street from the Museum of Fine Arts, visitors to the exhibit could plainly see that work had scarcely begun on the construction site. "Why is the territory of the Palace currently some sort of 'snow desert'?" one visitor demanded to know. "Are there reasons that construction has stopped? It is not only me who wonders this, but many thousands." As this visitor explained, it was not just the "toiling masses within the Soviet Union who needed this building."[53] The proletariat of all countries, he explained, was waiting for it to open. Vigilance was clearly needed in Soviet urban construction in the same way that it was necessary to ensure the country's industrial progress. For some, the lack of progress on the Palace of Soviets site, combined with the fantastical appearance of the chosen design, gave the project an unrealistic quality. As one museumgoer put it, "there are many people who look at the building as just showing off [pustoe shchegol'stvo]." The whole mess should be straightened out, they argued, with proper explanations and regular updates on the radio and in the press.[54]

It would not take long for the Palace of Soviets to become a familiar building. Discernible on the imaginary horizon, the Palace was the symbol of a new era. Soviet officials, for their part, worked to combat the perception that this was an era of empty promises. Although the Palace had not arrived on the cityscape by the time originally promised, its image circulated so widely as to create the impression that it had already been built.[55] Architectural drawings of the structure were put on display in 1934 in an October Anniversary exhibit held in the ground-floor windows along Moscow's Gorky Street; foreshadowing the Moscow General Plan unveiled in 1935, over a dozen images of the Palace, along with redevelopment plans for the surrounding area of the city, were included in the display.[56] The Palace of Soviets metro station (now Kropotkinskaia) was one of the first to open in 1935. The children's film *Kosmicheskii reis (Cosmic Voyage),* featuring an opening sequence showing the Palace of Soviets already built in Moscow, opened in theaters in 1935 and played until at least 1940. In 1936, Palace of Soviets chocolates were introduced on the assembly lines of the Red October Chocolate Factory.[57] In 1937, a model of the Palace of Soviets was on display at Moscow's Tret'iakov Gallery,[58] and in 1939, the model made its way across the ocean to be exhibited inside the Soviet pavilion, designed by Iofan, at the New York World's Fair. By the decade's end, the unbuilt tower had become an icon.

In Moscow's architectural circles as well, the design competitions for the Palace of Soviets were touted as a great turning point in the development of Soviet architecture and the building itself featured as the capstone project of Moscow's socialist reconstruction. In his speech at the All-Union meeting of architects held in Leningrad in May 1935, Moscow-based architect Nikolai D. Kolli proclaimed that "the announcement about the competition for the design of the Palace of Soviets marks a historic milestone in the reorganization of architectural production in the entire USSR." The "turning point in architecture" ushered in by the Palace of Soviets was for Kolli and other Soviet architects the start of a new era in design and practice, one that saw the architectural profession respond to the Communist Party directives laid out by Kaganovich at the June 1931 Plenum. Soviet architects, the party, and the state, Kolli proclaimed, had been tasked with "the establishment of an exemplary architecture [*polnotsennaia arkhitektura*], one that will combine complete utility with high artistry and emotionally-expressive forms."[59] Kolli asserted that the competition had opened before architects "wonderful possibilities for victories in socialist construction." But, Kolli chided, it had also "revealed the lagging behind and unpreparedness of the entire architectural front."[60]

In order to catch up, Soviet architects would have to go abroad. In March 1934, Mikhailov drew up a budget and requested a report from the USDS Engineering Office in preparation for the organization's first trip to America. Originally scheduled for May-August 1934, but delayed to late 1934, this journey was the first of several that USDS architects and engineers would take in the 1930s in their search for the expertise required to build Moscow's monumental Palace of Soviets.

SEEKING MODELS AND MARKETS ABROAD

The Palace of Soviets stood at the heart of Soviet efforts in the 1930s to transform Moscow into a socialist city. But that the building was meant to be "socialist" did not preclude the architects and engineers working at the USDS from openly borrowing foreign, non-socialist models for the Palace's design. Nor did it prevent them from engaging in the capitalist markets and transnational networks of expertise that they saw as necessary to the Palace's realization. The USDS was officially encouraged, authorized, and expected to act as a bridge between the capitalist building industry abroad and the non-market-based construction effort underway in Moscow.

Within a few months of announcing the winning design for the Palace, the USDS began preparing to send its first delegation abroad. The group would travel in autumn 1934 across Europe and over the Atlantic, stopping first in New York City, where it made its most fruitful connections with American engineers and building experts. The USDS delegation then travelled on to tour other American cities before returning again to New York, where they signed contracts with Moran & Proctor, one of the world's foremost foundations engineering firms. In 1935, an American delegation headed by Carleton S. Proctor himself travelled to Moscow to oversee work on the Palace of Soviets construction site directly. A second USDS delegation travelled to the US one year after the first, signing further contracts with Moran & Proctor for additional consultation work on the Palace.[61] The Palace of Soviets ensured that Moscow's Stalin-era development was tied in significant and lasting ways to global networks of expertise and to international technological advances. The very monumentality of the chosen design for the Palace demanded it.

Soviet architects and engineers of the 1930s were not unusual in their continued engagement with the world beyond Soviet borders. Similar trends carried on in other areas of Soviet life as well, from literature and the arts to economics.[62] In architecture and engineering, the model for this kind of international engagement, along with the institutions and connections that could easily facilitate it, was established during the First Five-Year Plan of 1928 to 1932. During the period of the Five-Year Plan, Soviet leaders intensified practices that they had begun during NEP, hiring increasing numbers of foreign experts and purchasing materials and machines from abroad. While German technology and economic assistance were dominant during the 1920s, by 1930 American technology took the lead.[63] American entrepreneurs were not dissuaded by the US government's policy of non-recognition of the USSR. Instead, they were keen to gain entry into the Soviet economy, especially during the period of intense industrial and agricultural development that began in the late 1920s. Both smaller firms (like Moran & Proctor) and large, leading American companies (including General Electric and Ford) signed technical-assistance agreements with the Soviet Union, as well as "pure" and "mixed"-company concessions that enabled foreign corporate bodies to invest capital, technology, and know-how into the Soviet economy and profit in turn.[64]

By the early 1930s, many of those who had become active players in the Soviet economy began to petition the US government to recognize the USSR. Moritz Kahn, for example, was quoted in *Izvestiia* in 1930 calling for diplomatic recognition, which had become especially important, Kahn argued, during the current economic crisis as the US was losing its position in the world economy.[65] Moritz was the brother of Albert Kahn, Ford's main architect in Detroit who had designed the Ford River Rouge Complex in Dearborn, Michigan. Between 1929 and 1932, Moritz ran Kahn Associates' Moscow office, coordinating a number of projects commissioned by the Soviet government, the first of which had been the Cheliabinsk tractor factory. This firm closed its Soviet branch and left Moscow after the Kahns could not agree on new terms set by the Soviet government in 1932.[66] Albert Kahn nonetheless maintained an amiable relationship with the Soviet Union, becoming an important contact for Soviet architects and engineers working on the Palace of Soviets. As early as 1931, long before a design for the Palace was chosen, USDS managers were in conversation with Kahn as they sought to "maximize the use of American experience in construction technologies." In 1931, it was Kahn who suggested that the office send its specialists abroad to consult with American experts directly.[67]

The USDS delegation was not the first Soviet group to cross the Atlantic in search of technical expertise. As American industrialists and workers were arriving in large numbers in the USSR during the period of the First Five-Year Plan, Soviet experts were also visiting the US, touring factories and industrial facilities.[68] The US Department of State kept a close watch on the back-and-forth of Soviet and American experts. Without an official embassy in Moscow, the State Department received its information through the US Legation in Riga, which subscribed to dozens of Russian-language newspapers and periodicals and was especially intent on following the Comintern's activities as closely as possible from the Baltic.[69] The Riga Legation was also an avid watcher of Moscow's "socialist reconstruction" effort. In late October 1931, the Legation wrote to the US Secretary of State to inform him, "in view of the interest expressed by American construction concerns," that the Metrostroi construction office had just been created and work on the Moscow metro had begun.[70] The punctilious aide who wrote this memo added in an aside that in February 1930, Pavel Rotert, who was now chief of construction of the Moscow metro, had "made a trip to the U.S.A. as representative of 'Dneprovsky Combinat' for the purpose of studying the construction of hydroelectric stations."[71] While it was Rotert's trip to America that was of interest to Washington, the consular aid had put his finger, inadvertently, on the close links that existed between the industrial construction projects of the First Five-Year Plan and Moscow's later urban development. Soviet personnel, like Rotert, moved fluidly in the 1930s from earlier posts overseeing big industrial projects in the Soviet hinterlands to positions managing large-scale infrastructural and politically symbolic projects in the capital.

The US government ended its policy of non-recognition on November 16, 1933. All memoranda regarding Soviet affairs were now sent to the State Department directly from the American Consulate General in Moscow. In May 1934, Washington received a memo about the Palace of Soviets from G. C. Hanson, the new Consul General. A few months after the final design for the Palace had been approved and announced, Hanson had visited Vasilii Mikhailov, Head of Construction for the Palace of Soviets, at his office in the city center. Mikhailov showed Hanson the project designs for the Palace and "intimated that much of the necessary machinery and technical assistance for the successful completion of such a project would have to be secured from abroad."[72] Hanson reported that most of Mikhailov's time was taken up not by the Palace but with "the administration of affairs in connection with the Dnieper Combinate,"[73] a hydro-electric plant on the Dnieper River. The Dnieper work would occupy Mikhailov for another year, Hanson noted, after which time the Soviet manager planned to "make a trip to the United States to make studies of the construction work there." Hanson felt Mikhailov's attitude to be courteous—"upon my departure he invited me to visit the Dnieper Combinate."[74] Like Rotert at Metrostroi, Mikhailov had moved from hydroelectric dam construction to the socialist reconstruction of Moscow. Although Mikhailov never did go to the US personally, his office was busy during spring and summer 1934 getting budgetary approval and visa papers in order to send USDS experts on their first trip to America.

The teams of Soviet architects and engineers who traveled to the US in 1934 and again in 1935 sought to gain expert assistance on a project that was neither industrial nor agricultural. They nonetheless used the same international networks mobilized for the First Five-Year Plan to do it, and they carried with them a long-standing Soviet reverence not just for American technology, but also for American managerial expertise.[75] It was the Amtorg Trading Corporation that formed the most important link between the USSR and the US. Created in 1924 and based in New York, Amtorg was, technically, an American corporation, but it represented the Soviet government in business dealings within the US.[76] As the seller of Soviet goods to the US market, Amtorg competed with other American companies. From its offices at the corner of Fifth Avenue and 29th Street in midtown Manhattan, Amtorg placed ads for Russian glassware, Bokhara carpets, and, prior to 1933, waged a campaign to persuade the US government to recognize the USSR.[77] But as a buyer, Amtorg had no competition from other Soviet agencies. As E. C. Ropes of the American Commerce Department wrote in 1943, Amtorg "represented a single huge purchaser, whose orders were at times and for certain firms the only large ones offered."[78] It was through Amtorg that American companies negotiated their technical assistance agreements during the period of the First Five-Year Plan, and it was through Amtorg that the USDS made its connections to the American architectural and engineering professions. From its offices in Manhattan, Amtorg was particularly well placed to introduce USDS experts to American skyscraper architects and engineers.

In September 1935, Petr A. Bogdanov, head of Amtorg from 1930–1934, gave a speech to a Soviet audience about his recent experiences in the US. "The essence of American efficiency," Bogdanov opined, was "simplicity and expediency; the ability to solve problems in the simplest and most effective manner with the smallest expenditure of means and labor and with the greatest results."[79] Bogdanov, an engineer by training, continued with the example of the Empire State Building:

> From my office window on the seventeenth floor of one of the skyscrapers along Fifth Avenue I was able to observe the daily construction of the biggest building in the world—the Empire State. Every day at specified hours, trucks brought separate metal structures that had been previously bolted together. A simplified derrick picked them up and raised them to the required height. The building grounds were never cluttered up, and the construction in no way interfered with the stream of pedestrians on the sidewalk.
>
> But one day I noticed that men were raising boards by hand. They started from the ground up and handed them from one story to the next in such a way that it was difficult to see just how they did it. Observing them more closely, I noticed that there were workers standing on each floor and handing the boards upwards. It seems that it would be necessary to build a special and very complicated machine to raise the boards mechanically [but], since boards are used only on a few rare occasions, the Americans had recourse to the most efficient method. They stationed twenty workers who raised the whole lot within half an hour. The Americans were not ashamed to use hand labor on a highly mechanized construction because in this case the hand method was the most rational. That's what I mean when I speak of simplicity in solving problems.[80]

Whether or not Bogdanov's view of rational methods, as seen from Amtorg's seventeenth-floor offices, was accurate, the proof of American efficiency, for Bogdanov and many others, was plain to see: the Empire State Building opened in May 1931 after being built at record speed.[81]

Before being recalled back to Moscow from his post in New York, Bogdanov had helped coordinate the USDS visit to the US in 1934.[82] Under Bogdanov's guidance, Amtorg negotiated contracts with American companies tapped to lend their expertise and efficiency to the construction of the Palace of Soviets. In addition to its role negotiating with and paying American firms, Amtorg had an important part to play in the transfer of information. As work began on the Palace of Soviets construction site, Amtorg handled communications between the site in Moscow and Moran & Proctor in New York. Most crucially, Amtorg translated important letters from Russian into English in which Soviet engineers asked questions of their American contractors about the ongoing project. They then sent translated responses back to Moscow. Amtorg was not just in the business of negotiating trade; it was also a vital node in the transfer of technical and cultural knowledge.

In autumn 1934, all three architects of the Palace of Soviets, Iofan, Shchuko, Gel'freikh, plus USDS engineer, Vasilii P. Nikolaev, made their way by train from Moscow to Western Europe. They visited Berlin, Leipzig, Paris, and London before continuing across the ocean to the US.[83] The main purpose of this first journey was to compare the proposed design plan for the Palace of Soviets with contemporary American building practices.[84] The delegation was tasked with studying the latest advances in foundations engineering, steel-frame construction, acoustics, and building materials.[85] In March 1934, the USDS Engineering Office had drawn up a draft itinerary for the trip. This itinerary saw the group criss-crossing Depression-era America, visiting important building sites and consulting with experts in Washington, DC, Philadelphia, Detroit, Chicago, Atlantic City, and, most important, New York City.[86] The USDS Engineering Office instructed the delegation, dubbed the "Architectural-Technical Commission," to conduct detailed studies of two to three major American building projects, and of four to five businesses supplying parts or materials for the US construction industry. The delegation would also hold a dozen or so consultations with American engineers, institutes, and firms on questions about the materials and methods to be used in the construction of the Palace. Specifically, USDS engineers wanted confirmation of the type of construction that should be used for the Palace's tower, topped by its enormous statue of Lenin. They also wanted to know whether their foundations, geotechnical, and electrical engineering plans, and their plans for the assembly of the building's steel carcass, were based on the latest construction methods.

The Architectural-Technical Commission set off in September 1934 with something to the tune of 26,000 US dollars (corrected for inflation, almost half a million dollars) to pay for hotels, meals, car rentals, and expert consultations.[87] The commission was given a list of specific buildings to visit during their voyage. In DC, it was the Capitol Building and the company town of the National Bureau of Standards, a government housing complex planned during the First World War. In Detroit, it was the Fisher, Union Trust, and General Motors Buildings; in Chicago the Tribune Tower and, of course, the Chicago "Century of Progress" World's Fair.[88] New York was the first city on the list, and it was also the city with the longest collection of must-see buildings. The Empire State Building and Radio City, which was still under construction, were at the top of the list, followed by the Chrysler, Woolworth, and Municipal Buildings. Since the Palace of Soviets presented a number of challenges in the areas of acoustics and lighting, large American theaters were also included as important sites to visit. The Palace of Soviets was, after all, to act as the Soviet government's primary stage before the people. The Palace's Great Hall had grown from a space holding 15,000 people in the original competition brief to one holding over 20,000. An enormous domed amphitheater, the Great Hall would sit at the base of the building beneath the statue of Lenin.[89] As the manager of the USDS would later put it, the "elimination of echo" in the Great Hall was "one of the most difficult [problems] to overcome in the designing of the Palace of Soviets."[90] In search of models in 1934, the commission visited the Paramount, Roxy, and Earl Carroll Theaters in New York. It also held consultations with Bell and Western Electric.[91]

The Architectural-Technical Commission's concerns about lighting and acoustics were secondary, however, to the information it had to procure in the area of foundations engineering. The commission signed a preliminary contract with Moran & Proctor in October 1934 that included a review, or "criticism," of the plan already prepared by Soviet engineers, as well as the drawing up of two new plans. The first of these new plans would be based on "the newest methods and equipment," the second was a low-budget option that would enable "the arrangement of work, eliminating the necessity of expensive equipment."[92] That the Soviet engineers working on the Palace of Soviets in Moscow already had advanced engineering knowledge is clear from their reports. The USDS engineering team sent a lengthy report to Moran & Proctor in 1935 detailing the surveys already conducted on the construction site to measure the types of soil that lay beneath the construction plot and from that to determine the logistics of construction work.[93] The files sent to New York also indicate that in addition to its knowledge of soil mechanics, the Moscow team was using modern engineering management practices. The materials sent to New York include, for example, Gantt charts showing projected timelines for construction. Moreover, the excavation process already underway in Moscow by 1935 made use of a combination of Soviet-made and foreign machinery—German-designed Orenstein & Koppel excavators were being used alongside *Mashinostroitel'* excavators.[94] The Soviet engineers were not novices, but they were convinced that a building like the Palace of Soviets required the technical expertise and managerial strategies that had evolved in the US over the course of dozens of construction projects.

In both the US and in the USSR, the 1930s was a decade of big building projects. From dams to bridges to skyscrapers, both American and Soviet engineers and architects sought to push beyond the limits of past achievements with large construction projects that were often as symbolic as they were functional. Carleton S. Proctor, hired by the USDS to work on the Palace, was among the world's foremost experts in the field of large-scale construction. During the 1930s his firm, which was founded in 1910 and specialized in foundations engineering, was also engaged in major building projects in the US. These included the George Washington Bridge of 1931, the Lincoln Tunnel of 1930 and 1937, the Colorado River Dam of 1937, the 1939 World's Fair site in Flushing New York, and the Golden Gate and San Francisco-Oakland Bay Bridges, built in 1933 and 1934 respectively.[95] In addition to their work on the Palace of Soviets in Moscow, Moran & Proctor were involved in the construction in 1935 of the United Fruit Company's Dock in Panama and the Malpaso Canyon Dam in Peru, built in 1936.[96] In September 1935, in an order marked "top secret," Molotov, in his position as Chairman of the *Sovnarkom*, approved payment of $18,000 to Moran & Proctor for foundations work on the Palace of Soviets site.[97]

Over the course of the following months, Proctor and his team made suggestions for the Palace of Soviets based on the particular assumptions the firm held from working mainly in the American context. Moran & Proctor's recommendations were based on knowledge of American equipment, which they recommended that the USDS purchase.[98] They also suggested ways to speed up the project. Excavation, the American engineers proposed, could be accomplished more quickly by adding additional steps to the logistics plan.[99] Moran & Proctor worked on the assumption that time and speed mattered—and they did in the Soviet context, though arguably in different ways than in America. Whereas in the US, investors turned to engineers to find ways to shorten the construction process in order to more quickly gain returns on their investment, a different logic seemed to be at work in the USSR. Upon his return from Moscow in 1935, Proctor interpreted this difference in a press statement. Framing the Palace as part of the broader modernization and development schemes underway in the Soviet Union, Proctor noted that "we [Americans] could not afford such production. To them [the Soviets] there is economic justification for this building. They must overcome the inferiority complex of the Russian peasant. And they are doing it."[100] Despite these apparent differences between the US and Soviet contexts, the approach to the Moscow project, from the engineering perspective, was not so different from one that might be taken in New York. For example, Moran & Proctor recommended a circular foundation footing for the Palace of Soviets based on the model they had used a decade earlier in their work on the New York County Courthouse in downtown Manhattan.[101]

Proctor was like many American experts who came into contact with the Soviet Union during the interwar period. He approached his work in the USSR with a sense of his own nation's superiority and mastery in the face of a developing but still "backward" country. To the American press, Proctor spoke highly of Iofan and his team of engineers. Ahead of his own trip to Moscow in 1935, Proctor was enthusiastic about the Palace project, and about the expertise awaiting him on the ground in Moscow. "In view of the difficult problems involved, the preparatory work done by the Soviet engineers in the subsoil investigation was outstanding," he told the *Herald Tribune* shortly before leaving for Moscow.[102] A Princeton Alumnus, Proctor was tied, however, to circles that would readily scoff at the Soviet Union and at the Palace project. The *Princeton Alumni Weekly* reported in its July 1, 1935 issue about Proctor's involvement on the project. "Proctor sailed for Russia on May 8 in order to put up a monstrous building for the Soviet Government," the *Weekly* stated. "Fairly near the Kremlin on the Red Square of Moscow, Carleton is going to toss up a shack that, without the slightest bit of exaggeration, will be big enough to house several structures the size of the Empire State Building. Just why the be-whiskered sippers of vodka think they want such a tower of Babel is a mystery to Carl as well as to us."[103] Although Proctor's own public statements about his experiences in Moscow were generally more diplomatic, the *Princeton* quip was likely not far from his own view. Later in life, Proctor would become a firm anti-communist. In his inaugural address as

President of the American Society of Civil Engineers in 1951, Proctor called on American engineers to "fight 'statism' and the intolerances that make us vulnerable to communism."[104] Basing this call on his experiences in Moscow in the 1930s, Proctor noted that

> ever since, in private conversations in Moscow 22 years ago, it was pointed out to me that ours was one of the most vulnerable societies to communistic encroachment—because our country harbored the greatest extremes in intolerance, religious, racial and sectional—ever since that time I have been trying to point out to engineers the power they possess to oppose intolerance in all its forms.[105]

Yet while Cold War-era posturing was where all of these relations were headed in the years after 1945, the interwar period still saw cooperation and even, in some cases, friendship between Soviet experts and their foreign colleagues.

There was considerable interest on the American side, both from the technical community and from the press, in the Palace of Soviets project and in the Soviet commission that toured the US in 1934. The Hector Hamilton scandal of 1932 had died down quickly, and soon major American papers printed stories that spoke of the Palace in favorable and excited terms. In 1934, with Iofan and company in New York, the *New York Times* reported that the city's Architectural League had entertained the visiting Soviet experts at a special tea held in their honor. The Soviet commission was warmly welcomed by Ralph T. Walker, then President of the New York chapter of the American Institute of Architects, who praised the Palace of Soviets itself as "thrilling and imagination stirring."[106] In 1935, with the headline "Huge Palace Held Feasible in Moscow," the *New York Times* publicly announced the American involvement in the project by reporting that Proctor had consulted on the Palace and found the plans sound and feasible.[107] A later issue of *Mechanix Illustrated* featured the Palace of Soviets, in a drawing by Douglas Rolfe, alongside the world's tallest buildings (fig. 2.6). The drawing captured the ambition and excitement, characteristic of the interwar period, of such large-scale and complex projects. Flying just above the enormous statue of Lenin is the DC-4, a plane that would be used extensively in World War II, but that was in 1939 still in the planning stages.

It is difficult for our eyes to reclaim this view of the Palace of Soviets, a building that prompts mainly laughter today, associated as it is with the failure of the Soviet project. The Palace has become, as Susan Buck-Morss notes, "the quintessential example of Stalinist monumentality, an icon of the architecture of dictatorship."[108] But the Palace of Soviets was understood in its time as one among many major building projects of its age. For many observers in the 1930s, the building's construction seemed possible and even desirable. As Ralph Walker put it, the Palace was a building that stirred the imagination. The excitement surrounding this building's construction was tied to a broader enthusiasm in the 1930s for large-scale projects that showcased the virility and might of world civilizations. Not everyone was happy with the chosen aesthetic—having seen the final design in the *New York Times,* a group of American workers wrote to the Central Executive Committee of the USSR beseeching it to "abandon this monstrosity . . . [this] bastard of bastards" that

WORLD'S TALLEST BUILDING

Figure 2.6: "World's Tallest Building," drawing by Douglas Rolfe. *Mechanix Illustrated*, September 1939.

"dim[ed their] faith in the success of the Workers' State"—but few argued against the need for monumentality.[109]

In 1935, once he was back in Moscow, Iofan prepared a report on the findings of the first Architectural-Technical Commission's trip abroad. Based on what it had seen, the commission was convinced that "American technology is the most applicable [model] in its pace, its approach to problem solving, in the precision of the model for carrying out work, and in the businesses that serve construction."[110] In laying out the work that needed to be done by the USDS for the Palace's foundations, acoustics, elevators, and air conditioning, and for the many other elements in the building's design, Iofan continued to correspond with many of the specialists he had met in the US, following up on specific discussions, asking new questions, and in some cases writing simply to express his thanks. In April 1935, Iofan wrote to Albert Kahn in Detroit to solicit advice on hiring an American lighting expert after receiving a letter from Stanley McCandless, Professor of Lighting at Yale Drama Department, who was "intensely interested in the Palace of the Soviets."[111] Kahn recommended some new studies on lighting, cautioned against hiring McCandless, and wrote to the National Electric Lamp Association in Cleveland on Iofan's behalf, promising to write again as soon as he had heard back.[112] In May 1935, Iofan wrote to John R. Todd, manager of John D. Rockefeller's construction empire in New York. "I recall with great pleasure," Iofan wrote, "the time spent in your company. The design of the Palace of Soviets is being worked out in detail now and we make use of your authoritative and helpful recommendations."[113] Iofan also sent sincere regards and best wishes from Shchuko, Gel'freikh, and Nikolaev. Todd sent a warm reply from his office at Rockefeller Plaza in return.[114]

Before Iofan received Todd's reply, a separate letter arrived in Moscow, this one from his son, Webster B. Todd. Webster also worked for Rockefeller, managing the Radio City (by now called Rockefeller Center) construction site between Fifth and Sixth Avenues in New York. "When your Commission was here last Fall," the younger Todd wrote to Iofan in his letter of June 6, 1935, "we had the pleasure of showing you about Rockefeller Center." Webster reminded Iofan that at that time work had just begun on the foundations and the steel was just being set for the 38-story building. "This building has now been completed and I thought you might be interested in some of the data showing the length of time it took to finish the work and put the tenants in their offices," Webster wrote. He laid out the figures for Iofan (136 working days between the setting of steel and the Certificate of Occupancy). "All this data will probably bore you," he wrote, "but you and your group were so interested and enthusiastic that I am taking the liberty of forwarding the information to you. Please give my kindest regards and best wishes to the other members of your Commission."[115] Iofan replied with enthusiasm, expressing his "admiration" at the speedy completion of the Rockefeller Center and saying that he remembered his visit to New York "with great pleasure."[116]

That Iofan and the Architectural-Technical Commission made friends and connections in New York, in some cases among the Rockefeller crowd, is not as surprising as it may seem. For one thing, the commission had something of a man on the inside in Viacheslav K. Oltarzhevskii, who at that time went by "Walter Oltar-jevsky." Oltarzhevskii had worked for Aleksei Shchusev in Moscow in the early 1920s before leaving the

Soviet Union in 1924 to study advanced building technology in New York. Oltar-zhevskii first found work at the firm of Helmie & Corbett, and then in the studio of Wallace K. Harrison. From 1931 he was involved in the construction of Rockefeller Center.[117] But more important, despite difficulties with language and some fairly substantial cultural differences, Iofan, Shchuko, and Gel'freikh shared with New York's skyscraper architects of the 1930s a common disposition toward architectural work. These were all men who shared a similar training, many of them spending their formative years studying in Italy or France. The relationships they forged in the 1930s were amicable and based on mutual understanding. This did not mean, however, that Iofan and his team were uncritical observers of America.

Iofan would write about his impressions of New York and other American cities in a handful of essays published upon his return in 1935 and 1936. In these essays, Iofan was critical of American cities in general, and of New York, with its slapdash and unplanned skyscraper layout, in particular. Yet this too should be seen as a disposition that Iofan shared with some of his American contacts. The Soviet architect returned to Moscow in 1935 articulating the same anti-urban critiques then being voiced in the US by figures like Lewis Mumford and Frank Lloyd Wright.

MOSCOW'S DUELING INFLUENCES

Technology transfer was a crucial component of the Soviet Union's self-fashioning and self-understanding during the 1920s and 1930s. The managers of the Palace of Soviets project, many of whom had worked on the large-scale industrial projects of the First Five-Year Plan, took it for granted that Moscow's socialist reconstruction would be undertaken with Western—in particular, American—technical assistance. This assumption was in part a product of the First Five-Year Plan period, but it was also the result of a broader cultural attitude in the 1930s that favored foreign ideas and connections. This is a decade that Katerina Clark has dubbed the "Great Appropriation." As Clark observes, "in building up its own image, Moscow appropriated both laterally (absorbing contemporary trends in other countries, primarily western European but also American) and diachronically (appropriating Great Russian and European culture of the past)."[118] A strong example of this dual appropriation, Clark notes, is the Palace of Soviets, which drew on American but also Italian influences.

In 1935, after his trip to America the previous year, Iofan commented in an essay printed in *Pravda* that "wherever I might travel, whatever I might see, I approached everything from a particular point of view: what of all this has to be 'taken home' to the Soviet Union."[119] Vladimir Shchuko harbored a similar instinct. Writing in *Arkhitektura SSSR*, also after the 1934 trip, Shchuko stated that "America can give our architects much in the field of building technology, in the knowledge of how to use construction materials, and more generally in the realm of bold solutions to architectural problems."[120] But in the realm of aesthetics, Shchuko cautioned, America should be avoided. The USDS's Architectural-Technical Commission had returned to the USSR via Italy, spending some weeks in that country reacquainting themselves with classical architecture at Pompeii and Herculaneum. Iofan and Shchuko had both studied and lived in Italy before the revolution.[121] Their commission now toured the country anew, visiting the amphitheater at Capua ("one of the world's largest," Iofan explained in his later report to Molotov) and the marble quarries at Carrara.[122] After a twenty-year absence, Shchuko, who had studied in Italy in 1905, was overjoyed by the trip. The return voyage "confirmed my belief that our youth who are studying architecture as an art can and should only do this in Italy with the best examples of classical architecture."[123] Having cleansed themselves of any lingering Americanism on the streets of Rome, Florence, and Naples, the Architectural-Technical Commission returned to their work in Moscow in early 1935. "My heart filled with pride," Iofan wrote in *Pravda*, "when I returned to Moscow and rode on our metro for the first time." A "strikingly beautiful and enormous construction," the Moscow metro, Iofan wrote, was quite superior to the drab New York subway.[124]

In their criticisms of New York City, Iofan and other Soviet architects of the 1930s drew on ideas and modes of expression that dated back decades in Russian literature. Like Iofan and his commission in 1934, Russian and Soviet writers had long expressed both adoration and disdain for the American city.[125] This genre included works like Maksim Gorky's 1906 poem "The City of the Yellow Devil," Mayakovsky's 1925 poem cycle "My Discovery of America," and Il'ia Il'f and Evgenii Petrov's American road-trip travelogue published in 1934.[126] In all of these works, descriptions of life in New York City served to fuel each writer's critique of American capitalist values more broadly. As Gorky wrote at the turn of the century:

> This is a city. This is New York. Twenty-storeyed houses, dark and soundless skyscrapers, stand on the shore. Square, lacking in any desire to be beautiful, the bulky, ponderous buildings tower gloomily and drearily. A haughty pride in its height, and its ugliness is felt in each house. There are no flowers at the windows and no children to be seen . . . Entering the city is like getting into a stomach of stone and iron, a stomach that has swallowed several million people and is grinding and digesting them.[127]

Two decades later Il'f and Petrov, the Soviet Union's most beloved satirists, would pick up the thread of Gorky's earlier critique in their description of a city now gripped by depression:

> The first impression of New York is that it is too big, too rich, too dirty, and too poor. Everything is too extreme. There's too much light on some streets, and not enough on others . . .
>
> Americans think that their technical skill has been raised to an unusual degree as a result of the advantages of the social structure of the United States. But in fact, American technical skill has needed the development of a new way of life for a long time now. The empty skyscrapers and factories working only three days a week testify to this.[128]

As the argument went, American technological prowess was undeniably impressive, but it could go no further under America's "stupefying social order."[129] With American development at a dead end, the Soviet Union would take on the mantle of leadership in all realms, including architecture and urban planning.[130] They would combine American technology with classicism under the banner of socialist development, and Moscow would serve as the model.

While Soviet architects of the 1930s drew on many of the same tropes as Gorky and Il'f and Petrov in formulating their criticisms they also drew on first-hand familiarity with depression-era America and on critical texts written by Americans themselves. The notion that the American model of urban planning was bankrupt could be found at the time chiefly in the writings of Lewis Mumford and Frank Lloyd Wright, both of whom were known to Soviet architects of the period. Frank Lloyd Wright was familiar with the Moscow architectural scene of the 1930s, having attended the Union of Soviet Architects' First Congress in Moscow in 1937.[131] Mumford, by contrast, had no direct dealings with the Soviet Union but was appreciated in Moscow through text. In 1936, the USSR Academy of Architecture Press published a Russian translation of Mumford's 1924 book *Sticks and Stones*.[132] In *Sticks and Stones*, Mumford charted the development of architecture in the US, from the forest huts of the first European colonists to skyscrapers. Soviet architectural historian and critic David E. Arkin, who wrote the preface to the Russian edition of *Sticks and Stones*, saw Mumford's book as "first of all a pamphlet, in which the theme of architecture is used merely as a motive for a more general theme: the analysis and criticism of the whole culture of American capitalism."[133] Mumford seemed to confirm for his Soviet readers that it was capitalism that had doomed American cities to failure.

In 1936, Iofan published an article based on his trip to the US and Italy in 1934, but also on his decade-long experience studying and working as an architect in Rome. (Iofan had returned to the Soviet Union from Italy only in 1924.) The purpose of Iofan's article was not to give a historical survey of past architectural development in America and Italy, but to highlight the "rich building experience" of the contemporary US and the "most interesting moments" of architectural development in Italy.[134] Concluding a long section on the American skyscraper, Iofan quoted Mumford's description of skyscrapers from the new Russian-language edition of *Sticks and Stones*:

> One need not dwell upon the way in which these obdurate, overwhelming masses take away from the little people who walk in their shadows any semblance of dignity as human beings . . . A building that one cannot readily see, a building that reduces the passerby to a mere mote, whirled and buffeted by the winds of traffic, a building that has no accommodating grace or perfection in its interior furnishing, beyond its excellent lavatories—in what sense is such a building a great work of architecture, or how can the mere manner of its construction create a great style?[135]

Praising Mumford as an "interesting and sharp architectural critic," Iofan used Mumford's condemnation of American architecture to bolster his own. Contrasting the American and Soviet city, Iofan argued that the chief difference lay not in building type or technique, but in the scale and scope of city planning. "For us [Soviets] the city is a grandiose complex, all parts of which are interdependent."[136] Only in combination with socialist city planning, Iofan asserted, could the virtues and values of the skyscraper be expressed. It was left to the USSR to find in the skyscraper a "great work of architecture." The great potential inherent in this monumental building type could only be realized, Iofan argued, in the socialist city.

There was one skyscraper in New York City that Iofan characterized in a positive light. In his 1936 article, Rockefeller Center received special attention from Iofan, just as it did in 1934 when his Architectural-Technical Commission was visiting New York. As the commission later reported, since work was still in progress on the Rockefeller site, they were able to see first-hand the organizational side of construction in the US.[137] While Radio City Music Hall, which was about the size of the smaller of the two Palace of Soviets auditoriums, served as an important model for acoustics and lighting, the tall Rockefeller skyscraper at the center of the vast complex, then called the RCA Building, was of greatest interest to the commission. Designed by Raymond Hood, this skyscraper was a close analogue to the Palace project in many ways. It was a monumental complex containing offices and theaters, like the Palace, as well as restaurants, shops, and radio broadcasting studios. The building's setbacks, and the opulence of its interior and exterior decorative sculptures, mosaics, and frescos were also very similar to plans for the Palace.[138] In the murals, sculptures, and friezes that were then being applied to the interior and exterior walls of the RCA Building and other structures in the complex, Iofan, Shchuko, and Gel'freikh may well have noticed a number of communist symbols snuck in by the left-leaning artists hired for the project. The Architectural-Technical Commission arrived in New York after Diego Rivera's mural, *Man at a Crossroads,* was hastily removed by sledgehammer from the RCA Building's main entrance—but only *just* after. And the lingering scandal of having had, however briefly, an enormous portrait of Lenin and an image of a May Day parade on Red Square in the entrance to the Rockefeller Center surely reached the ears of the visiting Soviet delegation.[139] But most important, Iofan observed in the Rockefeller Center a sharp criticism of American urbanism. Unlike the "fantastic disorder" and "merely commercial character" of New York City as a whole, Iofan saw in the Rockefeller Center planning elements similar to those increasingly favored in the Soviet Union. As Iofan wrote in *Pravda* in 1939, "one feels that here [in the Rockefeller Center] an attempt has been made to create an ensemble."[140]

By the late 1930s, the "ensemble" had come to dominate architectural discussions in Moscow. As David Arkin, who had written the Preface to Mumford's *Sticks and Stones*, explained to an American colleague during the flurry of correspondence exchanged between the US and the USSR during the wartime years,

> the distinctive feature of architectural work in our [Soviet] country is its close contact with town planning. Here an architect must be able to design not only separate residential and public buildings but entire streets, whole blocks and towns. We aim at achieving integral architectural "ensembles" in our cities. This is especially important now when many of our towns and cities have been razed to the ground by the Nazi aggressors.[141]

By the postwar period, the "ensemble" would become, as Soviet architects asserted, "one of the most important creative problems of socialist realism."[142] And when the Soviet state issued a decree in 1947 that called for eight additional skyscrapers to be built in Moscow, with the Palace of Soviets to stand as the ninth and tallest structure in the city center, it was the principle of the "ensemble" that underlay the project.

No USDS commission ever visited America again after 1935, but not for lack of trying. In late 1937, USDS officials wrote to Molotov to ask that Palace of Soviets specialists be sent on a three-month-long trip to the US. The request was never granted.[143] One year later, in 1938, Iofan himself wrote to Molotov from New York

City, where the architect was overseeing the construction of his Soviet pavilion at the New York World's Fair. Iofan urged Molotov to allow the USDS to send its experts back to America.[144] But once again, no measures were taken to make such a trip possible. By 1938, there were other events preoccupying Soviet officials back in Moscow—events that would make international engagement all but impossible.

THE TERROR

The USDS was not immune to the violence that swept across the Soviet Union in the late 1930s. Administrative staff and workers from various departments of the organization were purged and the USDS was left without a leader for a period of four months after Vasilii Mikhailov was arrested in June 1937.[145] Three months after his arrest, Mikhailov was executed for his alleged "sabotage and participation in a counter-revolutionary terrorist organization."[146] When Andrei Nikitich Prokof'ev replaced Mikhailov in October 1937, he too faced the threat of arrest.[147] Within months of becoming the USDS boss, Prokof'ev was denounced by his subordinates for rudeness, cronyism, and "suppression of self-criticism" in letters sent to Molotov and Stalin.[148] In 1938, Molotov ordered that Prokof'ev be discreetly investigated.[149] Soon, many of those close to the new boss were arrested, including Prokof'ev's direct assistant and others he had brought over to the USDS from his previous position at the "Builder" construction trust.[150] In November 1938, Molotov was handed a report that ostensibly confirmed the validity of many of the accusations leveled against Prokof'ev. In the eyes of his investigator, Prokof'ev was guilty of mismanagement and nepotism. Molotov's investigator also found that the new head of the Palace project was rude: his "sharp remarks" at party meetings frightened the construction workers.[151] The investigation into Prokof'ev implicated other top officials at the USDS as well, from low-level employees right up to architect Boris Iofan.

In the autumn of 1938, while the details of his life fell under scrutiny back in Moscow, Iofan was abroad, busily assembling the Soviet pavilion at the New York World's Fair. Iofan's New York pavilion was similar to the Soviet pavilion he had designed for the 1937 Exposition in Paris. Instead of Vera Mukhina's large steel sculpture of the *Worker and Kolkhoznitsa* that topped the Paris structure, the New York pavilion supported Viacheslav Andreev's *New Soviet Citizen*, an enormous figure with his right hand outstretched, raising a red star high up into the sky above. As the American journal *Architectural Forum* would report in June 1939, fair goers rated Iofan's pavilion first among all the foreign pavilions on display. The *Forum* described the pavilion as "a powerful, if occasionally naive, piece of monumental architecture."[152] Particularly impressive was the life-sized section of a Moscow metro station on display within the pavilion. And while the American pavilion included an enormous diorama of "Democracity"—the "city of the future"—the Soviet exhibition countered with images and descriptions of the 1935 General Plan for the Reconstruction of Moscow. At the center of this exhibit stood a model of the Palace of Soviets.[153] While Soviet curators hoped to emphasize that the socialist "city of the future" was already a reality back in Moscow, for Iofan, the pavilion in New York served primarily as a means to experiment with achieving a synthesis between art and architecture—an experiment that Iofan hoped to apply in the construction of the Palace of Soviets.[154]

Back in Moscow, the incriminating facts of Iofan's life, as uncovered in the 1938 investigation of Prokof'ev, were these: from 1914 to 1926, Iofan lived in Italy and when he returned to the USSR it was "on the invitation of Rykov."[155] Molotov's sleuth learned that, besides Rykov, Iofan was "also close to Bukharin and Radek."[156] Iofan, the investigator insinuated, owed his rise in the Soviet architectural profession to three Old Bolsheviks who had just recently been found guilty at the Moscow Show Trials. In addition to these incriminating connections, Iofan was known to avoid participation in communist party work on the Palace construction site. The architect had also hired employees who were now under arrest by the NKVD.

In the end, neither Prokof'ev nor Iofan were arrested. The Terror nonetheless disrupted the Palace project and left a mark on the USDS. Accusations like those waged against Prokof'ev and Iofan followed the same pattern across the Soviet Union. In 1937, the Central Committee promoted a campaign for "criticism and self-criticism," encouraging, as Wendy Goldman writes, "every self-styled crusader to step forward and expose abuse."[157] Bosses like Prokof'ev and Iofan were expected to play along, confessing to their mistakes publicly and penitently. Though it seems that neither Prokof'ev nor Iofan engaged much in this activity in the thirties, by the postwar years, the rituals of "criticism and self-criticism" would become routinized in meetings of the Palace of Soviets organization. And after the war, these two USDS leaders would take part regularly in their organization's party meetings.

The USDS faced a new set of challenges with the outbreak of war. In June 1941, work on the Palace was put on hold. Immediately after the German invasion, a wartime chain of command came into effect that placed the capital's building organizations, and all those who remained at work within them, under the direct authority of agencies like the local air defense office (*Mestnaia protivovozdushnaia oborona*, or MPVO). While large numbers of USDS workers and staff were drafted into the Red Army, those who remained on the Palace of Soviets construction site set aside their regular work and turned to other tasks: they installed bomb shelters on the site, and they ensured that the USDS's offices, factories, and the partially constructed Palace itself were fire-proofed and camouflaged.[158] The USDS's assets—its factories, materials, and personnel—were also diverted to the war effort. In some cases this meant that the organization lost some of these assets entirely, as in the case of the USDS machine shop, which was transferred to the People's Commissariat of Aviation Industries.[159] By December 1941, with Moscow under direct assault, USDS staff and equipment were evacuated East to head up the construction of the Urals Aluminum Factory, a USDS-led industrial-defense project overseen by Prokof'ev.[160] By keeping construction teams and design cadres together throughout the war, USDS leaders hoped that their organization might be strengthened by the experience.

Iofan, meanwhile, headed up the Academy of Architecture's division in Sverdlovsk, the largest city in the Urals, where, from late 1941, he oversaw the construction of housing for workers in the defense industry and the reconstruction of factories that had been evacuated from the front lines.[161] In his spare time, Iofan reworked the design for the Palace to suit the new ideological imperatives of the Soviet war effort. In the Sverdlovsk version, the Palace was transformed from a structure celebrating the October Revolution and the "construction of socialism" to one that also commemorated the Great Patriotic War. Yet, while Iofan made changes to the Palace's design in Sverdlovsk, back in Moscow the construction site lay barren. A diarist writing under the pseudonym K. Loriston recorded his impressions walking past the site on a warm day in early May 1942:

> On the road near the Palace of Soviets across from the Museum of Fine Arts I saw bombed-out houses, the bombs were probably heavy, windows knocked out, ceilings collapsed . . . I wonder what the fate of the Palace of Soviets will be, [they] had just installed the foundation footing, and on one side stands a steel skeleton of ten stories, rusting.[162]

The Palace of Soviets would remain in this ruinous state through the war and into the postwar years. The project lived on, however, in other ways. The technical expertise acquired by the USDS in the interwar period played a crucial role in Moscow's postwar skyscraper project. When Soviet Ministers gathered in January 1947 for the first round of planning meetings for the eight skyscrapers that would soon be under construction in Moscow, they raised questions once more of monumentalism and international engagement—old questions made new by the growing Cold War divide.

3

THE WAR

In the early hours of June 22, 1941, Germany invaded the Soviet Union. The Wehrmacht advance into Soviet territory was swift and brutal, and this war that would last until 1945 was a deeply transformative event for the USSR as a whole. By the winter of 1941, the German army had advanced as far as Moscow's northwest suburbs. Still, German forces never occupied the Soviet capital. Nor did Moscow ever sustain the level of damage inflicted upon cities like Leningrad and Kiev. The war was nonetheless a defining moment for the people of Moscow, as well as for the city's institutions, architects, and aesthetics.

As this chapter explores, the Great Patriotic War had a de-centering effect on Soviet architecture. Wartime exigencies took Moscow's architects away from the Soviet capital to the far reaches of the Urals and to other regions of the home front. There they embarked on entirely new projects, often, like their counterparts abroad, using standardized and industrialized methods and materials. New architectural institutions established during the war brought Soviet architecture still more firmly under the control and oversight of the state. On the international front, Soviet architects continued to engage, as they had in the 1930s, with their colleagues abroad. The wartime alliance between the US, the USSR, and Britain helped to foster these relationships, just as the Cold War that followed would stifle them.

Most important to Moscow's monumental redevelopment in the postwar period was the effect, both at home and abroad, of Soviet victory in the war. The Soviet Union emerged in 1945 as a world superpower. The postwar urban transformation of Moscow was one way that this war-weary country would communicate its newfound sense of security and self-confidence. More than ever before, Soviet leaders wished to develop Moscow as a showcase capital city. Unlike their efforts in the 1930s, architects working in the postwar period could no longer borrow so openly from American technological advances. Soviet urbanism would carve its own path—or so Soviet leaders would claim. With Moscow leading the charge, Russian national forms would take pride of place on architects' drawing boards in the postwar years. The war was a turning point in the history of Moscow's Stalinist skyscrapers. The event changed urban life in the capital in myriad ways, ultimately giving greater urgency to Moscow's monumental transformation.

FRONTLINE MOSCOW

Most Muscovites first learned about the German invasion on the radio. On June 22, 1941, Viacheslav Molotov announced across the airwaves that the USSR was at war. As People's Commissar of Foreign Affairs, Molotov had signed a secret non-aggression

Figure 3.1: "Defense of Moscow": anti-aircraft gunners on the roof of Hotel Moskva, August 1, 1941. Photographer Oleg Knorring. RIA Novosti archive.

pact with Germany two years before. Now, Molotov reported that the German army had crossed into Soviet territory. Addressing the country as a whole, Molotov reminded his listeners that "this is not the first time that our people have had to deal with an attack from an arrogant enemy. At the time of Napoleon's invasion of Russia our people answered by waging the Patriotic War and Napoleon suffered defeat and met his doom."[1] Molotov was not the only Soviet leader to draw the comparison with 1812. Stalin too worked to fuel the fires of nationalism, avowing in his early wartime speeches that Hitler would meet the same fate as Russia's historic enemies. In the coming years of war, the rise of Russian nationalist sentiment in the Soviet Union would shape developments in architecture and culture more broadly. Yet in 1941, in Moscow at least, the Napoleonic analogy sounded ominous: in 1812, after all, three-quarters of Moscow burned to the ground. The newly socialist city could not risk suffering the same fate.

From the moment of the invasion in late June 1941, Moscow was transformed by war. The capital shifted immediately from showcase socialist city to army command center. Moscow's "socialist reconstruction" was put on hold, with work on the Palace of Soviets and other projects of the Moscow General Plan suspended until peace returned.[2] Rationing was introduced in July, shop windows were boarded up, and street lamps were no longer illuminated after dark.[3] Although it would take many months for German troops to reach Moscow by land, within one month of the invasion the Luftwaffe had secured air bases within range of the Soviet capital. Soviet anti-aircraft defense units took up their positions on rooftops throughout Moscow and the skies above the city were filled with the enormous barrage balloons used to push German dive bombers up and away from the city and into the higher range of the anti-aircraft guns, each manned by seven or eight soldiers on the roofs below (fig. 3.1). Tethered down to the ground, dozens of bulky "refill stations" floated lazily along the city's wide boulevards (fig. 3.2).

By July, the Moscow Blitz had begun. During the first air raid against Moscow, on the night of July 21–22, nearly two hundred Luftwaffe bombers dropped 104 tons of

Figure 3.2: "Refill gas balloons for barrage balloons in Moscow," November 1941.
Photographer Oleg Knorring. RIA Novosti archive.

high explosives and 46,000 incendiary bombs in an assault lasting over five hours.[4] Londoners had already found words for the sounds these bombs made, from the *swish* of the incendiaries to the *woo-woo* of the German bombers overhead, and these sounds now became familiar to Muscovites as well. In the coming months, bombs would strike the main building of the Commissariat of Heavy Industry and the headquarters of the Communist Party Central Committee, which burned a full night long in the final days of October. The university building, located across from the Kremlin with its Imperial-era neoclassical façade, was also badly damaged. And gruesome rumors circulated that 200 people had perished in a single night alone from bombs that fell along Moscow's prestigious and newly renovated Gorky Street.[5]

The city's streets and buildings were transformed during the first months of the war in other ways as well. Using paint, plywood, and large swaths of canvas, Soviet architects and engineers camouflaged Moscow's main buildings and squares and built false structures that resembled factories and aerodromes in an effort to divert Luftwaffe pilots away from the Kremlin and other strategic, industrial, and cultural sites. The Bolshoi Theater, the Kremlin's churches and walls, and many other buildings were recast as nondescript two-story structures, barely recognizable through the camouflage (fig. 3.3).[6] While Muscovites took shelter in basements, bunkers, and metro stations waiting for the "all-clear," Germans listened to radio reports that exaggerated the level of destruction. "Factories and plants on the outskirts of Moscow are destroyed. The Kremlin is destroyed, Red Square is destroyed . . . Moscow has entered into a final phase of ruination," German listeners heard on August 5.[7]

The Kremlin was, in fact, not destroyed. Nazi pilots may have had a hard time spotting it, however, from the air.[8] As Reuters' Moscow correspondent Alexander Werth wrote in his diary on August 1, "the Kremlin is camouflaged with large splashes of black and yellow, and big canvases—with small houses and windows painted on them in what is said to be fireproof paint."[9] Werth, who had arrived in Moscow in early July, added that at Moscow's Malyi Theater "they are using the old stage scenery of Ostrovsky's *Forest* for camouflage."[10] On the night of August 8, Werth noted,

Figure 3.3: "Camouflaged building of the Bolshoi Theater," August 9, 1942.
Photographer Aleksandr Krasavin. RIA Novosti archive.

"a lot of incendiaries were dropped on the Kremlin, but were all put out."[11] In the end, the camouflage effort seemed to work; the dozens upon dozens of German air raids that sought to destroy Moscow between July 1941 to April 1942 left few major scars on the capital.[12] This reality did little, however, to diminish the psychological effect of the aerial campaign on the city's inhabitants.

Moscow would soon face the threat of invasion by land as well. By late September, German troops had captured Kiev, Minsk, and Smolensk. Wehrmacht forces had surrounded Leningrad to the north and were marching toward Moscow. On October 2, 1941, the Wehrmacht launched Operation Typhoon, the assault on the Soviet capital. Architects worked alongside ordinary Muscovites in their effort to fortify the capital. Neighbors joined together to dig up swaths of their own city in the hopes of saving it. Teams of men could be seen tearing apart the asphalt along the beautiful new boulevards of the 1935 General Plan to make way for anti-tank traps and trenches (fig. 3.4). On the outskirts of the city, residents were mobilized in the tens of thousands to build defensive structures and to dig trenches and traps in the mud of Moscow oblast'. Red Army Marshal Georgii Zhukov, commander of the Western front, remembered seeing "thousands and thousands of Moscow women, who were unused to heavy labor and who had left their city apartments lightly clad, work on those impassable roads, in that mud, digging anti-tank ditches and trenches, setting up anti-tank obstacles and barricades, and hauling sandbags."[13]

As German forces marched up the Mozhaisk highway from Smolensk to Moscow, the distinction between front line and city street began to dissolve. Photographers did not have to travel far to gather material for their reportage: *Pravda*'s 32-year-old Aleksandr Ustinov found that he could even take public transit to the front. Ustinov recalled receiving an assignment from his editor to photograph a reconnaissance team stationed near Moscow's northwest suburb of Khimki. "I called the garage," Ustinov wrote, "but all the cars were out. So I took trolleybus No 12 to Khimki." From there, Ustinov continued on foot to catch up with the reconnaissance division. "In those difficult days during the defense of Moscow," Ustinov wrote, "the front and the rear were so close together that sometimes I was able to shoot in both locations in a single day."[14]

Figure 3.4: "People digging trenches": Muscovites building antitank fortifications, November 15, 1941. Photographer Aleksandr Ustinov. RIA Novosti archive.

In mid-October white-collar workers, Communist Party officials, industrial managers, foreign embassy staff, actors, and professors from Moscow's cultural and scientific institutions were ordered to evacuate to the east. Panic descended on the capital as those left behind woke on October 16 to find shops, factories, and metro stations closed. The Soviet state had taken no measures to provide information or instructions for Moscow's general population. They were left to assume that German forces would occupy the city at any moment.[15] This was not an unreasonable assumption. Factories and other enterprises were rigged to explode the moment German forces entered the city. And those left to guard the Communist Party headquarters had simply vanished, leaving behind large piles of half-burned top secret documents and, as NKVD agents reported, hundreds of gas masks and typewriters, 128 pairs of felt boots, and a few tons of meat, potatoes, and other foodstuffs.[16] As the Moscow Communist Party office would report one month later, hundreds of party members in the city's factories and other institutions destroyed their party cards amidst the chaos.[17]

The October Panic was devastating to morale. Though order was quickly restored, the panic exacerbated social tensions as white-collar workers received privileged treatment over their blue-collar counterparts.[18] But on October 17, radio stations announced that Stalin was back in Moscow.[19] The Soviet leader quickly signed an order declaring that Moscow was officially in a "state of siege." With highways heading eastward still jammed with cars and people trying to get out, martial law was imposed in the city.[20] Yet, even as many Muscovites fled, rumors spread about others trying to get in. Mass document checks carried out over the following weeks turned up thousands of army deserters, draft dodgers, and other suspicious individuals hiding out in the capital.[21] A military tribunal was quickly set up to try those accused of being "violators of order."[22] Moscow became a militarized zone under strict oversight. By radio address, officials assured the city's inhabitants that rumors that Moscow would be surrendered to the Germans were lies spread by enemy agents. Moscow, Soviet officials pledged, would be defended to the last drop of blood.[23]

Over the course of the war, two-fifths of Moscow's inhabitants left, some evacuating to the safety of the East, others enlisting in the army. The population of Moscow dropped from just over 4.2 million at the start of the war to 3.1 million by October.[24] Evacuation from the capital had begun in the days immediately following the invasion, so that by the end of that first summer of the war over a million and a half Muscovites had been evacuated.[25] For those left in the city, the anniversary parade on November 7, 1941—the first held during wartime—was a defiant gesture. As new Soviet tanks drove up the snowy, stormy boulevards of the capital the effect was "impressive," wrote Leonid I. Timofeev, a professor of literature at Moscow's Maxim Gorky Institute.[26] Like many Soviet citizens, Timofeev began keeping a diary in June 1941 to document the "great historical break" (*bol'shaia istoricheskaia peremena*) that he sensed happening all around him.[27] There were no air raids at all on the day of the parade, Timofeev wrote. The parade was risky, he thought, given the threat posed by Luftwaffe bombers, but it was also smart: "its political effect will be equal to a military success and will be a strong blow against the prestige of Germany."[28] Indeed, this patriotic show of force in the besieged capital seemed to make a difference; Moscow's military censors noted a rise in "positive sentiments" in letters sent to and from the front in the weeks after the parade.[29]

The Red Square anniversary parade had been an impromptu celebration, announced unexpectedly at the last minute. *Pravda* photographer Aleksandr Ustinov recalled that on the morning of the parade, he was woken early by his colleagues: "Sasha, quickly wake up, we are going to Red Square!" The morning was unusually quiet. Large grey clouds hovered low on the horizon and thick flakes of snow fell softly over Moscow. "It was simply unbelievable," Ustinov recalled, "that three dozen kilometers away a bloody battle raged, but here on Red Square was a parade." Ustinov photographed soldiers, cavalry, and tanks as they paraded in the city center for a little over an hour. When the event was over, the *Pravda* group hopped on the metro, exiting at Belorusskaia station. By chance, Ustinov recalled, they caught a final glimpse of the tanks they had just seen on Red Square. Heading up battered Gorky Street, the massive machines were rolling straight to the front. "How resolute and formidable was their movement," Ustinov thought while photographing the scene.[30]

The Great Patriotic War was swiftly incorporated into the myth of the revolution, cast as a central event in the Soviet Union's coming of age. The war became, as Amir Weiner writes, "a weighty link in the revolutionary chain" reinforcing the Soviet project.[31] Yet it proved difficult, sometimes impossible, to fuse the chain of revolution from the wide range of experiences, narratives, and traumas that the war unleashed. The war saw a return to tradition, a resurgence of religion, and a terrifying level of violence and devastation that caused the loss of 26.6 million Soviet lives—three quarters of them men—over the course of just four years.[32] All of these transformations would force Moscow's administrators to rethink the physical shape and needs of their capital.

MOSCOW'S ARCHITECTS AT WAR

Stalin gave several speeches in honor of the Day of the October Revolution in 1941, and in each he underscored his physical presence in Moscow and thereby his confidence in the USSR's ability to withstand the German invasion. In addition to the speech he gave on Red Square, Stalin addressed the Soviet people from the bunker-like safety of the marble-clad Mayakovskaya metro station. While Red Square connected Soviet leaders to Russian Tsars and victories of the past, the Mayakovskaya metro station was a distinctly Soviet space. Located thirty-three meters underground, this station was designed by architect Aleksei N. Dushkin and completed in 1936. Elegant cupola vaults run down the length of the station, each one decorated by artist Aleksandr A. Deineka with a brightly colored mosaic celebrating Soviet aviation and other technological feats. On the occasion of Stalin's speech, on November 6, 1941, a large podium was set up at one end of the station. Stalin and other top officials arrived at this underground event on a private subway car. Two thousand guests had already gathered under the succession of domes and stainless steel arches lining the platform. The Soviet leader took his place at the raised podium, with his team seated behind.[33]

In his speech, Stalin summarized the losses suffered during the first four months of war, but stressed that the Soviet Union did not bear these sacrifices alone, flanked as it was by the USA and Great Britain, new partners in a coalition.[34] On this occasion, the Soviet leader stressed that technology was the key element that would enable the USSR to win the war. "The current war is a war of engines," Stalin asserted, standing beneath Deineka's mosaics hailing the country's recent technological advances.[35] Germany's industrial capacity might be vast, but it could not match that of the USSR, USA, and Great Britain combined. The side with the greater ability to build and power engines would win the war.[36] Stalin also announced that the USSR would soon receive aid in the form of raw materials from Britain (aluminum, nickel, tin, and lead were in scarce supply, Stalin noted) and 1 million dollars in hard currency from the USA, followed by shipments through the Lend-Lease program.[37] The target of Stalin's speech from Mayakovskaya station were the workers in the rear—those who would soon put these materials and funds to good use, and who included in their ranks architects and engineers. Alongside frontline soldiers, these workers of the rear would soon be celebrated as "heroes of the home front."

Stalin's November 6 speech was published the following day in *Izvestiia* and *Pravda*, together with photographs of the underground event.[38] It was also broadcast on loudspeakers and radios in apartment buildings, on street corners, in workers' clubs, factories, and theaters around the country, scenes that themselves became the subjects of newspaper reporting.[39] The new alliances with Britain and the US, and the celebration of defense industry work on the home front, were quickly incorporated into the October anniversary festivities. As Ilya Ehrenburg noted on November 6, in Moscow "a poster hangs on the façade of a building which has been half-destroyed by a bomb: 'Long live the fighting alliance between the U.S.S.R. and Great Britain!' In a small town in the rear . . . where the Moscow aircraft factory is situated now, sways a banner inscribed: 'Long live the United States of America!' This is for tomorrow's anniversary . . ."[40] Inside those factories, industrial managers and workers listened with rapt attention to Stalin's November 6 speech. *Izvestiia*'s correspondent in Sverdlovsk reported that the hall of the Opera and Ballet Theater in this bustling Urals town was completely full for the broadcast.[41] As the loudspeaker began to transmit the proceedings from Mayakovskaya station, "a wave of joy engulfed those present" in the Sverdlovsk auditorium. "All at once the hall grew as silent as could be," reported

Izvestiia. "Everyone stopped dead, waiting for the speech to begin."[42] The audience listened to Stalin's words with "undiminished attention."[43] These "Uraltsy," as the *Izvestiia* correspondent called them, erupted in loud, sustained applause in response to Stalin's call to action.

In fact, most of those present in the audience in Sverdlovsk that evening were not native to the Urals ("Uraltsy") at all. Many of them were newcomers who had only just arrived from Moscow and other cities and towns of the West. Among these new-comers in Sverdlovsk were the staff and workers of the Administration for the Con-struction of the Palace of Soviets (USDS). By the end of June 1941, the USDS had lost a good portion of its 3,600 workers in Moscow to the war effort as many were mo-bilized for Red Army service.[44] In autumn 1941, 600 additional Palace of Soviets workers joined Moscow's Fifth Home Guard Division of partisan fighters.[45] With work on the Palace temporarily suspended, those workers who remained at the USDS were initially assigned to defense-related tasks in the capital.[46] Boris Iofan, still the organization's Chief Architect, was in charge of camouflaging the Kremlin and Red Square.[47] But as German forces closed in on Moscow, USDS staff and 560 train cars worth of the organization's equipment were transported to the Urals.[48] By state order on August 28, 1941, the USDS was assigned to build up and run the Krasnogorsk Thermal Power Station (*teploelektrotsentral'* or TETs) and the Urals Aluminum Fac-tory (*Uralaliumin'stroi*) just south of Sverdlovsk.[49] Instructed by Molotov to evacu-ate, Iofan left Moscow for the Urals on October 16, accompanied by Sergei Merku-rov, sculptor of the gigantic Lenin statue that was to top the Palace of Soviets.[50] Once they arrived, Iofan would take on the position of head of the special wartime divi-sion of the Academy of Architecture in the rapidly growing city of Sverdlovsk.[51]

While Soviet artists, actors, and writers engaged in the important propaganda and morale-boosting work of wartime, the USSR's architectural workers, like their close cousins in engineering, had skills that made them indispensable members of the coun-try's defense industry. Many young architects joined the ranks of the Red Army as soldiers, sappers, and combat engineers, applying their knowledge of structures to the tasks of mine-laying and bridge-making. But for those who remained at the rear, there were other specialized jobs to be done. Architectural students training in Moscow's academic studios abandoned their drawing boards in June 1941 to join the city's vast network of defense workers. Vera Brovchenko, a 28-year-old apprentice in the studio of Dmitrii N. Chechulin, began working in the summer of 1941 in "en-gineering reconnaissance" (*inzhenernaia razvedka*).[52] Before the war Brovchenko had worked on the Dinamo, Komsomol'skaia, and Kievskaia metro stations. Now she worked as part of a small team based in a makeshift office located near the Moscow River, across from the House on the Embankment. From there, Brovchenko and her team waited by the phone for incoming reports of bomb damage. When a call came in, they would jump on their motorcycles and ride to the site to assess the damage, clear the rubble, rescue anyone trapped inside, and evaluate the structural integrity of the building to determine whether it could be quickly restored.[53]

Urban defense work drew on architects' existing knowledge of buildings and ma-terials. However, this type of engagement with the city was largely new to the So-viet architectural profession. As Brovchenko's studio master Dmitrii Chechulin put it in April 1942 at a meeting of the USSR Union of Architects, "the war has caused us architects to fundamentally transform our work."[54] The conflict required architects to retrain, learning a variety of new skills that opened them up to new aesthetic sensibilities. Brovchenko and many others attended special events organized by the Union of Architects, including lectures by military specialists on camouflage and fortification. They read about camouflage techniques being used by allied countries in special wartime editions of Soviet architectural journals.[55] But most of all, architects learned new methods on the fly. It was not just camouflage work that required them to retool. Students like Brovchenko had, up until the war, been trained in Moscow's architectural studios, where pupils studied and sketched examples of classical architecture from ancient Greece, Rome, and the Renaissance, before moving on to Russian classical models. The war changed this routine. And it required a different set of skills: a knowledge of industrialized and prefabricated materials, as well as standardized, simplified construction techniques. While these areas of design had grown in importance through the 1930s, the war pushed them to the forefront.

By late 1941, Moscow's architects were on the move, most of them assigned to new posts in the Urals and Siberia. Brovchenko was sent to Novosibirsk in December 1941, where her brigade worked for the Red Army's construction office, *Voenproekt*, converting a tractor factory into a factory for tanks.[56] The facility had to be expanded and an entire town built quickly alongside it, with two-story standardized brick housing for workers. "Everything was organized quickly-quickly, very quickly," Brovchenko recalled, "and within a few months the workers were there."[57] Now employed within the *Voenproekt* system, Brovchenko was sent with a construction brigade to Kiev in 1943. Working under the strain of wartime conditions in the devastated city, which had only just passed back into Soviet hands, Brovchenko's team built a factory out of whatever materials were available "despite the fact," as she would put it later, "that she considered herself an architect."[58] The "exceptionally curious" contraption that resulted "could not be found in any catalogue or in any textbook . . . it was concocted on-the-go so that it could be built quickly and with simple materials."[59] Architects joining the war effort in 1941 may have had little knowledge of or interest in this type of building. But by 1945, many of Moscow's leading architects had gained first-hand experience in the rapid, simplified construction necessary during wartime.

The new bond forged between architecture and the defense industry did not always make for a perfect marriage. In November 1941, Molotov received updates on the construction situation in the Urals from the bosses at the USDS. Andrei Prokof'ev, head of the USDS, reported that while *Uralaliumin'stroi* had enough materials and an excess number of workers on site, the construction teams lacked discipline and were too unprepared and undersupplied to carry out work during the winter.[60] Iofan in turn appealed to Molotov to intervene. The local foremen "still have not switched to fast, simple construction . . . to local materials for building factories and housing." Iofan reported that builders on the *Uralaliumin'stroi* site were still using steel and metal materials, and that housing was being built according to earlier designs for multi-story brick buildings. Iofan continued, with added emphasis: "it is clear that *what is needed now like never before is intervention from experienced designers and builders. A quick reorganization of design and construction is necessary.*"[61] Without this,

Iofan stressed, factories in the Urals would never be able to adequately support the war effort.

Iofan wrote to Molotov from his wartime office based at the headquarters of the People's Commissariat of Nonferrous Metallurgy (*Narkomtsvetmet*), now removed to Sverdlovsk. But the architect's agenda in November 1941 was not limited to concerns about the challenges of defense-related construction. Iofan told Molotov that, since the start of the war, he and his team had been continuing their work on the design for the Palace of Soviets. Though they had come up with "some new ideas," the team working in Sverdlovsk was limited by the fact that they had "neither working space, nor housing." Although the local authorities had "promised at first to help us, it is clear that some of the Comrades here do not understand the full importance of our work."[62] Iofan requested that Molotov issue an official Sovnarkom order granting the Palace of Soviets designers half of the living space in a dormitory newly built for *Narkomtsvetmet* technicians. Iofan also requested that thirty architects, sculptors, artists, and engineers, hand-picked by him, be exempted from military duty and reassigned to the Palace project.[63]

Over the next few years, Iofan would continue working on the Palace, bringing the earlier composition into line with the Bolshevik view of the war. Sculptural reliefs on the façade and interior walls were redesigned to include not only the "heroes of the Civil War" and the "heroes of the building of socialism," but also the "heroes of the Great Patriotic War."[64] In effect, the new design transformed the Palace into a monument to the war, as Iofan sought to capture in architectural expression the idea of a "call to action." As Iofan imagined it, "in the evening, the halls [on the ground floor would] be brightly lit and through the pillars and stained-glass windows murals dedicated to the capture of the Winter Palace in October 1917 and the Battle of Stalingrad in 1942 would be clearly visible."[65] While overseeing defense-related work in the Urals, Iofan allowed no one to forget that the Palace constituted a high priority. The architect wrote to Molotov and Stalin, petitioning to have the new Palace designs put on display in Moscow during holidays, and to have the new design reviewed for approval by Soviet leaders.[66] Iofan understood that monumental architecture, like a rousing speech, had the power to uplift the Soviet individual. Would the fact that the country's architects were already designing monuments to the war not serve to inspire victory in the battles yet to come?

CHARTING A NEW PATH THROUGH WAR

The war created innumerable shortages and roadblocks that the USSR's architectural institutions strove to anticipate and overcome. With transportation networks overburdened and materials like steel now reserved for armaments, the Union of Architects and the Academy of Architecture stressed the importance of learning to use local construction materials, untrained labor, and any and all tools available on site. The Union's new journal, set up specifically for war-related articles and discussions, explained: "we must make it our goal to free the transportation system from the need to move construction materials by using entirely local resources."[67] From its temporary wartime headquarters in Chimkent, in the Kazakh SSR, the Academy of Architecture printed a series of brochures for distribution among architects and laymen alike. Topics included "How to build with sun-dried earth or cob bricks" (4000 copies), "Housing and dormitories in gypsum bricks" (500 copies), "Earthen houses" (*zhilye zemlianki*, 1000 copies), and "Housing in panel-frame construction" (500 copies).[68] The Academy of Architecture also created temporary posts for its top architects in the major cities of the rear, especially in the remote cities of Siberia and the Urals, which became the center of architectural activity. When they returned to Moscow in the later years of the war, many architects would look for ways to integrate wartime lessons into their plans for postwar reconstruction.

The war prompted a move toward industrialization and standardization in Soviet architecture, but these initiatives did not merely result from the conflict. The Academy of Architecture's yearly plan for 1941, prepared in late 1940, had called for new research in the area of industrialized design. Main priorities for 1941 included "the question of mass construction in the areas of housing, public, and industrial buildings," and the related issues of industrialization and rationalization in the development of building types and construction elements.[69] The development of Moscow's southwest region was to serve as a case study in this new type of building.[70] The war interrupted these plans, but it also accelerated Soviet research and experience in standardized design, extending this expertise in unanticipated ways through calls for its rapid and widespread application.

Soviet architects were not unique in their wartime embrace of industrialization and standardization. Rather, they were part of a shift that was taking place internationally. Around the world, burgeoning defense industries prompted architects to mobilize in the early 1940s. In the US, prefabricated projects of the New Deal era were applied to the wartime building effort by institutions such as the Farm Security Administration and the Federal Works Agency. Often with the help of modernist architects, these and other agencies built low-cost mass housing for workers in the American defense industry. Anticipating a postwar building boom, American companies involved in wartime defense work also sought to adapt building techniques used during the war in the hopes of marketing them to American consumers once victory had been won. Some companies even tried to repurpose military-style metal huts as postwar dwellings. The Beech Aircraft assembly plant in Wichita, Kansas, for example, shifted its production after the war to manufacture the Dymaxion Wichita House, a round futuristic house that looked like the top of a grain silo. Designed by visionary architect R. Buckminster Fuller, the house was affordable, and easy to ship and assemble. Made of lightweight steel used for aircraft production, the house was widely publicized but never took off.[71] While the Dymaxion House experiment remained a prototype, in a more general way innovations spurred by the needs of war were adapted and repurposed in the postwar US.

In the American case, the transition from wartime to postwar building went hand in hand with the broadly popular acceptance of modernist aesthetics and design in American culture. The wartime application of standardized, prefabricated, and industrialized construction propelled the "victory of modernism" in postwar America.[72] American companies like Beech Aircraft, Revere Copper and Brass, or the US Gypsum Company sought to pivot from defense contracts to housing construction by selling their products through marketing campaigns that, as Andrew Shanken writes, "implicitly linked the war bonds with modern design, making modernization the payoff for the sacrifices of war."[73] In both the Soviet and American contexts, modernist ideals like flexibility and modularity in design found full expression during the war. And the immediate postwar years saw a real desire for knowledge exchange between urban experts from both countries on the potential postwar uses of prefabrication. But it would be another decade before Soviet architects took up prefabrication, and its corresponding modernist aesthetic, on the scale that it was applied in the immediate postwar years in Western Europe and in the US. The American embrace of modernism, by contrast, would hold widespread appeal for decades to come, paving the way for the rise of the International Style in the US after 1945.[74]

In the postwar years, Soviet architecture was characterized by the continued use of neoclassical styles and by a growing interest in national, vernacular traditions. Yet Soviet architects' commitment to stylistic traditionalism did not prevent them from also using modern building techniques and industrialized materials. Most Soviet architects simply saw nothing contradictory in a neoclassical approach to design that was rooted in the latest construction techniques. The doctrine of socialist realism, adopted in the mid-1930s, had in fact dictated this synthesis of up-to-date technology and classicism. In the 1930s, Soviet architects had begun to draw formal inspiration from the "best examples" of the classical past while also making use of new advances in construction. Moscow's Gorky Street, the penultimate site of Stalinist classicism and high culture in the 1930s, had been built with time-saving assembly-line construction, precast ceilings, walls, and decorative panels.[75] A single architectural studio might pursue a variety of approaches simultaneously, with some projects tending toward the classical and others toward the modernist. This was the case in Dmitrii Chechulin's Moscow studio.

By 1944, Vera Brovchenko was back in Moscow, working again for Chechulin. The studio was abuzz with activity in the final year of the war. Some of its architects had picked up the threads of prewar projects abandoned in 1941. Others, like Brovchenko, were assigned to work on new tasks that brought the principle of wartime austerity back home to Moscow. Brovchenko worked on a project using gypsum blocks for what she later called "the first microdistrict in the history of Moscow."[76] Housing construction had begun to pick up again in Moscow in 1944, and Brovchenko's housing district, located on Khoroshevskoe shosse in the capital's northwest region, was an experiment in rapid, low-rise mass construction.[77] While this project was underway, others working in Chechulin's studio were engaged in the same northwest region of Moscow on a different task, this one monumental and commemorative. The Leningrad Junction Bridge (*Leningradskii puteprovod,* soon renamed Victory Bridge) was among the first structures in Moscow to commemorate the war. Completed before the conflict was over and designed by Chechulin in collaboration with sculptor Nikolai Tomskii, the bridge was built in honor of the Battle of Moscow, fought in the autumn of 1941. Statues of soldiers, one male and the other female, flanked the entrance to the bridge, their arms outstretched, the woman raising her rifle high into the air.[78] These defenders of the city, who had pushed back the German assault on the capital, proclaimed a victory that would soon be achieved in reality.

By the time the war was coming to an end, Soviet architects found themselves working within a new set of institutions created in response to the conflict. On September 29, 1943, in anticipation of the massive tasks that lay ahead in postwar reconstruction, the Presidium of the Supreme Soviet created the USSR State Architecture Committee (*Komitet po delam arkhitektury pri Sovnarkome SSSR*). The Committee forged a more direct connection between architects and the Soviet state.[79] It reported to the highest state authority—the USSR Sovnarkom (renamed the USSR Council of Ministers, or Sovmin, in 1946). Like the multi-leveled system of artistic unions created in the early 1930s, the main (USSR-level) State Architecture Committee oversaw a complex network of sub-offices at the republic and at the municipal levels, but also at the levels of the regions and provinces within each Soviet republic. The State Architecture Committee would become the most important set of architectural institutions of the postwar period; even the USSR Academy of Architecture was subordinate to it after 1943. Its head at the USSR level for the first four years was the Moscow-based architect Arkadii G. Mordvinov.[80] Mordvinov acted as the primary go-between connecting Soviet architects to Soviet leaders. Mordvinov also oversaw the country's new Chief Architects. In Moscow, the post of Chief Architect was held starting in 1944 by Dmitrii Chechulin. Other prominent Moscow architects were assigned to Chief Architect positions in other cities located across the USSR. Appointed in the final months of the war, these men were tasked with creating and overseeing the development of General Plans for postwar reconstruction.[81]

As the extent of the damage in the Soviet Union's urban centers became apparent, the architect's role seemed all the more consequential. Mikhail I. Kalinin wrote in a letter to Mordvinov in October 1943 that "at the current time, in connection with the reconstruction of destroyed cities, among which are, for example, Stalingrad, which is being built entirely anew, it is necessary that in these matters Soviet architects take an active role and display broad initiative."[82] Their initiative would be carefully coordinated and supervised through the new state-architectural institutions. Architectural Councils were created within the new State Architecture Committee system at the municipal level. Their role was to ensure that each and every construction project undertaken in a given city was presented for approval before that city's Chief Architect and a board of experts. In Moscow, these experts were drawn from the ranks of the city's leading architects and engineers. Moscow's Architectural Council, made up of ten or so rotating experts and the Chief Architect, met twice a month on average to review construction designs. Moscow Council "experts" in the immediate postwar years included prominent figures like Boris Iofan and Vladimir Gel'freikh, Lev V. Rudnev, Nikolai Kolli, and Sergei Chernyshev.[83] The Council provided oversight as well as a forum in which architectural questions were regularly discussed between the city's leading figures in the profession. In theory, the State Architecture Committee was meant to streamline the reconstruction process. In practice, however, the Committee and its myriad sub-institutions often served to add chaos to an already confusing system made up of multiple architectural and construction institutions and competing jurisdictions.[84]

When it was created in 1943, the State Architecture Committee was instructed to take the lead in the protection and restoration of architectural monuments—a field of growing concern in the later years of the war. Among the first cities to be rebuilt was Istra, damaged during the German drive toward Moscow in autumn 1941. In early 1942, Moscow architect Aleksei Shchusev had already begun work on a new plan for Istra that drew on Garden City planning ideals.[85] Significantly, the heart of this reconstruction project was the restoration of the New Jerusalem Monastery, a Russian Orthodox site dating to the seventeenth and eighteenth centuries.[86] The journal *Arkhitektura SSSR* ran an article about the monastery's reconstruction in its first issue of 1942, describing it as "one of the most unique masterpieces of Russian art."[87] The article also included photographs that captured the extent of the site's wartime destruction, showing that the roof over the rotunda had been blown right off the main cathedral building. The photographs were taken by the team of preservationists from the Academy of Architecture working on site.

Architects like Shchusev saw in the war's destruction a call to action on the heritage front. As early as 1941, the Academy of Architecture began discussions about heritage conservation in light of the damage already inflicted by invading forces. A new Museum of Russian Architecture, created and headed by Shchusev, took on some of this work as well when it was founded in 1943.[88] The New Jerusalem Monastery at Istra was just one of a number of Orthodox sites that Shchusev and others saw as quintessential examples of Russian architecture. The close study and restoration of traditional Russian buildings in the early 1940s was in many ways a continuation of work begun in the 1930s. Socialist realism gave license for the broad and eclectic use of classical models, including the use of traditional Russian models. After the war the range of acceptable models narrowed considerably, with Russian forms taking pride of place. As Shchusev stated at a 1945 conference of architects, "just as the builders of the Renaissance drew lessons from the monuments of Rome and the Romans, so do our architects learn from the splendid monuments of Russian architecture."[89] Russian nationalism was a powerful force that continued to gain ground as the war dragged on. Still, like those "builders of the Renaissance," most major Soviet architects and artists continued to revere Italian monuments they had seen firsthand on study tours taken in the pre-revolutionary years and in the 1920s and 1930s.

Official statements made during and after the war by Soviet leaders supported the elevation of Russian national form above all else. On May 9, 1945, with the Red Army occupying Berlin, the Soviet Union had defeated Nazi Germany and the war in Europe was over. Two weeks later, Stalin gave his final wartime toast at the official celebration for Red Army Commanders held at the Kremlin: "I wish to raise a toast to the health of our Soviet people and, above all, to the Russian people." Loud applause erupted in the hall and the audience cried *Ura*! "I drink above all to the health of the Russian people," Stalin continued, "because they are the most outstanding nation of all the nations within the Soviet Union."[90] To the leaders of the war effort, the force that had saved the rest from certain destruction was the Great Russian nation. Stalin's speech would have widespread consequences for years to come. In architecture, it served to further bolster the turn to Russian heritage.[91]

As the war came to an end, Soviet architects found themselves at the intersection of two paths toward reconstruction. One direction saw architects prioritizing monumental prestige projects that symbolized that the nation remained strong and restoration projects that revived historical monuments destroyed during the conflict. The other path saw architects focusing on the more mundane reconstruction of housing, industrial facilities, and other urban amenities. These two paths could be pursued simultaneously, to be sure. But for a country so ravaged by war, with its economic and human resources devastated, these two directions in architecture would prove difficult to reconcile. In the Soviet capital—the symbolic heart of the country—the tension between monumentalism and the mundane would be especially fraught.

SOVIET INTERNATIONALISM AND POSTWAR RECONSTRUCTION

The war may have fostered nationalism, but it was also a moment of staunch internationalism. As they had done in the early to mid-1930s, Soviet architects once again engaged whole-heartedly in a transnational exchange of ideas with their colleagues abroad. The American-Soviet alliance was celebrated and nurtured in the realm of popular culture and in the halls of high diplomacy, and it was this wartime ally that proved particularly important for Soviet urban experts during the early 1940s. The wartime years saw a flurry of correspondence between American and Soviet architects. Beyond expressions of solidarity in the war effort, architects wished to send and receive new city planning literature. In both the US and the USSR, architects were busy preparing for the tasks that lay ahead in postwar reconstruction; this knowledge exchange was, for both sides, an important part of the preparation. Most of this correspondence passed through the offices of the All-Union Society for Cultural Ties Abroad (VOKS). This organization's Anglo-American Department, in particular its special Architectural Section led in these years by Moscow Union of Architects Head Karo S. Alabian, received, translated, and responded to hundreds of letters going back and forth between Soviet and American urban experts. The VOKS Architectural Section also issued its own English-language journal during the war. Called *Architectural Chronicle*, this journal made its way into the hands of American architects across the Atlantic.[92]

These transnational relations were pursued during the war both by organizations and by individual architects acting on their own behalf. In 1943, the American Institute of Architects reached out, sending material on American city planning to the USSR Academy of Architecture. In response, Viktor A. Vesnin, President of the USSR Academy of Architecture, sent the Institute several new publications from the Academy's press, along with expressions of gratitude and wishes that "our friendly exchange of letters and literature will continue with mutual benefit to our common cause."[93] Librarians at Columbia University and Swarthmore College wrote to VOKS, hoping to build up their collections with the latest Soviet architectural publications.[94] Letters also arrived from American architects working on defense-related projects. Catherine Bauer Wurster, an architect working on mass housing construction for the Federal Works Agency, wrote to VOKS in 1943, explaining that she was "doing research and writing in the housing and planning field once more, and would be very pleased to receive any material you might send me." A "beautiful volume" on the Moscow General Plan that Bauer Wurster had purchased while on a trip to Russia in 1939 was still "extremely interesting" to her. Nothing made her "happier or more hopeful about the future," she wrote, "than the improvement in USSR-USA relations." Bauer Wurster wanted "very much to renew my contact with the work and plans in the USSR." She hoped to return to Moscow soon after the war: "perhaps we will be able to motor up over Alaska and Siberia!"[95]

On the Soviet side, the new State Architecture Committee had a bureau specifically devoted to collecting the latest foreign publications and information as reference material for Soviet architects. From 1943 to 1947, this bureau was headed by Viacheslav Oltarzhevskii—the same "Oltar-jevsky," as he had reinvented himself in America, who worked in New York for a full decade in the 1920s and 1930s, part of which time he had spent at the firm of Harvey Wiley Corbett. Oltarzhevskii had returned to Moscow in 1935 to a prominent position at the All-Union Agricultural Exhibition only to be swept up in the Great Terror. Arrested in 1938, Oltarzhevskii worked for half a decade—while a prisoner—as Head of Construction and Chief Architect of the Siberian prison outpost of Vorkuta.[96] Born to a noble family in Moscow in the early 1880s, Oltarzhevskii trained in Petersburg and Paris.[97] By the time he was released from the Gulag in 1943, the architect was in his sixties. Some have claimed that W. Averell Harriman personally intervened on Oltarzhevskii's behalf. Harriman had been in Moscow in September 1941 to negotiate the extension of Lend-Lease to the USSR, and was appointed US ambassador to the Soviet Union in 1943.[98] Whatever the circumstances were for Oltarzhevskii's release, the architect made his way back to Moscow, where his international connections and knowledge of foreign languages assured him a good position in the country's new architectural institutions.

Oltarzhevskii found work quickly at the State Architecture Committee's Bureau of Scientific-Technical Information—an institution eager for foreign connections. There Oltarzhevskii collected materials from England, the US, and Sweden on urban reconstruction, wartime housing construction, and restoration projects.[99] He also worked to establish connections with other parts of the world. Writing to the Mexican modernist architect Carlos Obregon Santacilia, Oltarzhevskii aimed to establish an exchange of information about architecture and construction. The architecture of the Georgian, Armenian, and Azerbaijanian SSRs, Oltarzhevskii thought, would be of particular interest to Mexican architects.[100] Oltarzhevskii also reached out to his former New York mentors and employers. In a letter to Wallace K. Harrison, Oltarzhevskii wrote that "you will no doubt be surprised to hear from me after such a long interval, as what with the war and its contingencies, our correspondence lapsed."[101] He continued, writing that he would be "very pleased to hear how you are getting along and learn of the more interesting trends and events of recent years in the field of architecture and construction in America." Oltarzhveskii asked Harrison to update him about recent trends in architecture and construction and to send him American architectural periodicals, promising to send the latest publications on Soviet architecture in return. As a start, Oltarzhevskii sent Harrison a packet of several booklets on old Russian monuments.[102]

Oltarzhevskii also reestablished contact with his former New York employer, Harvey Wiley Corbett. As it turned out, Corbett was serving as Chair of the new Architects Committee of the National Council of American-Soviet Friendship (NCASF). The NCASF had been founded in 1941, its membership made up primarily of fellow travelers, some of whom had been involved in more or less radical wings of the American-Soviet friendship movement of the 1930s. The NCASF saw its primary role as "educational." As the organization explained to potential members in 1943, the NCASF would work to "promote better understanding and strengthen friendly relations between the United States and the Soviet Union," a task that they saw as "essential for winning the war and establishing an enduring peace."[103] So long as the USSR and the US saw a common enemy in fascism, the NCASF found that it could draw a wide and diverse membership of "sponsors" that included the Conductor of the Boston Symphony Orchestra, the Vice-President and Provost of the University of California, a judge in Pittsburgh, the President of the International Union of Mine, Mill and Smelter Workers, even Albert Einstein.[104] Most of the organization's sponsors would quickly lose their initial enthusiasm for the cause, demanding to be taken off the list of sponsors once the House Un-American Activities Committee began a formal investigation of the NCASF in 1946.[105] But for that brief wartime moment, the NCASF supported the genuine efforts of American and Soviet professionals to get better acquainted.[106]

The NCASF Architects Committee was founded in 1943, chaired by Corbett and supported more broadly by a large group of prominent American architects. On May 2, 1944, Corbett wrote to Karo Alabian at VOKS to let him know about this new American group, the purpose of which was to support "an exchange of technical information between members of the architectural profession of the USA and the USSR."[107] Corbett included in his letter a list of the Architects Committee's main members, some of whom were already connected to the Soviet profession from their work in the 1930s. Simon Breines, for example, had personally met Alabian, Iofan, and others when he attended the USSR Union of Architects First Congress, held in Moscow in 1937. Hans Blumenfeld, now with the Philadelphia Housing Association, had worked prior to the war for the Soviet City Planning Institute (Giprogor).[108] In his introductory letter, Corbett requested information from Alabian about plans for postwar reconstruction, the training of Soviet architects, how financing and ownership worked in the Soviet Union, and what types of organizations existed in the USSR for building design.[109] Materials could be sent in Russian, Corbett wrote, since the NCASF had the resources to translate everything they received into English.[110] The Architects Committee's first activity, Corbett told Alabian in that first letter, had been a showing in New York of "your tragic exhibit of Historic Monuments destroyed by the Nazis."[111] In return, the Architects Committee, in collaboration with the US Office of War Information, was preparing an exhibition to be shown in Moscow of American prefabricated housing.[112]

The NCASF exhibition of "Prefabricated Housing in the US" opened in Moscow in March 1945. But before making its way over to the Soviet capital, the exhibit was formally presented to Pavel Mikhailov, Consul-General of the Soviet Consulate in New York, at a large reception held in late 1944 and attended by hundreds of representatives from US companies that had contributed material to the exhibit. In a speech given at this event, Corbett expressed his enthusiasm for the venture and lamented the "centuries-long mutual heritage of isolation and lack of contact that have made us strangely unreal to each other despite the many similarities in our development and character."[113] The Soviet Consul-General echoed Corbett's friendly tone in his own speech, noting the special importance of technical exchange as the USSR was preparing to rebuild. The Soviet people, he stated, "plan to restore the country not only to pre-war conditions but to build finer, more beautiful and more livable cities than those before the war."[114] The US and the USSR would be jointly victorious in the war, he continued, and they would join together to rebuild in the coming years of peace.

The "Prefabricated Housing in the US" exhibition was officially opened on March 15, 1945 in the Great Hall of the Moscow Architects Club. The opening was attended by Soviet architects and officials, by VOKS President Vladimir Kemenov, and by W. Averell Harriman, who was by then the US ambassador to the the the USSR. Alabian wrote to Corbett in late March to tell him that the show had drawn a large number of visitors, with "the attendance between March 15 and 26 totaling 4,200 people."[115] In addition to the interest of members of the public, Alabian explained, a number of organizations, from the Moscow Building Institute to the People's Commissariat of the Building Industry, were making large group visits to see the show. The images on display introduced Soviet visitors to wartime innovations that would have seemed strange and novel to American audiences as well. Included in the show were examples of Sears-Roebuck prefabricated housing, projects by Albert Kahn Inc., and Buckminster Fuller's grain silo-shaped Dymaxion house.[116] "We have no doubt," Alabian wrote to Corbett, "that following this first exhibition acquainting the Soviet public with the development of prefabricated housing in America, we shall, with your kind assistance, continue familiarizing Soviet architects and builders with building methods in the USA."[117] In return, Alabian continued, Soviet architects were putting together a small photographic exhibit on "Russian Architecture of the Past and Present" to be shown to audiences in the US.

A few months after the American housing exhibition was held in Moscow, in early May 1945, a group of Soviet engineers and planners made their way to New York to attend another NCASF-sponsored event, the American-Soviet Building Conference. The event opened with a gala dinner held on the evening of May 4 at New York's Biltmore Hotel. Inside the opulent Jazz-era interiors, conference-attendees gathered to discuss postwar reconstruction. The Americans were especially eager to spread the gospel of prefabrication. John B. Blandford, Jr., of the National Housing Agency, and E. C. Ropes, head of the Russian Unit of the US Department of Commerce, both gave speeches, and a Soviet film "The Urals, Forge Shop of Victory" was screened.[118] On the following day, American and Soviet experts were paired together to lead panels on topics ranging from building industry organization to mechanical systems and utilities of the small house, industrial buildings, and, of course, prefabrication. On the Soviet side, in addition to engineers and technical experts, the new President of Amtorg, M. M. Gusev, was also present, showing that the Soviet Union was not only keen on fostering US-Soviet architectural friendship but also on supporting trade between the two countries.

Not long after the New York conference, in light of the high level of interest shown at that event from experts beyond the architectural and planning fields, the NCASF Architects Committee decided to change its name to "The Building Industry Committee."[119] Having learned about the change, Alabian wrote to Corbett with enthusiasm: "your report of the reorganization of the Architectural Committee into the Building Industrial Committee has coincided with our decision to increase the functions and composition of the Architectural Section of VOKS." A Building Engineering subsection had been created, Alabian explained, to ensure that those working in the Soviet building materials, plumbing, heating, ventilation, and other areas would also benefit from connection with American experts.[120] The continued desire on the part of the Soviet Union's architects to import American technology was as much a continuation of their earlier activities as it was a feature of the immediate needs of postwar reconstruction.

From its initial creation in 1943, the Architects Committee of the NCASF envisioned that their organization would facilitate relations between Soviet and American urban experts in ways identical to the ties pursued by both countries in the 1930s. That is to say, that American architects continued to think of their Soviet colleagues as professionals in search of foreign assistance that would help compensate for the backwardness of Soviet development. Many American architects, especially Corbett and Breines, were clearly motivated by real feelings of good will toward their Soviet colleagues and genuinely wished to foster "understanding and friendship between professionals in the building and planning fields" in the US and the USSR.[121] But they saw technology and knowledge transfer in this friendship as unidirectional. American technology would be adopted in Soviet cities, not the reverse. The Architects Committee's "purpose," adopted in 1943, was "to familiarize visiting Soviet specialists with American building developments relevant to Soviet reconstruction needs," and "to acquaint American architects, engineers and producers with the trade requirements in the Soviet building field."[122] The US would provide the expertise and perhaps even the materials, and the USSR, devastated by the war, would supply a *tabula rasa* for the widespread adoption and application of American-style construction.

The US was poised to carry out such an arrangement, having supplied expertise to the Soviet Union since the period of the First Five-Year Plan and, more recently, having administered Lend Lease during the war. Soon, the Marshall Plan would continue this vein of American internationalism into the postwar period in Europe. For their part, Soviet architects also fell into the rhythms of their earlier, interwar relations with American expertise. But within a few years, this entire transnational edifice would come crashing down when America's Red Scare and the Soviet Union's *Zhdanovshchina* wrenched these fragile ties apart.

THE FATE OF THE PALACE OF SOVIETS

In September 1945, *Pravda* journalist Lazar' Brontman attended one of the many VOKS receptions held that year. VOKS would remain an important organization after 1945, continuing to foster relations between the Allies even as the Cold War chill set in. In his diary, Brontman recorded numerous conversations, including a chat with composer Vano Muradeli about a new song he had written about Lavrentii Beria; a drink shared with the Director of the Marx-Engels-Lenin Institute; and another with architect Karo Alabian, who told Brontman about his design for the reconstruction of Stalingrad. Brontman also spoke with Boris Iofan, who was now back in Moscow. Brontman recalled having interviewed Iofan for *Pravda* years earlier about his design for the Palace of Soviets. "Now I barely recognized him," Brontman wrote in 1945. The architect had grown older; he was "small, thin, and had aged quite a bit." Iofan was, however, no less enthusiastic now about the work he was engaged in for the Palace of Soviets. Iofan told Brontman about the changes he had made during the war to the Palace's design. And when Molotov returned from London, Iofan asserted, he would look over the new design and approve it for construction.[123] Now that the war was over, Iofan was sure that construction of the Palace of Soviets would resume.

By 1945, Iofan and his colleagues had weathered nearly a decade of violence and instability. In the late 1930s, the USDS had been caught in the spiral of terror that worked its way through all Soviet institutions. The catastrophe of the war followed quickly thereafter. Yet, while the conflict interrupted the Palace project, it also served as a suspended moment of experimentation in the design studios of the USDS. In Sverdlovsk, Palace designers experimented with new glass lighting grates, mosaic techniques, decorative wood flooring, and textiles. Iofan had altered the blueprints of the Palace during the war so that it would be a shorter, squatter structure, but no less monumental than in prewar plans (fig. 3.5). And acclaimed artist Pavel D. Korin also continued working through the war on the enormous mosaic that was to fill the dome of the Palace's great hall. Brought onto the Palace project in 1940, Korin spent the wartime years sketching out the dynamic, muscular figures of his mosaic, called the "March to the Future." Art historian Vladimir Tolstoi recalled that in 1946, Korin had invited him to view a half-sized fragment of the full mosaic, which had by that time been assembled in a shed a few blocks away from the Palace of Soviets construction site in Moscow.[124] Tolstoi was struck first by the enormity and strangeness of the image: from floor to ceiling under the gables of the darkened shed, giant nude men marched forward, "their arms outstretched with pathos."[125] Tolstoi also noticed the dissonance between these figures' conventionally heroic poses and their all-too-familiar "modern" faces. For Tolstoi, Korin had perfectly captured the determined march "of our people" toward the bright and happy future.[126] What better time to build the Palace of Soviets than now—a moment when the Soviet Union had proven itself through war and was about to resume its march toward communism?

In the months immediately following the Soviet victory against Germany in May 1945, Iofan moved quickly to petition for work to resume on the Palace of Soviets. First, the USDS would need its Head of Construction back from wartime duty. On June 2, 1945, Iofan wrote to Molotov asking that Prokof'ev be relieved from his post overseeing military industrial construction in the Urals. Prokof'ev's wartime duties, Iofan wrote, had taken a toll on the USDS manager's health. And now, as large-scale work was set to begin again on the Palace of Soviets, Prokof'ev was urgently needed back in Moscow.[127] Next, Iofan appealed to higher-ups on the question of reestablishing foreign ties. On June 30, Iofan wrote to Kliment E. Voroshilov in the hopes of gaining passage for his team, once again, to go abroad. This time, Iofan requested that a group of twenty-some USDS planners, architects, engineers, and designers be sent to Vienna, Bucharest, Dresden, Budapest, Leipzig, and other cities to study the latest technical and material advances in construction.[128] Iofan does not appear to have been successful in sending his specialists to Central and Eastern Europe in 1945. The architect's first request, however, was granted and Prokof'ev was back in Moscow by summer.

Together, Iofan and Prokof'ev worked to secure state backing once more for the Palace project. First and foremost, the project required a dedicated budget line on Gosplan's Fourth Five-Year Plan. As Iofan and Prokof'ev would find for themselves,

Figure 3.5: Palace of Soviets model, Boris M. Iofan, 1947. V. Shkvarikov, *Sovetskaia arkhitektura za XXX let RSFSR,* Moscow: Izd. Akademii arkhitektury SSSR, 1950.

this was no easy task. There were countless other construction and reconstruction projects that required state financing. Moreover, the Palace of Soviets construction office had become an indispensable organization, routinely assigned at the behest of top Soviet leaders to work on projects that had nothing at all to do with the Palace. So useful was the USDS that in 1946 that it was engaged on restoration work on the

Kremlin and other prominent buildings in and around Moscow, including the Bolshoi and Vakhtangov Theaters. The USDS was also put to work on the construction of the Lenin Library, a building complex designed in the 1920s by Palace architects Vladimir Gel'freikh and Vladimir Shchuko.[129] By 1946, the USDS had grown into an extensive construction outfit, with 5,500 workers and staff. Yet, the organization had yet to obtain the official go-ahead to start work again on the Palace of Soviets.

It was in January 1947 that Iofan and Prokof'ev set aside their efforts to begin work again on the Palace of Soviets. That month, the USDS was assigned to build two of Moscow's eight new skyscrapers. As the organization's leaders well understood, these enormous new buildings would divert resources, labor, and expertise away from the Palace of Soviets for many years to come. Even so, the project was not yet cancelled and for the most ardent Palace devotees, the skyscrapers were seen as mere rehearsals for the even more monumental structure that would stand at the center of them all. As late as 1950, Iofan chastised a subordinate at a USDS communist party meeting for ignoring the Palace of Soviets project in his report on progress on the university skyscraper that was by then under construction on the Lenin Hills. "In his extensive report, Comrade Obshivalov did not find room [to mention] the work on the Palace of Soviets," Iofan began.

> He did not slip in even a word about this project, which has fallen out of the sphere of his attention. This is not right. At the current moment, our main goal is the construction of the university, but this is not the main goal of our organization. The construction of the university builds up strength and prepares us, in this way, for the construction of the Palace of Soviets. We must be ready, because at any moment we will be required to answer for the design of the Palace of Soviets and it will be very difficult if we are not ready.[130]

Iofan brought his remarks to a close in the manner of a speaker schooled in the art of "criticism and self-criticism"—a rhetorical tactic of increasing importance at such meetings in the late-Stalin years. Though he had begun by casting blame on others, Iofan now turned inward, reflecting on his own mistakes. "And then there is my great fault," the architect said. "I must fight more and indefatigably for recognition of the importance of our work. We must mobilize all of our strength," Iofan declared, "so long as we, a small collective, need to acquire space and people and properly prepare to pivot back toward working on the Palace of Soviets."[131]

Iofan's determination to complete the project he had begun in 1931 was not out of line with the purported desires of Soviet leaders. In 1949, at a Politburo meeting held on the topic of Moscow's new postwar General Plan, the Moscow Mayor Georgii Popov recorded Stalin's comments on the status of the Palace. "We will absolutely build the Palace of Soviets," Stalin stated, according to Popov, at that meeting in 1949. "Once we have finished the multi-story buildings," Stalin clarified, "then we will return to the Palace of Soviets."[132] In the postwar years in Moscow, a citywide skyscraper construction project was underway. When it came down to it, the Palace was a relic of an earlier moment and in the meantime the scope of Soviet leaders' plans for the capital had grown ever more ambitious. After 1945, Soviet leaders turned their attention to the construction of not just one skyscraper for their capital city, but nine.

4

MOSCOW OF THE PLAN

On January 13, 1947, the Council of Ministers of the USSR issued a decree (*postanovlenie*) calling for the construction of eight skyscrapers in Moscow.[1] Demobilization was still underway and bread lines and rationing were still a part of daily life. The failed harvest of the previous year was making itself felt in the capital; hunger and exhaustion could be seen on the faces of villagers who flowed into Moscow from the famine-stricken regions beyond.[2] Against this larger reality, Moscow's skyscraper decree of early 1947 was out of place. The order signaled to the few who first saw it that the Stalinist state was eager to return to prewar priorities while also rising to meet the demands of its new hegemonic status. The Soviet state would mark its wartime victory through a renewed commitment to monumental construction. In the process, Moscow would be reinvented as a world-class capital city—the "standard-bearer," as the line went, "of the new Soviet epoch."[3]

This chapter explores how Moscow was reinvented and reimagined in the postwar years. It looks at the city as it emerged in meetings and on paper—in designs and decrees, some of which were intended for public consumption. The skyscraper plans put to paper in the late-Stalin years reached well beyond the scope of what was realistic and achievable. The initial skyscraper decree of January 1947 pledged to "take up Comrade Stalin's proposal for the construction between 1947 and 1952 of multistory buildings in Moscow: one 32-story building, two 26-story buildings, five 16-story buildings."[4] This first line alone would prove difficult to achieve. The six-year timeline was too short and construction on most of the buildings lagged into the post-Stalin period. In the end, only seven of the decree's eight structures were built to completion. The failure to fully transform this plan into reality was, in part, the result of its sheer monumentality.

Enumerating the many ways in which the initial skyscraper decree fell short is not the goal of this chapter. That Stalinist "reality" failed to conform to "the plan" is as reliable a maxim as they come, and Moscow's skyscrapers were no exception. What is clear from the archival documents that remain from this ambitious and costly experiment in urban reinvention is that the officials, architects, engineers, and construction managers engaged in the project were never wedded to the integrity of that first skyscraper decree. Instead, they understood the urban building process as fluid. The initial skyscraper decree issued in January 1947 was the first of hundreds of orders printed by the USSR Council of Ministers as it sought to make the skyscrapers a reality. In the case of all but one—two if we include the Palace of Soviets—these buildings were built. This chapter begins to unravel the story of how and why these structures were constructed. From the orders issued to the disagreements aired to

the scandals that erupted in the process, this chapter examines the tremendous energy and resources devoted to making Moscow monumental in the years of high
Stalinism.

SKYSCRAPERS AND OTHER TALL BUILDINGS

In early 1947, Muscovites both ordinary and elite were not talking about skyscrapers. In the Soviet capital, as elsewhere in the first month of the New Year, it was the
mass political ritual of elections to the Supreme Soviets of the USSR's republics that
dominated the newspapers and took hold of public life. Beyond the rallies and elec-
tion activities held in offices and factories across the capital, bread lines and ration
prices of a country gripped by famine clouded the more intimate family conversations that could be overheard in the city's communal apartments, stairwells, and
shops. For elites, the most absorbing topic of discussion in Moscow at New Year had
to do with the spoils of war. Rumors spread through high society about the precious
objects moved quietly out of Germany and into Soviet territory in 1946. According
to *Pravda* editor Lazar' Brontman, who attended a private viewing of heaps of the
trophy art being stored at Moscow's Pushkin Museum, the whole city was talking
about German art.[5] Hundreds of thousands of priceless pieces, from the Sistine
Madonna to coffers of "Trojan" gold, were sequestered away in Moscow. The hungry
city was also a treasure trove.[6]

It was in late February 1947 that talk of Moscow's new skyscrapers made its way
onto the pages of *Pravda*.[7] Rather than announce the monumental construction project that had begun one month earlier to great fanfare and celebration, the skyscrapers made their first appearance buried in a third-page spread of transcripts of recent
speeches about the 1947 state budget. And so in this way, *Pravda*'s especially devoted readers learned that Stalin had decided to build tall buildings in Moscow "in
the coming years."[8] In information taken from the first skyscraper decree, *Pravda*
reported that the tallest, 32-story structure would be a hotel and residential building on the Lenin Hills.[9] The city's two new 26-story structures would include a hotel
and residential building near Dinamo stadium and an administrative building in
Moscow's Zariad'e district.[10] And the remaining 16-story structures would include
two administrative towers on Smolensk Square and Kalanchevskii Street, and three
residential buildings on the Kotel'nicheskaia embankment, on Uprising Square, and
at the Red Gates. As *Pravda* reported, these monumental multi-story buildings would
play a role in beautifying the city. They would also stand as central elements within
the broader reconstruction of Moscow.[11]

By March 1947 news of Moscow's skyscrapers reached American readers as well.
The *New York Times* broke the story with a front-page headline that read "Skyscrapers Gain Stalin's Approval."[12] The *Times* journalist quoted Chief Architect of Moscow
Dmitrii Chechulin, who provided the international press with information about the
intended heights and locations of the buildings. The article in the *New York Times*
also reported erroneously that "all buildings will contain living quarters, one of the
capitals' [sic] greatest needs."[13] In fact, the skyscrapers were never planned as a solution to the housing problem—though it was certainly true that Moscow faced a
severe housing shortage and that living conditions in the city's existing housing stock

had reached a crisis point. Ultimately, readers of both *Pravda* and the *New York Times* received few and, in some cases, misleading details about Moscow's new buildings. In the early months of 1947, Soviet officials, construction managers, and architects themselves had little notion of the shape the project would take over the following months and years.

The skyscraper decree of January 13, 1947 was impressionistic at best. The document gave little indication of the outsized role the buildings would come to play in Soviet life. The decree listed the desired heights and locations for each of the structures and it specified that steel frames be used to support them, the interiors of the buildings be comfortable and fitted with modern amenities, and the façades be made with "durable and stable" material.[14] It also assigned six institutions to build Moscow's new towers. Ranging in their power and expertise, these institutions were the USDS (Administration for the Construction of the Palace of Soviets), the MVD (or Ministry of Internal Affairs), the MPS (or Ministry of Railways), *Mintiazhstroi* (the Ministry of Construction of Heavy Industry), *Minaviaprom* (the Ministry of Aviation Industries), and *Minvoenmorstroi* (the Ministry of Construction of Army and Navy Industries).[15] The January decree thus set basic parameters for the project, but in order to transform the document into a plan that could be put into action, more such instructions were needed. Moscow's monumental new buildings would require a mountain of paperwork before they could come into being.

When the order to build skyscrapers in Moscow was issued, the Soviet Union was in the midst of a major ideological campaign that had begun the previous year. The so-called *Zhdanovshchina,* named after Communist Party boss Andrei A. Zhdanov but orchestrated by Stalin himself, had been launched in 1946 as an attack against Soviet writers. Within a year, official efforts to ensure ideological purity in Soviet culture by rooting out modernism, liberalism, and all things "Western" had spread swiftly through the literary arts and on to other fields, from opera and architecture to linguistics and biology.[16] Within this larger context, the skyscraper decree was strange. Skyscrapers were undeniably "Western" and the plan to build eight of them in the Soviet capital was plainly at odds with the campaign then being waged against Americanism and other foreign cultural influences.[17] The authors of the skyscraper decree were no doubt aware of this problem. In the text of their decree they presented Moscow's architects with a way to resolve the tension inherent in the city's new construction project.

The decree stated plainly that Moscow's new structures "must not repeat the famous examples of foreign multi-story buildings."[18] The document offered no additional clarification on this point, but in 1947 Soviet architects did not require it. Had a list of banned buildings been issued with the decree, it would certainly have included the skyscrapers of New York and Chicago—those same buildings to which Boris Iofan and others of the USDS had turned for inspiration in the 1930s. In earlier decades Soviet architects had, as Christina Crawford notes, "viewed American technological products as ideologically neutral."[19] But by 1947, these same architects were navigating the slippery terrain of the *Zhdanovshchina.* Pushed to prove and strengthen their adherence to the Community Party line, architects participated in the broader campaign against "formalism" and "kowtowing to the West." Public rituals like "honor courts" ensured that no one was immune and nothing was ideologically neutral in the new cultural atmosphere.[20] Soviet architects knew well that times had changed. In earlier years they had borrowed liberally from a wide array of foreign models, but now the range of acceptable influences had narrowed. And along with restrictions in style and design came limits in language. As the January decree signaled, in Soviet officialese Moscow's new buildings were not to be called "skyscrapers" (*neboskreby*). Instead, the decree referred to the buildings as "highrises," "multistory," or simply "tall" buildings (*mnogoetazhnye* or *vysotnye zdaniia*).

As Moscow's new building project got underway, the city's architects found themselves tasked with ensuring that there was a clear distinction between foreign ("*zarubezhnye*") skyscrapers and the Soviet Union's "tall buildings." New instructional guides and a new edition of the *Great Soviet Encyclopedia*, published in the early 1950s, aided in the effort to clear up any lingering confusions about building typology. The revised *Great Soviet Encyclopedia* helpfully defined the term "*neboskreb*" ("skyscraper") as a structure built in capitalist countries, in particular in the United States.[21] The encyclopedia's updated entry on "Architecture" similarly worked to disentangle tall buildings from skyscrapers. In the encyclopedia's first edition, published in 1927, architect Aleksei Shchusev had concluded his entry on "Architecture" with an account of the latest achievements in American skyscraper construction.[22] The revised entry of 1950, by contrast, culminated with images of the as-yet-unbuilt Moscow State University. This new history of architecture turned a building type closely associated with capitalism—the skyscraper—into an icon of communist triumph. The new history of architecture printed in the *Great Soviet Encyclopedia* also conflated communism with Russian national form. As the encyclopedia put it in its postwar entry, Moscow's new buildings had initiated "a wholly new Russian national tradition." The structures "architecturally express the greatness of Moscow—the capital of the world's first socialist state."[23] Russian nationalism had joined Soviet communism in its competition with the West.[24] And, as the argument went, just as A. S. Popov had been the first to invent radio and A. N. Lodygin had invented the lightbulb, Soviet architects and their leader Stalin had invented the "tall building."[25] In the same way that Soviet architects and engineers had gone abroad in the 1930s to learn from the skyscraper builders of New York City, now foreigners would flock to Moscow to study the Soviet Union's "tall buildings." The tables had turned.

For the most part, Moscow's architects would indulge the fiction that they were building "tall buildings" and *not* "skyscrapers." And yet, however much it was avoided in official directives and in the newspapers, the word "*neboskreb*" infiltrated closed-door discussions early on, whether Soviet officials liked it or not. In late February 1947, a group of engineers received an invitation for the first meeting of their "Committee on Heating, Ventilation, and Air Conditioning of the Tall Buildings (Skyscrapers)."[26] And in early March 1947, architect Arkadii Mordvinov could be heard discussing the "26-story skyscraper" planned for the Zariad'e.[27] That those involved in Moscow's new building project continued to use the word "*neboskreb*" during the first few months of their work is not wholly surprising, since by any standard definition Stalin's tall buildings *are* skyscrapers. Taller than they are wide, these structures continue to stand in Moscow today supported by steel frames, and they contain elevators connecting floors on which people live and work. The word "skyscraper" might also have been deployed in early discussions for rhetorical effect, signaling the significance and novelty of the work Moscow's architects were doing in 1947. Yet, however evocative and heroic—however accurate—the word "skyscraper" was, there was no denying its American origins. Tainted by its association with a rival economic system, the "skyscraper" had no place in the lexicon of socialist urbanism during the first years of the Cold War.

The skyscraper decree issued by the Council of Ministers in 1947 reflected a larger effort on the part of Soviet officials to put earlier patterns of Soviet internationalism to rest. Gone were the days when Soviet architects went abroad for assistance. Iofan's trip to America was a full decade in the past. As the order to build eight skyscrapers in Moscow came down, the Soviet Union was a more powerful, more self-secure state. Moscow had long been the target of urban beautifying projects, but these efforts took on ever greater urgency after 1945. The Soviet Union needed a capital that projected power and influence, a city to which experts from around the world would travel in order to study the latest advances in urban development. The tall buildings were the product of a new vision of the Soviet Union's place in the world—of a new, postwar internationalism that positioned Moscow at the center of world-historical development. They were also the product of a new, postwar anti-Americanism.

In the postwar years, it was not just the Soviet Union that had changed. The *Zhdanovshchina* at home, the Red Scare in the United States, and the start of the Cold War all worked to fracture the good will and productive networks of exchange that Soviet and American citizens fostered during the interwar and wartime years. Soviet engagement with foreign practitioners and their ideas did not cease entirely during the postwar period. Rather, Soviet architects found themselves engaging in a new, more scripted and less subordinate, way with their foreign colleagues. When, starting in 1946, Soviet architects participated in the creation and development of the International Union of Architects, they took the stock phrases of the *Zhdanovshchina* abroad with them, often eliciting confusion and hurt feelings from their foreign interlocutors.[28]

Skyscraper construction in Moscow served to support claims of Soviet greatness. But the project was also hampered by the anti-American sentiments that roared through Soviet culture in these years. Had Iofan and his team from the USDS traveled to America again in the late 1940s, they would have found that the latest trends in skyscraper building had moved on from the terracotta façades and neoclassical detailing that characterized interwar architecture. Sleek glass towers came to dominate American skylines in the postwar era. By 1947, the "International Style" had risen to prominence in the United States. The United Nations headquarters, built in New York City between 1948 and 1952, stood as a shining glass testament to the changing times. The Khrushchev era would see the Soviet Union and the US move closer again on questions of construction and architecture. But when Moscow's monumental new buildings began to rise up on the cityscape during late-Stalinism, American eyes would consider them hopelessly passé. Soviet and American architecture diverged in the postwar years as much for stylistic as for political reasons.

From the perspective of those working in early 1947 to ensure that Moscow's skyscraper decree would become reality, it did not much matter whether the new structures were "skyscrapers" or "tall buildings." Whether the structures would adhere to the dictates of the International Style or follow the neoclassical path of socialist realism was also not immediately important. No matter their style, the buildings would require expertise in steel-frame construction and knowledge in the latest developments in elevator and ventilation systems, among other modern technologies. Of the Soviet institutions assigned to build Moscow's new structures, the USDS brought prior experience to the project, having worked for over a decade on the Palace of Soviets. The five ministries named as builders offered managerial expertise and experience in industrial construction, but no direct knowledge of skyscraper building. And so, from the moment the skyscraper decree was issued, the USSR's economic base—and the Ministers who managed it—had to scramble to keep up with the vision for Moscow's postwar refashioning.

The organizations put in charge of building skyscrapers in the Soviet capital faced the tasks ahead of them with equal measures of agitation and bewilderment. What did they, the war-weary managers of the state's industrial economy, know about steel-frame skyscraper construction? One week after the skyscraper decree was signed, the Moscow Mayor Georgii M. Popov attempted to find out.[29] Hoping to coordinate the skyscraper project properly from the start, Popov convened a meeting on January 20, 1947 with all the institutions in charge of building Moscow's eight skyscrapers.

GEORGII POPOV'S MEETING

This first skyscraper meeting began with an argument between Illarion D. Gotsiridze, the Deputy Minister of Railways, and Popov. The January 13 decree had stipulated that the Ministry of Railways would head up construction of the 16-story residential building on the Red Gates plot, a piece of land already held (for all intents and purposes "owned") by the same Ministry. Gotsiridze asked for permission to build this skyscraper somewhere else in the capital. As he explained to Popov, the Ministry of Railways had already decided to erect a new office building for itself on the Red Gates plot, and the loose ground and the existing metro station below it made this location unsuitable, in any case, for such a tall and heavy building.

Gotsiridze was well positioned to provide such expert advice. An engineer by training, he had worked in the 1930s on the Moscow metro, including on the metro station at the Red Gates. Nevertheless, Popov responded by telling Gotsiridze to sit down and stop interfering with the meeting.[30] They had received an order; their meeting was not about changing a decree that had already been approved and signed, but about agreeing on general principles for the construction of Moscow's skyscrapers. After an exasperating exchange with Gotsiridze, Popov exploded: "This shows just what kind of love the Ministry of Railways has for housing construction. They have nothing against building an administrative complex but are against building housing."[31] Obviously preoccupied with the housing question, Popov would return to the issue later in the meeting, but for now, the floor passed to Vasilii V. Boitsov, the Deputy Minister of Aviation Industries.

Unlike his counterpart at Railways, Boitsov kept his remarks short and on point: the construction office at Aviation had started on the decree, they were still looking for an architect, and no, the bosses down at Aviation had not yet visited the construction site on Uprising Square, the one assigned to them for their 16-story building. "Your people at the Aviation Ministry need to visit the site personally," chided Popov. "I am certain that within the month Comrade Stalin will be asking for a report, so you have to go down there yourselves."[32]

Popov was a formidable figure who was cross-appointed as head of both the Moscow municipal and party governments. Born in Moscow in 1906 to a family of accountants, Popov was fiery and ambitious. He joined the Communist Party at the age of twenty, working as a Komsomol secretary and aviation engineer before rising swiftly through the ranks in Moscow.[33] Stalin, who saw Popov as "a businesslike man," personally nominated him in 1941 for membership in the Central Committee.[34] In December 1944 Popov was put in charge of city affairs as Chairman of the Executive Committee of the Moscow Soviet. And in May 1945 at the age of thirty-eight, he simultaneously became head of the Moscow party organization, a dual post that made Popov, essentially, the Mayor of Moscow.

Yet, Popov's power over Moscow affairs did not place him in a position above the country's powerful Ministries based in the capital. In the meeting he had called in January 1947 Popov was defensive, asserting control over the others present by repeatedly emphasizing his close connection to Stalin. Popov's frequent references to the thoughts and plans of the *vozhd'* added force to this municipal official's arguments, while also serving to clarify the monumental vision underlying the skyscraper decree. The idea to build skyscrapers in Moscow, Popov explained, had come from Stalin himself. "As Stalin says," Popov parroted, "people go to America and they return in amazement saying, 'oh, what enormous buildings!' Let them come to Moscow and see what buildings we have here—let them marvel at the sight of them."[35] Taking the performance further, Popov asked those present at the meeting to imagine a visitor arriving by train to Moscow: "from the station he sees a large building, rising up from the Red Gates, a beautiful large residential building. . . . Each plot was chosen to create a silhouette and to emphasize [the city's] architecture."[36]

The transcript of Popov's meeting in January 1947 contains rich passages in which the Mayor described in vivid, lyrical detail how the skyscrapers would be experienced and felt by those who encountered them. These passages show a leader anxious to convince a doubtful audience of the importance of the project set before them. Popov was in charge of a complex city that lacked a strong central planning agency and instead had a tangled mess of institutions often working at cross-purposes in the area of urban construction. As Popov was well aware, Moscow was a city in which urban development was never simple and straightforward. At that first skyscraper meeting, Popov stressed the importance of considering the needs of the city as a whole, but the Ministries saw the situation differently. Now saddled with massive new building projects that had little or nothing to do with their respective institutional goals, the Ministers and Deputy Ministers pushed back, searching for ways to combine their existing priorities with the monumental command. In order to become real, the skyscraper vision would have to contend with towering egos and cut across Moscow's myriad institutional divides.

Having lectured his audience on the aesthetic and ideological goals of Stalin's skyscrapers, Popov quickly returned to practical matters. This first meeting saw an extended discussion of technical problems that the group foresaw in areas such as the laying of foundations and the scarce availability in the postwar years of steel, non-industrial elevators, construction materials, and necessary equipment. The cityscape ideal underlying the entire project was exciting in theory, but in practice it presented enormous challenges, not least due to the lack of coordination, expertise, and experience on the ground.

The meeting convened by Popov in January 1947 was the first time that many of those in attendance had ever had to answer for such a large-scale highrise construction project. There were exceptions to this, of course, most notably Boris Iofan and Andrei Prokof'ev, respectively the chief architect and head of the USDS, both of whom were in attendance at Popov's meeting. The USDS had been assigned to build the 32-story skyscraper on the Lenin Hills and the 26-story building on the Zariad'e. The Ministry of Internal Affairs (MVD) also had experience in highrise urban construction. In fact, the MVD was already building a highrise structure on the very plot chosen for its Kotel'nicheskaia skyscraper. The 12-story building already underway on the Kotel'nicheskaia embankment had been started before the war. As the MVD's representative explained at the meeting, the war may have interrupted construction, but the foundation had already been laid and substantial progress had been made on the site.

The MVD tried to make the case that with minor changes, the earlier project could suit the needs of the new one: although the prewar design was not quite 16-stories tall, the MVD's man explained that with "the tower [it] will be 16-stories." Popov was skeptical. "We need the building as a whole to be 16-stories," he replied. The MVD assured Popov that the structure would be well built, with "the bottom of the building in granite, the façade . . . a ceramic in sixteen different colors."[37] Construction would be finished, he promised, in 1948. Although Dmitrii Chechulin and Andrei K. Rostkovskii, the same architects who had designed the earlier building, stayed on at the Kotel'nicheskaia site, this skyscraper would in the end be a different building than the first. It would be completed just a few months before Stalin's death in 1953.

Those at the first skyscraper meeting were also keen to discuss foreign knowledge and expertise. The USDS in particular had close ties to the American architectural community dating to the 1930s that might be made use of once again. The other institutions represented at the meeting also had a history of interwar exchange, ranging from the simple use of foreign technical manuals to face-to-face exchanges with foreign specialists. Given the long history of Soviet international engagement in the area of construction, the matter of foreign assistance was so obvious a topic that Popov likely anticipated it. But on this front, the Mayor dug in his heels, resisting any notion that Soviet architects and engineers would need to go abroad for technical assistance in skyscraper building.

The issue of foreign assistance was first raised at the meeting in a discussion about elevators. The initial skyscraper decree clearly stated that "the interior planning of the buildings must be suited for maximum convenience for work and mobility through the structures." And it clarified that "towards these goals, the planning of the buildings must make provision for the use of all the most modern technical means in elevator equipment, water supply systems, lighting, telephones, heating, air conditioning, and so on."[38] Yet, as some at the meeting stressed, without standardized dimensions for items such as elevators the design process would prove difficult.[39] "We should talk with Anastas Ivanovich [Mikoyan], so that he can help us buy samples of foreign elevators in America," suggested Innokentii A. Onufriev, the Deputy Minister of Construction of Heavy Industry—the organization in charge of building the skyscraper on Smolensk Square.[40] Popov was unconvinced. "Bear in mind," the Mayor replied, "that our country makes mine hoists, [and] in terms of speed they are much better, they go down 200 meters in 40 seconds, and our buildings will be about 70 meters."[41] The issue of elevators was returned to later in the meeting, with others also noting the importance of American advances in this area; no one, aside from Popov, seemed to think that mine hoists might prove useful for Stalin's skyscrapers.

MAKE NO LITTLE PLANS

Despite his active involvement in coordinating Moscow's skyscraper construction early on, Georgii Popov was never the man ultimately in charge of the project. The Soviet official whose job it was to oversee the skyscraper portfolio was Lavrentii Pavlovich Beria. A member of Stalin's small ruling group, Beria had come to Moscow from Georgia during the purges in 1938 to head up the NKVD. In the postwar years, Beria maintained a supervisory role over the Soviet security services, but he was chiefly involved from 1945 in overseeing the Soviet atomic bomb project. A shrewd manager and skilled administrator, Beria managed to maintain his close relationship with Stalin through the leader's turbulent final years.[42] He lived just inside Moscow's Garden Ring, not far from the site of the future skyscraper on Uprising Square. And as skyscraper construction in the city got underway, Beria received regular updates on the progress of each building site, compiled for him by one of his two main secretaries. In turn, Beria sent regular updates to Stalin, seeking the leader's approval on certain aspects of the project.[43]

Given the importance of the skyscrapers to Stalin himself, it is not surprising that oversight of the project was assigned to the highest level of government. Beria was no expert in highrise construction, but this new project begun in 1947 was not wholly unlike his other work. In the postwar Soviet Union, skyscrapers and atomic bombs shared a number of similarities. Like the atomic project, Moscow's skyscrapers were closely tied to Soviet foreign policy, as well as to state building and centralization. The goal of the skyscrapers, from Stalin's perspective, was to put Moscow on the map—to make the city the "capital of all capitals," as Stalin put it at a closed meeting in 1949.[44] According to the detailed notes taken at that meeting by Popov, Stalin argued that "without a good capital, there is no state."[45] "We need a capital that is beautiful," he continued, "one that all will admire . . . a center of science, culture, and art. In France there is Paris—that is a good capital."[46] Moscow had not always been the capital of Russia, Stalin acknowledged. "Leningrad was once the capital. There was a time when even Siberia wished to become the capital. It happened in this way because Russia was not united."[47] For Stalin, Moscow's urban development was inextricably tied to the nation's unity, as well as to the country's international status.

Despite his secondary role on the skyscraper project, Popov remains one of our most important—although not entirely reliable—sources on what Stalin was thinking as he made decisions about Moscow's postwar redevelopment. In particular, Popov's memoir, written with some twenty years' hindsight, provides a rare glimpse into the architectural ideas and motivations of the Soviet leader. According to Popov, it was Stalin himself who initiated the skyscraper project as a model for postwar re-construction in the Soviet Union as a whole. "Moscow, as the capital of the USSR," Popov explained, "was at the forefront, called upon to set the tone, to be the example for other cities." Placing himself at the center of the story, Popov recalled how "they called me from the Kremlin and asked me to come in to see the members of the Politburo . . . there I was shown a piece of Whatman paper on which was drawn in blue pencil a multistory building with a spire, on which fluttered a red flag, and next to which was written: 26–32 stories." "They explained to me," Popov writes, "that the drawing was done by I. V. Stalin."[48]

The notion that Stalin was the originator—the architect—of Moscow's tall build-ings was a powerful idea that guided those involved in construction at all levels. Popov's story of Stalin's drawing in blue plays on the cliche of the star architect who, in a moment of inspiration, hurriedly sketches the outlines of a new design on the back of a cocktail napkin. In Popov's case, the story served not just to signal Stalin's creative genius, but also to sweep away chaos and uncertainty with a narrative evok-ing the preordained and sanctified nature of Moscow's postwar transformation. Sta-lin as architect was, in Popov's account, a visionary with the Promethean ability to comprehend and dictate the development of Moscow as a whole. The skyscrapers were evidence of the power of the *vozhd'*.

Soviet architects attributed to themselves this same omnipotency. The very ability to imagine and thereby plan a city in its entirety was, Soviet architects claimed, a defining feature of socialist urbanism. Freed from the constraints of private property, individual interest, and capitalist investment, the Soviet architect asserted that he had the power not just to design individual buildings, but to shape and beautify cities as a whole. Yet attention to the cityscape—and the desire to shape the city in its totality—was not new, nor was it the preoccupation of socialism alone. At the turn of the twen-tieth century, American architect Daniel Burnham coined the phrase: "Make no little plans, they have no magic to stir men's blood."[49] Father of the "City Beautiful" move-ment, Burnham gave shape to the Progressive Era's goal of civic engagement by de-signing vast and monumental plans for Chicago, Washington, DC, San Francisco, and Manila. Just as Soviet architects took a page out of Burnham's book in the rhetoric they deployed, they similarly found that big plans did not translate neatly into reality. The *idea* to build skyscrapers in postwar Moscow may have been a bold plan hatched by a single individual, but the buildings would come to fruition through a flurry of little plans and through the work of many, many people. It was in the incremental steps of small decree after small decree that, little by little, the skyscraper plan fell into place. Skyscraper building in postwar Moscow was a gargantuan and unwieldy endeavor. And as Popov and others would quickly come to realize, this construction project begun in 1947 was so enormous that no single individual could possibly con-ceive of all of its moving parts, let alone manage it single-handedly.

LITTLE PLANS

After Popov convened the first skyscraper meeting in January 1947, the skyscraper-building ministers and their deputies, joined by architects and engineers, continued to meet and correspond through that spring and summer. With Beria's office coordinating the effort, these officials and experts worked to determine general principles and standards on a range of issues, from elevators to heating and ventilation, to building materials and labor. The result of many months of discussion and debate was a new decree, issued by the Council of Ministers on August 17, 1947. Titled "On the Measures for the Construction of Multistory Buildings in Moscow," this new decree was much more detailed and technically oriented than the first. At seventeen pages long, it contained fifty-five items and sub-items and twelve appendices. Unlike its January counterpart, the August decree was no lofty vision; it was a plan.

The new decree of August 1947 clarified important issues, from financing to staffing to who would supply bricks, gypsum, and limestone to whom and when. The document determined, for example, that the steel carcasses of the buildings would be prepared under the supervision of the Ministry of Construction of Heavy Industry in the factories of Ramenskoe, a town located just east of Moscow. The decree also noted that a selection of walnut, yew, sycamore, boxwood, chestnut, laurel, and white acacia woods would be brought into Moscow from the Far East, the North Caucasus, and the Georgian, Armenian, Azerbaijani and Kirgiz SSRs. The decree stated that the Soviet Ministry of Industrial Construction Materials would supply 5,200 washstands, 4,385 bathtubs, and 5,260 toilets. As for the municipal contribution to the project, *Mosgorispolkom* (the Moscow city government) would provide 2.7 million bricks, 1,600 tons of lime, and 700 tons of alabaster by the end of 1947.[50] The August decree was the culmination of seven months of meetings and correspondence, and in it, few matters were left unaddressed.

And so in August 1947 dozens of copies of this comprehensive decree were typed up and dispatched to all relevant ministries and organizations. Few recipients were privy to all of its contents, and most found their copies partially redacted, with three items containing no text beyond the word "secret." Those who ranked highly-enough to read the full document found in the first "secret" item an order requiring Nikita Khrushchev, then head of the Ukrainian SSR, to supply Moscow with 4 million square meters of gypsum planks from Ukraine. The second "secret" item was an order for the MVD, the Moscow city government (*Mosgorispolkom*), and the Moscow oblast' government (*Mosoblispolkom*) to allow 23,000 workers and their families to enter the city of Moscow and to be legally registered there to work on the skyscrapers. This line clarified that the Ministries and the USDS hiring these workers would be responsible for housing them, and Popov was tasked with finding plots in the region of Moscow for these new workers' districts. Finally, the third "secret" item of the August decree was an order requiring that ten engineers be sent abroad for six months to the US, England, and Sweden.[51] This last order does not appear to have been fulfilled.

The August decree was by no means the last word on Moscow's skyscraper project. Dozens of subsequent orders revised many of the items set out in the summer of 1947. Construction schedules would soon have to be extended and materials and labor requirements adjusted. But the August decree was nonetheless a comprehensive document with concrete instructions that helped to translate a hazy vision into an actionable plan. And now that the plan was set before them, the final piece construction managers faced was the matter of design: what would these buildings, with their steel frames, walnut panels, and modern elevators, look like?

Just as Ministry managers were meeting through the spring and into the summer of 1947 to discuss questions of management and construction, Moscow's architects and engineers also met in those months to grapple with the issue of design. Heading up the design discussions were Andrei Prokof'ev, boss of the USDS, and two of Moscow's top architects: Arkadii Mordvinov, who was head until 1947 of the USSR State Architecture Committee; and Dmitrii Chechulin, who had served as Chief Architect of Moscow since 1944. These men met first on February 6, 1947, along with delegates from the various Ministries involved, to begin establishing basic requirements for the designs. By the time this work was done, Moscow would have under construction eight structures that resembled one another so closely it seemed they had been designed by the same hand.

In truth, the path to uniformity was more complex. Prokof'ev, Mordvinov, Chechulin, and others had first to decide whether the design of Moscow's monumental new buildings would be assigned to architects specially selected in closed meetings, or whether there would be a competition held for the designs of each of the buildings. In May 1947, Beria received a draft list of architects hand-picked to design all eight structures, but in the end just three of the skyscrapers would be assigned to architects without competition.[52] By the summer of 1947, Chechulin had been chosen to lead the design teams of the skyscrapers that would stand closest to the Kremlin: the building on the Kotel'nicheskaia embankment and the one in the Zariad'e district. Boris Iofan, still head architect at the USDS, was assigned to design the skyscraper on the Lenin Hills, though within a year this commission was passed to Lev Rudnev. For the remaining five buildings, design competitions were held among preselected teams of architects specially invited to submit proposals. Supplying each team with a list of predetermined parameters for height, volume, number of rooms, and amenities, the ministries in charge waited in anticipation for the designs to come in.[53]

Despite hopes that Moscow's skyscrapers would arrive swiftly on the horizon, the design process took considerable time. As Prokof'ev, Chechulin, and Mordvinov explained to Beria in the spring of 1947, reviews of the architectural proposals would proceed over the next four to seven months. This would be followed by reviews of corresponding technical design proposals drawn up by engineers.[54] All told, it would take at least a year before construction work could begin. The process dragged on so long that in January 1949 the Council of Ministers issued a decree titled "On the Approval of Design and Technical Projects of the Multistory Buildings." Back in 1947, however, fantasies about the speedy arrival of a new, monumental Moscow prevailed.

When the first architectural designs for Moscow's skyscrapers were unveiled in the late summer and autumn of 1947, they were not well received. Reviews of the competition entries for Moscow's 16-story skyscrapers began in mid-August and carried on until early September 1947. Each team of architects presented their designs for evaluation at the offices of the USSR State Architecture Committee. The reviews were presided over by the chairman of this institution, architect Grigorii A. Simonov, who assembled review panels made up of Moscow's top architects, engineers, and construction experts. In architecture, masters including Ivan Zholtovskii, Nikolai Kolli, Aleksei Shchusev, Karo Alabian, and Boris Iofan evaluated the designs. The

Figure 4.1: Nikolai D. Kolli, Lev V. Rudnev, Karo S. Alabian, and Grigorii A. Simonov in 1947. Collection of the State Central Museum of Contemporary History of Russia.

sculptor Vera Mukhina and the painter Aleksandr Gerasimov also took part in these reviews.[55]

In the first round of evaluation, the review committees reacted tepidly to the designs set before them. Chechulin, in collaboration with architect Andrei Rostkovskii, presented three different variations on their 16-story building on the Kotel'nicheskaia embankment. The reviewers faulted all three proposals on a variety of fronts, from an overabundance of north-facing apartments to a lack of standardized elements.[56] But, most troublingly, in all three cases Chechulin and Rostkovskii had exceeded the preset parameters for height, volume, and number of apartments. In their most deviant proposal, the architects had more than doubled the number of apartments from the 300 called for in the brief to 616. While the architects had striven for monumentalism by way of sheer size, the reviewers found that "the exaggerated volume of the building was one of the reasons that the building expanded in breadth [but] lost the character of "verticality" [*vysotnost'*], which it must have."[57] All three of Chechulin and Rostkovskii's designs were rejected by the committee.

The other architects working on the other buildings were met with similarly tepid responses. Proposals were submitted by three separate teams of architects for the skyscraper on Uprising Square. But these designs were found to be "primitive" and "cumbersome." One was especially offensive, with its "crude" (*grubyi*) silhouette and the "archaic" architectural detailing on its façade.[58] The designs submitted for the Red Gates building, by four different architects, were also found to be unacceptable.[59] One had raised the height of the building to 18 stories rather than the prescribed 16; another had no separation between the residential and office spaces; and yet another looked like a "lumbering, expressionless mass."[60]

By the time a new team of reviewers assessed the reworked design for the Kotel'nicheskaia skyscraper in late 1948, the earlier problems with massing had been resolved and the building's silhouette was now seen as "picturesque."[61] Still, the reviewers noted in their report that the "excessive number . . . of large and small turrets and towers" that topped the building gave it an "alien" (*nesvoistvennyi*) and "historical" appearance. In pen on the typewritten report, someone clarified this last comment by crossing out the word "historical" and replacing it with "Gothic." The reviewers were not anti-historical, as such. Rather, they were opposed to the incorporation of foreign historical, or Gothic, motifs into a Russian cityscape. This sentiment, expressed in a closed report, mirrored the ideas then being articulated in the public arena, where a firm link was being forged between Moscow's skyscrapers and the deep Russian past.

EIGHT HUNDRED YEARS OLD, AND THIRTY YEARS YOUNG

While Moscow's architects met to present their preliminary skyscraper designs in the late summer of 1947, the city prepared to celebrate its 800th anniversary. This new holiday was set, on Popov's initiative, for Sunday September 7, but Muscovites banked on a full weekend of festivities.[62] And so, as the capital's architects met behind closed doors to imagine the future shape of Moscow, the public out in the streets broke from their routines to commemorate the city's history. Their still vivid memories of the recent war and the suffering endured in those early postwar years would be temporarily supplanted by a collective celebration of the distant past. The anniversary celebrations would also serve as the occasion to properly announce Moscow's skyscraper project in the press in articles that tied the city's postwar construction to earlier periods of development.

In the weeks before Moscow's 800th anniversary celebrations, the American writer John Steinbeck spent time in the city while traveling in the USSR. Steinbeck had visited Moscow in 1936 and he immediately spotted a number of changes on this second trip. Accompanied on his travels in 1947 by the Hungarian photojournalist Robert Capa, Steinbeck wandered the streets of the capital, observing that "whole sections of the narrow, dirty districts of old Moscow had disappeared." The city, as Steinbeck saw it, was cleaner. Moscow's muddy streets were now paved and there were "hundreds of tall new apartment houses, new bridges over the Moscow River, the streets widened, and statues every place."[63]

Steinbeck also noticed that work on the city continued. Scaffolding was up in various places, buildings were being painted and repaired, and lights were strung up along the Kremlin, on bridges, and on public buildings. "And this work did not stop in the evening," Steinbeck wrote. "It went on with floodlights all night, this painting and grooming of the city for its first non-war celebration in many years."[64] As Steinbeck had learned, the attention that was being lavished on the Soviet capital was for the upcoming celebration of Moscow's 800th anniversary—a holiday that would be quickly followed in November by the thirtieth anniversary of the Bolshevik Revolution.

What Steinbeck and Capa saw when they visited Moscow in 1947 was the result of the Moscow General Plan of 1935. Although work on the plan had been interrupted by the war, the widened boulevards, bridges, and new public buildings were all hallmarks of that interwar beautification program. But the two foreigners were also witness in 1947 to Soviet society as it made its way through the slow and difficult transition from war into peace. In addition to the many changes and improvements that Steinbeck saw in Moscow, the writer also noticed exhaustion and stress on the faces of those around him. "In spite of the bustle and preparations," wrote Steinbeck, "the people in the streets seemed tired." The women wore little makeup, Steinbeck observed, and their clothing was, in his opinion, "adequate but not very pretty."[65] Many men were still wearing their uniforms, often with the insignia missing. Steinbeck figured that these uniforms were the only clothes they had.[66]

In the Soviet Union, the postwar period was a time of great hope, but also deep disillusionment. Wounds both physical and psychological were all around, as ordinary people and officials alike resigned themselves to the struggles of postwar life. The Soviet Union had won the war, expanded its territory and influence in Eastern Europe, and emerged as a superpower on the world stage. But what this victory might mean for Soviet society, culture, and politics remained uncertain. While many Soviet officials and large numbers of ordinary citizens counted on seeing greater liberalization and continued cooperation with the West in the postwar years, Soviet leaders pushed instead for a return to the repressive and insular politics of the 1930s. As Stalin, the architect of Soviet victory, turned his attention to the tasks of reconstruction, he also renewed the call for vigilance and struggle against enemies of the Soviet state.[67]

The Moscow anniversary celebrations offered a brief reprieve from this tense atmosphere. Physicist Sergei I. Vavilov, who as president of the Academy of Sciences was ensnared in the heated scientific debates of the time, described the weather in Moscow that holiday weekend as "radiant."[68] With not a cloud in the sky above them, crowds of people were out in Moscow's streets and parks, enjoying the sunshine and the endless sequence of activities. Red silk banners with slogans painted in old Slavonic script fluttered in the warm breeze. Large crowds of people streamed onto Gorky Street, where on Soviet Square, as Vavilov recorded in his diary, they paid homage to Yuri Dolgorukii, founder of Moscow. The twelfth-century Prince was present only in the form of a foundation stone marking the site of an equestrian statue to be erected in his honor. But Vavilov and others gathered there anyway, on that site across from Moscow's city hall (Mossovet). There, a revolutionary monument—the Obelisk to the Soviet Constitution—had stood from 1918 until it fell into disrepair in 1941.[69] Now, in celebration of Moscow's 800th year, a statue honoring the pre-revolutionary past would replace this monument to the Bolshevik Revolution.

There was no denying that something was off in Moscow's 800th anniversary celebrations. Even as he had pressed forward with preparations for September, Georgii Popov had not been able to allay concerns from both officials and ordinary citizens that this new holiday was problematic, if not outright blasphemous. In May 1947, Popov received updates from the city's regional officials on their preparations for the anniversary holiday. The Mayor learned about the wide range of planned activities, from historical exhibits and lecture cycles to the weaving of traditional cloth at local factories and the restoration of the homes of Griboedov and Gogol'. Moscow's neglected pond, *Chistye prudy*, would be cleaned for the holiday and there was talk of restoring some of the city's manor houses and monasteries as well. Officials in Moscow's Stalin district excitedly reported that they had chosen Peter the Great as the guiding theme for their planned events.

Not everyone was satisfied with this historical medley. One city district official concluded that they were all making a "serious mistake when speaking more about the 770-year period [before the revolution] while less attention was paid to the question of how Moscow lived during the Soviet period."[70] In the months to come, in response to local officials' "fixation on the distant past," Popov would have to remind municipal officials time and again that the most recent thirty years were the most important.[71] Making light of what were in 1947 quite serious ideological contradictions, the cartoonists of *Krokodil* would print a joke on the magazine's cover in August 1947 that read: "Just think, Moscow is 800 years old. But by the looks of her, she can't be over 30!"

Municipal officials were not alone in their concerns about the celebration of Moscow's 800th anniversary. In late August 1947, Popov received transcripts of workers' comments recorded in the lead-up to the holiday. Some of Moscow's factory workers pledged to work twice as hard in honor of the city's anniversary, but others took issue with the event. Aside from the vexing problem of which era or historical figure, specifically, was to be commemorated in September, there were questions of ideological hierarchy. "Won't it be the case," asked one worker, "that the holiday for the 800th anniversary of Moscow might eclipse the holiday for the thirtieth anniversary of the Great October socialist revolution?"[72] Moscow's holiday should be delayed, this worker suggested, until after November 7. The new holiday's proximity to October was an issue that officials grappled with as well, but perhaps more troubling was the fact that the anniversary opened the door to yet more severe forms of criticism.

As Muscovites saw which buildings were being restored and which walls were being painted in preparation for the holiday, their anger swelled. "When will prices go down for potatoes and vegetables?" asked one worker at a textile factory near Moscow's Kursk Station. "Will there be, for September 7, an increase in the allocation of bread," this worker continued, "or will changes be made to the rationing system?" Across town, workers similarly held out hope that Moscow's 800th anniversary would see the state take measures to ensure that basic foodstuffs, like bread, sugar, and grain, were easier to come by. But aside from concerns about the country's continued rations regime, Muscovites also drew connections between the city's beautification efforts and their own dismal living conditions. Women at the Red Seamstress factory asked if they could address those officials planning the holiday celebrations "on the question of apartment repairs," since no one else seemed to care.[73] And then there was Senadskii, an engineer who delivered an especially poignant rebuke when he told Moscow party officials that "the celebration of the 800th anniversary of Moscow is premature." "Since the war," Senadskii explained, "we have not been able to grow stronger. We do not [yet] see a better life. There is not enough food, shoes, raw material, everything is expensive. And here is a State Committee spending large sums of money on celebrations . . ."[74] Popov, who received transcripts of each of these complaints, carried on with the program, perhaps hoping that, in the absence of bread, the circus would suffice.

Figure 4.2: Georgii M. Popov at the celebration of Moscow's 800th anniversary, September 1947. Collection of the State Central Museum of Contemporary History of Russia.

The 800th anniversary of Moscow served as the occasion to officially announce the skyscraper project to the broader Soviet public. The first round of design meetings had only just begun, but the new skyscrapers nonetheless formed a key component of the anniversary celebrations. In the lead-up to the holiday, the editors of *Pravda* printed a "conversation" with Dmitrii Chechulin, who, in his capacity as Chief Architect of Moscow, explained that "it was Stalin's idea" to build 16, 26, and 32-story tall buildings in the city. With talking points taken directly from the January 1947 decree, Chechulin added that the buildings would "be original in their artistic composition" and that they would "not repeat foreign examples."[75] Further details were disclosed on the radio when, on the eve of the holiday, Boris Iofan gave a fifteen-minute talk on "multi-story buildings in Moscow"—a segment followed by music and readings from Tolstoi's *War and Peace*.[76]

The capital's architectural establishment played a central part in curating the holiday festivities, with the Union of Soviet Architects coordinating 200 lectures in 25 different regions of the city on topics that celebrated both the city's recent and distant past. The Union also created exhibitions and brochures, like the one on "Moscow in the Past, Present, and Future" and another on "The Architecture of the USSR over 30 Years."[77] Beyond these educational activities, Moscow's architects had begun work through the summer of 1947 restoring key monuments throughout the city. In response to a decree "On the Preservation of Architectural Monuments" issued by the RSFSR Council of Ministers in May 1947, Chechulin compiled a list of three of Moscow's churches that were in need of restoration.[78] Just as the war had served in earlier years as the impetus for action on the heritage front, so too did the city's anniversary celebrations provide a crucial opening for architectural preservation.

In September 1947, Moscow's past and present were celebrated in restorations, exhibitions, and tours but the future was also honored in the form of small placeholders laid throughout the city. Just like the foundation stone placed on the spot of the future statue of Dolgorukii, city officials positioned special markers on the sites of Moscow's future skyscrapers. In the popular imagination, at least, the weekend of Moscow's 800th anniversary would be remembered as the starting point of the city's skyscraper construction project. And by unveiling the skyscrapers on the city's anniversary, Soviet officials signaled their desire for these structures to compliment the existing urban terrain. Yet however much architects strove to ensure continuity in their designs, the city's eight new highrises would necessarily stand in tension with the past.

In the placement and configuration of the buildings themselves, the skyscraper project worked to fracture the Kremlin's hold on Moscow's city center, transforming the 800-year-old city into a distinctly "socialist" cityscape marked by its Stalinist construction. The skyscraper project did not disavow Moscow's long history. Rather, it sought to co-opt the Russian past in service of the Soviet present. As the initial skyscraper decree stated, "the proportions and silhouettes of these buildings must be original and their architectural artistic compositions must be drawn from the historical character of the city's architecture and from the silhouette of the future Palace of Soviets."[79] While the creation of a definitively socialist cityscape that would rival other world capitals was the primary goal of the exercise, equally important in this postwar moment was the act of rooting the project firmly in the past. In the coming years, Moscow's skyscrapers would be discussed as the crowning achievements in a long line of Russian architectural monuments.

Moscow's skyscrapers were the most widely discussed and broadly influential architectural projects of the postwar Stalin era. These buildings, mockingly called "wedding cakes" abroad, would be duplicated in Soviet and post-Soviet architecture for years to come.[80] As early as September 1948, the USSR State Architecture Committee requested that all design materials and sketches for the buildings be put in the Academy of Architecture's museum. The materials were considered "of great value to the study of creative development of Soviet architecture and in the museum they will be preserved in the appropriate manner," as the Committee's official put it in a note to Beria.[81] Soon these materials were displayed for professional study, and the distinctive Stalinist spires and tiered step-like recessions were repeated *ad infinitum* in diploma projects by students of the Moscow Architecture Institute and other architectural schools across the Soviet Union and throughout the growing socialist world. As with the Palace of Soviets in the 1930s, images of Moscow's skyscrapers circulated widely to a popular audience as well. But unlike that earlier project, the buildings begun in 1947 were soon made real in steel and stone on the horizon.

MONUMENTALISM STEP BY STEP

As architects, engineers, and Ministry officials debated questions of design through the late 1940s, their plans for Moscow's new buildings shifted. The decree of January 1947 called for the construction of a 26-story building on Leningradskoe shosse in the region of the 'Dinamo' stadium that was to hold apartments and hotel rooms.[82] Within a few months, a new location was selected along the Dorogomilovo embankment near the Kiev train station for this building, which would in the end become the Hotel Ukraine. As Beria told Stalin in a letter of July 1947, Nikolai A. Bulganin, then Minister of the Armed Forces, and Konstantin A. Vershinin, Commander of the Soviet Air Force, had requested that the Council of Ministers reconsider the location near Dinamo stadium, due to its proximity to the airport and aviation factory.[83]

The five 16-story structures were also altered as time went on. The building at the Red Gates, for example, would contain apartments as intended, but also offices. The building on Smolensk square would rise to 22-stories instead of 16 and it would hold only administrative offices, not residential apartments as originally planned. The 16-story administrative building in the region of Kalanchevskii Square (known from 1933 as Komsomol Square)[84] became, in the end, a 17-story hotel.[85] And in 1948, a significant change was made to the structure on the Lenin Hills. Originally slated to serve as a hotel and residential building, it was recast in 1948 as the new site of Moscow State University.[86]

According to Popov, the decision to build a university on the Lenin Hills came from Stalin himself. Before the Soviet leader ordered changes to the plan, Popov recalled Stalin saying, "You mean, in Moscow we have a pitiful, beggarly, unauthoritative Cathedral of Science? And we tolerate this?"[87] While Stalin was responsible for this important decision, Popov took credit for the removal of Boris Iofan as head architect on the project. As Popov wrote in his memoirs, "I suggested that a stronger group of architects and engineers be assembled to build the MGU building complex."[88] Iofan was replaced in 1948 by Lev Rudnev. Shocked by his removal, Iofan appealed to Stalin in July 1948 to request that he be put back on the project: "I appeal to you in a difficult moment of my life," Iofan wrote. "Today, the head of construction at the USDS Comrade Prokof'ev informed me of a decision on the project of the new building of Moscow State University, which I will finish in two weeks, to give the project to architect Rudnev."[89] Iofan's request that Stalin allow him to remain as chief architect on the project was not successful. And although he would stay on at the USDS, the head architect of the Palace of Soviets would not directly oversee the construction of any of Moscow's postwar skyscrapers.

On March 15, 1948, the Council of Ministers issued a new decree that built upon and amended the orders put into place in August 1947. With this new document, Moscow's leaders committed to beginning construction work first on the buildings

Figure 4.3: Head architect of Moscow State University Lev V. Rudnev (second from the left) at work in the studio, 1951. Collection of the Museum of Moscow.

on the Lenin Hills, Smolensk Square, at the Red Gates, and on the Kotel'nicheskaia embankment. Construction work on the remaining four buildings on the Zariad'e, on Dorogomilovo embankment, and on Komsomol and Uprising Squares was to begin only in 1950.[90] This March 1948 decision arose as a result of shared concerns among officials that complications would arise if construction began on all eight buildings at once. One year into the project, it was clear that Moscow's monumental transformation could not possibly take place as quickly as planned. The Soviet Union had only just emerged from a global conflict that left it impoverished in labor and construction resources. While the March 1948 order suggests a degree of cooperation between the various institutions involved in building Moscow's skyscrapers, the document was ultimately an imperfect solution to the competition over resources inherent in such a large-scale building project. No decree could fully succeed in preventing some Ministers from hoarding labor and materials; no order could fully alleviate the imbalances that existed across the skyscraper ministries.

The lack of coordination among the various skyscraper construction sites in the Soviet capital was distinctly at odds with the aesthetic coherence that had been achieved by 1949 across the designs for all eight buildings. In June 1949 the design sketches for Moscow's skyscrapers were finally revealed to the public on the pages of the journal *Arkhitektura i stroitel'stvo* (*Architecture and Construction*) (figs. 4.4–4.11).

Figure 4.4: Design for the 26-story building of Moscow State University on the Lenin Hills. Architects L. V. Rudnev, S. E. Chernyshev, P. V. Abrosimov, A. F. Khriakov. *Arkhitektura i stroitel'stvo*, June 1949, 4.

Figure 4.5: Design for the 32-story Administrative Building in the Zariad'e, towering over the Red Square and the Kremlin to the left. Architect D. N. Chechulin. *Arkhitektura i stroitel'stvo*, June 1949, 9.

Figure 4.6: Design for the 26-story hotel on the Dorogomilovo embankment. Architect A. G. Mordvinov. *Arkhitektura i stroitel'stvo*, June 1949, 10.

Figure 4.7: Design for the 20-story administrative building on Smolensk Square. Architects V. G. Gel'freikh and M. A. Minkus. *Arkhitektura i stroitel'stvo*, June 1949, 14.

Figure 4.8: Design for the 17-story hotel on Komsomol Square, with Moscow's Kazan Railway Station by A. V. Shchusev on the left. Architects L. M. Poliakov and A. B. Boretskii. *Arkhitektura i stroitel'stvo*, June 1949, 17.

Figure 4.9: Design for the 17-story residential building on the Kotel'nicheskaia embankment. Architects D. N. Chechulin and A. K. Rostkovskii. *Arkhitektura i stroitel'stvo*, June 1949, 18.

Figure 4.10: Design for 16-story residential building on Uprising Square. Architects M. V. Posokhin and A. A. Mndoiants. *Arkhitektura i stroitel'stvo*, June 1949, 20.

Figure 4.11: Design for the 16-story residential and administrative building at the Red Gates. Architects A. N. Dushkin and B. S. Mezentsev. *Arkhitektura i stroitel'stvo*, June 1949, 22.

Impressive in their height and monumentality, the skyscrapers' designs gave the appearance of having been created by the same hand. More changes would be made in the coming years to bring each building into line with the next. In 1951, for example, the Ministers of Railways, Aviation, and Construction of Heavy Industry approached Beria with plans to add spires to the tops of their respective skyscrapers. These elongated pinnacles would not only add height to the buildings, they would also bring them more into line with their sister structures. Beria signed off on the request, agreeing that the Red Gates, Uprising Square, and Smolensk Square buildings were incomplete without this final, vertical touch.[91]

THE POPOV AND CHECHULIN AFFAIRS

Postwar Stalinism was a tumultuous and uncertain time for Soviet architects. The *Zhdanovshchina* saw these experts engage in intense debates on questions of ideology and style. But the political dramas unfolding during these years also found their way to the doorstep of Soviet architecture. During his final years, Stalin oversaw a series of high-level purges, of which the Leningrad Affair is the most well known. In 1949, officials in the Leningrad Communist Party committee were arrested, interrogated, and charged with having formed a regional conspiracy.[92] The purge spread beyond the former capital when Nikolai Voznesenskii, head of the State Planning Commission (Gosplan) in Moscow, was arrested and executed in connection with the Leningrad Affair. This, in turn, led to a purge within Gosplan.[93] And as all this was happening, in October 1949—the same month that Voznesenskii was arrested—Georgii Popov found himself at the center of a related purge known as the Moscow Affair.[94]

The Moscow Affair began in October 1949 when three anonymous "communist engineers" in Moscow sent a letter denouncing Popov to Stalin and members of the Politburo. The three engineers accused Popov of "stifling self-criticism" in the Moscow party ranks "to the point that nobody dares say a word to the person above them."[95] They also accused the young Moscow party boss of placing his own cronies in positions of power, of being "lazy by nature" and "illiterate in Leninism," of enabling an "epidemic of dacha construction" that served Soviet elites, and, worst of all, of harboring fantasies of one day becoming leader of the Soviet Union. As evidence of Popov's thirst for power, the engineers relayed an episode from a banquet held for the 800th anniversary of Moscow, at which one of Popov's lackeys had made a toast "to the future leader of our party, Georgii Mikhailovich." Popov, the anonymous engineers alleged, "paid no heed to the comment, as if in agreement with the prognosis."[96]

Having read the engineers' letter, Stalin ordered that Popov be officially investigated. Penning his own denunciation of Popov in late October, Stalin provided clear guidance to the investigators. "I consider it my duty," Stalin wrote, "to point out what appear to be two utterly self-evident and, for me, grave features of the Moscow party organization, which highlight a deep flaw in comrade Popov's work." First, in agreement with the three engineers, Stalin maintained that self-criticism had indeed been stifled in the Moscow party apparatus. Second, Stalin continued, "it is clear that the Moscow party leadership has taken to usurping the role of the ministries, the government, and the Central Committee and to issuing direct instructions to enterprises and ministries, and that when ministers choose to stand up to those practices, they are mocked and humiliated in public by comrade Popov."[97] Those skyscraper ministers and their deputies who had been in attendance at Popov's meeting of January 1947 would likely have agreed with this second charge.

By early December 1949 Popov was stripped of his dual position as head of the Moscow party leadership and city executive. Demoted to the post of Minister of Urban

Construction, Popov would remain involved for a time in Moscow's skyscraper project, though he was soon demoted further to Minister of Agricultural Machine Building before being transferred to a position outside Moscow.[98] The Politburo decree summarizing Popov's dismissal, along with announcements put out by the Moscow party organization, were circulated and widely discussed at party meetings.[99] Popov's demotion was of special interest to those working on Moscow's skyscrapers.

In January 1950, over 300 Communist party and candidate members of the USDS met to discuss the Moscow Affair and the recent Moscow party committee's pronouncement on "mistakes in the work of Popov."[100] Popov had played a direct role in the skyscraper project from the start and in their work building the Zariad'e skyscraper and MGU many of those at the USDS had had direct dealings with the fallen Moscow mayor. It was surely no secret that Popov had angered the Ministries in charge of skyscraper construction by doing precisely what he was accused of doing: "usurping the role of the Ministries," as Stalin had written in his letter. In the course of early skyscraper discussions, Popov had berated Ministers and their assistants. He had publicly mocked them and attempted to pull rank in planning discussions by emphasizing his close relationship with Stalin. When they came together in January 1950, USDS party members pledged their agreement with the Moscow party committee's decision on Popov and they made speeches calling for higher levels of criticism and self-criticism within their own organization. There were other issues on the minds of those USDS employees who gathered in 1950, however. Popov was not the only figure to fall in the preceding months—the Moscow Affair had hit even closer to home.

For Soviet architects, Popov's demotion was seen as part of a chain of events that culminated with the fall of the most prominent figure in Moscow's architectural scene: the Chief Architect of Moscow, Dmitrii Chechulin. Chechulin, who was head architect of both the Zariad'e and the Kotel'nicheskaia skyscrapers, had immense power in Moscow in the postwar years. The architect was closely connected to Popov—a link that became a liability in 1949. The Chechulin Affair started in June 1949, two years into Moscow's skyscraper construction project, when a disgruntled engineer, L. M. Gokhman, sent a letter to Stalin. Gokhman was the chief engineer on the MVD's skyscraper on the Kotel'nicheskaia embankment and he had grown tired of Chechulin's penchant for changing designs and shifting plans at will. Gokhman wrote to Stalin in 1949 to expose the architect's mismanagement and capriciousness.

Gokhman opened his letter to Stalin by expressing his admiration and gratitude for the leader. "I write to you as a communist, an engineer, the chief engineer of the tall building of the MVD," Gokhman led off. "There is no greater happiness for the Soviet individual," Gokhman wrote, than to work at the behest of the leader himself— the leader who "saved our nation, our women and children from disgrace and slavery." Moreover, Gokhman continued, "there is no greater happiness for the Soviet engineer than to engage in competition with that 'much-vaunted' American technology and to demonstrate to the world that we are not only spiritually and morally superior to the 'American way of life,' but also technologically superior."[101] Drawing directly on the language of the first skyscraper decree and of the *Zhdanovshchina* more broadly, Gokhman assured Stalin that "the fundamental structural scheme of the building is *original* and in no way can it be seen as drawing on the standard

American solutions."[102] Gokhman proudly added that the method he was putting to use on the Kotel'nicheskaia building was not only saving the country 1,500 tons of steel, but that the rigidity (*zhestkost'*) of the Kotel'nicheskaia tower was "four times greater than any of the other tall buildings under construction in Moscow and *eight times* greater than any American skyscraper."[103] Having established his ideological loyalties, Gokhman came to the point. The engineer denounced Chechulin, along with Andrei Rostkovskii, the other top architect working on the Kotel'nicheskaia building. Both in their forties and trained after the revolution, Chechulin and Rostkovskii had together been awarded the Stalin Prize in 1948 for their design of the Kotel'nicheskaia skyscraper.[104]

By Gokhman's account, although Chechulin and Rostkovskii were officially the "authors" of the Kotel'nicheskaia building, they were rarely present on the construction site. Since both architects were engaged in many other building projects throughout the capital, they made an appearance, according to Gokhman, only about once every few weeks. The engineer complained that Chechulin's work on other projects, from the Zariad'e skyscraper to a residential complex on Gorky Street, left him too little time to devote to any one site. The worst of it, in Gokhman's view, was that when Chechulin did show up he pulled rank. The architect appeared on the building site only to issue directives left and right that interrupted construction. In some cases, Chechulin's orders had caused long delays and in others they had led to the waste of large quantities of materials, most troublingly of steel. It is no surprise, Gokhman wrote, "that this 'impromptu' on-the-fly planning, in the place of professional work alongside the collective, leads to many unnecessary alterations to the design."[105] Gokhman was not the first engineer to take issue with an architect over questions of cost and managerial style. In this case, however, the feud had also become personal.

Before sending his letter to Stalin in the summer of 1949, Gokhman had written to other higher-ups imploring them to act on his behalf against Chechulin. Gokhman relayed his past attempts to draw attention to Chechulin and Rostkovskii's behavior in his letter to Stalin. "As a Communist," he wrote, "I was obliged to bring to the attention of the party organization the outrageous behavior of the architects, especially Chechulin, who, using his position as chief, does whatever takes his fancy."[106] But having taken his complaints to party officials, Gokhman found that "Chechulin began in every way to harass me." Seeking to discredit the engineer before the collective, Chechulin had apparently tried to have Gokhman replaced.[107] From party officials, Gokhman was told that "although *on points of fact* I am indisputably correct . . . *tactically* [*takticheski*] I am incorrect and I must grit my teeth and work so as not to 'annoy' Chechulin with complaints to the Central Committee."[108] By the time he wrote to Stalin, Gokhman was at his wits' end: "I am literally in despair [*bukval'no v otchaianii*] from these words and am ready to kill myself if there is even one percent of truth in them. I cannot and do not even want to hear about such 'tactics' . . ."[109] Whether for his vehemence or because he timed it right, Gokhman was rewarded for his efforts: an official investigation into both Chechulin and Rostkovskii was launched in the summer of 1949.

When Soviet officials began to the pull on the threads of corruption and mismanagement on the Kotel'nicheskaia site, all manner of "unbolshevik-like" behaviors and practices began to come loose. Investigators found that Chechulin took an impulsive approach to design, was inattentive in his work, and was far too well compensated. The architect's "impromptu" approach to construction was demonstrated by various incidents. In one, Chechulin was alleged to have ordered that 63 steel columns making up the first four floors along the façade of the Kotel'nicheskaia building be taken down because they intruded by 35 centimeters into the floor plan of the building—an order estimated to cost 1 million rubles to carry out.[110] The order was seen as outrageous, and indeed it was this particular episode that had prompted Gokhman to write to Stalin in the first place.

Chechulin's lack of attention to the buildings under his supervision was confirmed by the simple fact that in 1949 the architect was in charge of seven separate construction projects in locations throughout Moscow. All of these projects were large state commissions for buildings that included, in addition to the two skyscrapers, a residential building for Gosplan, a hotel for the MVD, and an officers' residential district on Khoroshevskoe shosse.[111] While this workload had obvious consequences for the level of oversight that could conceivably be brought to each project, it raised flags in terms of Chechulin's finances as well. The way that financial compensation worked for architectural commissions in Moscow in the postwar period was such that Chechulin was making between 25,000–30,000 rubles each month for all of his commissions combined.[112] Compared to the average wage for workers in the construction industry across the USSR in 1950—565 rubles per month—this was quite a sum.[113] And while earning commissions on individual construction projects was the norm for Soviet architects, the sheer number of these commissions and the sums paid out for each individually were found by the architect's investigators to be extraordinary.[114]

The Chechulin Affair had major implications for planning in the capital city more broadly, as municipal officials took notice that their Chief Architect was neglecting his primary duties. Chechulin had become the Chief Architect of Moscow in 1944. And the Chief Architect's primary role, as it was determined during the war, was to oversee the implementation of his city's master plan and to head up the office of the city-level State Architecture Committee. But by late July 1949, just when Chechulin was found absent from his managerial responsibilities on the skyscraper construction sites, he was also found to be neglecting the implementation of Moscow's General Plan. In what ought to have surprised no one, given the priority assigned since 1947 to Moscow's skyscrapers, the city's design studio, Mosgorproekt, was in 1949 being "managed by Chechulin simply as a part of the project for the tall buildings."[115] The various branches of the city's State Architecture Committee, from the studio for standardized design (*masterskaia tipovogo proektirovaniia*) to the office of regional architects (*otdel raionnykh arkhitektorov*) were found to have little or no supervision.[116] Although Moscow's skyscrapers were envisioned as a totalizing plan for the capital, in practice these buildings were diverting resources and time away from citywide planning.

In their investigation of Chechulin, Soviet officials came face to face with the failures of master planning in Moscow. They found in July 1949 that over the previous two years, Moscow's State Architecture Committee "has as a whole never held a meeting and no goals have been set for it by anyone."[117] Lacking oversight, the Architectural Construction Control Office, a body in charge of inspecting building work in the city, had been taking bribes. More damaging still to the material state of the capital city were the effects of policies introduced during the war that allowed residents to take on the burden of building housing and other amenities themselves. With the help of a state loan program initiated in 1944, Soviet citizens could build their own homes on land leased from the local soviet.[118] Still, in the late 1940s, Moscow's Architectural Construction Control Office documented numerous instances of illegal individual construction (*samovol'noe stroitel'stvo*), including 146 instances in 1948, with 34 cases of unsanctioned new homes and 56 cases of newly built administrative buildings and children's establishments.[119] The first quarter of 1949 had seen 37 instances of unsanctioned individual construction, including 27 cases of individually built homes, garages, and children's nurseries. In the absence of leadership from Chechulin's office at the top, Moscow was building itself from the bottom.

The investigation into Chechulin and Rostkovskii was brought to a close with a Council of Ministers decree issued in September 1949, titled "On the work of architects D. N. Chechulin and A. K. Rostkovskii." The probe had been carried out so swiftly that Chechulin's own rebuttal to Gokhman's accusations arrived too late.[120] In the decree of September, both Chechulin and Rostkovskii were severely reprimanded for their activities on the Kotel'nicheskaia skyscraper.[121] Chechulin lost his position as Chief Architect of Moscow and Rostkovskii was relieved of his duties as head of a design studio. (As fate would have it, all three men would soon be neighbors on the Kotel'nicheskaia Embankment. Gokhman and Rostkovskii would both be granted apartments in 1952 in the Kotel'nicheskaia skyscraper; Gokhman an eighth-floor apartment for his family of four, and Rostkovskii a second-floor apartment for his family of six.[122] Chechulin lived there too.)

The Chechulin affair was widely discussed at meetings of the organizations in charge of building Moscow's skyscrapers. And at these meetings, the fates of Chechulin and Popov were discussed in tandem. At the USDS party meeting of January 1950, Boris Iofan denounced both men, "whose work," Iofan claimed, "is characterized by complacency and smugness."[123] In 1948, Iofan had been unceremoniously removed, likely on Popov's urging, from the commission to design the skyscraper on the Lenin Hills. Now, as an active member of the presidium of the USDS party organization, Iofan publicly declared that neither Popov nor Chechulin was "concerned with criticism, with the opinions of the masses, they forgot that Soviet construction is powered by the strength of the people, the strength of the collective."[124] The Chechulin Affair had preceded the purge of Popov by some weeks—Chechulin was removed from his position as Chief Architect of Moscow just as the Moscow Affair began. But the timing of these two cases was more than sequential. As the Moscow party committee saw it in late 1949, Popov had long served as Chechulin's patron, silencing any and all criticism waged against the Chief Architect.[125]

What had come to light in the Chechulin Affair was damning not just to the architects involved, but to the Soviet architectural profession as a whole. Even so, the Chechulin Affair appears to have had only minor consequences, both for Chechulin himself and for Soviet architecture more broadly. Chechulin maintained his position as one of the Soviet Union's top architects and he would go on to design some of the most important buildings of the late-socialist period. In the 1950s, Chechulin built the Hotel "Rossiia" (on the same plot chosen in 1947 for his uncompleted Zariad'e skyscraper). He also built Moscow's Hotel Peking and designed the Moscow Pool, an enormous open-air swimming pool constructed on the spot of the unbuilt Palace of Soviets. From 1965 to 1979, Chechulin oversaw the construction of the RSFSR House of Unions. Known as the Russian White House, the building today holds the offices of the Russian Prime Minister. Chechulin was a prolific and talented architect who retained his power and notoriety through decades of cultural and political upheaval.

The investigation and demotion of this architectural heavyweight nonetheless ushered in a new moment in Moscow's planning history. The year 1949 saw new figures entering Moscow's political and architectural arena. Popov's former post as Moscow party boss passed to Nikita Khrushchev, whom Stalin had summoned back to Moscow from Ukraine. Khrushchev would later remember his transfer back to the capital as "partly a consequence of the sickness which began to envelop Stalin's mind in the last years of his life." Khrushchev was "sure that Popov is no conspirator," but the future Soviet leader nonetheless thought that the young Moscow party boss "carried himself stupidly and his work hasn't been up to snuff."[126] Khrushchev arrived to his new post in Moscow just in time to appoint a replacement for Chechulin. For the position of Moscow's Chief Architect, Khrushchev brought Aleksandr V. Vlasov back to Moscow from Ukraine. Khrushchev and Vlasov had worked together on the reconstruction of Kiev's main thoroughfare, the Kreshchatik.[127] Vlasov had the right experience for the job, having worked in Moscow in the 1920s and 1930s and having more recently served as Chief Architect of Kiev from 1944 to 1950. When he returned to the Soviet capital, Vlasov found that his new office was engaged in the creation of a new General Plan for Moscow.

MONUMENTALISM AND MOSCOW'S NEW GENERAL PLAN

When Soviet officials investigated Chechulin in 1949, they found that an "impromptu" approach to planning characterized his tenure as top architect of Moscow. Chechulin's last-minute alterations on the Kotel'nicheskaia skyscraper and his apparent lack of oversight in city planning offices more broadly were symptoms of the larger chaos that gripped urban planning in Moscow in the postwar period. The investigation into Chechulin created an opportunity for discussion among officials about the lack of centralization and the unruly nature of planning in the Soviet capital. While the celebrated construction of Moscow's skyscrapers gave the impression of a coordinated plan, in reality the city's urban terrain, not to mention its urban planning offices, were in disarray.

The Chechulin Affair revealed the need for greater oversight and coordination in Moscow's urban development. But even as the investigation of Chechulin was underway in the summer of 1949, Moscow's architects and planners were working to accomplish what the Chief Architect had not: creating a new General Plan for the city. The impetus behind the city's new master planning document was a joint USSR Council of Ministers and Communist Party Central Committee order issued in February 1949. Moscow's new General Plan was initially envisioned as a document that would carry the city through the next 20–25 years, though this would be shortened by August 1949 to ten.[128] The team assembled to bring it to fruition was composed of key figures from the USSR State Architecture Committee, including Arkadii Mord-vinov and Grigorii Simonov. They were given just a few months before they had to present their General Plan to state and party officials for approval.[129]

As Moscow's officials came together through the summer of 1949 to create a new planning vision for the Soviet capital, they would first have to reckon with the accomplishments—and failures—of the city's first General Plan, adopted in 1935. This earlier planning document was intended as a ten-year program for urban ex-pansion and development, but, interrupted by the war in 1941, the plan of 1935 was never completed. Rather than being updated to suit the changing circumstances and new technologies of the postwar years, this earlier document had simply remained in effect as Moscow's guiding text through to the late 1940s. The General Plan of 1935 had established a comprehensive urban program for Moscow that saw the city's boundaries widened, its waterways, transportation, and energy infrastructures ex-panded, and its boulevards and vistas made more prominent through beautification projects. Moscow's skyscrapers fit well within this preexisting scheme, but an up-dated General Plan was clearly needed as the city approached the new decade.

The order issued in February 1949 calling for a new Moscow plan provided few instructions to planners, but it did clarify the official position on the city's earlier planning document from 1935. Hailing the 1935 General Plan as a success, the order of 1949 highlighted the various ways in which the earlier plan had been "overful-filled." The construction of the Moscow metro, the expansion of gas lines, and the building of bridges were all noted as key accomplishments. Claiming that the "main tasks" of the 1935 General Plan would be completed "within the next 3–4 years," state and party officials in 1949 were encouraged to view Moscow's second General Plan as one that would build upon the strong foundation laid by the first. This cele-bratory language made for good copy in *Pravda*, but behind closed doors the city's architects and urban professionals would offer a more sober assessment of what had truly been accomplished since 1935.

As the team of architects and planners assembled in 1949 set to work, they quickly found that large swaths of the 1935 program had never been implemented. Those working on the draft plan printed their findings and recommendations in booklets marked "secret" that include a document on the "Achievements of the General Plan for the Reconstruction of Moscow." On the lefthand side of this document were listed each component of the 1935 plan, point by point. On the righthand side were notes listing the degree to which each point had been accomplished. The notes made visi-ble a long line of unfulfilled promises. While progress had been made on the metro, gas lines, and bridges, dozens of other elements of the 1935 plan were "not carried out," "not realized," and "not finished." Some roads, like the Sadovnicheskaia Em-bankment, had not been resurfaced, while others, like a section of Volkhonka Street, had not been been widened. Moscow's famous Gorky Street had been expanded and built up, but not to completion. And the city's other boulevards (*magistrali*), like Len-ingradskoe shosse and the Garden Ring, were similarly unfinished.[130] The city's fleet of trams, trolleybuses, buses, and taxis remained numerically below targets set in 1935. And the centerpiece of the 1935 Plan—the Palace of Soviets—had "not yet" been built.[131] Of greatest consequence to the average resident, though, were the un-fulfilled targets in housing construction. Less than twenty percent of the residential construction called for in the 1935 plan had been achieved.[132] Hospital and school construction fared even worse.

As Moscow's second General Plan took shape, city officials worked to make up for lost time. Housing became the centerpiece of the postwar program. In their draft recommendations, those working on this new plan called for the construction of 115,000 new apartments in the first five years alone, and 300,000 total by 1959.[133] While this was nowhere near the scale of Nikita Khrushchev's countrywide mass housing campaign, initiated in 1957, the second Stalinist General Plan for Moscow acknowledged, on paper at least, that officials understood the city's most urgent need: housing.[134] In March 1950, as Moscow's new party boss, Khrushchev gave a speech on steps that had been taken toward the creation of the city's second General Plan. As the future Soviet leader put it, "housing construction has now become one of the most important priorities of the party and Soviet organizations."[135]

There was no fanfare or celebration accompanying the unveiling of the new General Plan when the document was publicly released in 1952. In speeches at the Nineteenth Party Congress in October of that year, officials repeated Khrushchev's pledge that housing, as well as hospitals and schools, would be central components of the new plan.[136] When all was said and done, Moscow's postwar General Plan would cover the ten-year period of 1951 to 1960. As Timothy Colton notes, "the document was not the ode to monumentalism that might have been expected."[137] Instead, the second and last Stalinist General Plan for Moscow broadly reflected the real needs and concerns of the city and its citizens.

Still, the vision for Moscow that was put to paper in the late 1940s and early 1950s was caught between two opposing impulses, one mundane and the other monumental. By placing housing at the center of the postwar General Plan, officials acknowledged the crisis in living standards that residents of all social groups faced in the Soviet capital. At the same time, however, Moscow's planners were beholden to the promise of architectural monumentalism. Just as the Palace of Soviets had served as the showpiece structure of the 1935 General Plan, Moscow's second Stalinist General Plan positioned the city's eight skyscrapers as the pivot points for urban development. As a result, housing was pitted against monument in a battle that skewed in favor of ideological rather than practical concerns. As with the General Plan of 1935, the postwar plan highlighted the city's southwest as the area that would see the greatest extent of new housing development. When the new General Plan was unveiled, Moscow State University was still under construction in this southwest region. The skyscraper was to serve as the focal point for expansion. Uniform neoclassical residential blocks would help to frame the university building, and the needs of residents were placed second to this monumental aesthetic. Ultimately, the gargantuan structure on the Lenin Hills, along with its sister highrises, would divert resources away from housing construction.

In April 1950, Lev Rudnev, the head architect of the university skyscraper on the Lenin Hills, met with his colleagues at the Moscow Union of Architects. Describing his recent ascent to the top of his new building, which was still under construction, Rudnev noted his surprise at what he could see from the newly built sixteenth floor. "I have never seen how Moscow unfolds in all its grandeur," the architect stated.[138] Rudnev did not divulge much more detail about what he saw, but he no doubt noticed

Figure 4.12: View from the Moscow State University building in 1951. Still under construction, the university building is flanked by temporary barracks-style structures. Collection of the Moscow City Archive GBU "TsGA Moskvy."

the sprawling and unkempt nature of the city below. Moscow's skyscrapers were contributing to a disorder that long predated them. The new vistas that emerged as a result of skyscraper construction revealed the unintended consequences of Stalin-era monumentalism: the chaotic networks of roads and railway tracks built to supply construction sites, the barracks and dormitories hastily assembled for both regular and Gulag workers (fig. 4.12), and, far in the distance, the new residential districts under construction that were to house the many Muscovites displaced from the city's skyscraper construction sites. Moscow's monumental new buildings, conceived to bring order to the Soviet capital, were creating chaos instead.

5

MOSCOW OF THE SHADOWS

That the locations chosen for Moscow's skyscrapers were not empty—that they were inhabited by tens of thousands of Muscovites—was a fact not addressed in the first skyscraper decree of January 1947. The enormous task of evicting and resettling those who inhabited the city's skyscraper plots was considered only after the skyscraper project was already underway. Each of the ministries and organizations in charge of building Moscow's new towers would thus find themselves responsible in the coming years not just for building skyscrapers, but also for constructing housing, schools, clinics, and other amenities for displaced Muscovites. By 1949, the resettlement of residents displaced by Moscow's skyscrapers would come to preoccupy Soviet officials at all levels of the bureaucracy, from administrators working in special resettlement offices to Lavrentii Beria, who oversaw the skyscraper project until his arrest in June 1953.

When it began in 1947, the skyscraper project introduced into the planning and governance of Moscow a permanent conflict between the symbolic needs of Soviet power and the practical needs of urban life. The remaining chapters explore the numerous ways in which this conflict took shape. This chapter focuses on the irreconcilable tensions that emerged in the late 1940s between what I am calling Moscow of the plan and Moscow of the shadows. These two cities, one ideal and one real, were inextricably bound together. Monumental Moscow, as envisioned in idealized plans, could take shape only with the support of a vast shadow city—a city of workers, supply lines, and displaced residents.

Architectural drawings of Moscow's future cityscape, like those by Dmitrii Chechulin and Mikhail V. Posokhin, rendered tensions between these two Moscows all but invisible. But the conflict is legible all the same in surviving letters written by residents eager to voice their discontent. This chapter examines the experience of displacement, which prompted ordinary citizens to write to officials demanding that state agencies be held accountable for providing adequate housing. Many also complained about being moved from their former homes in the center of Moscow to new settlements on the outskirts of the city. In the coming years, hundreds of Soviet elites would benefit from skyscraper development, receiving luxury apartments in three of Moscow's new highrises located in the city center. Yet in the late 1940s and early 1950s, tens of thousands of their neighbors were relocated to the periphery of the city. Through this process, social stratification and class identity took on a new spatial dimension in Moscow, as inhabitants of the Soviet capital came to understand their own lives and fates in relation to the skyscraper project.

Ultimately, the skyscrapers raised questions about who belonged in a city like Moscow and what it meant to be a Muscovite in the waning years of the Stalin era. But the buildings also highlighted problems of belonging of a more historical nature. As objects from the past were literally unearthed during the excavation process, Soviet architects and officials were forced to consider not just who, but *what*: what belonged in a city like Moscow? Which buildings, monuments, and streets would be saved, and which would be discarded? These questions were especially acute on the central-most skyscraper plot in the Zariad'e, a historic district near the Kremlin. Archaeological excavations carried out on the Zariad'e site interrupted skyscraper construction, ensuring that carefully laid plans gave way to the dictates of historical preservation. In contrast to the many buildings and homes unceremoniously destroyed in the Zariad'e to make way for the neighborhood's new skyscraper, the material remnants of a more distant, pre-Soviet past were deemed worthy of conservation by late-Stalinist officials. The value attributed during late Stalinism to sites of Russian national heritage both shaped and complicated Moscow's monumental transformation.

MONUMENTAL MOSCOW AND THE SHADOW CITY BEYOND

The displacement of tens of thousands of people was one of the most significant effects of Moscow's skyscraper project. But when Soviet officials began working on the building project in 1947, the issue of displacement was far from their minds. Focusing their discussions on questions of style and symbolism, the Soviet Union's leaders and architects paid scant attention to the broader implications of their monumental vision for the capital. To be sure, Moscow's eight skyscrapers were always intended to be more than stand-alone buildings. These towers were positioned at locations across the capital in order to reshape the city as a whole. Those who designed Moscow's skyscrapers understood well that their buildings would serve as pieces within a broader architectural ensemble. Architect Mikhail Posokhin's perspectival drawing of the skyscraper destined for Uprising Square captured this totalizing ambition well (fig. 5.1).

Posokhin's residential building in the center, and her sister structure, the hotel on the Dorogomilovo embankment across the river, stand as pivot points in a rational city plan made up of neoclassical buildings, gardens, parks, and boulevards that continue on into the distance, as far as the eye can see. Still a child when the Bolsheviks took power, Posokhin was in his thirties when he became head architect of the skyscraper on Uprising Square. He would serve a long tenure later in life, from 1960 to 1982, as Chief Architect of Moscow, but Posokhin's career began not in the capital, but in the Siberian city of Tomsk. There, when not busy reading novels by his favorite author, Jack London, Posokhin studied painting with Vadim M. Mizerov, a watercolorist who painted mainly in the impressionist style. Posokhin went on to study at the Academy of Art in Leningrad, where he wandered the city alone with his sketchbook "absorbing the harmonious character of the architectural environment" and finding himself for the first time "face to face with a big city with its unique beauty, architecture, and scale of life . . ."[1] While Posokhin's early education was in the fine arts, the future architect, like so many of his generation, cut his teeth on the indus-

Figure 5.1: Skyscraper on Uprising Square, architect M. V. Posokhin, 1951.
Collection of the Shchusev State Museum of Architecture.

trial construction of the First Five-Year Plan. In the early 1930s, Posokhin returned to Siberia to work as part of a team of topographers and geodesic specialists at *Kuznetskstroi*. This construction outfit was in charge of building a large metallurgical factory, with a socialist city ("Sotsgorod") alongside it, in the city of Stalinsk.

When Posokhin moved to Moscow in 1935, he was determined to become an architect. While this vocation would bring together both the artistic and the scientific sides of the young man's training, it was Posokhin's watercolors, which he showed to Aleksei Shchusev, that got him in the door. The monumental architecture that had become popular in Moscow by the mid-1930s made this career choice especially exciting. Posokhin would later recall his certainty that one day he "would design something like the Palace of Soviets."[2] Sure enough, Posokhin would rise to the top, winning the competition to build the skyscraper on Uprising Square just over ten years later.

Posokhin's image of his skyscraper on Uprising Square rendered the urban fabric of postwar Moscow, as it really was, unrecognizable. But if reality was of little matter to Posokhin, realism by contrast was of central importance. In his image, Posokhin used a number of devices to convince the viewer that his sketch was an accurate picture of the cityscape. The photographic details of the foreground against the blurred background work to this end, as do the details on the ground that invite the viewer to lean in for a closer look: small cars driving along the Garden Ring Road, tiny people gathering outside the enormous building in the center, dramatic shadows cast by the structure's setback silhouette.

Figure 5.2: Skyscraper on Uprising Square, architect M. V. Posokhin, June 1952,
I. Petkov photographer. Collection of the Museum of Moscow.

Posokhin's skill as a draftsman, his careful geometry and precise detailing, conceal the dreamlike qualities of his image. The architect chose to position his residential skyscraper off-center and at an angle on the page, inviting the viewer to focus first on the park in front of the building before gazing upwards, scaling all sixteen floors of the skyscraper to the star perched atop the spire. The image's strong diagonal axis and the curving loop in the river add yet more dynamism to the static page. Beyond all practicality, Posokhin bent, pushed, and distorted reality, painting over Moscow's spontaneous and organic urban development with a rational, linear plan. In contrast to what really stood on the construction site at Uprising Square (fig. 5.2), and against what was possible to build in reality, Posokhin's design sketch was a utopian fantasy, unsullied and antiseptic.

By their own account, Soviet architects of the late-Stalin era were not utopians. In fact, in the postwar years, Stalin-era architects abhorred utopianism. In September 1947, on the occasion of Moscow's 800th anniversary, architects at the Soviet Academy of Architecture gathered to celebrate and toast to their capital city. Those in attendance praised the many projects that had been realized in Moscow's "socialist reconstruction." The Moscow General Plan of 1935 served as the primary point of reference in many of their anniversary-day speeches. As the architect of that General Plan, Sergei Chernyshev, himself stated, "there is a feature of particular significance that characterizes the General Plan for the reconstruction of Moscow and differentiates it from reconstruction plans for cities in foreign countries: this feature is our plan's reality, in contrast to others' utopianism."[3]

Soviet architects saw in the postwar reconstruction plans then underway in England, France, and elsewhere nothing but "naive daydreaming and blatant utopianism on the one hand, and the typical social-reformist demagoguery on the other."[4] Yet Moscow's architects, as Posokhin's sketch indicates, were also avid practitioners of "naive daydreaming." Like architects elsewhere they were utopians. In setting their sights on the ideal of the plan and excluding its consequences, Moscow's architects failed to grasp until later the immense effects their designs would have on the Soviet capital.

Architectural drawings like those by Posokhin rendered invisible the lines that were beginning to form between Moscow's skyscrapers and the shadow city that the skyscraper plan required. But if Soviet architects seemed oblivious, state officials working in other city offices began to notice that Moscow's monumental new building sites were causing unanticipated ripple effects on the city as a whole. In early 1949, the RSFSR-level building inspectorate reported that, in connection with construction that had begun the previous year at five of the skyscraper addresses, "a whole range of housing settlements for construction workers and for those displaced from their homes . . . as well as various types of infrastructure are being built."[5] As the city developed vertically, it expanded horizontally as well.

In the postwar years, Moscow was swiftly expanding into *podmoskov'e*: the forests and villages that lay in the vicinity of the capital but were beyond the city limits. From 1948 onward, the towns of *podmoskov'e*, places like Liublino and Cheremushki, Kuntsevo and Tekstil'shchiki, could be seen scattered throughout state orders pertaining to Moscow's skyscraper development. These places would soon be built up with housing for workers and displaced Muscovites, and with the factories, warehouses, and other facilities necessary to support the capital city's skyscraper development. Yet for Moscow's architects, these elements which proved to be so central to skyscraper building were also the most difficult to see.

In the 1930s, Stalin-era architects had developed a new way of looking at urban space, an approach that Heather DeHaan has called "iconographic" planning. Unlike the more scientific approach that dominated in the 1920s—an approach in which, as DeHaan writes, "planners had deployed the tools of scientific perception, treating the city as an object to scrutinize, research, and rationalize"—the new approach of the 1930s saw planners engage in "a different form of visual transcendence." "The present," DeHaan writes, "melted away, defamiliarized and 'de-realized' by visions of a radiant future."[6] This way of seeing carried into the postwar period, as architects continued to focus on the city that would be instead of the city that was.

By early 1948, it was clear to Soviet leaders that work on the skyscrapers was proceeding at too slow a pace. According to the plan, all eight buildings were to be completed by 1952, but one year into the project the plots had yet to be cleared and construction work had not yet begun. Hoping to speed up the process, the Council of Ministers issued an order in March 1948 focusing on the demolition and construction required before building could begin. The order stated that by year's end the Administration for the Construction of the Palace of Soviets (USDS) would need to build 3,500 square meters of housing for those living on the plot selected for MGU on the Lenin Hills. The Ministry of Construction of Heavy Industry would have to build 1,200 square meters of housing for those living on the plot at Smolensk Square. The Ministry of Internal Affairs would build 1,000 square meters of housing for those living on the place of the future Kotel'nicheskaia residential skyscraper. And the Ministries of Railways and Aviation, would build 1,500 and 1,200 square meters, respectively, for those then living on their two plots along the Garden Ring Road at the Red Gates and on Uprising Square.[7] In the coming months, similar orders went out to the Ministry of Construction of Military and Naval Industries for its 16-story building on Kalanchevskii Street and for the USDS's building in the Zariad'e district.

But this new housing for displaced residents was not nearly the extent of the additional construction that would have to be done. Building skyscrapers in the socialist city required the concomitant creation of a vast infrastructure to supply and transport building materials and laborers. For example, in addition to the 1,000 square meters of housing for those displaced by the Ministry's Kotel'nicheskaia tower, the Ministry of Internal Affairs (MVD) was also ordered to build factories to produce reinforced concrete and ceramic building parts, as well as a mechanical workshop. All three of these facilities were to be located in Likhobory, northwest of the city center.[8] Also to the city's north, the MVD built a metalworking factory in Khovrino, and to the west a brick factory in Istra and, in Guchkovo, one for ceramic tiles and alabaster for the Kotel'nicheskaia building's façade. It built a mechanical factory in Rybinsk east of Moscow and maintained a construction yard at Luzhniki within the city itself.[9] Finally, there were the new railroad tracks that would link these factories to the city, like the one from Likhobory station to the Kotel'nicheskaia embankment.[10] These would have to be built too.

Creating a new infrastructure to produce and transport building materials was a time-consuming and complicated task that slowed construction schedules significantly. But the eviction and resettlement of residents living on the plots chosen for skyscraper development was equally complicated and far more sensitive. Resettlement offices were created for this task as well, and the secretaries and bosses in those offices quickly found themselves on the front lines of disputes between the Soviet state and its citizens over what kind of city Moscow was and should be. The most densely populated of all the skyscraper plots was the one selected in Moscow's Zariad'e district, an area in the center of the city that was home to just under 10,000 people in the late 1940s. The Zariad'e building project was managed by the USDS. Like the Palace of Soviets, this skyscraper—also never built to completion—had a very real effect on the future shape of the Soviet capital.

THE ZARIAD'E

Had Moscow's skyscraper project been undertaken at a different time, Soviet leaders might have gone to some trouble to draw attention to urban destruction, using demolition to demonstrate the state's power, ambition, and benevolence. Stalin might have posed as a Haussmann or a Mussolini, pick in hand, ready to clear away the dilapidated buildings of old Moscow to make way for a modern, rationally-planned city.[11] Or, to draw a different comparison, Soviet leaders might have aped their immediate contemporaries abroad, championing the skyscrapers as "slum clearance" projects like those undertaken in the postwar years in the New York of Robert Moses and the Pittsburgh of David Lawrence and R. K. Mellon.[12]

Nowhere in Moscow would the opportunity to publicly combat "urban blight" while lauding the virtues of "urban renewal" have presented itself more clearly than in the Zariad'e. This neighborhood, located just east of the Kremlin, was known to be one of the more miserable parts of town. But with the destruction of the recent war still so close and with the Soviet housing crisis so widespread, demolition was not a spectacle in the postwar Stalin era. Instead, popular articles about Moscow's upward expansion of the late 1940s focused on the great buildings that would emerge on the skyline, paying little heed to all of the other construction and destruction that was necessary to bring these buildings into existence.

The Zariad'e was one of Moscow's oldest neighborhoods. It was still bordered in 1947 by some of its sixteenth-century stone walls (fig. 5.3). Kitai Gorod stretched to the north and east, and the Moscow River bordered the neighborhood to the south. The Upper and Middle Trading Rows, which had stood in various forms since the fourteenth century, had once separated the Zariad'e from the Kremlin and Red Square.[13] The neighborhood drew its name not from any distinguishing features of its own, but from this location adjacent to Moscow's central trading district (*za riad'e,* or "behind the rows"). Before the Bolshevik Revolution, the Zariad'e was home to craftsmen and small-scale traders, including at one time a large Jewish population.[14] Tailors, shoemakers, spinners, hat makers, furriers, button-makers, and typographers lived in the second and third floors of the neighborhood's buildings and sold their wares in shops along the narrow lanes below.[15] These roads dated back many centuries and most of the buildings along them had been constructed well before the revolution.

As writer Leonid M. Leonov put it in his 1924 novel *The Badgers*, the Zariad'e "was no place for sensitive nostrils."[16] Describing the neighborhood on the eve of the revolution, Leonov wrote, "the smells hereabouts were many. . . . Now it was the brisk, pleasant, rustling scent of leather that burst upon the passer-by from the open doorway of a warehouse. Then it was the rich Russian reek of the kitchen that enveloped him as he passed the eating-house . . . Or he would recoil under the impact of the odours flung out like slops from Dudin the furrier's cellar window."[17] Leonov knew the Zariad'e well, having grown up there himself. And he wrote about the neighborhood of his youth again in a short story titled "The Fall of Zariad'e," published first in 1936 and then again in 1947. "Walk along Red Square," Leonov began his account of the Zariad'e's decline,

past the holiday tribunal and the Lenin mausoleum, past the opulent and magnificent mass of St. Basil the Blessed . . . go along Varvarka to the first street

Figure 5.3: Entrance to the Zariad'e. Photograph from album of construction in the Zariad'e, 1950. Collection of the Moscow City Archive GBU "TsGA Moskvy."

on your right, step aside so as not to get knocked down by the lorry, and look down. Behind you the noisy streets of the proletarian capital will rumble, a demonstration rattles past or long elegant cars glide by. If it interests you to take a peek at how life in the great capital has changed, descend down that craggy old Moscow pavement. Twenty years ago you would have seen sunken, ungainly buildings, churches, barricaded passageways, crumbling walls.[18]

In fact, in 1947, many of the neighborhood's sunken buildings, its churches and crumbling stone walls were still there. The Moscow General Plan of 1935 had promised to liberate the Zariad'e from "petty buildings" (*melkie postroiki*), but the liberation had yet to take place.[19] By the late 1940s and early 1950s, the social composition of the Zariad'e had changed, but its roads and many of its buildings were the same.

The postwar period was not the first time that Soviet officials had set their sights on redeveloping the Zariad'e. The neighborhood was partially demolished in the 1930s in preparation for an earlier construction project that was never built.[20] And as residents would later report, once the Zariad'e was slated for redevelopment, Moscow city authorities had refused to invest in any infrastructural improvements at all (fig. 5.4). In the 1930s, Zariad'e residents of course endured far worse than deteriorating living conditions. As the Great Terror swept through the city, dozens of Zariad'e residents were arrested and executed.[21] The years of war that followed saw the neighborhood continue to decline.

Despite its decrepitude, the Zariad'e remained into the postwar years a densely populated and lively neighborhood. According to the tally drawn up by the Zariad'e skyscraper construction office in September 1949, there were 9,512 people living on

Figure 5.4: Mokrinskii Pereulok, house at the corner of Pskovskii pereulok, Zariad'e, 1930s.
Collection of the Museum of Moscow.

the site.[22] When counted again in March 1950, the neighborhood's population had grown to 9,650. In this second tally, the construction office classified the inhabitants of the Zariad'e by occupation. Workers were the largest professional group, numbering 2,245, but alongside this proletarian majority the Zariad'e was also home to four Stalin prize laureates, two writers, 58 workers in the arts, 51 academics, one Deputy in the Supreme Soviet, and one decorated athlete. Dozens of doctors and other medical professionals lived in the Zariad'e in 1950 as well, along with hundreds of pensioners. The largest category of people in the Zariad'e by far were the children. They numbered over 4,500 and their voices could no doubt be heard echoing through the streets and courtyards below.[23] Before the Zariad'e skyscraper could be built, these residents would have to be removed and their homes would need to be cleared from the site. Just how exactly to carry out this task took some time to decide.

Between October 1949 and August 1950, USDS officials worked to establish suitable guidelines for the displacement and resettlement from the Zariad'e of all residents and other facilities. The result of this effort was a short, four-page order issued by the Council of Ministers on August 25, 1950, the terse lines of which obscure the months of back-and-forth between the USDS and the Council of Ministers.[24] At the heart of the matter was a legal question: how should the USDS compensate displaced residents? Once this problem was posed, related questions emerged: were certain groups of residents entitled to more compensation than others? Should compensation be offered in the form of new housing, or could lump-sum payments be made instead to those evicted from their homes? No matter how these questions would ultimately be answered, all parties at the table were in agreement that the USDS and the other ministries building the skyscrapers were obligated to find housing for displaced residents. This responsibility was unquestioned.[25]

K. D. Vinokurov, deputy head of the USDS, began these deliberations in October 1949 when he sent a draft of his displacement order to Konstantin M. Sokolov, the USSR Minister of Urban Construction. In the coming months, Sokolov would look over this draft and make substantial edits. In their draft order, the USDS proposed separating Zariad'e residents into different categories to determine the level of compensation each resident would receive. The first category would be made up of the families of soldiers, the families of wounded warriors, invalids of the Great Patriotic War and their families, and workers ranking no lower than the sixth or seventh skill grade.[26] To replace the housing they would lose in the Zariad'e, this highest category of resident would receive an equal amount of living space in housing specially built either within Moscow city limits or in the Moscow oblast'. A second class of resident followed the first. This second group, made up of disabled workers, pensioners, and the single elderly, would be compensated similarly to the first, with equal amounts of living space in residential settlements built within 40 kilometers of Moscow. Finally, a third category of resident, made up of anyone not included in groups one and two, would be evicted without being provided any new housing at all. Residents in category three would instead receive monetary compensation in the amount of 5,000 rubles per person.[27]

This solution proposed by Vinokurov reflected a Soviet reality in which social differentiation existed and membership in an entitlement group determined one's access to goods and services provided by the state. Vinokurov's scheme did not, however, square with the letter of the law. In examining the draft order sent over by the USDS, Sokolov was quickly advised by a legal expert at the Ministry of Urban Construction that the document was "in contradiction to the applicable legislation."[28] Precedent was found in state decisions dating to the 1930s that protected all tenants' rights to be rehoused.[29] Vinokurov's draft order was also inconsistent with Soviet norms in that it positioned veterans and their families as a status group. This may well have been considered the correct course a few years, or even months, earlier—and indeed, the USDS order on the resettlement of residents from the skyscraper plot on the Lenin Hills, issued in May 1949, did refer to veterans and their families as members of a special status group.[30] But, as Mark Edele writes, with mass demobilization carried out in 1948 the Soviet state stopped granting veterans special privileges.[31] Vinokurov's displacement order of 1950 would be rewritten.

When it was officially issued and signed in August 1950, the USSR Council of Ministers order on the displacement of Zariad'e residents treated all equally, making no special allowances to any one group in particular. In the end, no resident would be compensated monetarily; all would instead be resettled in newly-built housing equal in size to their current residence—although, in keeping with Soviet law, this new housing would not exceed the nine-square-meter sanitary norm and would not be smaller than five square meters per person. In addition to these provisions, the de-

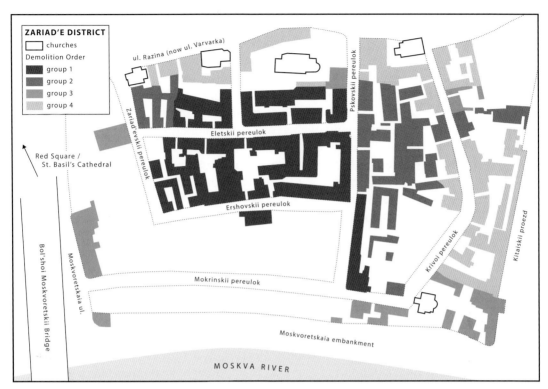

ZARIAD'E DISTRICT
☐ churches
Demolition Order
■ group 1
■ group 2
■ group 3
▨ group 4

ul. Razina (now ul. Varvarka)

Pskovskii pereulok

Red Square /
St. Basil's Cathedral

Zariad'evskii pereulok

Eletskii pereulok

Ershovskii pereulok

Krivoi pereulok

Kitaiskii proezd

Bol'shoi Moskvoretskii Bridge

Moskvoretskaia ul.

Mokrinskii pereulok

Moskvoretskaia embankment

MOSKVA RIVER

Figure 5.5: Reproduction of the displacement map drawn up in 1950 for the Zariad'e plot. Designed by Gregory T. Woolston. Based on the original color document held in RGAE f. 9510, op. 1, d. 107, l. 163.

cree stated that new housing would be built for Zariad'e residents both within the city of Moscow and in the nearby settlements of Kuntsevo to the west and Tekstil'shchiki to the southeast.[32] With the question of compensation squared away, USDS officials could get down to the business of resettling the nearly 10,000 residents of the Zariad'e.

While Vinokurov and Sokolov were deliberating, construction managers at the USDS were busy deciding how to demolish the Zariad'e. In March 1950, they created a map of the neighborhood (fig. 5.5). The map outlined what remained of the Zariad'e. The neighborhood's curving streets, narrow passageways leading to a maze of interconnected courtyards, buildings haphazardly arranged—these were marked on the map in red, blue, yellow, and green, the colors indicating where a structure stood in the sequence of demolition. Residents of the Zariad'e were not pictured on the map, but their fates were tied to the colored zones all the same. Those living in the buildings of groups one and two—red and blue on the original map—were to be resettled by December 1950. Those in groups three and four (green and yellow) were to remain in their homes as construction work began on the site. This arrangement would be "expedient," wrote construction managers in early 1950, since it allowed for the relocation "at a later date" of some 3,445 people still living in the Zariad'e.[33]

The Zariad'e residents living in groups three and four saw nothing expedient in having to remain in derelict housing that was now located within a construction zone. Still living on the site in May 1952, the residents of 3, 4, and 6 Zariad'evskii Lane (*pereulok*) wrote a collective letter to Stalin, asking when they would be resettled and "when, finally, will we be able to catch a breath in real human housing [*v nas-toiashchem liudskom zhilishche*]."[34] These residents lived communally, in conditions common across Moscow in the postwar years, though they had no shared kitchen, no heat, and a single toilet and sink for neighbors collectively occupying some thirty rooms.[35] As this group reported in their letter to Stalin, the floors of their building were rotten, the pipes leaked, and the dampness and lack of sunlight were the cause of serious health problems, including tuberculosis. Conditions had grown worse when construction of the Zariad'e skyscraper began. Construction work, the residents told Stalin, was being carried out directly under their building. The noise was unbearable; the trenches, pits, and electrical cables were a danger to the children; a layer of soot now covered everything; and there had already been two deaths among the construction workers from poison gas on the site.

In their letter, the residents of Zariad'evskii Lane demanded to know "why we—who have lived all our lives in the center of Moscow, having survived continuously through privations and the hardships of war—must go live out of town while many newcomers from different cities receive housing in the center of the city."[36] These neighbors desperately wished to see their living conditions improve, but they were also opposed to being moved from central Moscow to the city's outskirts. "We wait, if possible" they signed off, "for a positive answer with regard to our resettlement into new housing within Moscow [*imenno v Moskve*]."[37]

Soviet officials were not unsympathetic to this type of appeal. The collective letter sent to Stalin from the residents of Zariad'evskii Lane made it all the way to Mikhail T. Pomaznev, the head of the chancellery of the Council of Ministers, who quickly sent it on to the RSFSR procurator, Pavel V. Baranov, who was asked to "investigate and take action."[38] One month later, Baranov reported on what he had found. The procurator confirmed that the residents of Zariad'evskii Lane were indeed living in unsafe and unsanitary conditions, just as they had described in their letter. It was also clear that the resettlement process was taking much longer than planned. In Baranov's opinion, the residents should be resettled as soon as possible. The residents' request that they be resettled *within* Moscow, however, was ignored. In the summer months of 1952, the neighbors of Zariad'evskii Lane were moved to the district of Kuntsevo, located just west of Moscow.[39] Once part of a gentry estate owned by the Naryshkin family, the dacha village of Kuntsevo was, in the decades before the revolution, as Stephen Lovell writes, "an enclave for Moscow's merchant elite."[40] Known by the 1940s as the location of Stalin's "nearby dacha," Kuntsevo soon became home to thousands of displaced Muscovites, many of whom would carry on writing to state officials in hopes of seeing some improvement in their new circumstances on Moscow's outskirts.

The process of eviction and resettlement could not come soon enough for Zariad'e residents eager to escape the rapidly deteriorating conditions of the neighborhood. Still, many were none too thrilled by the prospect of living in suburban Moscow. A far cry from the amenity-rich suburbs then emerging in the postwar United States, the Soviet suburb of late Stalinism was barren and unappealing. The new residential districts in which those expelled from central Moscow found themselves in the early 1950s were poorly planned and hastily built. Located in *podmoskov'e*—in outlying villages that would become part of the city only in the coming years—these peripheral places were never featured in architects' drawings of Moscow's monumental new cityscape, but were an integral, if shadowy, part of Stalin's skyscraper project just the same.

THE DIVIDED CITY

The state order dictating the resettlement of Zariad'e residents of August 1950 did not, in the end, divide the neighborhood's inhabitants into different categories of entitlement. Instead, state officials opted for a uniform solution that provided each resident, regardless of social status or wartime service, with new housing located either elsewhere in the city or in the Moscow oblast'. Yet residents of the Zariad'e themselves worked to undercut this egalitarian approach by appealing to state officials for preferential treatment. In their letters, residents mobilized the very categories of entitlement and social differentiation that officials were keen to avoid. While narratives of wartime sacrifice are the most common theme in these letters, others are prominent as well. Soviet intellectuals and artists, for instance, saw well-appointed housing as a right tied to their professional productivity and accomplishments.

Mikhail A. Arutch'ian, an award-winning Armenian artist, and his wife Tamara Bedzhanian, a prizewinning singer, wrote to Beria on December 31, 1952. The couple was still living in their apartment in 6 Eletskii Lane in the Zariad'e, and they dreaded being moved to a far-flung district like Kuntsevo or Tekstil'shchiki (fig. 5.6). Bedzhanian had sung in Tbilisi and Erevan before performing in the theaters and concert halls of Moscow, while Arutch'ian, a stage designer and cartoonist, had been since 1949 the head artist of the Armenian pavilion at Moscow's All-Union Agricultural Exhibition (the city's socialist realist fairground showcasing the agricultural and national architectural achievements of the Soviet Union's republics). "We live in the Zariad'e," Arutch'ian and Bedzhanian wrote, "in the very center of Moscow, in a single-family three-room apartment." "Moving to Kuntsevo or Tekstil'shchiki would mean for us," they continued, "the total loss of connection with the organizations where we are assured work." Housing in those regions, they explained, was "connected only with great difficulty to transportation networks"—a point of particular concern for artists who worked late into the night—not to mention, they continued, "the total lack of telephone connection and other amenities."[41] Moreover, if moved to the outskirts, they would also be far from the medical services available in Moscow, which Arutch'ian relied on for treatment of hypertension. As the couple knew, the USDS had a number of buildings in the city—"tall buildings," they added parenthetically in a reference to the city's new skyscrapers. Could they not be settled in one of those?[42]

As members of Moscow's cultural elite, Aruch'ian and Bedzhanian's sense of entitlement was rooted in legal and cultural norms that sanctioned privilege in the Stalin period. Starting in the 1930s, members of certain professions—scientists and writers, for instance—were granted larger amounts of living space than the average urban resident. Arutch'ian and Bedzhanian had contributed for many years to the cultural life of the Soviet Union and it was on this basis that they felt deserving of sizeable, well-appointed, and private housing in central Moscow. That they already occupied a three-room apartment all to themselves was a testament to their high

Figure 5.6: Map of Moscow as it developed into the mid-1950s. Map by Cox Cartographic Ltd.

social status. But to further strengthen their appeal, the couple appended a note from Moscow's Chief Architect, Aleksandr Vlasov, attesting to the fact that Arutch'ian had worked on camouflaging Moscow in 1941, a task for which Arutch'ian was awarded a medal in 1947 on the occasion of the city's 800th anniversary.[43] In the end, however, the couple's appeal was of little use. Arutch'ian and Bedzhanian were resettled in late January 1953 in Tekstil'shchiki, where they were given a two-room apartment.[44]

The district of Tekstil'shchiki drew its name and identity from the textile factories prominent in Moscow's southeastern region by the late nineteenth century. The area had been built up in the decades prior to Zariad'e resettlement, but, as Arutch'ian knew, the neighborhood remained poorly connected to the urban grid. By 1947, there were an estimated 25,000 residents living in 1,359 apartments in the area. But officials did not begin the process of extending gas lines out to Tekstil'shchiki and other outer regions of Moscow until 1948.[45] That same year, the Moscow city government gave the USDS seven hectares on which to build housing for those displaced from the Zariad'e.[46] In 1949, the USDS continued the process of connecting the area chosen for residential construction to the urban grid.[47]

The USDS settlement in Tekstil'shchiki was built up on the city's outskirts, foreshadowing in its density and speed of construction the development of mass housing districts during the coming Khrushchev era. The new residential district extended southeastward from the intersection of Ostapovskoe shosse (now Liublinskaia ulitsa) and Proezd No. 1906 (now Saratovskaia ulitsa). It consisted of over a dozen four-to-five-story silicate brick buildings of different sizes.[48] Each building would contain between 36 and 59 apartments. Rounded pediments over first-floor windows and doors and other classical detailing made Tekstil'shchiki typical of Stalin-era housing developments, but the new district was still viewed as being out of sync with Moscow's urban plan. Since a new General Plan for Moscow was also in the works in 1949, as construction got underway in Tekstil'shchiki architects at the Ministry of Urban Construction expressed concerns that the new district not only violated earlier planning documents, but contradicted their vision for Moscow's future development.[49] The fact that this newly and hastily built district was not part of the plan was plainly obvious to residents of the Zariad'e as well.

Unlike their counterparts outside the Soviet Union, Moscow's displaced residents could not form residents' associations to fight intrusive construction in their neighborhoods. Nor could they stage public protests or work collectively to oust local politicians from office for supporting the desires of developers over the needs of residents. The tool that Soviet citizens did have at their disposal was the letter. Letter writing was, in the late Stalin era as in earlier and later Soviet periods, an accepted means by which to express one's discontent. The experience of displacement prompted ordinary residents to write to top Soviet leaders, demanding that local officials be held accountable for providing new and adequate housing in a timely manner. Many couched their complaints, requests for assistance, and denunciations in an emotional and autobiographical language that had been typical of public letter-writing in the Soviet Union since at least the 1930s.[50] Thus when Zariad'e residents mailed their letters of complaint or denunciation to authorities they were participating in a highly ritualized practice.[51] Writing to state officials and newspapers to report on poor living conditions and corrupt housing officials was a routine activity for many throughout the Soviet period.[52]

In these letters, displaced Muscovites in the late 1940s and early 1950s engaged with the Soviet state through narrative descriptions of their family's past and present and through sincerely articulated hopes for the future. Through these descriptions citizens interacted directly with the state and, for its part, the state was responsive. Letters were received, read, discussed, and responded to, sometimes harshly and at other times benevolently. Given the vast apparatus that existed to receive and process residents' letters, it is clear that the Soviet state got something out of these exchanges. Letters, of course, served as an important form of information gathering. They allowed higher-ups to keep tabs on middle managers. But letter writing also encouraged residents to act like citizens, taking an active role in the political life of the state.

While some Muscovites, like Arutch'ian, appealed to state officials on the basis of their achievements and accolades and with the support of powerful patrons, others relied chiefly on personal narratives of wartime sacrifice and descriptions of their day-to-day suffering. Anfieva K. Vikhoreva wrote to Stalin in November 1950, in the hopes of receiving a single-family apartment in Kuntsevo, rather than the single room she had been assigned in an apartment shared with three other families. At the time she wrote to Stalin, Vikhoreva was still living in the Zariad'e, just down the road from Arutch'ian and Bedzhanian at 12 Eletskii Lane. Vikhoreva's husband, a worker, had died in 1929, leaving her to care for their three young sons. Her first son had died in 1939, and the second had been killed at the front in 1944. The third son, who had joined the army in 1943, had only just returned from duty in October 1950. Writing in November, Vikhoreva requested a separate apartment for the two of them.

In her interaction with the Soviet state, Vikhoreva displayed a savviness typical of less well-connected Zariad'e residents. She made sure to display her knowledge of the relevant housing law and to show that she knew the precise amount of living space to which she was entitled, in accordance with the official displacement order. "According to the Council of Ministers order," Vikhoreva wrote, "they must give the exact same amount of living space that we have now, or 9 meters per person plus 4 1/2 square meters of sanitary norm or communal norm altogether 22.5 square meters must be given to us." Although her separate apartment on Elekskii Lane was 33.6 square meters, Vikhoreva would agree to one of just 21 square meters, so long as it was theirs alone. "Insomuch as my son has returned from the Soviet Army where he was [enlisted] for seven years, he will now begin to study and work," Vikhoreva wrote, "and this will be very difficult for him when there are three families in the apartment."[53] The recipient underlined this last part of the letter. But Vikhoreva was ultimately unsuccessful in her attempt to secure a better arrangement for herself and her son. Rather than the separate apartment she had hoped for, she was given a 17.3 square meter room in a communal apartment in Kuntsevo. According to the Deputy Chief of the USDS, Vikhoreva accepted her lot "without complaint" (*pretenzii ne imeet*).[54]

The displacement orders issued by the Council of Ministers mattered well beyond the narrowly bureaucratic domain in which they were created. These documents quickly became public knowledge, serving to make the difficult and uncertain circumstances of displacement at least somewhat more predictable. Whether a state order divided residents into separate entitlement groups or treated them all equally, these documents were popularly understood as legally binding contracts between state and citizen. While some residents worked to subvert these texts by requesting preferential treatment, many of their neighbors strove to ensure that the stipulates of these documents were followed to the letter. And when reality departed from the procedures laid out in the official order—as it so often did— residents expressed their anger and resentment in letters to officials. While some letter-writers took a biographical approach, appealing to state officials on the basis of their personal circumstances and privileges, others wrote denunciations, singling out culprits guilty of transgressing the bounds of fairness and legality. The denunciatory approach was especially common in letters sent by residents who had

had recent first-hand experience with mid-level officials. In particular, it was the managers of the USDS's Resettlement Office (*Upravlenie po pereseleniiu*) who were the focus of most denunciations.

LIFE IN THE SHADOWS

Many Zariad'e residents found the prospect of moving from the heart of Moscow to the undeveloped outskirts troubling. In October 1951, Beria received a collectively written and typed letter signed by 26 frustrated residents of the Zariad'e. According to the displacement order, these residents were to have been resettled by December 1950 from their homes at 8 Eletskii Lane to new housing built for them in Tekstil'shchiki. As they explained to Beria, while some of their neighbors had been moved as planned in 1950 over one hundred people remained in the Zariad'e well into the following year. Tired of being told month after month by officials at the Resettlement Office that they would be moved "in the coming days," the residents appealed for swifter evacuation from a neighborhood that increasingly resembled a war zone.[55] Their apartment building shook from blasting work on the construction site, the bare-boned roof was no hope against the elements, the ceilings tumbled down into the apartments below like an avalanche, and water had not run through the building's pipes for months. With winter fast approaching, these residents—most of whom were either invalids of the war or family members of soldiers killed in the conflict—were getting anxious. They had heard that others not connected with the Zariad'e at all had been given rooms in three of the new buildings in Tekstil'shchiki.[56]

These residents from Eletskii Lane went further than most in demanding that Beria set up a commission to inspect their present living conditions, to "swiftly and thoroughly monitor" the proper execution of the displacement order, and to look into the improper allocation of housing to non-Zariad'e residents.[57] These demands were taken up and once again Pavel V. Baranov, the RSFSR procurator, was brought in to investigate. It did not take long for USDS officials to respond once the procurator was involved. As Baranov reported, by late November 1951 the 26 residents and their families had been resettled into new housing.[58] As for the question of the unsanctioned distribution of housing in Tekstil'shchiki to individuals not connected with the Zariad'e, Baranov confirmed that this claim was true.[59]

Baranov had seen this all before. Just a few months earlier, in July 1951, the procurator had been following up on an earlier complaint from a different set of residents when he found evidence of similarly unsanctioned allocation of housing, this time in Kuntsevo. A letter from six Kuntsevo residents to Stalin prompted this earlier investigation. In this case, the letter-writers had been resettled in Kuntsevo one year earlier and "consequently," they wrote, "we find ourselves suburban residents [*zagorodnye zhiteli*]."[60] The writers, two women and four men, had come to Kuntsevo not just from the Zariad'e, but also from the Lenin Hills—the USDS's other skyscraper construction site. Now, these neighbors who had moved from different parts of Moscow banded together to expose the corruption of managers in the Resettlement Office who had "contorted and systematically violated the decree, granting living space not according to legal principles but according to their own discretion."[61] It had become clear to these new Kuntsevo residents that the Resettlement Office "is made up of treacherous people."[62]

In their letter, these residents complained about a V. M. Brezhneva, an MVD employee who had received an apartment all to herself. They also complained about a comrade Petrakov, a USDS official who the residents accused of bribery, while warning that it "was not comrade Petrakov alone. This disease has infected the entire apparatus of the USDS management."[63] But most of all, these residents of Kuntsevo complained about the man in charge of resettlement, E. P. Popov. Popov was rude, haughty, and abusive toward Kuntsevo inhabitants, and even worse he had given his own brother (who had arrived recently in Moscow from the Urals) an apartment intended for Moscow's displaced residents. "Our party and our government display daily concern and responsiveness to the settlers [*pereselentsy*]," these residents wrote, "creating for them all the conditions for a better life, but some '*chinovniki*' from the USDS, like comrade Popov, distort and trivialize such an important matter of state."[64] Not only had the new residents of Kuntsevo been unwillingly transformed from urbanites into suburbanites, but the unfair allocation of housing threatened to turn law and order on its head. It must have been at least some consolation, then, when E. P. Popov was expelled from the Communist Party for his conduct in Kuntsevo.[65]

While some residents focused their attention on rooting out corruption among state officials, others wrote letters to alert Soviet leaders to the more mundane challenges of life on the outskirts. In July 1952, Beria received a letter from a Major Rekin who lived in Kuntsevo and had witnessed the district's development firsthand. Rekin began by praising the "great government work by which thousands of Muscovites resettled from the Zariad'e are given new houses, rooms, and separate apartments with all amenities."[66] Rekin described the new settlement at Kuntsevo, with its asphalt streets and sidewalks, green lawns, laundry facilities, and new movie theater. Those who lived in this new district, Rekin wrote, "are thankful to the Party and the State, for their attention and concern that all are resettled into good conditions."[67] The only problem was that the settlement was too far from the train station connecting it to Moscow. According to Rekin, "the new settlement stands like a distant island, far from the railway platform." In order to reach the platform, residents had to trek through the mud wearing tall rubber boots and old rags to prevent their clothes from getting dirty.[68] It was nearly impossible, Rekin asserted, to make it into Moscow from Kuntsevo cleanly dressed. The whole affair was "utterly unsanitary." Worse, it was "simply humiliating going into Moscow looking like that."[69]

It was not only residents who were alarmed by the mud and filth that characterized Moscow's suburban districts. A few months later, in late 1952, Beria heard from doctors working at the Kuntsevo Regional Health Office. The head of the office wrote to Beria requesting that the Ministry of Health be permitted to intervene in construction in Kuntsevo to address serious health concerns. Although a school, a preschool, a nursery, a workers' club, a *banya*, and a laundry house were nearing completion in the new settlement, construction of a medical clinic had been repeatedly delayed. In the time being, a makeshift clinic with four cots had been set up, but this was not enough. Beria learned that the residents of Kuntsevo were complaining in large numbers about the need for a proper clinic to treat tuberculosis, dysentery, and other serious ailments. For this oversight in the settlement's construction, the health officials blamed Aleksandr N. Komarovskii, the powerful boss at the USDS who was heading up construction on both the Zariad'e Building and on Moscow State University on the Lenin Hills.[70] Advocating for their patients, the Kuntsevo health officials were outraged. As they saw it, "constructing housing without building any social-cultural amenities in an entirely new settlement, leaving workers' children without supervision, is out of the question and unjust."[71]

Kuntsevo's health office had butted heads with Komarovskii before. The same two health officials who wrote to Beria in 1952 had written one year earlier as well; this earlier letter had likely prompted much of the progress that had been made by 1952 on Kuntsevo's schools, *banya*, and laundry construction. In their earlier letter, Kuntsevo health officials described Komarovskii as cold-hearted and strange. They had repeatedly approached Komarovskii directly about the poor state of health services and sanitation in the new district. "But in response to our requests," they wrote, "we were rejected and given a very odd, heartless answer."[72] Komarovskii had apparently replied: "Don't chase the crane in the sky, catch the sparrow instead."[73] It was a variation of the Russian expression: "better a sparrow in hand, than a crane in the sky."[74] Komarovskii wanted the health officials to be more realistic and not strive for too much. He recommended that they make do with what they had: a makeshift five-room clinic for a population of 20,000. Komarovskii, a central figure in charge of building skyscrapers in postwar Moscow, had perhaps grown tired himself of chasing impossible dreams, or as he put it, "cranes in the sky."

Komarovskii replaced Prokof'ev as head of the USDS in October 1948. Prokof'ev was by then in his early sixties and in poor health; he died a year later.[75] Twenty years his predecessor's junior, Komarovskii had made a name for himself building the Moscow-Volga Canal in the 1930s. Following in the footsteps of his father, a railroad engineer, Komarovskii studied at the Moscow Institute of Transport Engineers before beginning work on the canal in 1931. Komarovskii rose quickly through the ranks. By 1944, he had joined the Communist Party, acquired a military title, and become head of the industrial construction wing of the Gulag. When he took over at the USDS, Major-General Komarovskii continued to hold this position as head of the Department of Industrial Construction (Glavpromstroi) of the MVD USSR.[76] As such, he was also engaged during these years in the large-scale, Gulag-run construction efforts of the Soviet atomic project.[77] The two projects—skyscrapers and atomic bombs—were closely connected: as beautiful as the university skyscraper would be, it was the new physics and chemistry labs that stood out for many Soviet officials as the central attractions of this building.

Thinking back later to this period of his life, Komarovskii was proud to have led the construction of MGU. "Many foreign guests to Moscow marvel at the university ensemble on the Lenin Hills," he wrote in 1972. Yet, Komarovskii also recalled the shadow city that had emerged around Moscow as a result of the skyscraper project. "Speaking of the construction of MGU," he wrote, "it is necessary to talk also about the resettlement of residents from the territories surrounding MGU and its facilities, and also from the territory for the construction on the Zariad'e, which was full of old buildings."[78] Komarovskii remembered this as a difficult and intensive assignment, since "in fact all residents had to be given new housing with amenities, which had to be built from scratch with all utility connections, roads, and so on."[79] Komarovskii recalled that one housing district had been built to the north of Moscow, near the Lobnia railway station, another in Tekstil'shchiki, and yet another in Cheremushki. By 1972, Komarovskii seemed to have forgotten about Kuntsevo.

Komarovskii remembered best of all the residential construction at Cheremushki. The housing in Cheremushki was mainly allotted to construction workers, not to those displaced from the Zariad'e, but the development of this region followed the same ad hoc pattern of construction in places like Kuntsevo and Tekstil'shchiki. As Komarovskii himself noted, the Cheremushki region of Moscow would become famous in the post-Stalin years as the site of the Soviet Union's showcase microdistrict: the main building block of the mass housing campaign initiated in 1957 by Nikita Khrushchev. Indeed, as Komarovskii wrote, by the late 1950s, "Cheremushki" districts, named after the one in Moscow, began to appear in cities all over the Soviet Union. Thinking back to the earlier years of the late Stalin period Komarovskii wrote, "with a smile, I remember now what harsh criticism was voiced for the fact that 'instead of rebuilding the central part of Moscow the workers are stuck out at some-such Cheremushki' [lezut v kakie-to Cheremushki]." The development of these peripheral regions of the city, Komarovskii acknowledged, was at the time "not so much part of the creation of the new microdistricts of Moscow, but a result of the impossibility of building new housing in the center."[80] Though all this would change in the Khrushchev era, in the late Stalin period life on the outskirts was an afterthought, not a central part of the plan.

One of Moscow's eight skyscrapers was, in fact, built on the outskirts of the city. This was the showpiece building of the lot, the skyscraper to top all skyscrapers: Moscow State University. While the Zariad'e was densely populated, the site chosen for skyscraper development on the Lenin Hills was leafy and pastoral. Most inhabitants of this village-like corner of Moscow lived in small wooden houses. The southwest region of Moscow, where the tall university building would stand, had been slated for redevelopment in the 1930s as part of the Moscow General Plan, but substantial work in this direction began only in the postwar years. By the USDS's official count, there were over 4,000 people living on the new university's plot.[81] Among the existing structures that would have to be demolished to make way for the MGU complex was wooden housing belonging to the Red Proletariat Factory, brick housing belonging to the MVD's gold mining research institute, and two farms—the 12th Anniversary of October kolkhoz and the Lenin Hills sovkhoz.[82]

A number of the wooden houses nestled among the Lenin Hills were found to be in decent condition. The USDS therefore decided simply to pick these houses up and move them, along with their residents, to a new location by the Lobnia railway station north of Moscow. While this removed the burden of having to build new housing for these residents, it also meant that USDS officials entered into the realm of Soviet homeowners and their renters. Many of the wooden homes on the Lenin Hills were communally occupied, owned by one resident who rented rooms to others. One such tenant was Maria Kalinkina, who had two children and rented one-tenth of a house on Vorob'evskii (Sparrow) Lane. Agaf'ia Kozlova, an elderly "mother-heroine" whose two sons were killed in the war, owned the house. Kozlova lived entirely off her garden plot, with no pension. Kozlova and her family, a daughter, two sons, two daughters-in-law, and four grandchildren, lived in the other nine-tenths of the house.[83]

While the Kozlov family would move with their wooden house up to Lobnia, Maria Kalinkina looked for an alternative solution to her displacement. In January 1951, after USDS officials had offered her a "Finnish cottage" north of Lobnia at the Katuar station, Kalinkina wrote to Stalin, pleading for him to find a way to allow her to stay in Moscow. "Lobnia is unacceptable for me for a number of reasons," she wrote. Kalinkina was taking typing classes, with still five months to go. "And after studies, there is work," she wrote, "there will be a lot of time spent in transit, the children will be completely neglected." Moreover, Kalinkina's son had studied French for three years already in school, but in the school near Lobnia, they studied German. "He won't be able to take his exam," she wrote. Finally, Kalinkina appealed to Stalin on the basis of her husband's twenty-five-year service in the Soviet Army. Before he had passed away in 1947, he was a decorated soldier who had fought in the Civil War and in the more recent conflict, "freeing South Sakhalin from the Japanese aggressors" and earning the "personal thanks of the Generalissimus, of You Comrade Stalin."[84] In the end, Kalinkina was given new housing in Kuntsevo.

Unlike at the Zariad'e, those living on the Lenin Hills were divided into various entitlement groups by the office in charge of evictions and resettlement. The Lenin Hills was a more complex space, home to both owners and renters, collective farm workers and workers from various Ministries that had built housing in the area.[85] Individual ownership was partly the result of wartime legislation, further developed in a state decree of 1948 that required city and district officials across the USSR to allot plots of land to individuals wishing to build one- or two-story houses for themselves.[86] In an effort to make sense of the wider variety of residents and housing types in this location, the Council of Ministers issued an order in May 1949 titled "On the resettlement of citizens living on the plot for the construction of Moscow State University on the Lenin Hills and Adjoining Territories." In addition to providing residents who were also "owners" with the option of moving their home—a home they had likely built themselves—the order also made concessions to those who would choose instead to be resettled in new housing. Renters (s'emshchiki) would be compensated not with new housing, but with 5,000 rubles, unless they were members of the following groups: the families of soldiers, wounded warriors, and invalids of the war, as well as disabled workers (invalidy truda), pensioners, and the single elderly.[87] These groups of renters—which included Maria Kalinkina, who received her husband's pension—would be given new housing elsewhere in the city.[88]

The long process of displacement and resettlement from the Lenin Hills and from the Zariad'e carried on into the post-Stalin period. As late as June 1953, the ski champion and coach Dmitrii M. Vasil'ev and his wife Vera Evgen'evna, a doctor, wrote to Beria to express their dissatisfaction about having to relocate to Kuntsevo.[89] Still living in the Zariad'e, the couple told Beria that "relocation to the far edge of the city, beyond city limits, will create more difficult conditions for our work and life as we will spend so much time in transit to and from work."[90] Aspiring to the "middle class" lifestyle promised to cultural leaders, doctors, and other elites in the postwar years, the Vasil'evs asked Beria to help them acquire a more central apartment: "if possible," they wrote, "in a skyscraper [v vysotnom dome]."[91] The Kotel'nicheskaia embankment skyscraper, visible just down the Moscow River from the Zariad'e, had just been completed by the time the couple wrote to Beria. But apartments in that new residential tower had already been allocated. And in any case, approaching Beria for assistance in June 1953 was of little use: the Soviet official who had long been overseeing Moscow's skyscraper construction project was arrested that very month.

UNEARTHING THE PAST

There was nothing especially unique or unusual about Moscow's expansion into *podmoskov'e*. Growing cities tend to overrun their rural hinterlands. Moscow's rapid urbanization followed a pattern that would have been as familiar to a Roman in the second century or to a Londoner in the nineteenth as to a Muscovite in the twentieth century. In the early nineteenth century, the poet William Blake watched as the northern part of London crept into the nearby countryside, a movement he dramatized in his poem *Jerusalem*. Blake found the expansion of London into its hinterland troubling. As Elizabeth McKellar writes, "past and present were fused in Blake's imagination with the northern edge of the city representing an idealized landscape of pastoral perfection just at the moment it was being snatched away irrevocably by the march of bricks and mortar."[92] In the Soviet imagination, urban expansion was more positively associated with modernization and progress. Still, the pace of Moscow's growth in the postwar years was unnerving from the perspective of those living on the capital's outskirts.

A cartoon printed in the Soviet magazine *Krokodil* in 1951 satirized this discomfort (fig. 5.7). "Good heavens! [*Batiushki!*]" says an old woman who is out picking mushrooms in the forest, "the mushrooms are growing [as fast as] the new construction!" The cranes and skyscrapers in the background have so encroached into the forests of *podmoskov'e* that they now set the pace for nature's own development. In *podmoskov'e*, the natural and built environments trade places; skyscrapers have become the standard by which all other things grow.

For their part, Soviet architects and officials saw little tension, initially, between tradition and progress in Moscow's skyscraper project. Designed in stylistic reference to the Kremlin towers, Moscow's postwar skyscrapers were seen not as tools of erasure, but as monuments that, in their form and symbolism, seamlessly connected the deep Russian past with the Soviet present. And yet, past and present did collide during Moscow's skyscraper development when in 1949 Moscow's past was unearthed by workers digging the Zariad'e building's foundation pit. Though skyscraper construction was clearly a priority in postwar Moscow, so too was uncovering the historic roots of the Soviet capital. Between 1949 and 1950, six large-scale archaeological excavations were conducted on the Zariad'e construction site.

Archaeologists working in the Soviet Institute for the History of Material Culture had had their sights set on the Zariad'e since the early 1940s.[93] Starting in 1941, this Institute, together with the Academy of Architecture, began recording details about buildings in the Zariad'e and collecting materials from the parts of the neighborhood closest to the river that had been demolished earlier. The skyscraper decree of 1947 offered an unprecedented opportunity to carry out a full-scale dig on the site. The Institute for the History of Material Culture and the Museum for the History and Reconstruction of Moscow jointly organized the excavations in 1949 and 1950 (fig. 5.8). The Zariad'e dig was one in a series of excavations carried out in Moscow—collectively

Figure 5.7: "In a Forest of *Podmoskov'e*." *Krokodil*, July 30, 1951. Caption reads: "Good heavens! The mushrooms are growing [as fast as] the new construction!"

dubbed the Moscow Archaeological Expedition—that was headed from 1946 to 1951 by Mikhail G. Rabinovich, a young archaeologist in his early thirties.[94]

The archaeological agenda fit well within the cultural atmosphere of the postwar years. Archaeological study of the Zariad'e was part of the broader elevation of Russian national culture after the war.[95] Despite opportunities for excavations on Moscow's many construction sites of the 1930s, Soviet archaeologists had paid little attention to the city in the interwar years.[96] But scholarly attitudes toward Moscow changed during the ideological campaigns of the late 1940s. The celebration across the USSR of Moscow's 800th anniversary in 1947 stood out to many as one of the first postwar holidays, but the event also signaled a deeper political and cultural shift. The anniversary was part of a larger effort to secure Moscow as the symbolic center of the Soviet Union and the expanding socialist world. As Mikhail Rabinovich recalled, Moscow's 800th anniversary celebration caused some uneasiness in Aleksandr Udal'tsov, the

Figure 5.8: Excavation in the Zariad'e, 1950. Collection of the Moscow City Archive GBU "TsGA Moskvy."

Director of the Institute for the History of Material Culture. "Moscow had still not been studied archaeologically," Rabinovich explained, thinking back in the early 1980s to the postwar moment. "In this first city of the world, there had not been a single excavation, as there had been in dozens of other large and small cities—starting with Kiev and ending with Zvenigorod . . ." "The solution to this problem," Rabinovich wrote, "was simple: organize excavations in Moscow."[97]

In the postwar years, Rabinovich headed the work of the Moscow Archaeological Expedition, first along the Iauza River, then in *podmoskov'e* (in Sokol'niki, Cheremushki, and Fili), and finally in the Zariad'e itself.[98] As Rabinovich recalled, it was here that his team made its most successful discoveries. Lying beneath the Zariad'e, some four to six meters down, was a layer of soil preserving fragments of clay dishes from the tenth to thirteenth centuries. Also among the relics unearthed were earthenware vessels, glass bracelets, and slate spindle whorls. But the excavations did not only uncover small items from the past. An entire network of houses, streets, and walls had been preserved underground. The Zariad'e settlement, as it turned out, dated back to a time before Moscow's founding father, Yuri Dolgorukii.[99]

Although his work uncovering the deep Russian past was a success, Rabinovich quickly became the victim of the very forces that had prompted the archaeological digs in Moscow in the first place. In 1951, Rabinovich's boss, Udal'tsov, summoned him to his office. As Rabinovich recalled, Udal'tsov broke the news awkwardly. Rabinovich's demotion would be purely "perfunctory," Udal'tsov explained. Rabinovich was not suited to be head of the Moscow Expedition because, for one thing, he was too junior. Everyone was "very satisfied" with Rabinovich's work, but the fact that the young archaeologist was not ethnically Russian but Jewish complicated matters. "It was obvious," Rabinovich recalled, contrary to Udal'tsov's assurances, "that the issue was precisely my last name."[100] The archaeological work carried out in the Zariad'e during late Stalinism was inextricably tied to the anti-cosmopolitan campaign of the postwar years.[101] The destabilizing force of the *Zhdanovshchina* made the past a dangerous terrain to navigate.

What archaeologists found below ground in the Zariad'e added greater certainty to Moscow's long historical narrative. But above ground, as well, experts began to petition the state for historical work of a different kind. Also on the Zariad'e plot, preservationists engaged in a battle to record and preserve Moscow's architectural heritage before it was swept away by Stalin's tall buildings. The Section for the Study of Architectural Monuments, part of the Moscow branch of the Union of Architects, met in 1951 to discuss the need to incorporate older architectural monuments into the Soviet Union's new urban ensembles. This group noted the many instances of "inexcusable relations between a number of urban planners and the architectural heritage of the past," and they called on architects to become more aware of how their designs might work with, rather than against, existing city spaces.[102] Moscow's skyscraper plots were key sites for this work: what was to be done with the Kitai-gorod walls in the Zariad'e, for example, had yet to be answered.

During the later Khrushchev era, the demolition of large parts of Moscow's Arbat neighborhood would see preservationists loudly voicing their discontent and demanding greater public involvement in decision-making about the built environment.[103] By then, preservationists had grown stronger and more emboldened by the shifting politics of the Thaw. But in the years of late Stalinism, it was Moscow's top architects who largely drove the effort to preserve the city's historical monuments. For the most part, architects worked to embed preservationism into the city's socialist reconstruction. The displacement order for the Zariad'e of August 1950, for example, included a list of buildings on the site that were recommended for preservation. Among them were the Chambers of the Romanov Boyars, as well as the Church of St. Barbara, the Church of St. Maksim, the Znamenskii Monastery, the Church of St. George, and the Church of the Conception of St. Anna.[104] Valued by Soviet architects and officials in the 1950s as monuments of Russian national heritage, these ecclesiastical structures remain on the site today.[105]

As architects built a ring of modern skyscrapers in Moscow, they also sought to preserve the past. Efforts to unearth and protect the materials and monuments of Russian history were carried out against the larger transformation of the Soviet capital.

While the history unearthed and preserved at the sites was material worthy of public consumption, the architectural and popular presses remained silent on the fact that tens of thousands of Muscovites were being shifted from center to periphery. They were city dwellers turned villagers overnight. Disconnected from the city center, those who were resettled traveled against the flow of modernization, as if backwards through time. On the periphery they would be joined by tens of thousands of construction workers, many of whom were brought to the capital specially to build the skyscrapers. Unlike their new neighbors, many of these workers would see and experience Moscow for the first time.

6

THE *VYSOTNIKI*

The young welder E. Martynov would never forget his first day of work on the university construction site. Winding his way through small mountains of freshly dug dirt, Martynov glanced up at the metal columns that had recently been planted into the ground below and now stretched far up into the sky. It was a clear spring day and Martynov could feel the air around him vibrating from the clanging, clattering, screeching sound of the machines that were hard at work nearby. Martynov handed his documents to comrade Fedorov, a Stalin-award-winning foreman, who carefully looked over the papers, sizing up the young man with a sideways glance before giving him an easy task to start. Martynov would later admit that he was a little nervous on that first day.[1] This was not just any construction site, after all. This was the future site of the 32-story Moscow State University (MGU), a building known at the time as the "Palace of Science." And those who worked on this building were not just ordinary construction workers; they were "*vysotniki*."

Martynov's account of life on the MGU construction site is, of course, an idealized one. It was published in 1952 in a special collection of narratives written by workers, foremen, and architects printed by the Soviet trade union press one year before the new university building opened its doors to the first cohort of students. There was a ready audience both in Moscow and beyond for the fifteen thousand copies of this booklet that celebrated the achievements of the builders of MGU. The Soviet satirical magazine *Krokodil* highlighted the publication of the booklet in its August 1952 issue, announcing to its readers that "the young workers of the tall building of the Moscow university have written a book that shares the experiences of their work."[2] In the accompanying cartoon image, an older reader seated on a park bench holds a copy of the book in his left hand (fig. 6.1). Glancing up at two healthy young workers, the old man congratulates them: "A rare piece of work!" he exclaims. "In it, they come up with so much yet at the same time don't make anything up!"[3]

The publication and celebration of narratives like Martynov's in 1952 was part of a larger project to make popular heroes out of Moscow's skyscraper construction workers. This chapter examines these heroic narratives and the ideological work they did in the postwar Stalin era, but it also considers the silences and absences in such texts. Accounts of the mismanagement, faulty work, accidents, and reprimands that were a part of daily life on the construction site are not printed in that 1952 booklet. The real difficulties of carrying out such monumental construction projects are acknowledged in Stalin-era workers' narratives, but these texts aim to convey to the reader how challenges were overcome, usually in stories about workers banding together to succeed against all odds. Published narratives about the university's

Figure 6.1: "New in Literature."
Krokodil, August 20, 1952.

construction repeated a familiar set of literary conventions established across decades of socialist realist works.

Also not printed alongside Martynov's account are the experiences of Gulag workers and former Gulag inmates whose sentences had been reduced in exchange for their work building up postwar Moscow. Like Martynov, Ismail G. Sadarov worked on the university skyscraper project, though he did not freely wander onto the construction site to report for his first day of work. Sentenced in 1947 in the North Ossetian ASSR to seven years imprisonment for military desertion, Sadarov was given early release in 1950 in exchange for working on the construction of Moscow State University.[4] Sadarov's experience building the university skyscraper survives in a slim historical record that is a faint whisper when held up against Martynov's much louder voice. And yet, these men, along with thousands of other men and women like them, inhabited the same small world of the university construction site. Weaving together their voices is the goal of this chapter, which examines how the vysotniki were idealized in Soviet popular culture and how they lived and worked in reality.

BUILDERS AS HEROES

The word "vysotnik" is derived from the Russian word *"vysota,"* or "height"; it was a term applied to all construction workers engaged in building Moscow's skyscrapers. They included in their ranks both skilled and unskilled laborers and as a group were counted among the heroes of the postwar era. Each of Moscow's eight skyscraper construction sites employed a variety of vysotniki, from those who worked at the top of the structures to those working closer to the ground, digging foundation pits and fixing in place the metal matrices needed to reinforce concrete. But as the nickname implies, "vysotniki" were best known and most celebrated for their work scaling the tall buildings. From the early 1950s, these men and women could be seen climbing up the tall metal carcasses of Moscow's enormous new structures to carry out their work as welders, granite workers, stuccoists, and steeplejacks (*verkholazy*). Craftsmen like E. Martynov secured, sculpted, and shaped the spires of Moscow's skyscrapers (fig. 6.2). And in the process, they were some of the first to see Moscow from the new vantage points created by the city's tall buildings.

Whether gazing out across the city from the outlying tower on the Lenin Hills or from the more central spire on Smolensk Square, the vysotniki saw Moscow in an entirely new way. This fact was often used as the basis of metaphor in vysotnik narratives, like Martynov's published account from 1952, which culminates with the young worker triumphantly gazing out across the cityscape from just beneath the newly-installed gold star atop the university skyscraper. "The fog faded away, and all of Moscow became clearly visible," Martynov wrote. From the top of the building, Martynov could see that "the Soviet people are building their own beautiful future! They are dreaming not of war, but of peaceful, happy lives!"[5] A keen observer not just of the built environment but of Soviet society as a whole, the figure of the vysotnik was endowed with special powers of perception. From his or her unique vantage point, the skyscraper builder was able to assess the state of affairs below. Not all vysotniki, of course, would see the world through the optimistic eyes of the young Martynov.

Moscow's vysotniki of the late Stalin era were idealized and celebrated in popular culture in the mold of Soviet heroes before them. The term "vysotnik" had an earlier usage that ensured that Moscow's skyscraper builders were closely associated with the heroic. In the 1930s, it was in most cases used to refer to Soviet aviators (*letchiki-vysotniki*). In the Soviet Union, as in the United States, the interwar period was the age of great aviator-explorers. In the Soviet case, the aviators of the thirties conquered the popular imagination with their daring flights to the arctic. (In 1937, against the backdrop of the purges, Soviet aviators first landed an aircraft at the North Pole and then broke the world record in long-distance flying by traveling over the arctic from Moscow to the United States.[6]) From 1941, aviator-vysotniki featured as key figures of the Soviet war effort. But by the late 1940s, the word "vysotnik" had come to refer, in Moscow at least, mainly to the workers involved in skyscraper construction. Like the aviators before them, these builders captured popular attention by reaching for new heights.

That aviators and skyscraper builders were so closely linked in the Soviet imagination is not surprising, given the symbolism attached to their respective achievements.

Figure 6.2: Welder E. Martynov building Moscow State University. *Dvorets nauki: rasskazy stroitelei novogo zdaniia Moskovskogo gosudarstvennogo universiteta*, Moscow: Profizdat, 1952.

Their shared goal of reaching for new heights—whether by plane or by skyscraper—was rooted in the same inclination. This was not a uniquely Soviet phenomenon. As Adnan Morshed writes, in the early- to mid-twentieth century "the skyscraper was popularly seen in the role of the airplane's urban alter ego."[7] In both airplane manufacturing and skyscraper building, planners combined technology with human force and bravery to create spectacles in the sky. Airplanes and skyscrapers alike were at once beautiful and sublime, awe-inspiring and terrifying.

Those who built these structures could be similarly described. In New York City in the 1930s, newspapers tracked the construction of the Empire State Building day by day in serialized accounts of the brave workforce of the city's "sky boys" and "poet builders."[8] These men, immortalized in the photographs of Lewis Hine, were as diverse in ethnic origin as their Soviet counterparts were two decades later. And any New Yorker who found themselves in Moscow after the war would have been reminded when hearing stories about the vysotniki of similar narratives from the interwar years back home. The Soviet Union was nonetheless keen to emphasize the differences between its monumental building projects and skyscrapers built abroad. While one group of skyscraper workers built in the name of capitalist "progress," the other labored in the pursuit of "communism." But perhaps the key difference was that the vysotniki understood their work as an extension of wartime sacrifice.

Figure 6.3: "My father defended Stalingrad, and I am building [it back] up" / "*Moi otets otstaival Stalingrad, a ia otstraivaiu.*" *Krokodil,* May 20, 1953.

Moscow's vysotniki were swiftly incorporated in the late 1940s into the pantheon of Soviet revolutionary and wartime heroes. Construction workers were important figures in the Soviet imagination in the 1930s, but the immense tasks of postwar reconstruction served to move this category of worker to center stage. Soviet writers and officials worked to forge strong associative links between postwar building and wartime heroism. As the construction worker pictured on the May 1953 cover of *Krokodil* put it, "My father defended Stalingrad, and I am building [it back] up" (fig. 6.3). Many of Moscow's young vysotniki had similar stories about their fathers' and mothers' heroism, and many more had fought in the war themselves. These wartime experiences remained relevant in the work being done on the construction site, where large banners were hung from the steel carcasses of the buildings with war-related and patriotic slogans, including "In peaceful days" (*V mirnye dni*) and "Glory to Comrade Stalin" (fig. 6.4).

Fedor Lagutin, a master concrete worker on the university construction site, recalled in 1952 that nine years earlier he had been stationed with his battalion far from Moscow, on the Rybachii Peninsula up north. Knowing that Lagutin had worked before the war in the capital city, the other soldiers in the battalion, none of whom had ever been to Moscow, asked Lagutin to describe it. "I began talking about the

Figure 6.4: Red Gates skyscraper with banner and text reading "Glory to Comrade Stalin," April 1950. Collection of the Shchusev State Museum of Architecture.

Kremlin," Lagutin recalled, "about the wonderful stations of the metro, about the wide and spacious streets and squares, and the new beautiful buildings." But Lagutin's description of Moscow was quickly cut short as German artillery began to shell the unit. "Everyone rushed to their positions . . ." he recalled. Then, "when the enemy guns fell silent, one of the soldiers piped up: 'Just you wait," he exclaimed, "we'll finish fighting this war, and then we'll build such palaces that you will sigh in amazement.'"[9] For Lagutin, whose leg was amputated during the war, the university skyscraper on the Lenin Hills was one of these palaces. After the war, Lagutin was determined to continue working in construction, despite the challenges presented by his disability. "I will build again!" Lagutin told himself. If the Soviet flying ace Alexei Mares'ev could get back up into the sky with two prosthetic legs, so could Lagutin, the concrete master resolved. In 1949, Lagutin was put in charge of the concrete division at the building site of Moscow State University.[10]

Older workers like Lagutin tied personal frontline memories to the construction site, but for the younger Martynov, it was the act of bearing witness to wartime destruction on the home front that spurred him on in his work. Still a child when the war began, Martynov remembered the year 1941, when his father left for the front and his mother started work at a factory. The family had moved just a few years before to the outskirts of Moscow. They settled in a little house with a small yard next to the construction site of a new school. As a child, Martynov would wander out of his yard and onto the construction site next door to watch the builders at their work; sometimes the workers would allow the boy to help out by holding bricks and tools. Each day Martynov would return home covered in dirt until the school was finally finished and the boy was old enough to enroll. When the school was destroyed in that first winter of the war by the Germans, Martynov was crushed. "She was demolished by the bombs that were thrown down and tore through the outskirts of Moscow by fascist pilots," Martynov recalled in 1952. "Tears welled up in my eyes," he continued, "at the sight of the mound of broken bricks."[11] A few months later, Martynov joined the ranks of the city's construction workers, training to mend his broken city by becoming a welder. A decade later he would pay homage to his lost school by helping to build the country's premier university.

Soviet skyscrapers served as a means through which both the state and the self could be rebuilt after the war. It was often the able-bodied male builder who featured on magazine covers and in published texts. But, as even the most idealized vysotnik narratives attest, the skyscraper construction sites were filled with the scarred bodies of shell-shocked warriors who had lost far more than limbs in the recent war. Wartime trauma runs throughout the construction worker narratives printed alongside Lagutin's and Martynov's in that small booklet of 1952. While Moscow's skyscrapers stood as monuments to Soviet victory in the war, their construction also served as the means through which builders could overcome past grief and loss. Those wishing to take up the metaphor might make themselves whole again through work, rebuilding the self along with the city. Soviet production novels of the twenties and thirties could serve as the model for a vysotnik wishing to reforge himself on the construction site. Only instead of returning home after the Civil War to rebuild a cement factory, like Gleb Chumalov in the novel *Cement*, decorated veterans now returned from the Great Patriotic War to build skyscrapers in Moscow.[12] As *Ogonek* magazine put it in 1952, "before our eyes Moscow is transforming, enormous bright buildings are climbing up to the sky, and alongside Moscow, together with her buildings ordinary Soviet people grow—the rank and file builders of communism."[13]

WOMEN ON THE CONSTRUCTION SITE

The idealized stories and images circulated in the press portrayed the skyscraper construction site as a predominantly male space. But in reality, newly demobilized soldiers and other men on skyscraper building sites worked side by side with women (figs. 6.5–6.8). The number of Soviet women working in the construction industry had risen significantly during the First Five-Year Plan and remained high through the war and into the wartime years.[14] Unlike in England or the United

Figure 6.5: Construction of the skyscraper on Uprising Square, 1951.
Collection of the Museum of Moscow.

Figure 6.6: Construction of Moscow State University, 1949.
Collection of the Moscow City Archive GBU "TsGA Moskvy."

Figure 6.7: Construction of Moscow State University, 1951.
Collection of the Moscow City Archive GBU "TsGA Moskvy."

Figure 6.8: Construction of Moscow State University, 1951.
Collection of the Moscow City Archive GBU "TsGA Moskvy."

States, Soviet women were not pushed out of the workforce after 1945. In archival photographs of Moscow's skyscraper construction sites, women can be seen digging foundation pits, laying bricks, checking column verticality, and raising reinforced-concrete slabs with the help of telpher hoists.[15] Women worked on Moscow's new buildings in both skilled and unskilled positions, and they faced burdens that were uniquely theirs to bear. As a housing official employed by the MGU construction office observed in 1950, there were not enough kindergartens and daycares to serve the population of workers employed to build the university. "We have a larger number of women at home not working for six months," the official noted, "because there is nowhere to put their children."[16] Dislocated from their extended families and lacking support from the state, builders who were also mothers faced intense and unique forms of pressure. In the late-Stalinist period, women faced contradictory demands; they were expected to help rebuild the country while also repopulating the Soviet Union.[17]

Posters and newspaper reports of the postwar years rarely, if ever, depicted women working in skyscraper foundation pits. Instead, women were shown working as bricklayers or more commonly as stuccoists or modelers (*lepshchiki*), adding the final decorative touches to a building's façade. By locating women on the façades of Moscow's skyscrapers, artists and writers worked to reinforce traditional gender roles after a war during which female combatants and partisans on the frontlines, and women workers on the home front, had interrogated those roles. In a painting created in the late 1940s, for example, the artist Georgii Satel' pictured a young woman on one of Moscow's skyscraper sites; wearing summer shoes and a clean white smock over her dress, she is shown taking instruction from an older male craftsman. The painting, titled "The Komsomol-Builders of Moscow," was shown at the All-Union Art Exhibition in 1949 and published in *Ogonek* the following year. The men in Satel''s painting give direction and they do the heavy lifting, passing up the premade acanthus leaves that will decorate one of the building's columns. The woman in white, by contrast, stares intently at a spiral-shaped corner volute of a Corinthian capital while being shown how to carve it. Her clean, white drapery looks nothing like the quilted jackets (*telogreiki*)—or even the lighter jackets and overalls for warmer weather—worn by the typical *vysotnitsa*, but this was of little matter. Like so many women draped in white before her, the figure in Satel''s painting is an allegory for peace and the purity of the tasks that lay ahead.

Both women and men worked on the façades of Moscow's skyscraper construction sites as modelers. Photographs taken on the MGU site in 1951 show a group of workers arranging ceramic tiles atop rows of bricks. One of the workers assembles a floral medallion. All are wearing matching dark coveralls (fig. 6.9–6.10). Elsewhere on the MGU construction site, archival photographs seem to confirm the more idealized images produced by artists like Satel'. In a photograph taken in 1950, women are shown working in clean light clothing and high heels, with hair tied back just so (fig. 6.11); the woman in the white top in the foreground has mislaid her gloves. The contrast in dress and facial expression between the two women in front and the other seven in the back gives the image a staged quality. Whether the women pictured traded in their work boots and headscarves of their own ac-

Figure 6.9: Construction of Moscow State University, 1951.
Collection of the Moscow City Archive GBU "TsGA Moskvy."

Figure 6.10: Construction of Moscow State University, 1951.
Collection of the Moscow City Archive GBU "TsGA Moskvy."

Figure 6.11: Construction of Moscow State University, August 5, 1950.
Collection of the Moscow City Archive GBU "TsGA Moskvy."

cord, or whether they were asked to do so ahead of the photographer's visit to the construction site, photographs like this one show the importance of making women visible on the construction sites, even if this visibility was accompanied by unrealistic representation.

Idealized images of life as a *vysotnitsa* worked together with narratives about the privilege and access that the city of Moscow could offer young workers. For M. Nakonechnaia, who began work as a stuccoist on MGU in February 1951, life as a skyscraper builder was rewarding insofar as it provided a path toward future social mobility. Nakonechnaia had arrived at the MGU site skilled in construction, having trained in school as a modeler prior to joining her brigade at MGU. Yet she saw in this work an opportunity for even greater fulfillment. As she wrote in 1952, "'We build—we study!' These words became a motto for many young builders . . . In our brigade almost everyone dreams about studying at the university and in institutes." Nakonechnaia was already studying part-time by correspondence, and just as soon as MGU was ready, she wrote, she would begin studying in the university's Geography department.[18]

The idea that young builders would one day become university students found broad appeal in the late-Stalin era.[19] A cartoon printed in *Krokodil* in 1950 developed this theme, showing a young woman like Nakonechnaia laying bricks on the MGU construction site (fig. 6.12). "When will you be finished?" asks the young man standing below her. "The building," she replies, "in 1951; university, in 1956!" In creating the archetype of the upwardly mobile vysotnik, writers and cartoonists drew parallels between Moscow's postwar skyscraper builders and the *vydvizhentsy* of the

НА ЛЕНИНСКИХ ГОРАХ

Рис. В. КОНОВАЛОВА

(По теме студента МГУ В. ШУБКИНА)

Многие молодые строители нового здания МГУ имени
Ломоносова готовятся к поступлению в университет.

— Когда вы окончите?
— Здание — в 1951 году, а университет — в 1956!

Figure 6.12: "On the Lenin Hills." *Krokodil*,
September 30, 1950.

Caption reads at top: "Many young builders of the
new MGU building are preparing to enroll in the
university."

Caption reads at bottom:
—When will you be finished?
—The building, in 1951; university, in 1956!

early 1930s—those workers swiftly promoted to managerial positions on the industrial sites of the First Five-Year Plan.[20] The promise implied by this comparison was ultimately an empty one. Upward mobility on the scale seen in the 1930s was simply not on offer in the postwar years. The Soviet state in this later period was more intent on cementing its relationship with those who had risen a decade earlier than it was on welcoming a new generation of workers into the ranks of the managerial and intellectual classes. As Vera Dunham observed, the "Big Deal" struck between the postwar Stalinist state and the Soviet "middle class" came at the expense of workers.[21] The low wages and poor housing workers endured in the 1940s were matched only by increasingly punitive laws that criminalized absenteeism and job changing.[22] In reality, ascending the social ladder during late Stalinism was no easy task, even for Moscow's vysotniki.

BOOTS ON THE GROUND

Just as the Great Patriotic War served to motivate Soviet skyscraper construction, it also left a legacy of loss and devastation that made large-scale building projects difficult to achieve. Postwar shortages resulted in intense competition over materials, equipment, and labor between managers working across Moscow's different construction sites. Building materials often arrived late or not at all, and construction equipment and gear were in short supply. Managers at all skyscraper sites complained about a shortage of skilled workers.

Having grown accustomed to shortages and late deliveries, some building managers were caught by surprise when all went according to plan. In October 1947, Andrei Prokof'ev, head of the Administration for the Construction of the Palace of Soviets (USDS), appealed to Molotov in a panic over a boot shortage. Prokof'ev, in charge of building both MGU and the skyscraper on the Zariad'e, was so surprised by the prompt arrival of workers on site that he wrote to Molotov to report shortages in gear that had not yet arrived. The USDS was in need of 500 extra pairs of boots, immediately.[23] Next, mere days after the boot shortage was resolved, Prokof'ev wrote to Beria to request that the MVD allocate 4,900 inmates (*spetskontingenty* or ITKs) to the Zariad'e and MGU projects. The USDS was still short on laborers, even as it struggled to clothe those already working on site. In this instance, Prokof'ev needed workers not for skyscraper construction, but for building housing for the vysotniki in the district of Kuntsevo and for working at the USDS's industrial and wood processing plants outside Moscow.[24]

The struggle to secure the human resources needed to build Moscow's tall buildings was unceasing. The war had caused a sharp decline in the number of working-age men able and available for employment in the immediate postwar years in the Soviet construction industry. Beyond the issue of the USSR's postwar population crisis, construction workers in this moment were just plain hard to recruit. As Donald Filtzer notes, construction sites proved especially difficult to staff in the immediate postwar years. The Ministry of the Building Materials Industry, for example, found that it was "virtually impossible to persuade about-to-be-demobilized soldiers to take jobs on their construction sites."[25] The work was hard and the wages were low. Still, Moscow's skyscraper construction managers had access to labor reserves in ways few other project managers did in the postwar years.

Moscow's skyscrapers were top on the list of construction endeavors of the postwar period. The Council of Ministers made the importance of the capital's monumental development clear in its repeated commitment of large numbers of workers to skyscraper construction. In its decree issued in August 1947, the Council of Ministers stated that 23,000 new workers and their families would be permitted entry and residence in Moscow over the years 1947 and 1948.[26] This was followed by an order in March 1948, calling on the Ministry of Labor Reserves to supply 6,000 workers drawn from the rural population.[27] And in August 1948, an order titled "On Measures to Quicken the Construction of the New Building of MGU" made the Ministry of Labor Reserves responsible for supplying the USDS in particular with 2,000 workers from both the rural and urban populations of the Vladimir oblast' just east of Moscow and from the Belarussian SSR.[28] In 1949, a new order called on the Ministry of Labor Reserves to supply yet more workers for the MGU project. This time, it would include workers to be sent to the USDS's lumber camps in Kostromskaia oblast' and Gor'kovskaia oblast', plus the supply of one hundred or so young recruits straight out of the country's trade schools.[29]

As any Soviet manager knew, commitments made on paper were not always fulfilled in reality. As early as April 1948, Prokof'ev, still head of the USDS until he was ousted that October, wrote to Beria to complain. Prokof'ev reported that the Ministry of Labor Reserves had not only neglected to send 2,000 new workers from the countryside to work on MGU, but that they had refused to supply any workers at all.[30] Again in 1950, the USDS's Second Construction Office, dedicated primarily to work on the Zariad'e skyscraper, reported that it faced an "acute deficit of labor power."[31] Although the Second Construction Office began that year with a labor surplus (745 workers in place of the 616 required) by year's end, the office had less than forty percent of the workforce needed (965 workers instead of the 2,516 requested). The construction office also complained about having to take on low-skilled workers out of desperation, as well as those without any qualifications at all. Despite these difficulties, the USDS was on the whole better supplied than most other skyscraper ministries.

Moscow's skyscraper project may have been imagined as a unified citywide plan in architects' drawings, but in practice resources were allocated unevenly, with certain construction sites better supplied than others. While there were over 10,000 workers employed on the MGU construction site in mid-1949, the buildings at Uprising and Komsomol Squares had fewer than 1,000 workers combined.[32] By 1950, the MGU site boasted over 14,000 workers, while the residential building on Uprising Square had just over 900 and the Komsomol Square hotel fewer than 700.[33] The university building had been given priority, with its managers gaining greater access to labor and materials. But beyond official sponsorship of this project over and above the others, a key feature that separated one construction site from the next lay in a manager's ability to use forced labor. Gulag labor was used at the Moscow State University site and on the MVD's Kotel'nicheskaia building. But on these sites too, managers repeatedly complained of a shortage of workers.

Just as they competed with one another over scarce materials and human resources, construction managers also sought to overcome the labor shortage by mobilizing the existing workforce in staged competitions. The vysotniki working on one site, for example, would routinely engage in a "socialist competition" with those on another in a race to see who could build their skyscraper the fastest. Similarly, brigades might compete with one another on the same construction site to reach unreasonably high production quotas. In this arena, the role of the Communist Party was key.

LOCATING COMMUNISM ON THE CONSTRUCTION SITE

As Iakov Tsytsarkin, a mason working on MGU, put it in 1952, the university skyscraper was being constructed "for the happiness of the people, in the name of the radiant future—communism."[34] The local Communist Party office on the MGU site would have approved of this sentiment. It worked tirelessly to strengthen the thread linking communism to the construction site. But to the frustration of local party officials, the Tsytsarkins were few and far between. Instead, Communist Party leaders found that few workers conformed to the model communist builder and that not all communist members set good examples for the rest. Reconciling the skyscraper project with communism was a constant struggle in the final years of the Stalin era.

Local Communist Party organizations were active on each building site, with construction managers, along with architects and engineers, incessantly working to mobilize workers (fig. 6.13). Construction managers and architects also attended regular party meetings to discuss a wide range of issues, from workers' morale to workers' housing. One of the key problems that skyscraper building managers faced was the considerable challenge of motivating workers to fulfill, even over-fulfill, construction quotas. One approach was to offer higher wages and better housing to Stakhanovites, shock workers, and the highly skilled Engineer-Technical Workers (*Inzhenerno-tekhnicheskie rabotniki* or ITRs).[35] This practice, dating to the 1930s, was used widely on USDS construction sites, where Stakhanovites in 1950 saw their wages reach up to about 1,400 rubles a month—a sum three or so times greater than that received by the average worker.[36] But skyscraper construction managers also relied on their local communist party offices to provide the spiritual motivation that, they hoped, would counteract the lack of productivity among a largely disunited, unskilled, and resentful workforce. As Prokof'ev at the USDS put it in 1947, it was the local party office's job to "work on the political education of our cadres and above all to raise party propaganda to the level of the tasks set before them, to cultivate love and patriotism."[37]

Despite the high level of communist party activity on each construction site, only a small minority of vysotniki were themselves members of the Communist Party. In 1951, the construction site on Uprising Square had 704 workers of whom 38 were communists; on the Red Gates site communist party members made up just three percent of all workers.[38] The numbers on the MGU site were similar: in 1951, 656 party members participated in the local party office out of a total of 23,495 workers engaged on the building site.[39] And so, in addition to holding regular party meetings for card-holding members, local party leaders also sought to shore up the ideological and political education of others in the hopes that they too would opt for party membership.

To this end, various activities were organized both on the construction site and in workers' living spaces. In 1949, the party office at the Red Gates construction site reported on a study circle organized for workers who were reading the Short Course on the History of the Communist Party. Fifteen communists and fourteen non-party construction managers and Stakhanovites attended the study circle. In the end, two of those who attended had, a report determined, "raised their political level" enough to become party candidates, in hopes of one day joining the party as full-fledged members.[40]

In theory, a worker's membership in the Communist Party was directly related to their performance on the construction site. As an official from the Red Gates party office put it in 1949, "the communists of our party organization play a vanguard role in production, serving as examples for the entire collective."[41] But in practice, the correlation between party membership and work ethic proved difficult to guaran-

Figure 6.13: Architect Lev Rudnev speaking on the construction site of Moscow State University, 1949. USDS Head Aleksandr Komarovskii is standing in the foreground on the right. The sign reads: "At a high caliber and ahead of schedule we build the hearthstone of world culture–Moscow State University." Collection of the Moscow City Archive GBU "TsGA Moskvy."

tee. The Red Gates party office in particular struggled to maintain the truth of its pronouncements. Communist party member Khabarov, who worked on the Red Gates site, over-fulfilled construction targets each month by 140–180%. Another party member, Ovchinnikov, similarly over-fulfilled the plan, for his part by 120–160%. Yet, while their productivity was laudable, the party office found that this pair nonetheless "worked poorly as agitators."[42]

Khabarov and Ovchinnikov were not alone in their low level of agitational work. Comrade Malyshev, another party member working on the Red Gates skyscraper, regularly overfulfilled production quotas, but the party office still saw him as not just a poor agitator but an all-out embarrassment. Malyshev's rudeness and aggressive behavior seemed at odds with his productivity. The party office grew so concerned about this worker's conduct among his fellow laborers that it issued a "severe party reprimand" to Malyshev. But even this seemed to have no effect. Not only did Malyshev continue to insult his fellow workers on the construction site, but "in gross violation of party and work discipline," he reportedly began to drink heavily while at work.[43] The Red Gates party office complained in 1949 that all attempts to set Malyshev straight were unsuccessful. This party office was not alone in finding that its best workers were not necessarily good communists.

Both on and off the construction site, local party organizations tried to encourage better behavior among workers by connecting with them through "mass-agitational work." Each construction site contained spaces that were marked as distinctly communist, and in addition to lectures and study circles the party offices staged agitational conversations and printed agitational newspapers. In addition to agitation in the workplace, dormitories and housing districts were to have newspaper walls, "red corners," and, if possible, workers' clubs. On May Day holidays and October Revolution anniversaries, local party offices organized the celebrations. Other holidays were also marked by communist party activism. In 1949, for example, on the occasion of Stalin's seventieth birthday, the USDS party office organized a range of activities, including a lecture on "Stalin the Great Successor of Lenin" in the red corner in the workers' dorm in the Zariad'e. They held a youth night at the USDS workers' club and a readers' conference on the theme of "The Image of Comrade Stalin in Artistic Literature." On this occasion, party leaders also read excerpts from Stalin's biography in the red corners of the Zariad'e, Izmailovo, and Luzhniki workers' districts.[44]

Despite all of these activities and efforts, local party officials still struggled in their attempts to reach workers. While the party wished to intervene in ordinary workers' daily lives, it more often than not stood at a distance from day-to-day activities. When party bosses bothered to look, they found that those in charge of "mass-agitational work" tended to avoid workers' homes and private spaces entirely. The USDS party office noted in 1948 that agitation in the dorms of the Zariad'e construction workers was "being carried out unsatisfactorily."[45] The dorms had no radios, no newspapers or magazines, no games, no mobile libraries, and the red corner—that primary space "for carrying out mass-political work"—was non-existent.[46] In 1949, the USDS party office reported on similar problems in its workers' districts throughout the city. Taken together, USDS workers' housing was not only lacking mass-political activities and red corners; living conditions in the material sense were abysmal.

The blame on all fronts for failures in USDS workers' housing fell squarely on the shoulders of two officials: G. I. Gulynin, head of the USDS housing office (zhilishchno-kommunal'nyi otdel or ZhKO), and Comrade Evstigneeva, the chief party organizer in affairs relating to the ZhKO. In late 1949, the party office reprimanded Gulynin and Evstigneeva. "In knowing about the unbelievable crowding in the dormitories," Evstigneeva was chastised for not having "sent signals to the party office [and] not bringing these questions for discussion during meetings." She had also "not intervened in the needs of the workers and had not taken an interest in their daily living conditions," thereby covering up Gulynin's negligence.[47] But reprimands did not immediately solve the problem and the USDS continued to face challenges in upholding even the most basic levels of cleanliness—let alone communist party agitation—in workers' housing districts.

It was in their mass-agitational work on the construction site that the local party offices were, by their own measures, more successful. By the summer of 1950, workers had built the steel frame of the university building on the Lenin Hills up to a height of one hundred meters. As V. Grushkin recalled, the builders were now faced with the question of how to carry bricks and other construction materials up to the top of the structure. Grushkin was head of the party organization on the MGU construction site. According to his account of these events, published in 1952, it was the communist construction workers who came up with the solution, requesting permission to borrow one of the tower cranes in use elsewhere on the site.[48]

The crane operators agreed, but the work would have to be done quickly. "Many builders remember the enormous poster that was hung on the construction site," wrote Grushkin. "Comrade Builders!" it said, "Standing on the Stakhanovite Watch for Peace and intensifying our working day, we, the Zhvoronkov, Skomarov, and Repetskii brigades, are undertaking to free up our crane for the duration of one shift in order to move no less than 20 thousand bricks in a day. We call on the builders to ensure that these bricks are laid on the walls of the Palace of Science!" As Grushkin recalled, this call to arms was also published in the construction site's newspaper, *Stroitel' Universiteta* (*The University Builder*). The bricklayers came through, Grushkin wrote. Next, they would "fulfill their obligation to finish building the walls by the end of the year," building right up to the twenty-sixth floor of the new university.[49]

The Stakhanovite Watch was a frequently-employed and exhausting form of worker mobilization that was often carried out in honor of an important event or cause. Workers were required to heroically push themselves to the limit, working ceaselessly until an unreasonably high production quota was met. On this occasion in 1950, the backbreaking labor of MGU's bricklayers was carried out in honor of the activities of the World Peace Council, an international organization founded by the Cominform in 1948. Over on the Red Gates construction site, workers similarly pledged their support of this cause (fig. 6.14). The World Peace Council's activities were all over the news in the summer of 1950, as were the numerous Stakhanovite Watches for Peace being carried out at the time in factories and on building sites throughout the Soviet Union.[50]

There were other ways to motivate builders to work overtime as well. Socialist competitions (*sotsialisticheskie sorevnovaniia,* or simply *sots-sorevnovaniia*) were held between brigades of workers on the same construction site, or between workers across different sites. In July 1949, vysotniki building the Kotel'nicheskaia residential skyscraper entered into a socialist competition with those building the administrative skyscraper on Smolensk Square. The competition was announced ritualistically, with specific targets set down on paper and signed by construction managers, party bosses, Stakhanovites, and brigade leaders. "We, the builders of the MVD USSR," the Kotel'nicheskaia pledge began, "workers, ITRs, and administrators, are proud of the honorable tasks entrusted in us by the state for the construction of one of the first tall buildings in Moscow."[51] The Kotel'nicheskaia workers pledged to fulfill the year's construction plan, while also undertaking additional work. Instead of raising just ten stories of steel frame by the end of the year, as the plan called for, the vysotniki would over-fulfill the plan by building an additional two stories, making it up to twelve altogether by year's end.

While this kind of mobilization ensured that the skyscrapers would arrive more quickly on Moscow's horizon, the impact on workers' health and morale was less inspiring. In late 1949, Beria's office reported that on the Smolensk Square construction site, between July and October of that year alone, there had been twenty-one injuries and accidents. Though Beria's secretary could not confirm it, an anonymous letter had arrived alerting them to the fact that there had also been "accidents with fatal outcomes."[52] Although accidents and injuries were rarely reported to those at the top, dangerous working conditions were a major concern affecting health, safety, and morale at every skyscraper construction site.

Figure 6.14: "On the construction site of the tall building at the Red Gates. Collecting signatures in support of the World Peace Council on the conclusion of a Peace Pact between the five great powers." Moscow, September 8, 1951. Photograph by Valentin Konstantinovich Khukhlaev. Collection of the Museum of Moscow.

The workers who labored to make Moscow monumental in the late Stalin period may have been driven in part by the desire to contribute to the "building of communism," but many were also motivated simply by the need to earn a wage. While construction was one of the Soviet Union's major spheres of priority after the war, wages in this area were low compared to other sectors: in metallurgy and coal mining, for example, wages were on average twice as high.[53] Yet, while poorly paid, construction workers depended on this income to eke out a basic living.

Officials from the local Communist Party offices that dotted Moscow's construction sites worked hard to bring the vysotniki together under the banner of communism, but few factors helped unite the collective more than the issue of pay. On October 12, 1948, three workers' brigades—48 people in total—refused to show up for work. The workers did not report for their shifts in Kuntsevo, where they were building a housing district for the USDS. And when the USDS party office met to discuss the situation two days later, one brigade was still absent. There was some debate at the meeting about whether to refer to this as an instance of "mass absenteeism" (*massovyi nevykhod*) or whether to use the more serious term "strike" (*zabastovka*). But there was no doubt what had caused this collective action: the workers were not being properly paid.

For months, the USDS accountant had been making mistakes, reducing workers' already low wages significantly. Groups of workers had brought their complaints to management, but nothing had been done. Instead, the workers were met with hostility from their boss, a Comrade Iung, who responded rudely, calling them "unmentionable words" too obscene to be repeated at the party meeting.[54] USDS officials worked quickly to fix the problem and to get the work going again on the construction site. But the workers' actions showed that those building the premiere structures of the Stalin era were sometimes willing to take great risks to improve their meager lot, especially when empowered by their place in the broader collective.

EVERYTHING IS MORE VISIBLE FROM THE TOP

Moscow's vysotniki were celebrated in the popular press of the late-Stalin era. As a collective, they were hailed as heroes of the sky—men and women who skillfully braved the elements in the pursuit of impossible heights. By the early 1950s, it was the notion that these workers had gained a new outlook on Moscow, and on the Soviet Union more broadly, that most captured the imaginations of Soviet journalists. The underlying assumption was that the gigantic skyscrapers that were rising taller by the day on Moscow's cityscape would make the world more legible. As the rest of Moscow gazed up at the skyscrapers, the vysotniki peered down, seeing their country in a new way.

Iakov Usov was featured in a 1952 issue of *Ogonek* magazine, interviewed while at work atop the Uprising Square building alongside his younger apprentice. Holding a masonry pick in his right hand, Usov was photographed for *Ogonek* while gazing out at the city below. Behind them, the silhouette of a second skyscraper was just visible through the fog in the background of the photograph. As *Ogonek* explained,

> each morning, setting to work, Iakov Grigor'evich sees Moscow before him, lively and noisy, despite the early hour. And the building-giants, like watchmen, tower over her. They stand at different ends of the great city—on Smolensk [Square], the Lenin Hills, Kotel'nicheskaia embankment, the squares of three train stations, at the Red Gates. Usov himself works at the top of yet another tall building that is growing on Uprising Square.[55]

Before arriving in Moscow to work as a vysotnik, Usov had spent four years rebuilding Stalingrad. Though he started out on Uprising Square as a mason, when the brickwork was finished Usov requested that he be allowed to train anew as a facing expert (*oblitsovshchik*). He would train with the brigades at MGU before returning to work on the façade of the Uprising Square building. From high up in the air, Usov would spend the years of late Stalinism gazing down on Moscow, admiring the view from the top.

While vysotniki like Usov were regularly featured in state and party newspapers of the postwar years, each skyscraper construction site also had its own newspaper dedicated to exclusive coverage of vysotnik affairs. On the Uprising Square building site, the wall newspapers *Vysotnik* and *Molodoi vysotnik* (*Young Vysotnik*) were printed monthly.[56] At the Red Gates site, the newspaper *Mnogoetazhnik* (*The High-riser*) was, in 1949, only issued "from time to time," though party officials pledged to do better.[57] Over at MGU—the building site with the largest number of workers—the most important paper was *Stroitel' universiteta* (*The University Builder*). A number of wall newspapers were also posted in common areas on the MGU site for workers to read. As propaganda tools of the local communist party offices, construction site newspapers were intended to motivate and inspire workers. In 1951, the *University Builder* was credited with playing a "significant part in disseminating the progressive role of the best Stakhanovites on the construction site."[58] Occasionally, the newspaper's stories were shared with a broader audience, as articles and other content from the *University Builder* were reprinted in the national Soviet news outlets.

The editorial office of the *University Builder* was located directly on the university construction site, in a temporary building in the so-called Fifth Settlement—a ramshackle collection of administrative buildings and offices that would disappear once the skyscraper was completed. The newspaper office, dwarfed by the gigantic structure emerging on the horizon nearby, was a squat, unremarkable single-story wood structure with tiny windows in brown wooden frames. The building may have been nondescript, but the vysotniki knew exactly where to find it, and they dropped in regularly to report their accomplishments and to submit their own poems and essays to be published in the paper. As the writers of the newspaper *Sovetskaia kul'tura* described it in 1953,

> you would not find this little building in the thousands of photographs and drawings printed daily in the country's newspapers, or in the articles and essays that describe completely, in minute detail, not only what was and what is on the Lenin Hills, but also what will be. The crowded excursions [to the site] do not visit this little building. And yet, from the first days of construction on the university, during the heated workdays, builders have often come down here—masons and carpenters, electricians and stuccoists, assemblers and parquet layers, drivers and workers of all kinds. They come in and share the joy that they take in their victories at work.[59]

It was a small editorial office and workers often relayed their accomplishments and adventures to Matvei Kriukov, the editor of the paper.

In addition to running articles that celebrated workers' achievements, newspapers like the *University Builder* also set about exposing faulty work and mismanagement on the construction site. In the spirit of the "criticism and self-criticism" that one would find at a local communist party meeting, the writers for the local newspaper saw it as their duty to report on mistakes, mismanagement, and corruption. Writers for the construction site newspapers did not need to go far to find content for these investigative reports. This sort of content, in fact, came straight to them from the many workers eager to voice their discontent. The *University Builder* in particular was known for its "real and easy-to-understand content" that, as one party report put it, "attracted a significant number of readers." Receiving around 200 letters a month from its readers, the *University Builder* played an important role in adjudicating worker complaints and publicizing instances of corruption and negligence reported by readers.[60] As V. Grushkin, the head of the party organization at MGU, put it in 1952, construction site newspapers informed vysotniki about the accomplishments of their "comrades in labor," but also served as a mechanism for circulating criticism against "careless workers."[61]

It was not just workers who found themselves targeted in the vysotnik press. An exposé published in the *University Builder* in early 1950 led to an immediate communist party investigation of Maria M. Goberman, who worked in the office of the USDS design department. The local party office confirmed a number of the accusations made in the newspaper, finding Goberman guilty of having made serious errors in payroll accounting, having dispatched the design office's courier to pick up her groceries, and having assigned the design office's cleaner to wash the floors in her apartment.[62] The party office also pinned blame on Boris Iofan, head architect of the USDS. Not only had Iofan failed to maintain careful oversight of Goberman, but he had regularly awarded her unmerited bonuses.[63] Few on the skyscraper construction sites were shielded from the scrutiny of the muckraking vysotnik press.

Construction site newspapers like the *University Builder* were tools used primarily to motivate workers to fulfill their quotas, thereby making monumental Moscow a reality all the more swiftly. Alongside the ritual celebration of builders' accomplishments, the journalists and editors of these newspapers worked to subvert hierarchies in their reporting, giving their vysotnik-readers a greater sense of power and control. Articles like the one published about Maria Goberman in 1950 used folksy adages and moralizing tones to harp on the failings of a favorite target of the Stalin era: the bureaucrat. Against the grueling reality of work on the skyscraper construction site, stories that took administrators and even party leaders down a peg or two could only be good for morale.

By late 1951, the university building was taking shape. The thirty-fourth anniversary of the October Revolution was celebrated on the Lenin Hills that year with great fanfare. The skyscraper itself was illuminated, its gold star lit up brightly for the first time, and an enormous portrait of Stalin was hung along the building's façade. In an article written for the occasion by the *University Builder* and printed for a wider readership in *Krokodil*, writers and workers summed up the accomplishments and shortcomings of this monumental building project. The heroic undertaking had almost been accomplished. The skyscraper had almost been built. And yet, there was a sense among the vysotniki that work was not proceeding at a quick enough pace. In this article, titled "Up to the Mark," the *University Builder*'s editors explained that they had set out "to clarify the question of what is up to the mark and what is not."[64]

"Up to the Mark" was written jointly by *University Builder* editor Matvei Kriukov, his coworker at the paper B. Turovetskii, and the popular Soviet satirical writer Leonid Lench. Their article combined the denunciatory elements typical of the *University Builder* with the humor of *Krokodil*.[65] For these three writers, the answer to the first part of their question—what was "up to the mark" at the MGU site—was obvious. It was the university building, of course: "there she is, up to the mark—the thirty-eight-story central part of this grandiose building, topped by a spire with a shining star!" This star, they continued, was visible for all to see, shining "as a symbol of labor and peacefulness."[66] Also worthy of praise were the Stakhanovites on the construction site. And it was to them—to the "famous steeplejack" Aleksandr Patrikeev, and to the very same modeler who carved the star atop MGU, Sergei Solomentsev—that these writers turned to for advice on where to find what was "not up to the mark." "It all depends on your point of view," the Stakhanovites replied.

Just as Moscow's monumental new buildings spoke loudly to the people below, so too could the modelers and façade-shapers of these structures speak volumes from their elevated positions up top. The point of view of Solomentsev and his fellow vysotniki was that there were many aspects of the construction project that were not "up to the mark." "For us, from our thirty-eight-story 'mountain,'" they stated, "we can see a lot. We see our suppliers, Muscovites, Ukrainians, and Belorussians: you know, the entire country is building MGU, and building it superbly! And we clearly notice which factory suppliers are up to the mark," they wrote, "and which are not."

According to Solomentsev and his fellow Stakhanovites, the university building's suppliers were often lacking in both enthusiasm and ability. Over at the Moscow factory for asphalt slabs, the director had apparently received a large order from MGU and "immediately burst into tears: 'We won't manage it! How could we?! They want non-standard slabs . . . come on! Release us from this, please!'" the factory director cried. As a result of his whining, claimed the Stakhanovites, the asphalt factory director was relieved of part of that order. In response, the university builders took their concerns to the Ministry of Industrial Construction Materials, but to no effect. This Ministry, the Stakhanovites said, had forgotten "the good Russian expression: 'Moscow does not believe in tears.'"[67]

In this article of 1951, the Stakhanovites listed others who were also "not up to the mark." They named so many that the writers eventually asked them to stop: "'That's enough!' we said, 'That's enough for now. But how can we find a solution to this?'"[68] According to Solomentsev and the others, the solution was for all to work together. "Up to the Mark" ended on a happy collectivist note, but the article's unflattering portrayal of faltering supply chains and sniveling bureaucrats hinted at very real grievances felt across Moscow's eight skyscraper construction sites.

HOUSING THE VYSOTNIKI

While they spent their days building Moscow's monumental new skyscrapers, the vysotniki made homes on the city's outskirts, their lives spilling out beyond the frame of architects' carefully drawn sketches for the Soviet capital. Many of the vysotniki working on the hotel on Komsomol Square lived in a few dozen two-story wood buildings in the southeast region of Liublino. Others from that construction site were assigned to dozens of two- and three-story buildings in the eastern suburb of Ismailovo.[69] Workers from the Kotel'nicheskaia building also lived in Ismailovo, as did some building MGU and the skyscraper on the Zariad'e.[70] Still more vysotniki from the MGU and Zariad'e sites lived in Khlebnikovo to the north, Kuntsevo to the west, and Cheremushki and Ramenka to the southwest.[71] Remnants of these settlements linger in Moscow today, like the vysotnik House of Culture, which still stands on Ramenka Street, its portico and pediment newly restored.

If skyscraper building in the capital was based, as the claim went, on the latest technologies and advances in building, the construction of workers' housing drew by contrast on the simplified materials and rapid construction methods of the war-time years. Workers were housed in wooden huts like the forty or so built in Cheremushki, in stone houses like those built in Tekstil'shchiki, and in yurts like those in Luzhniki.[72] On the whole, the vysotniki lived in deplorable conditions, with many of them appealing to state officials to intervene with construction and housing managers on their behalf.

Nadezhda A. Shuliakovskaia lived in the USDS workers' district in Cheremushki, a village located southwest of Moscow, just beyond city limits. Not far from the construction site of the new university, the housing in Cheremushki had been designated specially for workers with families. On paper, at least, the region was built to include a workers' club, a banya, a clinic, and a nursery. There was also a school for up to four hundred children, like those of Nadezhda Shuliakovskaia.[73] This school would prove to be a sore spot for the vysotniki and their families.

The Cheremushki school had been built by 1950, but in the summer of 1952, it had yet to open its doors to students. Instead, the school was being used as a storage space for the high-quality, expensive furniture destined for Moscow State University. In the place of four hundred students sat 4,530 chairs, tables, and office sets.[74] By 1952, the vysotnik-parents of Cheremushki were irate. "I have four children who go to school in the city—to different schools," Shuliakovskaia and her husband wrote to Beria in August 1952. In Cheremushki a school had been built, "but it is not open," they wrote. "What is the reason for this?" they asked, rhetorically. "It is closed," they explained, "because MGU has turned it into a warehouse for furniture. And because of this, our children must again walk in the winter through the city to different schools kilometers away." The "Shuliakovskii Parents," as they signed their letter, asked Beria to do everything in his power to ensure that the school be emptied of furniture and made ready for the upcoming school year.[75]

Sergei I. Verzilin, another Cheremushki resident, was also angry. He wrote to Beria on the same day as the Shuliakovskiis. Verzilin's son Leonid was also forced to walk to a school many kilometers away, in his case in rubber boots that were needed to wade through two ravines. These ravines were always full of water, Verzilin explained to Beria, and Leonid would return home late, at 9 o'clock at night, wet and muddy. "Not just once has he fallen into the water and mud," wrote Verzilin. "And it is not only my child," Verzilin continued, there were hundreds of children who could not go to their local school because it was being used as a storage space for MGU.[76] While their parents worked hard to build the Soviet Union's premiere university, the children trekked long distances to school through the muddy outskirts of Moscow. In all likelihood, the children used the tall steel frame of Moscow State University in the distance to orient themselves through the marshy tracks of *podmoskov'e*.

In addition to the complaints sent by parents, the Cheremushki school's director had also written to the Kremlin, pleading for the school to be opened for the 1952–1953 academic year. In the end, these complaints were delegated to USDS head Aleksandr Komarovskii. Komarovskii was having none of it. The furniture would stay where it was, he decided, until it could be moved into MGU, at the earliest at the end of 1952. In his report back to the Council of Ministers on the issue, Komarovskii suggested that the younger children could attend the middle schools for girls and boys located not far from the workers' settlement in Cheremushki.[77]

Like the Muscovites displaced from the Zariad'e, the skyscraper workers living in Cheremushki raised their voices in protest on a range of issues from access to schools to lack of cleanliness and poor amenities. Workers also complained to top Soviet officials about middle managers, often using the bygone trope of the "beneficent Tsar." The two men ultimately in charge of housing MGU's workers—and therefore those ultimately to blame, in the eyes of workers and their families—were USDS chief Komarovskii and G. I. Gulynin, manager of the USDS housing office. As Moscow's skyscraper builders knew, Beria and other top Soviet officials could, and sometimes did, overrule decisions made by Komarovskii and Gulynin. This intervention could take a legalistic form when top officials forwarded a worker's appeal to the offices of the state procurator, who had the power to intervene through the force of Soviet law. But intervention could also be improvised and personal, stemming from an arbitrary act of mercy on the part of an official who held the power to overrule a decision already made below. Nataliia M. Gotovskaia took this second, more personal, approach, at least initially.

In late December 1952, Gotovskaia wrote to Beria appealing for help in settling a disagreement she was having with the USDS housing office. Gotovskaia had taken up residence in Moscow illegally with her husband, Ivan F. Korolev—a Gulag inmate sent from Karaganda to Moscow in 1950 to work on the construction of MGU. A former Gulag inmate herself, Gotovskaia had brought her two young children all the way to Moscow from Karaganda in 1951 so that they could be reunited with Korolev.[78] Gotovskaia had moved to Moscow without permits or permission. Her husband worked as a modeler, and she too was trying to find work for herself on the MGU site—work that would come with housing. Gotovskaia explained all of this in her letter to Beria in December 1952. In asking him to help her find both work and housing, Gotovskaia pleaded with Beria not to allow her family to be split up. "I beg you," she wrote, "not to make orphans of my children and my children ask you to allow them to live with their father, so that our children will be happy . . ."[79] Beria forwarded Gotovskaia's letter to Komarovskii, who agreed to find Gotovskaia work on the construction site and family housing in the Cheremushki district.[80] It seemed to Gotovskaia that her ordeal was finally over.

Within days of the decision, Komarovskii's deputy at the USDS, Aleksei V. Voronkov, wrote to his boss to share his concerns. Already familiar with Gotovskaia, Voronkov informed the USDS chief that Gotovskaia was not to be trusted. For one thing, Voronkov wrote, her marriage to Korolev was not registered and they were therefore not legally a family qualifying for family housing. For another, Gotovskaia did not hold a valid permit allowing her to live in Moscow.[81] In fact, she had not been working or registered anywhere for over a year. But beyond these established facts, Voronkov had done some digging of his own. Having found another Gulag worker from the same camp in Karaganda, Voronkov reported that not only did Gotovskaia have a "real" husband back in Kazakhstan, she was also the daughter of kulaks who had been sent to Karaganda in 1929–30.[82] On the basis of this new information, Komarvoskii reversed his earlier decision.

Gotovskaia was desperate to remain in Moscow, but her luck was quickly running out. Losing hope, she wrote to Beria once again. In her second letter, Gotovskaia mobilized the full force of Soviet rhetoric, appealing to Beria "as an uncle" to ask for his permission to stay in Moscow. Gotovskaia knew that Komarovskii had initially permitted her to stay in the capital, granting her both work and housing, but that his subordinates had intervened against her. Recounting her negative experiences with officials at the USDS housing office, Gotovskaia complained that the administrators there lacked all compassion. In her interactions with them, Gotovskaia had been mocked for her poor level of literacy and reproached for thinking herself worthy of living in Moscow. Perhaps they were right and "I am really not a Soviet woman," she wrote, and "it is really forbidden [for me] to arrive in our beautiful capital of Moscow, in which the beloved uncle of all the people, Iosif Vissarionovich Stalin, lives."[83] Gotovskaia well understood that exile from Moscow would reflect the level of value attributed to her by the Soviet state. In the end, Beria seemed to agree with the housing office's characterization of Gotovskaia. She and her children were sent back to Karaganda, far from Moscow.[84]

Nataliia Gotovskaia was one voice among many connecting the skyscraper construction site to the world around it. This wife and mother from Karaganda moved across boundaries that were supposed to be fixed, revealing in the process just how porous the lines were between Moscow and the world beyond, between worker and civilian, and between Gulag and non-Gulag. Although construction managers and housing administrators struggled to maintain dominance over their domains, Moscow's skyscraper project was too monumental to fully control. Each skyscraper was like a whirlwind casting matter outward while also pulling new forces into the capital.

THE URBAN GULAG

The USDS began using Gulag labor for skyscraper construction in Moscow in 1948. Already in October 1947, Andrei Prokof'ev, then head of the USDS, had written to Beria requesting that the MVD allocate 4,900 inmates (*spetskontingenty*) to help build MGU. Prokof'ev informed Beria that the USDS faced an "acute shortage" of labor and he noted the speed with which the skyscrapers were to be constructed.[85] As Prokof'ev envisioned it, the majority of these *zeks* (inmates) brought in to strengthen the labor force would live and work near Moscow—2,000 in Kuntsevo and 1,500 at Vodniki station in Moscow oblast'. The rest would work at the USDS's lumber camps in Kirovskaia oblast' and Kostromskaia oblast'. Prokof'ev's early request that the skyscraper on the Lenin Hills be built by forced labor was just the beginning of a longer institutional relationship forged between the USDS and the Gulag. And when Komarovskii replaced Prokof'ev in October 1948 the USDS became inextricably tied to the Soviet Union's carceral system. This relationship was embodied in Komarovskii himself: while serving as head of the USDS, Komarovskii also retained his earlier post as head of Glavpromstroi (*Glavnoe upravlenie lagerei promyshlennogo stroitel'stva*)—the construction wing of the Gulag.[86]

There is, of course, a much longer history of the use of forced labor in construction work in and around Moscow. In her book *Building Stalinism*, Cynthia Ruder examines the Dmitlag camp that held over 198,000 forced laborers, or "canal soldiers," who built the Moscow-Volga Canal in the early 1930s.[87] In the postwar years, the number of construction projects built by Gulag laborers in the Soviet capital expanded.

Glavpromstroi, created in 1941, became a major force in Moscow's construction industry.[88] In Moscow, Glavpromstroi was not only active in the area of skyscraper building. By 1952, Glavpromstroi's construction office No. 560 oversaw thousands of prisoners working on thirty-four separate sites throughout the city.[89] In addition to a large number of USDS-related jobs, this work also included the construction of thermotechnical, electrothermal, and geochemical facilities for the Academy of Sciences and other research institutions in Moscow.[90]

That Moscow's skyscrapers were built in part by incarcerated laborers did not, then, make these sites unique. Rather, these prestigious buildings were nodes within a dense constellation of projects unachievable in the postwar years but for forced labor. By the late 1940s, there were multiple Glavpromstroi factories and construction offices involved in different capacities in Moscow's skyscraper project.[91] Glavpromstroi's Rybinsk factory No. 1 was tasked in 1949 with assembling the metal skeleton of the Kotel'nicheskaia skyscraper, while Glavpromstroi's construction office No. 833 (later renamed construction office No. 620) supplied workers to build MGU.[92] The larger construction office No. 90 (renamed construction office No. 560 in 1949 and amalgamated into office No. 565 in late 1952) was also engaged in building MGU, along with housing for workers in the nearby areas of Kuntsevo, Cheremushki, Tekstil'shchiki, and Vodniki.[93]

Glavpromstroi's presence in postwar Moscow ensured that the Gulag was not just a system "over there." The number of prisoners in this branch of the Gulag rose rapidly after the war and in addition to the large-scale industrial projects built by Glavpromstroi in remote regions of the country, the organization was also responsible for building hundreds of residential and cultural structures in urban areas where the lines between camp and city blurred. Although Gulag bosses took pains to maintain barriers between the "zones" that were inhabited by inmates and the outside world beyond, the physical proximity of regular and Gulag workers on the skyscraper construction sites was a stubborn reality. And along with the advanced skills that many of these inmates brought with them to the skyscraper construction site came their experiences of incarceration.

Maintaining a clear separation between Gulag "zones" and the city beyond them was, of course, most easily achieved on paper. A map of the MGU construction site created for internal use in 1949 shows an enclosed zone adjacent to the footprint of the future skyscraper.[94] In this image, a neatly fenced enclosure separates the prisoners from regular workers and included within the fenced zone are the physics and chemistry buildings of MGU—structures built by Gulag workers. The inmates who worked on MGU lived close to the construction site, in a camp built for 3,000 people. In 1950, the camp would be expanded to accommodate 8,000.[95] Still more housing was set up to accommodate this growing population near Cheremushki and Tekstil'shchiki—locations that were also home to both regular construction workers and to Muscovites displaced from the Zariad'e.[96]

A steady flow of Gulag workers arrived on the MGU site through the early 1950s. In May 1951, the Council of Ministers issued an order intended to strengthen the university construction effort. The order called for new workers to be brought into Moscow from technical schools across the country and requested an additional 2,000 prisoners for work on the site. The latter would include first-time offenders only, except those convicted of especially dangerous crimes.[97] With this influx of workers—both incarcerated and not—arriving on site, officials worked to stem the flow of people, goods, and information between zone and city. Reports filed by camp bosses in May 1952 describe wooden fences, guards, gates, and watchtowers at three camps on the Lenin Hills that held collectively over 7,000 men and women. A fourth camp in Tekstil'shchiki was similarly zoned in and housed nearly a thousand men and women. And at a fifth MGU camp at the village of Karacharovo to the east, 1,376 men were housed.[98] An additional camp, named the "Vysotnyi," was set up on the twenty-third floor of MGU. There, 208 female and 160 male prisoners lived in the rooms and corridors of the unfinished building while they worked on completing the upper floors of the skyscraper. While they ate in cafeterias set up on the top floors of the building, these inmates would have to descend to one of the camps below in order to wash.[99]

While the MGU and Kotel'nicheskaia construction sites were divided between *zeks* and regular workers, there were also gradations in between. The zoned landscape of skyscraper labor was further complicated by the nearly 2,000 prisoners granted early release by the MVD on June 24, 1950 in exchange for building Moscow's skyscrapers.[100] This group would work on the university construction site for the remainder of their sentence, or until the building was completed. Those chosen for early release were to already possess skills needed on the construction site and they could only be selected from the ranks of first-time offenders. Beyond these requirements, the MVD issued a list of the crimes that, if committed, would exclude a prisoner from qualifying for the skyscraper posting. While someone convicted of the abuse of power or position (Article 109) would qualify for early release, someone convicted of embezzlement (Article 116) would not. A conviction of theft of personal property (Article 165) made the inmate ineligible, unless what had been stolen was horses or livestock (Article 166). And an individual charged with military crimes, such as desertion, could qualify, unless the conviction was for passing information to a foreign government, enemy army, or counter-revolutionary organization (Article 193, point 24). Special settlers, Vlasovites, and counterrevolutionaries, as a rule, were ineligible.[101]

In the end, finding enough skilled builders who had committed the "right" kind of crimes proved difficult. MVD officials complained that this was too tall an order, and out of the millions of prisoners who were in the Gulag system at that time, they turned over a few hundred workers fewer than the 2,000 requested.[102] Of the 1,774 individuals released in 1950 and transferred to Moscow, many would never arrive on the MGU site. In some cases, the opportunity to flee was too great. This was the case with a dozen of the newly freed, who simply took this as an opportunity to run away. A further thirty-four people from the group were arrested soon after their arrival in Moscow. And then there were the seventy-nine individuals who were not permitted to enter Moscow when they arrived, due to passport restrictions. This last group would be sent on to serve out their "early release" in the gold-mining industries instead.[103]

Those newly freed builders who did arrive in Moscow in the late summer months of 1950 came from all corners of the country. By nationality, the group included Russians, Bulgarians, Ukrainians, and Azerbaijanis. They came from places as far away as the Molotov oblast' in the Urals, the Altai Krai in Siberia, and the Odessa oblast' in the Ukrainian SSR.[104] Though there was at least one watchmaker and one zoo technician among them, many came to the site, as requested, already skilled in construction. Nikolai Mikhailovich Svernik, for example, had worked previously on the construction of the closed resort town of Tskaltubo in Georgia. Helpfully, from the perspective of the foremen on the construction site, there were many young men in this group, like Aleksei Grigor'evich Maksimov, born in the Leningrad oblast'. At 23 years old in 1949, Maksimov was sentenced to five years' imprisonment near Stavropol' for failing to report for active duty. Maksimov joined his brigade at MGU in February 1951, and by August he had distinguished himself as efficient and harder working than most. In his first summer in Moscow, Maksimov got married to a woman named Maria Ivanovna.[105]

Alongside Maksimov worked the plasterer Nurmukhamed Gudbaevich Gil'manov, who would be reprimanded for rudeness to the guards. Others would find themselves swept up in the penal system again, like Anatolii Sergeevich Shorokhov from Arkhangel'sk oblast' who was arrested by the Moscow city police for hooliganism. Many of these workers requested, and were sometimes granted, time off to visit ailing parents elsewhere in the country. In at least one case the mother of one of these builders wrote to MGU officials directly to inquire about her son. In June 1951, Zoya Palkina had not heard from her son for months. "As his mother, I am very worried about the health of my son," she wrote to the cadre office at MGU. "I ask you to write and tell me what is going on with him, where is he, is he even alive and healthy?" she begged to know.[106]

Ismail Guseinovich Sadarov, who had been imprisoned in 1947 in the North Ossetian ASSR for military desertion, also found his sentence commuted in 1950. Sadarov worked as a painter on the MGU site starting in September of that year. At twenty-six years old, he was described by his superiors on the university site as conscientious, disciplined, and efficient. A few months into his time in Moscow, in late December 1950, Sadarov received a letter from his mother in Baku. "I am glad that you are in Moscow," she wrote, "alive and healthy, working, just watch that you obey your bosses, work honestly, be an example," she advised.[107] Sadarov's mother had not seen her son in the decade since he had joined the army, and now although he was far away she needed his help. In her letter, Sadarov's mother asked him to see if he could take a short leave of absence to visit her in Baku. His presence would help her to resolve a dispute she was having with the other occupants of her apartment, who were trying to evict her. Sadarov was granted leave and spent the New Year's holidays back at home.

Receiving a commutation in exchange for work on the university skyscraper seemed to offer some a chance to reunite with family members. The bricklayer and brigade leader Sergei Ivanovich Tsarev appealed to MGU construction officials soon after arriving at the site in 1950 about his young son. Tsarev's wife had died during the war, leaving him with three nearly grown children and one young child. But when Tsarev was arrested in 1947, the boy was sent to a children's home (*detskii dom*). Now, having been released from the Gulag, Tsarev wished to fetch his son and bring him to Moscow, so that he himself could "raise and educate him."[108] While there is no indication in the file as to whether Tsarev was successful in his appeal, others like him did manage to bring their families to Moscow. Georgii Klement'evich Volynkin found accommodation while working on the MGU site for himself, his wife, and their two children. While Volynkin spent his days laying parquet flooring at the new university, he returned home each night to the abysmal living conditions of the USDS's women's dormitory at Cheremushki. In May 1953, Volynkin implored MGU officials to grant his family new housing. His request was denied.

Historians have long noted the porousness of the boundaries between Gulag "zones" and "ordinary" Soviet life—a feature of the country's forced labor system that became particularly evident in the postwar years.[109] The Gulag system grew to its largest size in the final years of the Stalin era, a period that also saw Soviet officials experimenting with ways to maximize the labor productivity of this system in order to meet the needs of postwar reconstruction. Moscow's postwar growth and expansion was heavily dependent on Gulag labor. In the years after 1945, a growing number of camps were built in and around Moscow, most supporting the city's building industry. By 1949, there were 31,692 Gulag prisoners in the Moscow oblast' alone.[110] Their growing presence on building sites throughout the capital was part of a larger trend by which the economic function of the Gulag trumped its punitive role. And as this happened—as economic imperatives outweighed efforts to isolate prisoners—a new type of relationship between the Gulag and the city emerged during the waning years of the Stalin era.

Did Gulag laborers and those workers granted early release in 1950 see themselves as vysotniki? Incarcerated workers certainly contributed, like regular workers on Soviet construction sites, to Moscow's "socialist reconstruction." As Anna Tsepkalova writes, "Gulag inmates, in the minds of camp authorities, were to become 'builders of a new society'."[111] The educational and corrective function of the camps was wrapped up in the act of building itself—an act that helped to reforge "'malicious transgressors of the regime' into 'people of a new epoch'."[112] Yet, while Gulag workers might have had the potential to remake themselves into iconic vysotniki, their accomplishments, as Tsepkalova notes, were neither celebrated nor showcased by state officials. Unlike their free vysotnik counterparts, the incarcerated workers who helped build MGU and the Kotel'nicheskaia skyscraper left behind not proud narratives of heroic feats, but faint traces of their experiences.

The GULAG History Museum in Moscow, founded in 2001, contains in its collection a piece of the Kotel'nicheskaia skyscraper. The slim board of wood that once made up part of a door jam in the building was reportedly found by a workman when renovating one of the apartments. The wooden fragment was deemed too precious to be thrown away because one of the skyscraper's incarcerated builders had inscribed a trace of his existence on it. "Astakhov Ivan Emel'ianovich," he had written in a spot on the underside of the wood where nobody would notice it:

> Year of birth 1896
> convicted by order to 10 years
> put finishing touches (*otdelyval*) on the tall building
> That is how we lived
> in this country (*vot kak my zhili v strane*).[113]

Three weeks after Stalin's death, on March 27, 1953, the Supreme Soviet ordered that an amnesty be granted to Gulag prisoners who "posed no great danger to the state."[114] With certain exceptions, the amnesty was granted to inmates whose sentences were less than five years, women who were pregnant and women with children under ten, anyone under the age of eighteen, men over fifty-five, and women over fifty. Amnesty was also granted to those who had been imprisoned for certain offenses while serving in the military or at work. The amnesty, along with two other events that closely followed it—the release and acquittal in April of the physicians arrested in the Doctors' Plot, and Beria's arrest in June—signaled, as Miriam Dobson writes, "the emergence of a new political culture, founded on the law (rather than a single leader's wisdom) and pride in the state's own 'humane' treatment of its citizens."[115]

Yet, while the amnesty ushered in profound political, social, and cultural changes in the first months of the post-Stalin era, for many of the Gulag workers building Moscow's skyscrapers amnesty, in the immediate moment at least, changed very little. With Moscow's skyscraper project still underway in March 1953, the amnesty threatened to slow the pace of construction. Many of the prisoners working on MGU were granted amnesty but were compelled to stay on in Moscow, working on the building site until the project's completion. Many of those whose sentences had been commuted also stayed on at the site. By September 1953, the university would, in any case, be completed.

REACHING NEW HEIGHTS

In June 1952, the Soviet writer Marietta Shaginian made her way from Moscow's Kiev station toward the Lenin Hills. She walked southward along the Moscow River embankment, past the large "Tets-12" electric power station, and then up into the hillside where the river loops back northward. She passed the little wooden houses of "semi-dacha type" that still dotted the Lenin Hills "but were already condemned." Up atop the hills, Shaginian felt a fresh breeze on her face as she took in the scene: "before me was a fantastic [*skazochnaia*] panorama of construction, on a scale that you have to first get used to." The scene was disorienting and exciting:

> You've just moved your eyes away from the little wooden houses with their two to three little windows, where 'suburban [*prigorodnye*] Muscovites' live, and there before you is a building that is impossible to take in as a whole, without directing your eyes from top to bottom, from right to left and from left to right.[116]

The enormous building was of course the new university skyscraper—a structure that appeared even larger than it was in its location on the elevated and desolate Lenin Hills.

After recovering from the initial feeling of vertigo—the "muscular reaction to the space," as Shaginian put it—the writer walked over to the small temporary wooden building on the site that housed the MGU Construction Office. On the second floor, Shaginian found who she was looking for: Sergei I. Balashov, the chief engineer of MGU, a "large, broad-shouldered, and hospitable" man who could tell the writer all that she wished to know about the new construction technology that was being used on the site and the effects that this technology was having on the vysotniki themselves.[117]

Figure 6.15: View of the Moscow State University construction site in July 1950, with the USDS construction offices in the foreground. Collection of the Moscow City Archive GBU "TsGA Moskvy."

This was not the first time that Shaginian had visited a major Soviet construction site. From 1926 to 1928, the writer had observed the Dzoraget hydroelectric plant in the Armenian SSR. Her involvement on that site was the basis for her production novel, *Gidrotsentral'*, published in 1931.[118] A symbolist poet before the revolution, Shaginian was drawn to large-scale engineering projects, for it was there that she felt closest to discovering the linkages between new technologies and the New Soviet Man. In 1952, Shaginian had done her research before arriving on the university construction site. In the weeks leading up to her expedition to MGU, Shaginian had read everything she could find about the construction of Moscow's skyscrapers and had cleared two weeks in her schedule to devote exclusively to observing Moscow's vysotniki. Shaginian was inspired to visit the site after reading the booklet of workers' experiences on MGU published that year—the same booklet with the young welder Martynov's memories of his first day of work.

And so, on that June day in 1952, Shaginian met with MGU's chief engineer for a half hour. He would be the first of many to greet Shaginian on the site, and though Chief Balashov was busy, he made time to sit down with the writer to answer some of her questions away from the mountains of papers, plans, and people who filled his office. Balashov rattled off some numbers as Shaginian took notes. Of particular importance were elements such as elevators. As Shaginian learned, there would be 108 elevators in the structure, 66 of which would serve the building's main corpus. These elevators would run seven to eight times faster than the average, so that it would not take long to travel from the first to the thirty-sixth floor.

But it was not just the engineering technology that was impressive. When speaking with the young workers on the site, Shaginian had the impression that the carpenters, masons, stuccoists, and painters before her had been transformed into entirely new people. Just as technology improved with each new Soviet building project, people too were elevated to new heights. There was no room in Shaginian's account of this experience for the labor camp on the twenty-third floor of the building or the Gulag zones on the ground below. This writer saw her world through the lens of socialist realism.

By the time that Shaginian climbed up the Lenin Hills in the early summer of 1952, the first of Moscow's skyscrapers were nearing completion. As the journal *Sovetskoe*

Figure 6.16: Skyscraper on Smolensk Square, 1952.
Collection of the State Central Museum of Contemporary Russian History.

iskusstvo (*Soviet Art*) announced in August 1952, "the 27-story building on Smolensk Square is ready! It is the first among the tall buildings of the capital to have been put into operation! . . . The large asphalt courtyard, not so long ago a construction yard, is decorated with posters glorifying the valiant work of the builder-vysotniki."[119] *Sovetskoe iskusstvo* gave an account of the opening ceremonies, at which workers of all types gathered together to celebrate with architects, state and party officials, and others invited from Moscow's factories. The terrace above one of the building's stairways was turned into a makeshift tribunal from which speeches were delivered and a banner was hung: "Glory to the Great Stalin!" There were many young workers present, the article noted, "for whom construction of the tall building was a serious school where they mastered new construction science and refined techniques, becoming highly-qualified master-vysotniki."[120]

In the coming years, similar ceremonies would be held at the other buildings as they were completed, one by one. As the next chapter will discuss, the Kotel'nicheskaia residential skyscraper would receive its new tenants in early 1953, followed quickly by the residential skyscraper at the Red Gates and later by the residential skyscraper on Uprising Square. Moscow State University would open its doors to students on September 1, 1953. During the early months of the post-Stalin era, both students and elites moved into the skyscrapers. These monuments that stood at the heart of the Stalinist vision for Moscow became useful, in ways beyond mere symbolism, right at the moment that Stalinism was beginning to fade from view.

7

THE VIEW FROM THE TOP

The Kotel'nicheskaia building, located just down the Moscow River from the Kremlin, was the first of the city's residential skyscrapers to be completed. Starting in late 1952, apartments in this highrise were given to members of the Soviet Union's cultural, scientific, and bureaucratic elite. At around the same time, apartments were also granted to these same groups of Soviet citizens in the nearly completed skyscraper at the Red Gates, located not far from a trio of railway stations in Moscow's northeast. Muscovites' dreams and desires of living in one of the capital city's skyscrapers can be found in hundreds of surviving letters. Written by high-ranking members of the city's elite and addressed to Soviet leaders, these letters offer a glimpse into the lives of the beneficiaries of the skyscraper project. They also afford us a view into the relationship between the Soviet state and the individuals who served it at the highest level in the postwar period. Just as Moscow's monumental skyscraper project prompted displaced residents to articulate their hopes and concerns to state officials, so too did the skyscrapers open up a discursive space in which elites could perform and reassert their higher status.

Hopeful skyscraper residents drew on rhetoric that was not unique to the postwar years. Like their non-elite counterparts, letter writers used patrimonial forms of address and mobilized personal networks in ways that harkened back to the pre-revolutionary era.[1] In their sense of entitlement to domestic comfort and their striving for a "cultured" way of life, writers drew on the mores of prewar Stalinism.[2] Yet, while in the 1930s, the high salaries and good apartments given to elites were, as Sheila Fitzpatrick writes, "only dimly reflected in the newspapers," in the postwar years, the privilege of this group had risen tall on the skyline for all to see.[3] As Vera Dunham notes, what made the late Stalin period distinct from the 1930s was that "the worker was now excluded" and a new partnership—what Dunham calls the "Big Deal"—was forged between the state and the professional class.[4] By 1953, this partnership had been made plainly visible on the capital's monumental new cityscape. The Moscow of high Stalinism had no qualms about flaunting the privileged status of its most elite residents.

The skyscraper project was a public celebration of luxury at a moment of widespread depravation. In their letters requesting skyscraper apartments, Stalin's postwar elites shared their dreams of living in healthy and happy homes. Yet, as this chapter explores, their letters also included detailed accounts of existing living conditions. A strong anti-urban critique weaves its way through these many descriptions of the squalid rooms and difficult lives of the Stalin era's top scientists, painters, and bureaucrats. These groups saw the skyscrapers as the antidote to a derelict and diseased urban space. But for most who hoped to receive a skyscraper apartment, their requests remained unfulfilled. In this city, home to the country's top bureaucrats, scientists, and artists, there were simply not enough apartments to go around.

ELITES AND ENTITLEMENTS UNDER STALIN

On October 12, 1952, Lily Brik wrote a letter to Lavrentii Beria requesting that she and her husband be permitted to trade their apartment in the Arbat for a place in one of Moscow's coveted new skyscrapers. Although she had been married since 1938 to literary critic Vasilii A. Katanian, Brik was known among friends and Soviet higher-ups alike as "Mayakovsky's wife." However inaccurately this described the former relationship between the futurist poet and his muse, the epithet was Brik's bargaining chip in her attempt to gain greater material comfort from the Soviet state. Brik's letter to Beria arrived quickly at the Council of Ministers, where it was routed to a special office handling the distribution of apartments in Moscow's new skyscrapers. Like so many others whose letters reached the apartment allocation office in the early 1950s, Brik appealed for new housing on the grounds of her continued contribution to Soviet intellectual life. Brik demonstrated her need for a new apartment by describing the inadequacy of her existing living conditions, and she further bolstered her request by noting the amount—and it was quite a substantial amount, for the time—of living space she had to trade. "Dear Comrade Beria, forgive me for bothering you," Brik began.

> I, (L. Iu. Brik) and the writer V. A. Katanian have lived for over twenty years in a very good apartment (71 square meters), the first monthly payment for which was made by V. V. Mayakovsky. We could not have dreamed for the rest of our days for a better apartment. *And yet, this apartment is on the fifth floor with no elevator.* Last year I developed severe heart disease and was laid up for several months. Now I suffer repeated seizures. *The doctor says that a fifth-floor apartment with no elevator will kill me.* Comrades who are already living in the tall building on the Kotel'nicheskaia embankment have told me that there are some 3-room apartments there still unoccupied. We would like to request that you not deny us permission to trade in our apartment for rooms on the first or second floor of that new building. It stands by the river, and from there I could breathe in the fresh air without ever having to leave home.[5]

Like many of the other appeals that reached the office handling the allocation of the capital's new high-rise apartments, Brik's letter was accompanied by a note of support from someone higher up in Moscow's elite. For Brik, this was Nikolai K. Cherkasov, the actor famous for playing Aleksandr Nevskii and Ivan the Terrible in the Eisenstein films who was, by then, also a Deputy in the USSR Supreme Soviet. Cherkasov explained that he had been working on Mayakovsky's oeuvre for three years with "Mayakovsky's wife Lily" and her husband Vasilii. Together, Cherkasov told Beria, the three of them had been preparing Mayakovsky's poems for performance on the radio. From his involvement in this "increasingly engaging work," the movie star could vouch for the importance of Brik's work, for the severity of her heart condition, and for her need for a new apartment at the Kotel'nicheskaia residence.[6]

Brik's appeal was one of hundreds of requests for apartments sent in 1952 to the Council of Ministers by Moscow's cultural, scientific, and bureaucratic elites.[7] Their letters were addressed most often to Beria, but also to Stalin, Molotov, Kaganovich, and other prominent Soviet leaders.[8] Taken together, the correspondence follows certain conventions: most letters were typed, many were written on office stationery, professional achievements and awards were listed carefully, while biographical information about class origins, wartime participation, or party membership was included sparingly (though the last was most commonly included of the three). Existing living conditions were described in detail and the majority of letters noted the exact amounts of square meters of space the writer currently held. Many letter writers wrote about their own or their family members' health problems; in a few cases doctors' notes were appended. Individuals like Brik sent letters, as did individuals or groups on behalf of friends or colleagues, as well as institutional leaders. For example, the President of the Academy of Sciences requested 26 apartments for academicians and their families in March 1952, the Procurator General of the USSR wrote that same month requesting seven, and the Minister of Cinematography requested 14 later that year.[9] Just a small handful of letters were sent from construction workers, themselves eager to be granted a skyscraper apartment—in some cases these were apartments that the letter-writer had himself built, and in no case were these appeals successful.

The majority of elite letter writers in 1952 justified their entitlement to skyscraper apartments by demonstrating that they belonged to the ranks of Moscow's managerial, cultural, or intellectual workers, yet appeals were also couched in popular ideas about healthful living, convenience, comfort, and centrality within the city. While it seems that most of the Ministers and institutional leaders at the top had already secured decent housing in the capital for themselves, many of their immediate subordinates, including their deputy Ministers, had not. Most of the artists, writers, scientists, and bureaucrats appealing to the state in 1952 for new apartments complained about the quality of their housing in the capital. Brik's "very good" private apartment of 71 square meters was a rarity, and it is perhaps for this reason that her name does not appear on the list of recipients of new apartments drawn up in the autumn of 1952. More likely, though, Brik had simply written too late. Official authorization notices were sent out starting in September 1952 to those well connected and fortunate enough to have been granted new apartments in the skyscrapers. Most of the Kotel'nicheskaia building's first inhabitants had moved in by early 1953.

The Kotel'nicheskaia skyscraper was located, as Brik noted, on the Moscow River not far from the Kremlin (fig. 7.1). In early 1953, new neighbors on the sixth floor of the building included Arkadii Aleksandrovich Plastov, one of the Soviet Union's leading socialist realist painters, as well as two professors from the Moscow State Conservatory—Dmitrii Mikhailovich Tsyganov and Konstantin Georgievich Mostras, both violinists. Down the hall was V. I. Gostev, the Deputy Chairman of the Council for the Affairs of Religious Cults. On the thirteenth floor the Deputy Commissioner for the Protection of Military and State Secrets in the Press, I. A. Isachenko, found himself the neighbor of E. N. Bueverova, Manager at the Inspectorate for the Quality of Champagne Wines, N. N. Blokhin who was Director of the Institute of Experimental Pathology and Cancer Therapy, and Daniil L'vovich Sagal, a prize-winning

Figure 7.1: Skyscraper on the Kotel'nicheskaia Embankment, 1952.
Collection of the State Central Museum of Contemporary Russian History.

Figure 7.2: Skyscraper at the Red Gates, 1952. Collection of the Shchusev State Museum of Architecture.

actor, then at the Red Army Theater.[10] Films starring Sagal would play at the Kotel'nicheskaia skyscraper's movie theater, the *Illiuzion,* located on the ground floor. Similar apartments were granted to similarly high-ranking Muscovites in a second skyscraper, the dual-purpose residential and administrative building at *Krasnye vorota* ("Red Gates"). This building stood on the hilly northeast curve of Moscow's garden ring and it was, after the Kotel'nicheskaia tower, the second skyscraper to be completed in Moscow (fig. 7.2).

While the Kotel'nicheskaia building took its name from the seventeenth-century smithies that once stood on this shore where the Moscow and Yauza rivers meet, the "Red Gates" building was connected instead to the high culture and military history of the Russian Tsars.[11] The Red Gates building took its name from the eighteenth-century triumphal arch that once stood on the site. The Red Gates arch had been built first in wood and then in stone before it was demolished in the late 1920s during the expansion of the Garden Ring road that winds around central Moscow. In 1935, a metro station bearing the dismantled arch's name was opened beneath the site where Moscow's Red Gates skyscraper would stand two decades later. From 1953, this skyscraper was home to residents including A. N. Bakulev (Chief Surgeon at the Kremlin hospital), M. F. Strepukhov (Chief Editor of *Trud*), and Aleksei Dushkin (Chief Architect of the skyscraper itself).[12] Apartments at this second residential building were assigned at the same time as those in the Kotel'nicheskaia tower, with residents lists drawn up simultaneously for both.[13] The third residential skyscraper—standing on Uprising Square (now Kudrinskaia Square) on the northwest curve of the Garden Ring—was completed only in 1954.

The lists of residents drawn up in late 1952 at the Council of Ministers classified the majority of officials having been granted apartments in these first two buildings—the Kotel'nicheskaia and the Red Gates—as "workers in science and the arts" (*rabotniki nauki i iskusstva*), and "managerial and engineering-technical workers" (*rukovodiashchie i inzhenerno-tekhnicheskie rabotniki*).[14] These were the two largest categories of apartment recipients overall, though dozens of new apartments in the Kotel'nicheskaia building were also given to officials from the security services: from the Ministry of Defense, the Ministry of Internal Affairs, the Ministry for State Security, and to Commandants in the Kremlin Garrison.[15] The Ministry of Railways, the institution in charge of building the Red Gates skyscraper, received a whopping 35 apartments for its staff in this building (the Minister had requested 100) along with all of the office space. Members of the Communist Party's Central Committee were, notably, not the intended recipients of any of the apartments in these buildings. In March 1952, the Secretary of the Komsomol wrote to Beria asking for ten apartments; he received six. By early February 1953, all but nine of the 600 apartments in the Kotel'nicheskaia and Red Gates buildings were occupied.

SOCIAL HIERARCHY ON THE SKYLINE

The reconstruction of Gorky Street two decades earlier had transformed Moscow's central commercial thoroughfare into a socialist realist boulevard housing the city's elites, and the skyscrapers built after the war on the river and on the hill were part of a project to push this vision further. Moving beyond the transformation of single streets, the skyscraper project asked architects to consider the city as a whole and to treat the entire capital as one enormous socialist realist ensemble. While in reality Moscow's late Stalinist beautification program was applied unevenly across the cityscape, the capital's new skyscrapers did have a noticeable effect on the look and feel of the city. The novel vertical points on the landscape served as new centers of power and culture, while also displaying late-Stalinist social hierarchies openly on the cityscape.

In the letters written by Soviet elites hoping to receive new apartments in Moscow's skyscrapers, the aesthetic vision driving the construction of these buildings showed up very little. Few, if any, of the letters spoke in the architectural language of socialist realism. None of Moscow's letter writers, for example, expressed a desire to live in beautiful buildings that were part of rational ensembles that built on the legacy of Russia's historic architectural tradition. Instead, Moscow's elites expressed their desire to experience the more banal elements of skyscraper design: single-family apartments, elevators, reliable electricity, and plumbing. In doing so, however, letter writers tapped into a broader socialist realist rhetoric—one that extended beyond the realms of art and architecture and into the very grammar and fabric of daily Soviet life.[16] In their letters, Moscow's elites channeled and shaped ideas about what a home was supposed to be. They justified social hierarchies and upheld ideas, commonplace since the 1930s, about the role of architecture in enabling feelings of happiness and well-being.[17]

The allocation of private family apartments to Moscow's bureaucratic and cultural elites was a practice in keeping with the policies of prewar Stalinism. Housing for Soviet officials was typically handled through an individual's place of employment. The highest members of Soviet officialdom and their families lived in private apartments in Moscow's House of Government, built across from the Kremlin in 1931.[18] Others lived in the Kremlin itself. And still more lived in hotels or in buildings that had been turned into cooperatives or dormitories to house the staff from various state agencies and artistic unions.[19] Members of certain professions (scientists, writers, artists, and sculptors) were, from the mid-1930s, entitled to larger living spaces than other citizens. A state decree of 1933, for example, gave scientific workers (*nauchnye rabotniki*) the right to an extra room for use as an office, or to the equivalent of twenty square meters of extra living space (in the absence of a separate room).[20] But Moscow was a city full of artists, scientists, and top state officials and the number of those entitled to more dwelling or specialized space far outstripped what was available in the housing stock.[21] It is clear from the desperate attempts to gain access to skyscraper apartments in 1952 that the city's chronic housing shortage rendered entitlements primarily symbolic. Only a small number of those who, by their profession, had access in theory to better apartments were in reality able to live at the capital's best addresses and in the most desirable neighborhoods in the city center. Given the housing shortage in the Soviet capital, entitlements served more as status markers than as a surefire means by which elites secured housing in accordance with their status.

The most famous of Moscow's elite neighborhoods in the 1930s was Gorky Street, the artery running northwest from the Kremlin, cutting through the Garden Ring before reaching Belorusskii train station. A nineteenth-century commercial and artistic hub, Gorky Street was widened and transformed into a model socialist realist boulevard as part of the Moscow General Plan of 1935. Yet the report drawn up in the late 1940s in preparation for the second Moscow General Plan found that Gorky Street's transformation had only been partially completed.[22] While 17 buildings on Gorky Street had been built or remodelled by 1949, 6 more were still under construction, and the groundwork had yet to be laid on another 8 that would complete the program set by the 1935 General Plan.[23] By the postwar years, even Gorky Street's model buildings contained communal apartments and malfunctioning elevators, and residents complained that their apartments had no hot water. In 1952, some of this famous boulevard's residents, like actor Boris Olenin of the Mossovet Theater, were writing to state officials to request a new apartment in Moscow's skyscrapers.[24]

Olenin complained in his letter to the Council of Ministers of October 1952 of the lack of space in the two-room apartment that he and his wife shared with another family at 6 Gorky Street. Their single room, measuring 22.75 square meters, deprived Olenin, he argued, of the ability to "carry out creative work at home and to get a reasonable amount of rest."[25] Appeals for new housing from the city's intellectuals and experts rested on the idea that the home was a space for both work and relaxation. Letter-writers like Olenin envisioned their new skyscraper apartments as clean, modern, peaceful retreats, but these domestic spaces would also double as offices, libraries, rehearsal spaces, and laboratories. The Soviet Union's creative workers would carry out their service to the state even when settled comfortably at home, or so they promised in their letters. State officials, for their part, took these claims seriously but were in no position to grant better housing to all, or even most, of those who were by law entitled to it. Olenin, like so many of those who wrote in in 1952, did not receive a skyscraper apartment. If raising all of Moscow's elites out of the immediate effects of the USSR's housing crisis had been the goal of the decision in 1947 to build skyscrapers in the capital, the project's managers and architects might have ensured that there would be enough apartments to go around.

In truth, solving Moscow's housing crisis was never a goal expressed by those involved in the city's skyscraper project. These buildings served a different, symbolic purpose. And as Mark B. Smith notes, in the postwar years, the Soviet state "did not face up to the housing crisis with the systematic approach that would have come from sustained interest at the top."[26] While Moscow's second General Plan, created starting in 1949, did address housing directly as the most significant challenge that the city faced, municipal officials did not see the city's new skyscrapers as part of the solution. Any role that the skyscrapers could play in solving the housing crisis was a happy accident. Nevertheless, that these buildings were connected in some way to the goal of raising living standards in the capital was an idea both popularly held and widely circulated in the press. At a meeting in 1949 of the Communist Party office for Moscow's Molotov district, a young worker named Korovaeva expressed her hope that better housing was just around the corner. "Comrades," she said, "our government is continually taking care of us, creating for us the best living conditions. Our capital, Moscow becomes more beautiful by the day. Alongside low-rise buildings, gigantic large residential buildings are emerging with full amenities in which we workers will live."[27] Speaking to an audience of just over a thousand workers, Korovaeva seamlessly connected the capital's aesthetic project with the housing question.

As it turned out, the beautiful new buildings described by Korovaeva were not for Moscow's workers at all. The city's skyscrapers, in particular, would be exclusive spaces reserved for elites. Unlike the cheap imitations of luxury goods—what Jukka Gronow calls "democratic luxury"—that the state produced starting in the 1930s for mass consumption, Moscow's skyscrapers were expensive to build. Ordinary Muscovites might buy new "Pobeda" ("Victory") wristwatches, produced on a mass scale

Figure 7.3: Skyscraper at the Red Gates, 1951. Collection of the Shchusev State Museum of Architecture.

starting in 1947. They might even be able to afford a bottle of perfume, a box of chocolates, or champagne and caviar for special occasions. Democratic luxury goods like these were made widely and cheaply available, serving, as Gronow writes, as "concrete proof of the fact that everyday life in the Soviet Union was a feast."[28] Communism promised abundance not just for the few but for everyone. But a skyscraper was not a wristwatch. These buildings posed a challenge to the democratic luxury model introduced in the 1930s in that they served as proof, in steel and marble, that everyday life in the Soviet Union was a feast for the few, not for all.

I. G. Kartashov is one of the few workers whose letter to the Council of Ministers survives in a collection of otherwise elite voices. Kartashov wrote to Beria in 1952 to request an apartment in the Red Gates building that he himself had built. "I took part in the construction of [the Red Gates]," Kartashov wrote, "and the whole time I cherished a dream that I might be lucky enough to live out my old age in that building."[29] This dream was perhaps inspired by the enormous architectural drawing reproduced for all to see on the wall of a neighboring building along the Garden Ring Road (fig. 7.3). Kartashov enjoyed none of the amenities offered by the Red Gates skyscraper. Living with his family in a damp communal apartment, he wanted the opportunity to live in decent housing and to maintain his health for longer so that he might "work for the benefit of our beloved homeland."[30] Few of the elites who wrote letters requesting apartments in 1952 used such patriotic language. Most of them demonstrated service to the state by their rank or position or in lists of awards they had received. Only Kartashov expressed his desire to live in one of Moscow's skyscrapers as "a dream"—other supplicants understood it instead as an entitlement.

ALLOCATING APARTMENTS

The Ministries and institutions in charge of building Moscow's skyscrapers were not given the power to oversee the allocation of spaces in their buildings or, indeed, to manage them in any way. In June 1952, the Office for the Use of the Tall Buildings (*Upravlenie po ekspluatatsii vysotnykh domov pri Sovete Ministrov SSSR*) was created for this purpose. After managing the distribution of apartments and offices in the skyscrapers, this office remained active for the next forty years as the body in charge of staffing and repairs in each of Moscow's skyscrapers.[31]

In the months after it was established in 1952, the Office for the Use of the Tall Buildings mitigated the various conflicts that arose over housing requests and took over the management of all affairs having to do with Moscow's new towers. One by one, the Ministries and the USDS that had built the skyscrapers transferred the products of their labor to the Office, which was overseen by the Council of Ministers. The Kotel'nicheskaia building was the first residential skyscraper to be completed, and the MVD that had built this structure transferred the building's 364 apartments to the Office. The Office also took control of all repair shops, warehouses, materials, products, and supplies designed for the building. A Director, V. P. Bogdanov, was appointed as manager of the skyscraper. On the grounds that the Kotel'nicheskaia building was located in the center of the city, that it was equipped with all manner of amenities, and that the apartments were of high quality, rent for the building was set at 3 rubles per month per square meter of living space.[32] Bogdanov, the Office determined, should operate the building at a profit of at least 350 thousand rubles per year. By the Office's initial calculations, the revenue from this building would be somewhere in the range of 1.6 million rubles annually—a healthy sum to keep up with the high cost of maintaining this luxury structure.

Rent was to be the largest contributor to the Kotel'nicheskaia building's revenue stream, but the skyscraper was not just a place of residence. The building also contained shops, a post office, a bank (*sberkassa*), a telephone exchange, parking garages, and a movie theater, all of which would bring in additional revenue. Such amenities were found in all of the skyscrapers: for example, the building at Uprising Square would boast an especially opulent grocery store on its ground floor (fig. 7.4). The Kotel'nicheskaia building had considerable expenses, however, and by the Office's own calculations, these would leave little in the way of profit. As Director, Bogdanov was in charge of recruiting staff for the skyscraper—82 staff members to start, and then a total of 120 once the building was running at full capacity. Bogdanov himself would make 24,000 rubles per year, while his deputy (an engineer by profession) would make 18,000. The first round of hiring included three more engineers to work onsite, four elevator masters, eighteen elevator operators, an accountant, six *dvorniki*, two laundrywomen, and fourteen maids. The majority of these employees would live in a dormitory, and the rent they paid there would also be collected as part of the skyscraper's revenue.[33]

Figure 7.4: Skyscraper on Uprising Square, store interior, 1955.
Collection of the Shchusev State Museum of Architecture.

Other building directors and staff were soon appointed for the other skyscrapers completed in 1952 and early 1953: these were the Red Gates residential and administrative structure on the Garden Ring and the office building that stood on Smolensk Square at the top of the Arbat. By September 1952, the Kotel'nicheskaia and Red Gates Directors were given instructions for moving residents into the buildings. First, an official order granting an apartment would be sent out to each new tenant. Upon receipt, the tenant was required to provide the building directors with documentation, including their passport or military card, a certificate from their current place of residence listing current square meters of space held with details about all family members who also resided with the recipient, and a certificate from their place of employment.[34] While these instructions were being implemented in the autumn of 1952, a growing number of letters requesting apartments poured in each month, and letters of rejection were sent out by the dozen in reply. The 600 apartments that had been created so far in Moscow's new skyscrapers could not satisfy the demand for better living conditions in a city of over 4 million.

The majority of those who were granted apartments in Moscow's skyscrapers saw an improvement in their living conditions and an increase in the square meters of living space they held. In a number of cases, however, hopeful residents refused skyscraper apartments on the grounds that they were too small. The physicist and Stalin Prize laureate Aleksandr Savvich Predvoditelev had a family of eight (three generations of physicists, mathematicians, and chemists, plus a maid) living in one home. He wrote to complain in September 1952 about having been given one apartment in the Kotel'nicheskaia building (a rare 5-room, 80 square meter luxury), which the Office had then changed to a 3-room apartment measuring 42 square meters in the Red Gates building. The decision to reassign Predvoditelev this second apartment "not only did not improve [his] living conditions, but made them practically impossible."[35] If his family currently had three rooms of 56 square meters and still some of them had to live in the attic, how, he asked, could they possibly all fit in a 42-square-meter apartment? Predvoditelev also had a specialized library of 3,000 volumes (14 bookshelves-worth), collected over the course of his 30-year career and "without which [he could] not carry out his scientific work."[36] Predvoditelev's name does not appear on the list of apartment recipients drawn up a few months later, and in the end his 3-room apartment in the Red Gates building was given to someone else.

Most of those categorized as "workers in science and the arts" did see the size of their living quarters expand after moving into the Red Gates skyscraper. Prior to moving into this building, the average square meters of living space among scientific and artistic families was just over 7 square meters per person. This rose to just over 12 square meters a head once these families were settled in the Red Gates.[37] This was considerably higher than what most Muscovites enjoyed at the time. But some in the city were even more successful in making the square-metered logic of Soviet housing work to their advantage. In 1952, for example, Pavel Nikolaevich Blokhin, engaged the state in an elaborate game of musical apartments by which he attempted to improve his family's living conditions and increase their living space by a third.

As Director of the Academy of Architecture's Research Institute on Housing, Blokhin knew his way around Moscow's complex web of municipal, federal, and institutional housing authorities.[38] Blokhin was married and had two daughters, the eldest of whom was married with a newborn baby. In June 1952, Blokhin was granted a 2-room apartment measuring 35.6 square meters in the Kotel'nicheskaia skyscraper. But like many savvy Soviet citizens, Blokhin had sent out more than one apartment request to more than one institution. By a stroke of good fortune, he received not one but two apartment offers. The second, measuring 32 square meters was allocated through the housing office of Mossovet. Although neither of these new apartments was as large as the sizable apartment the Blokhin family currently held, this double offer presented Moscow's foremost housing expert with an opportunity to bargain with the state.

In his letter to the Office for the Use of the Tall Buildings, Blokhin set aside justifications he might have made on the grounds of his state service and laid out his case in numerical terms:

At the current time, I live in a three-room apartment of 48.4 square meters on 17 Bol'shoi Karetnyi Lane. In this apartment, which is held in my name, live [the following]: in one room—my daughter, her husband, and their 9-month-old baby (my granddaughter), in the other two rooms—my wife and me, and our youngest 19-year-old daughter.

When we leave this apartment, another family, strangers to my [eldest] daughter, will likely be settled into my two rooms and the space will be turned from a single-family into a communal apartment. As a result, the living condi-

Figure 7.5: "From the point of view of the gossip," drawing by V. Dobrovol'skii. *Krokodil*, February 28, 1953. Caption reads: "I don't envy the residents of that building. How can you possibly find out what's going on in each of those apartments?"

tions of that part of my family remaining in our old apartment will worsen. (In this communal apartment, my eldest daughter's family will continue to live in their one room, along with a nanny.)

Since I do not expect it will be possible to receive a larger apartment in the skyscraper, with room for my entire family [of seven] [39], I ask that you permit me to trade in to Mossovet *not* my two-rooms, but just one of them, measuring 16.2 square meters. The remaining two rooms from my old apartment (a total of 32.2 square meters) will then be transferred to my daughter Alla Pavlovna Sarukhanian (postgraduate student at the Pedagogical Institute). Within this space, she will reside with her husband (engineer-lieutenant R. L. Sarukhanian, who works at Tsentrovoenproekt), my granddaughter, and a nanny, that is to say 4 people in 32 square meters.

I will live with my wife and youngest daughter in our 36 square meter apartment in the Kotel'nicheskaia building.[40]

While Blokhin figured that he could not save his eldest daughter from the fate of living in a communal apartment, he could attempt to help her gain more living space, and more privacy, than she would otherwise have in a single room.[41]

It was no secret that the capital's new skyscrapers were full of single-family apartments. The mass housing campaign of the Khrushchev era would soon make single-family housing more widely accessible, but in the final years of the Stalin period, communal living remained a reality for the majority of Soviet citizens.[42] A cartoon printed in February 1953 in the Soviet satirical magazine *Krokodil* showed a woman (a gossip, we are told) gazing up at the Kotel'nicheskaia building from across the river (fig. 7.5). "I don't envy the residents of that building," the gossipmonger in the cartoon exclaims. "How can you possibly find out what's going on in each of those apartments!"

Figure 7.6: Skyscraper on the Kotel'nicheskaia embankment, interior, 1957.
Collection of the Shchusev State Museum of Architecture.

The cartoon lightly mocked the reality of communal living, where privacy was all but nonexistent. Most Soviet citizens would not be able to escape from the gossipy neighbors in their communal apartments until at least a decade later. In the last years of the Stalin era, single-family apartments were a luxury in Moscow enjoyed by a small number of the city's residents. Few in Moscow had access to the private kitchens, bathrooms, and dining rooms on offer in the skyscraper apartments (fig. 7.6).

The letter writers of 1952 expounded on the myriad benefits of living in single-family apartments. Many noted that though they currently resided in communal apartments, they deserved single-family housing by virtue of the nature of their work. The Stalin-prize-winning legal historian, Mikhail Nikolaievich Gernet justified his request on the grounds that a new apartment would provide more space for his scholarly work, and more sunlight. Writing to Beria in December 1952, Gernet explained that he wished to trade his family's two rooms in a communal apartment for a home in one of Moscow's skyscrapers. Not only was there no daylight in the rooms in which he lived (because the neighboring building obscured his windows), but Gernet had no private space to work. He carried out his work in the hallway, where, due to his blindness, he dictated his work to a secretary. "The presence of other residents left and right further intensifies the need for a special room for scientific work" Gernet wrote.[43] As proof of the severity of his living conditions, Gernet supplied a certificate from the sanitation inspector and a doctor's note. Gernet, who was born in 1874 and was busy researching the history of the Tsarist prison system, received a two-room apartment on the fifteenth floor of the Kotel'nicheskaia building.

The Deputy Chairman of Gosbank, N. V. Smirnov, appealed on the grounds of having "no opportunities for recreation" in his apartment, which was home to three families and a total of 17 people.[44] Moreover, with eight young children in the home, Smirnov was not able to sleep normally—a condition seriously affecting his health. Not long after Smirnov's request came in, two ballet dancers from the Bol'shoi Theater wrote to Beria requesting a new apartment on the grounds that they lived over 10 km from the city center. With a workday beginning at 10 in the morning and lasting until midnight, such a long distance meant that they could not spend break times, lunch, or dinner at home. And given the physical exertion of their work, they wrote, their health was beginning to show the effects of the poor location of their housing. A home closer to the theater would be preferable. Beria sent the request down the chain of command, with the note "consider, and help."[45] In the end, Smirnov and his family found themselves in the more restful Red Gates building, and the ballerinas were housed in the Kotel'nicheskaia tower.

HAPPINESS AND THE SOVIET SKYSCRAPER

By the early 1950s, Moscow's skyscrapers were as visible on the city's horizon as they had long been on the pages of Soviet magazines and newspapers. As cranes lowered the steel girders of these buildings into place, architects continued to ply their rhetoric for a popular Soviet audience. In *Ogonek* in September 1952, readers learned the many ways in which Moscow's tall new buildings surpassed similar structures found in the United States. Architect Karo Alabian explained that although residents in American skyscrapers could feel their homes swaying in the air at the slightest hint of wind, Moscow's skyscraper residents would be spared such frightening sensations due to the technological improvements made in Soviet design.[46] A few months later in *Literaturnaia gazeta*, readers learned that although the "bulk of skyscrapers in Manhattan and Chicago [stand as] symbols of the enslavement of man to the soulless machine of business," Moscow's tall buildings were located "at points [chosen as] most favorable for the buildings themselves and for the city."[47] Soviet skyscrapers "did not squeeze out existing residential neighborhoods by robbing them of light and air. Surrounded by open areas stretching for long distances, Moscow's skyscrapers were positioned throughout the city in order to form a new panorama."[48] As the first of Moscow's new towers were completed, architects returned to the Cold War rhetoric with which they had begun the project in 1947.

Like other Soviet newspapers and magazines, *Krokodil,* the USSR's most popular satirical paper, printed numerous cartoons and stories in the early 1950s on the skyscraper theme. The skyscraper silhouette came to signify the revolution in Soviet material culture and living conditions that was underway in the postwar capital. The coveted central location of the Kotel'nicheskaia embankment residential tower was

Рис. В. КОНОВАЛОВА

— Из окна нашей квартиры видна Красная площадь.
— А где ты живёшь!
— В высотном доме на Котельнической набережной!

Figure 7.7: Cartoon by V. Konovalov. *Krokodil*, September 30, 1952. Caption reads: "From the window of our apartment you can see Red Square." / "Where do you live?" / "In the tall building on Kotel'nicheskaia embankment!"

the subject of one cartoon published in 1952 (fig. 7.7). "From the window of our apartment you can see Red Square," says one young girl to another as they walk home from school on an autumn day. True to form, *Krokodil* also set about gently parodying many of the promises of Soviet skyscraper life. In a cartoon by Iu. Cherepanov published in the magazine in 1950, a skyscraper still under construction is shown to have its own weather system (fig. 7.8). Taller than anything Moscow had ever seen, these buildings, Cherepanov joked, would need a separate weather forecast. And in all likelihood, the cartoon suggests, the view from the top would always be cloud-free.

Krokodil did not limit itself to images in its coverage of the skyscraper motif. In 1951, years before the buildings were completed, the magazine published a poem titled "With All Amenities" written by a "future skyscraper resident (*zhilets-vysotnik*)":

Figure 7.8: Cartoon by Iu. Cherepanov. *Krokodil*, September 20, 1950. Caption reads: "The weather forecast has proven accurate, but not up to the highest level."

The skyscraper is growing and reaching for the moon.
An apartment in that building will be given to me.
On the top floor I'll settle in with my wife,
I'll joyfully take note of the move-in date.
It will be pleasant for us under that very moon
As we listen to the Moonlight Sonata.[49]

Alongside the poem was a drawing of the Kotel'nicheskaia building in a special two-page spread in honor of the thirty-fourth anniversary of the October Revolution. Like the promise of the revolution itself, Moscow's new skyscraper apartments, this poem suggested, would provide joy, comfort, health, and culture.

In descriptions that circulated in the press about Moscow's skyscrapers, a close connection was drawn between the aesthetics of the skyscraper and the effects these buildings would have on the health and happiness of those who would lived in them. That these buildings would be among the healthiest places to live in the capital was an idea promoted in the press and subsequently advanced by letter-writers of the early 1950s. Like Lily Brik or Mikhail Gernet, a sizable percentage of those who wrote to the Council of Ministers asking for apartments in 1952 justified their requests on the grounds that the buildings would provide relief from their various ailments. As was the case for Brik, elevators were one of the main draws in this regard.

Health was similarly a concern for Vladimir Gel'freikh, architect of the adminis-trative skyscraper on Smolensk Square. As part of the trio that had designed the Pal-ace of Soviets in the 1930s, Gel'freikh appreciated the skyscrapers from an architec-tural perspective, but it was still the healthy life that the buildings seemed to promise that was a primary draw. In October 1952, Gel'freikh wrote to Beria to request an apartment in the Kotel'nicheskaia building. Gel'freikh and his wife lived just a few blocks from Lily Brik in a large (63.5 square meter) apartment on the sixth, and top, floor of 45 Arbat Street. Gel'freikh had been given this apartment after moving from Leningrad to Moscow in 1935—a privilege that came from his work on the Palace of Soviets. But while in 1935 the building had been brand new, seventeen years later the roof was leaking, the elevator was permanently in disrepair, and "life there has become difficult."[50] Walking up and down six flights of stairs was hard for the aging architect and his wife, and his current home did not have room for a proper office. Although his request came in rather late, Gel'freikh was nonetheless granted one of the largest skyscraper apartments available: a four-room space on the twelfth floor of the Kotel'nicheskaia building. Luckily for Gel'freikh, someone else had only just declined this apartment, through which Gel'freikh gained an extra 15 square meters of living space for his family.

Letter writers' obsession with air flow, sunlight, and cleanliness was partly shaped by the information publicly circulating about the skyscrapers as they were being built, but it was also the result of the dirt and disease that were central components of every-day life in postwar Moscow. Just as Brik had envisioned "breathing in the fresh air without ever having to leave home," other letter writers imagined similar futures in the skyscrapers.[51] Whether the skyscraper apartment would relieve hypertension or allow for a better night's rest, the concern with health did not subside once residents moved in. Some would write to request that they be moved from one skyscraper apartment into another one that was sunnier, quieter, or larger. The Deputy Manager of Kholkhoz Affairs, with a family of seven, wrote that he would even downgrade to a 2-room apartment instead of the 3-room space he had been assigned, in order to obtain rooms for his sickly daughter on the sunnier side of the Kotel'nicheskaia building.[52]

Related to residents' worries about health were their concerns about the techno-logical advances found in the buildings. That the skyscrapers would be built with the most advanced technologies in heating, sanitation, lighting, and air circulation systems was decided from the outset of the project. While the original decree of Janu-ary 13, 1947 did not specify the size or quantity of apartments each residential skyscraper would contain, it did require that the designs for the buildings make use of the "most modern technical means in elevator equipment, water supply systems, lighting, telephones, heating, air conditioning, and so on."[53] These amenities were part of what made the skyscrapers so desirable, but they also presented challenges.

In September 1952, while requests for the apartments were still flooding in, newly settled residents were already writing in to complain about faulty amenities. Noisy elevators were high on the list of complaints. A resident in the Red Gates building noted that his apartment was filled with noise around the clock "due to the proximity of the elevator engine room (above the apartment)." Because this resident had hypertension, he argued, the "noise is extremely harmful and any resulting sickness could abruptly progress for the worse."[54] Another resident, also complaining about noisy elevators in the Red Gates building, made sure to include in his letter information about his recent health problems and visit to a sanatorium. As they settled in, Moscow's new skyscraper residents sought to hold those in charge to account for the promises that seemed to have been made about a new life in these monumental new buildings.

Faina G. Ranevskaya, who lived in the Kotel'nicheskaia building, jokingly described her living conditions with a play on the phrase "Bread and Circuses." One of the Soviet Union's greatest actresses, Ranevskaya was known on and off screen for her aphorisms, many of which have been recorded and published posthumously. "The windows of Ranevskaya's apartment in the skyscraper on the Kotel'nicheskaia Embankment opened onto the [building's] stone interior courtyard," begins one of these anecdotes:

> And there is the exit from the movie theater and the place where they would unload the bread trucks. Faina Georgievna full of loathing would hear the familiar folksy expressions of the drivers, distinctly audible beneath her window at the break of day. And in the evening, she would witness in anguish the loud mob of movie-goers heading home from the *Illiuzion*.

I live above bread and circuses, Ranevskaya complained.[55]

While Ranevskaya was surely glad to move from her communal apartment into the Kotel'nicheskaia building, her humorous account of life in a skyscraper apartment was not far removed from other residents' complaints.

For the duration of the high Stalinist period, Moscow's skyscrapers were incomplete carcasses on the skyline of the capital, symbols of a future that was just around the corner but had not yet arrived. The symbolic work done by these buildings in the late Stalinist period was carried out in texts and images circulated in the popular press. And by 1952, the tropes that had been repeated in newspapers and magazines about modern amenities and healthful skyscraper living had made their way into Muscovites' own appeals for apartments. Soviet citizens could imagine, based on the many sketches and written descriptions they had read, what their future lives as skyscraper residents would feel like. But the dream of living in a skyscraper apartment became a reality only for a small group of elites in the final months of the Stalin period.

Given the limited number of apartments available in these buildings, Moscow's skyscraper project had the potential of creating a crisis of legitimacy for the regime: too many elites were entitled to better living conditions, and too few were successful in their appeals. The unsteadying forces latent in these structures were tempered by the death of Stalin. The symbolic power that Moscow's monumental new structures held over the city was broken—or at least diminished—at the very moment that they came into being. No sooner had they been completed, these buildings became targets in Nikita Khrushchev's de-Stalinization program. Khrushchev was quick to disassociate himself from the skyscraper project. By late 1954, he had rebranded Moscow's skyscrapers as symbols of Stalinist "excess" (*izlishestvo*). Targeting the architects of the buildings directly at the All-Union Builders' Conference held in the capital in December 1954 Khrushchev accused Soviet architects of being "stumbling blocks on the road to the industrialization of construction."[56] In the coming years, the new path in architecture pursued by Stalin's successor—one that prioritized prefabrication and standardization over "individual" and "excessive" designs—would radically transform the way Soviet cities were built and experienced.

While Khrushchev immediately tried to distance himself from Stalinist monumentalism, he nonetheless inherited these seven important institutional structures, completed just in time for a renewal of Moscow's openness to the outside world. In the 1950s and 1960s, Moscow State University would host international conferences, a youth festival, and other events; the Hotel Ukraine and Hotel Leningrad would host international dignitaries in lavish interiors; and the residential skyscrapers on Uprising Square, at the Red Gates, and on the Kotel'nicheskaia embankment would continue to serve as symbols of Moscow's status as a world-class socialist city. The building on Smolensk Square, for its part, would also connect the Soviet Union to the international sphere by serving as the headquarters of the Ministry of Foreign Affairs. In Moscow, Stalinist monumentalism would never be wholly eclipsed.

8

DE-STALINIZATION AND
THE BATTLE AGAINST "EXCESS"

Moscow's skyscrapers took their places on the horizon of the city in the last months of the Stalin era. The enormous weight attached to the construction project and the large sums dedicated to its completion ensured that three of the eight buildings were finished before Stalin's death in March of 1953. The office tower on Smolensk Square and the residential skyscrapers on the Kotel'nicheskaia embankment and the Red Gates were up and running by early 1953. Over on the Lenin Hills, Moscow State University was nearing completion. This building would welcome its first cohort of students in September 1953. Construction of the remaining skyscrapers lagged in the post-Stalin years and the tower planned for the Zariad'e was never built to completion.[1]

The first inhabitants of the residential towers on the Kotel'nicheskaia embankment and at the Red Gates learned about the death of Stalin just as they were settling into their new lives as skyscraper residents. They may have been listening to the radio in the early morning hours of March 4, 1953, when the Soviet government announced that Stalin had suffered a brain hemorrhage and lost consciousness the night before. They likely heard about Stalin's death over the airwaves on March 6 and they may have brought home that day's issue of *Pravda* with its front page dedicated to the Soviet leader's passing. The skyscraper residents, along with those now at work in their new skyscraper offices on Smolensk Square, were surely among the crowds of mourners who streamed toward the House of Unions to view Stalin's body lying in state. On March 9, they lined the streets of the capital to watch the funeral procession go by.

In the coming weeks, the skyscraper residents would learn that Lavrentii Beria—to whom many had addressed their requests for skyscraper apartments—had been arrested. On the pretense that he was planning a coup, Beria was arrested on the orders of Nikita Khrushchev and other top officials on June 26, 1953. The skyscraper project, with five out of eight buildings yet to be completed, was passed from Beria to Georgii Malenkov. A new, collective leadership took charge after Stalin's death, composed of Khrushchev and Malenkov, as well as Lazar Kaganovich, Anastas Mikoian, Nikolai Bulganin, and Viacheslav Molotov. In late December 1953, the collective had Beria executed and over the next few years, Khrushchev would rise to replace Stalin as sole leader of the USSR.

This chapter examines Khrushchev's first public salvo against Stalinism—his speech at the Builders' Conference in December 1954. At this event, Khrushchev rehearsed his program of de-Stalinization by attacking the architecture of the Stalin era. Later, in his Secret Speech of February 1956, Khrushchev would rail against Stalin's cult of personality, lashing out at the former leader for his "grave abuse of power" and deviation from the principles of Leninism.[2] Khrushchev thereby opened the door to increased international engagement and a period of cultural liberalization known as the Thaw. But by the time these well-known events unfolded, Soviet architecture had already been shaken to its foundations. In the months following the Builders' Conference, the main institutions of Stalinist architecture were dismantled. Khrushchev's attack on the preeminent architects and structures of the Stalin period steered Soviet architecture away from monumentalism, allowing a different approach to architecture and urban planning to rise to prominence in the 1950s—one based on prefabrication, standardization, and mass housing construction. At the very moment that Moscow's skyscrapers made their appearance on the cityscape, they were cast as villains in a battle against architectural "excess."

NEW PROTAGONISTS

Given his prior experience overseeing major construction projects in earlier years, Khrushchev was well positioned, once in power, to bring swift changes to Soviet architecture. The new leader was neither an engineer nor an architect, but he knew the building industry well. Earlier in life, Khrushchev had overseen major building projects, from the Moscow metro in the 1930s to the reconstruction after the war of Kiev's main thoroughfare, the Kreshchatik.[3] Yet however well informed he was, Khrushchev did not wage his attack on Soviet architecture alone. He found allies among urban professionals eager to supply information and ammunition that would prove valuable when the time came to publicly unveil major changes in the way Soviet cities would be built. One of these allies was an urban planner named Georgii A. Gradov.

On November 30, 1954, Gradov, a relatively young and fiercely oppositional figure in the building profession, attended the first day of the Builders' Conference.[4] Held in Moscow in the lavish interiors of the Grand Kremlin Palace, the Builders' Conference brought together urban experts from across the Soviet Union for eight days of speeches, meetings, and panels. While most in attendance did not realize it beforehand, it would be through these deliberations that Soviet architecture and urban planning would shift course away from Stalinist monumentalism and toward the prefabricated modernism of the Khrushchev period. When they returned to their hometowns and offices after the final day of the conference on December 7, 1954, the 2,200 delegates who attended this event were well aware that the winds had shifted. As Mark B. Smith has shown, Soviet urban professionals had long been developing prefabricated techniques and standardized plans, but the political will and coordination needed to implement them on a mass scale was absent during late Stalinism.[5] Suddenly, all of that changed. For figures like Georgii Gradov, the Builders' Conference marked the start of the revolution in architecture that he had been waiting for for quite some time.

While Gradov would attend the Builders' Conference in late 1954, his name was not included on the initial list of conference invitees.[6] The pages of names compiled in advance of the conference in early November included the most prominent experts and decision-makers in Soviet architecture, from engineers and architects to those working in the building materials industry. Also on the invite list for the conference were journalists, foreign guests from the People's Republics, and top Soviet officials.[7] Gradov himself made it onto the list only days before the Builders' Conference began. His name was tacked on as a belated thirteenth addition to the group of invited delegates from the Academy of Architecture.[8] He was listed beneath the more recognizable names of Pavel Blokhin, Ivan Zholtovskii, and Arkadii Mordvinov, as well as the Presidents, Vice-Presidents, and Directors of the Architectural Academy. In ink that was slightly lighter and not in line with the rest, the typist had made space at the very last minute for this thirteenth invitee: "Gradov, Georgii Aleksandrovich, no date; Research Institute of Public Buildings; head of department." Had the typist known Gradov's birthdate, its inclusion would have shown him to be the youngest man on the list.

The Builders' Conference was an early exercise in de-Stalinization that preceded Khrushchev's Secret Speech by fifteen months and that caught most who witnessed it by surprise. Also surprising to many was the outsized role that Gradov played in the events of late 1954.[9] As his pseudonym suggests, "Gradov" was a city devotee. His commitment to urbanism extended well beyond his chosen *nom de guerre*—a surname derived from the Slavic root for "city" ("*grad*").[10] Born in 1911 in the Ukrainian part of the Russian empire, "George of the City" was by training both a civil engineer and an architect. A graduate in the early 1930s of the Higher Construction Institute in Moscow, Gradov began his career working for Voenproekt, where he built standardized projects ranging from dorms for Red Army soldiers to canteens for senior officers. In 1934, Gradov was accepted to the graduate institute at the Soviet Union's new Academy of Architecture in Moscow. Finding himself among the first cohort at this school, Gradov was swept up in the spirit of the times, consumed by the search for a new, distinctly socialist architecture. Gradov was also engaged in these years in heated debates with his teachers—in particular with Ivan Zholtovskii about the role of classicism in this "search for the new." Zholtovskii and other studio masters at the Academy knew their fiery young student as Georgii "Sutiagin." It was not until 1940 that Sutiagin became "Gradov."[11]

Gradov's ideas about architecture and urban planning took shape during his years at the Academy. There, Gradov railed against the status quo, developing a strong distaste for classicism and an antipathy for the tendency among his teachers and peers to pursue, as he saw it, "purely aesthetic" questions. Gradov would later characterize the 1930s as a time of "phony decorative ornamentalism that snowballed into unrestrained archaic excess."[12] But during these years, the young architect-engineer found important mentors. He found solace in the studios of the Vesnin brothers and Alexander P. Ivanitskii, whose studio was located within the Moscow State Institute of City Planning, or Mosgiprogor. It was from the Vesnins and Ivanitskii that Gradov learned, as he later recalled, to find "the organic interconnections between new social-functional content and form, naturally bearing in mind modern technology and economic requirements."[13]

This commitment to reconciling form and function and to mobilizing scientific knowledge in urban planning was a hallmark of Ivanitskii's approach. Ivanitskii was the lead planner for the city of Nizhnii Novgorod from 1928 until his resignation in 1935. He was a pragmatic planner who valued scientific objectivity and research over politics and symbolism. As Heather DeHaan writes in her study of urban planning in Nizhnii Novgorod, "Ivanitskii rejected the idea that the city plan should serve as an image of power, transmitting state authority through its political aesthetic."[14] But by the mid-1930s, science had given way to symbolism in Stalinist master plans projecting the power and authority of the Soviet Union and Stalin.[15] At the same moment, then, that Gradov found inspiration in Ivanitskii's approach to planning, Ivanitskii found his influence in the profession diminished. Out of step with the Stalin era, Gradov would find his footing only in the decades to come.

In later years, Gradov would describe himself as an architect who had always tried to carry out the credo of Constructivism. He was especially interested in building collective structures inspired by the *doma-kommuny* of the 1920s and in carrying on the trends of the experimental design of the first Soviet decade. As Gradov would later recall, "taking such positions" in the 1930s, "amidst the general slide into eclecticism and imitation [*epigonstvo*] was very hard."[16] In the late 1950s and 1960s, Gradov would be given license to take up Constructivist-inspired design again.[17] But in the formative years of his career, Gradov's way of thinking about architecture made him ill-suited to the time. While those around him pursued neoclassicism and monumentalism in city building, Gradov eschewed historicism and struggled to maintain scientific rigor and ideological commitment in his work. Gradov's notebooks of the 1940s show him searching for tangible links between Marxism-Leninism and the built environment. Gradov also found inspiration in those years in the work of the Moscow Party boss, Nikita Khrushchev, whose words Gradov copied out in his notebook: "It is necessary to note," Khrushchev had said in the 1930s, "that a number of architects get a bit carried away with the exterior side of things and not infrequently do they worry merely about creating a beautiful façade, a beautiful picture. The questions of building construction and interior planning of apartments are shunted to the rear of the plan. This is a big problem."[18] Khrushchev's distaste for the path taken by Stalinist architecture in the 1930s was well documented and served, for Gradov, as a source of inspiration.

Throughout the Stalin era, Khrushchev had voiced his concern with the way urban planning was conducted in the Soviet Union. At a meeting on "Questions of Construction" held in 1935 by the Communist Party Central Committee, Khrushchev stole the show with a fiery speech on mass housing.[19] "It has to be said openly," the future leader exclaimed, "that architects often don't think about the cost of the housing they design, they don't worry about the Soviet *kopek*, they completely separate their designs from economic questions." "This harmful phenomenon must be liquidated," Khrushchev declared in 1935.[20] And as Stalinism came to a close, Khrushchev would attempt to do just that.

In the years between Gradov's studies in the 1930s at the Academy of Architecture in Moscow and his attendance in 1954 at the Builders' Conference, the young architect-engineer worked on major city planning projects outside Moscow. Starting in 1937, Gradov worked for four years in Frunze as director and chief architect of *Kirgosproekt*, the planning office of the Kirgiz SSR. His colleagues there would look back favorably in 1960 at Gradov's work in Frunze, where he "achieved positive results" in his Summer Theater in the city's central Panfilov Park.[21] While in Frunze, Gradov also worked on plans for other Kirgiz cities, including Osh and Karakol.[22] In 1941, he left the Kirgiz SSR to voluntarily enlist in the Red Army. Serving until 1945 as a sapper along the Karelian Front, Gradov's commanders found him to be a highly-disciplined and strong-willed subordinate who was "politically literate, ideologically mature, [and] devoted to the Party of Lenin-Stalin."[23] These traits made Gradov particularly well suited to wartime service, but they would also serve him well in peacetime; his doggedness and ideological commitment would gain the attention of higher-ups in the years of transition between Stalin and Khrushchev.

In 1945, following his demobilization, Gradov found a position back in Moscow in Giprogor, the Soviet city planning institute. From there, he worked on the creation of a postwar General Plan for Stalinsk, an industrial city in Siberia that had grown rapidly during the First Five-Year Plan. Moving next to a post within the Academy of Architecture's Institute of Public and Industrial Building in Moscow, Gradov found himself working in an organization that he loathed with increasing intensity. The direction that Soviet architecture took in late Stalinism did not square with Gradov's ideas about urban planning. The skyscrapers that were being built in Moscow symbolized all that was wrong, in Gradov's eyes, with Soviet architecture. Finding the atmosphere in Moscow's postwar architectural and planning circles stifling, Gradov began to search for an official outlet for his many critiques.

ARCHITECTURE AS ART AND AS SCIENCE

In the years of late Stalinism, Moscow's top architects focused their energies on the problem of "ensemble development" (*ansamblevaia zastroika*). This approach, dedicated not just to modernizing but also to sculpting and beautifying cityscapes, motivated Moscow's skyscraper project. Stalinist architects drew on the historic built environment for inspiration in crafting architectural ensembles. As Aleksandr Vlasov explained in a speech that he gave as Chief Architect of Moscow in 1953, "the historic architectural ensembles of Leningrad and Moscow, Paris and Vienna, Peking and Venice are preserved in the history of architecture not as dead memorial monuments, but as examples of the high art of composition."[24] Vlasov pointed to the harmony and balance achieved in spaces like the sacred complexes of Egypt and the Acropolis of Athens, the squares of Florence, and the Kremlins of Moscow, Novgorod, and Pskov. These were examples that could be looked to when planning new city ensembles. In its contemporary manifestation, Vlasov continued, the residential block had become an integral part of the ensemble. Where church steeples and palace spires had once served to orient citizens with the horizon, residential towers now served as pivot points on the cityscape. In Moscow, Vlasov noted, the skyscrapers on Uprising Square and the one on the Kotel'nicheskaia Embankment stood as shining examples of ensemble development.

Yet, Moscow's skyscrapers could just as easily serve as evidence of the chaos of Soviet city planning. The sheer number of stakeholders involved, from the Ministries in charge of building each skyscraper to the factories supplying materials to the institutions providing labor, made the citywide skyscraper project begun in Moscow in 1947 extraordinarily complex. The architectural ensemble—a feature

composed in Moscow of a skyscraper plus boulevards, parkland, or riverside embankments extending outward—could take years to achieve. The ensemble was an
ideal and only rarely did it appear as planned in reality.

Georgii Gradov was keenly aware of this problem. Working in the immediate postwar years at Giprogor, the Soviet city planning agency, Gradov was frustrated by
what he saw as the overly abstract and unscientific approach to urban planning being
carried out at his institution. In late 1949, in his third year at Giprogor, Gradov wrote
a letter of complaint to the Soviet Ministry of City Planning. As the head of Giprogor's
fourth architectural studio, Gradov was a knowledgeable informant. In his eleven-
page letter, he not only described the shortcomings in Soviet city building but proposed a number of possible solutions. Focusing on Giprogor specifically, Gradov
made the following arguments: the General Plans of cities tended to be too abstract
and were not rooted in reality; there was a lack of integration in urban development
across various projects being undertaken in a single city; and, more broadly, there
was a lack of established norms and no real scientific methodology underlying Soviet urban design.[25]

In his letter of 1949, Gradov claimed that over the course of its twenty-year existence, Giprogor had failed to develop the most basic standards for city planning.
"There are no firm provisions on zoning, the economy of urban construction has not
been developed at all, and there are no scientifically and legally valid standards for
density of construction, parkland, or for cultural and children's institutions," Gradov lamented.[26] Giprogor, Gradov continued, worked in "complete isolation from the
scientific institutions of the country—the USSR Academy of Sciences, the branches
of the Academies, the institutes . . ." That is to say, Gradov wrote, that "Giprogor is
stewing in its own juices." Cut off from external technical debates and from reality,
the organization was caught in a loop of "endless stamps and streams of paper."[27]
Gradov asserted that Giprogor should design "not General Plans on paper [*bumazh-
nye genplany*], divorced from life, for the archive, but real-technical and working projects." "It is necessary," he argued, "to change the very method for designing General
Plans."[28] In Gradov's opinion, plans had to be subordinate to the requirements and
conditions of real life.

For Gradov, the heart of the problem was not the boldness of "ensemble development," but the inability of Soviet architects to truly realize their lofty and monumental goals in reality. The problem lay in a lack of coordination across the many
planning offices at work in the country. As Gradov saw it, individualism reigned in
the institutions of late Stalinism. To get his point across, Gradov parodied "typical"
city builders, who were individualistic and narrow-minded: "it's my money—where
I want, how I want, that's how I'll build," sneers one builder; "I need to build a house
for *my* workers, not to design and build a city for someone else," whines another.
Gradov offered in his letter of 1949 a scathing criticism of Soviet architecture and
planning, but he refrained from naming names. This would change after his move
in the early 1950s to the Academy of Architecture's Research Institute for Public
Buildings. At the Academy, things got personal.

Gradov would continue to lodge complaints with higher-ups at the Academy, but
his concerns seemed to have no effect. As Director of the Academy's Research Institute for Public Buildings, however, Gradov found that he was surrounded by like-

minded colleagues. In particular Konstantin A. Ivanov, the Associate Director of Gradov's institute, shared his boss's convictions. Together, Gradov and Ivanov sent one letter of complaint to the newspaper *Bolshevik* and another one to *Literaturnaia gazeta*, but neither was published by the editors.[29] In 1952, the pair wrote to Yuri A. Zhdanov, head of the Agitational and Propaganda Administration's Science Sector. Gradov and Ivanov appealed to Zhdanov on the grounds that the Academy of Architecture had neglected its scientific mandate. The Academy, "which 17 years ago was assigned by the government the task of developing architectural science, has not achieved its mission," they wrote.[30] Not only that, the pair contended, but with architects like Karo Alabian and Arkadii Mordvinov at the helm, the Academy had been actively steered in the opposite direction. A firmer link was needed between science and architecture.

Over the following years, Gradov practiced sparring directly with Mordvinov, President of the Academy of Architecture. Gradov argued openly with Mordvinov at official meetings and he debated his opponent silently, in commentary scribbled in the margins of his personal copies of Mordvinov's publications.[31] In a speech that he gave at the Academy in 1952, Gradov criticized Mordvinov and others for getting caught up in eternal discussions about mass construction, rather than taking action. The country's leading architects, Gradov argued, were taking a back seat in this important area of city planning.[32] While architects staged interminable debates, builders lacked standardized, up-to-date plans. Gradov used schools and hospitals—public buildings from his area of work—as examples. The Academy had decided three years earlier, he explained, that every new school should have a gymnasium, but it had not created any updated designs for such schools. And so "schools are being built," Gradov reported, "according to the old design without gymnasiums." Worse, Gradov claimed, hospitals were being built, in the absence of any standardized designs at all, on the plans for schools—adapted on the fly to include, presumably, operating rooms instead of classrooms.[33] The Academy's apparent inability to translate idea into practice was causing chaos on the ground.

In Gradov's eyes, the blame for all of this lay squarely on the shoulders of those men in charge of the Academy of Architecture. Long in the habit of writing letters of complaint to newspaper editors and state officials, Gradov carried on this work as the Stalin era came to a close. In February 1954, with the support of Ivanov and a small group of co-conspirators, Gradov wrote an open letter to Nikita Khrushchev, now the First Secretary of the Communist Party of the Soviet Union. For years, Gradov's letters had gone unanswered; his warnings unheeded. It must have come as some surprise to the disgruntled city planner when he caught the attention in 1954 of the incoming leader of the Soviet Union.

GEORGII GRADOV GOES TO THE BUILDERS' CONFERENCE

The open letter that Gradov sent to Khrushchev in February 1954 was hard-hitting and inflammatory. In his letter, Gradov denounced leading Soviet architects by name for not making full use of the industrial and scientific advances available to them and, more generally, for deviating from the Communist Party line. Gradov addressed the First Secretary directly in four introductory pages that summarized his principal complaints. But the real impact came in the enclosure: a one hundred-page letter in which Gradov spun a rich tale of intrigue and conspiracy that was sure to catch the attention of a leader like Khrushchev, whose appetite for drama was high and whose interest in such "signals from below" was piqued at this uncertain moment of political transition.[34]

This report was the work of a patient and meticulous mind that had been waiting years for the opportunity that post-Stalinism now presented. While Gradov could not have imagined, two years before the Secret Speech, that he would contribute to the effort of "de-Stalinization," his words were easily taken up in service of that cause. Nothing if not consistent, Gradov repeated a script that he, Ivanov, and others had rehearsed in their earlier letters and speeches. Soviet architecture had taken a wrong turn in the 1930s, Gradov argued, a turn away from technological and scientific advancement and toward "the slavish admiration of the archaic, the widespread unscrupulous copying of architectural features and forms dug up from the past, the cult of privileging unique architecture over mass [architecture]."[35] All of this, Gradov asserted, "is not in accordance with the ideals of our society and it contradicts the directives of the Party and of Lenin on the creation of a new socialist material and spiritual culture."[36] For twenty years, Gradov wrote, innovation in architecture had been liquidated. Who was responsible for this state of affairs was, for Gradov, plain to see.

Gradov may have found his audience at last in the era of de-Stalinization, but his letter to Khrushchev was, in its rhetoric, a Stalinist text through and through. Gradov explained to Khrushchev that "in the sphere of architecture a monopolistic Arakcheevist regime of ornamentalism and imitation reigns."[37] At the top of this "Arakcheevist regime," Gradov continued, was Mordvinov (fig. 8.1), who had surrounded himself with "unprincipled" architects, including Sergei Chernyshev, Nikolai Kolli, Nikolai Bylinkin and their "toadies." Standing in opposition were "active communists who raise their voices in criticism," like Gradov, but who were repeatedly thwarted in their attempts to redirect and save the profession.[38]

Gradov's letter was sent to the right person at the right time. Khrushchev was likely already preparing to wage a full-scale attack on Stalin's chief architects—an attack that would culminate at the Builders' Conference in Moscow in late 1954. But Gradov's letter provided the fuel for him to do it. At the Builders' Conference in December, Khrushchev would directly attack the leading architects of the Academy, including those who had built—and were, like Mordvinov, still building—Moscow's skyscrapers. In Khrushchev's attack on the profession, these monumental structures would serve as representative examples of Stalinist "excess."

Over two thousand representatives from the Soviet building industry from across the USSR were present for the week-long Builders' Conference that lasted from November 30 to December 7. In the coming days, the Soviet Union's newspapers would print excerpts of the major speeches delivered at the conference for the whole country to read. News of the drama that was unfolding in Moscow would quickly reach foreign observers as well.

Had Khrushchev not intervened so directly in the affairs of the city building professions in 1954, the Builders' Conference might have proceeded in the usual scripted fashion. In the weeks leading up to the event, speakers drafted and re-drafted their

Figure 8.1: Arkadii G. Mordvinov, architect of the Hotel Ukraine on the Dorogomilovo embankment and then-President of the USSR Academy of Architecture. Pictured in 1951 with his collective and a model of the hotel. The Hotel Ukraine was under construction until 1957. Collection of the Museum of Moscow.

speeches, rehearsing their lines in front of colleagues who gathered behind closed doors to provide feedback and criticism well ahead of the official proceedings. On November 18, 1954, a contingent of architects met to hear the draft speech of Mikhail Posokhin, head architect of the skyscraper on Uprising Square. Subjecting himself to this routine form of peer review, Posokhin heard the usual rebukes, with Mordvinov noting that there was not enough self-criticism (*samokritika*) in the speech.[39] But if Soviet architects were accustomed to criticism from their peers, nothing would prepare them for the tongue-lashing they would receive at the Builders' Conference from the incoming head of state. Khrushchev would deliver his address to the conference only on its final day, but this did not prevent him from weighing in earlier. From his seat in the hall, Khrushchev interrupted speakers at will throughout the proceedings.[40] The resulting spectacle, in which the heavyweights of the profession found themselves bewildered and speechless, was no doubt as unsettling as it was amusing for the others seated in the hall.

On the second day of the Builders' Conference, Georgii Gradov delivered what served as the first volley in Khrushchev's battle against Stalin's chief architects. From his place at the podium, Gradov made his usual complaints, attacking the Academy of Architecture for deviating from party directives in their pursuit of "artistic-decorative problems." This time, however, Gradov's words were bolstered by a powerful voice from the audience. Khrushchev roused the auditorium, interjecting enthusiastically in support. The two men played off each other in a carefully choreographed routine that aimed to root out the perpetrators of architectural "excess": "there, where you work, there are such people," Khrushchev said, interrupting Gradov, "so tell us . . . tell us your secrets."[41] The audience moved in their seats. "Comrades," Gradov continued, "the secrets that Nikita Sergeevich is talking about, if we can call them secrets, are that one part of the Academy of Architecture of the USSR—and not just the Academy, but also the Union of Soviet Architects—is of the opinion that the basis of architecture must lie not in pure aesthetics, but in a concern for the material-technical aspects of architecture."[42] The other part of the profession, however, believed "that architecture is first and foremost a creative art [*khudozhestvennoe iskusstvo*]."[43] For too long, Gradov claimed, this second approach to architecture had dominated.

Khrushchev pressed on: "Who's leading the charge in this way of thinking?" he demanded to know. Gradov was quick with a reply: it was Arkadii Mordvinov. "As Mordvinov emphasizes in his book," Gradov said, "'architecture is art'." Mordvinov had elevated monuments—and the monumental—to a higher status than industrial and agricultural construction, Gradov claimed. But there were others to blame as well. The architectural historian and theorist Ivan L. Matsa, Gradov noted, had also contributed to the lowly status of mass construction when he argued that "between 'high architecture' and 'simple' mass construction there is a difference akin to that between a person and a monkey."[44] The audience erupted in laughter at this line, but Gradov was not amused: "Comrades, I would not have drawn your attention to [these phrases] if they were not having serious negative effects on our architecture," he stated angrily.[45]

Gradov carried on with further examples, partly in response to Khrushchev's continued prodding but also because this was in fact the speech that he had prepared. He turned next to the sorry fate of party doctrine at the hands of the country's architectural aesthetes. The Academy's Institute of History and Theory had, in Gradov's view corrupted "one of socialism's fundamental economic laws." Setting the issue of "material need aside," the institute's new adage was: "Soviet architecture solves its problems with the goal of maximally satisfying the growing *aesthetic* needs of the whole people."[46] The auditorium erupted in laughter again, but to Gradov this aesthetic encroachment into sacred revolutionary texts was blasphemy.

When asked by Khrushchev who had coined this new adage, Gradov pointed to the director of the institute Comrade Kurochkin. "What if we were to give [Kurochkin] 'aesthetics' instead of an apartment, how do you think he'd react?" Khrushchev joked. "It's possible," replied Gradov, "that he doesn't feel the full sting of this incorrect understanding of architecture because he has an apartment."[47] Laughter burst forth from the auditorium once more. But now the comedic duo were getting to the heart of the matter. Soviet architecture was on the brink of a reformation that would see it eschewing aesthetics to focus instead on material need.

For Gradov, all of this boiled down to moral questions of Soviet citizens' access to housing and services. "Even in 1944–45," Gradov lamented,

when the country was faced with the urgent task of rebuilding cities and settlements destroyed by the war, when many of our people were living in dugouts and it was necessary to make good use of every ruble in construction, a number of leaders [in the profession] . . . concentrated their attention on the artistic problem of city planning, calling on architects to beautify cities, to build masses and monuments not justified by practical need. Given priority were questions about creating a showy effect, about the emotional impression of the natural landscape, about the color of buildings, about the creation of ocular accents, and so on.[48]

It was "just like Manilov," Gradov added, referring to the figure of the sentimental and ultimately foolish landowner in Nikolai Gogol's *Dead Souls*. Soviet architects, in Gradov's reading, had abdicated their duty to the people, opting to build monumentally instead of practically in the moment of the country's greatest need.

Underlying Gradov's attack on the Soviet Union's leading architects and theorists was a more fundamental criticism of Stalinism itself. De-Stalinization had scarcely begun in 1954, but the Builders' Conference provided a forum to test and rehearse criticisms of Stalin's legacy. Khrushchev's powerful predecessor had left an indelible mark on the cityscapes of the country. And it was no accident that in his own remarks at the Builders' Conference, Khrushchev targeted Moscow's skyscrapers specifically, directing his fiercest criticism toward the architects who designed and built these quintessential examples of Stalinist monumentalism. When Khrushchev took to the podium on the final day of the conference, he would continue Gradov's attack on Moscow's architects. But he would also, in targeting Stalin's tall buildings, lay blame at the feet of the former leader himself.

When Khrushchev spoke on the final day of the Builders' Conference, he called for greater efficiency in construction, increased use of industrialized and prefabricated materials, and an end to unnecessary decorations and embellishments in design that, as he stated, caused "unnecessary expenditures."[49] Like Gradov, Khrushchev singled out Mordvinov and others by name, targeting Moscow's top architects directly for their involvement in costly, impractical construction. "Comrade Mordvinov's report," Khrushchev stated, "and the speeches of some architects at this conference showed that they avoid the questions of economics in construction and are not interested in the cost per square meter of residential space."[50] "Architects, like all builders," Khrushchev noted,

> must make a sharp turn toward problems of construction economy, must study them thoroughly. It must always be remembered that one of the most important is the cost of erecting the building, the cost per square meter of space. An architect, if he wishes to keep abreast of life, must know and be able to use not only architectural forms, ornaments and various decorative elements; he must know the new progressive materials, reinforced-concrete sections and parts and, most of all, must have an excellent understanding of construction economy.[51]

Mordvinov and his colleagues, Khrushchev asserted, had neglected to consider the cost per square meter of space. Listing the exorbitant costs racked up in the construction of Moscow's skyscrapers, Khrushchev noted that "certain architects have been carried away with putting spires on buildings, with the result that such buildings resemble churches." This was not just a question of economics, but also of aesthetics: "Do you like the silhouette of a church?"[52] Khrushchev asked the audience.

Khrushchev also criticized Mordvinov for stifling criticism within the Academy of Architecture. Claiming that Gradov had sent a letter to the Communist Party "in which he set forth his critical observations on architectural problems"—and that Mordvinov had received it, but done nothing about it—Khrushchev sought to "eliminate every manifestation of monopolism and suppression of criticism" in the Soviet architectural profession.[53] According to Khrushchev, Mordvinov had actively worked to prevent Gradov from speaking at the Builders' Conference. "You, Comrade Mordvinov, and your assistants," Khrushchev stated, "have stifled the voices raised against embellishments and sham details in architecture."[54] Excesses, embellishments, redundant features, and architects getting "carried away by needless adorning of façades"[55]—this was the new language used to describe architecture once seen as beautiful, monumental, and majestic. Khrushchev avoided the Stalinist lexicon, in some cases clarifying ("we are not against beauty, but against superfluities")[56] but in most instances simply avoiding its terms altogether. Notably absent from Khrushchev's speech at the Builders' Conference was the word "happiness"—a word so central to Stalinist architectural development.

Within months of the Builders' Conference, major changes would be brought to the Soviet Union's architectural institutions. The event marked a radical break between Stalinist and post-Stalinist urbanism. Still, there were continuities to be observed at the conference as well. The criticisms that Khrushchev and Gradov brought to the fore in late 1954 were neither new nor original; as Daria Bocharnikova writes, the twin goals of industrialization and standardization in mass construction were "widely acknowledged in the profession and remained among the priorities of Soviet architecture before and after 1932."[57] And as postwar reconstruction got underway in the 1940s, these priorities only gained new urgency. In their theoretical debates, at least, Soviet architects never abandoned industrialized and standardized construction. It was undeniable that there were figures in the building profession, mainly architects, who embraced the artistic, expressive potential of architecture. But there were many others besides Gradov who advocated for a different approach.

The concerns raised by Khrushchev and Gradov at the Builders' Conference mirrored those stated by figures from outside the architectural profession. Present alongside the country's top architects at the conference were Ministry heads and construction managers like Nikolai A. Dygai, who oversaw the first three years of construction of the Leningrad Hotel skyscraper, Pavel A. Iudin, who oversaw the construction of the skyscraper on Smolensk Square, and David Ia. Raizer, who also oversaw the construction of the Smolensk Square skyscraper, along with the first years of the design and construction of Mordvinov's Hotel Ukraine. Dygai, Iudin, and Raizer all gave speeches of over an hour each, in which they advocated—albeit less colorfully—many of the same changes called for by Gradov and Khrushchev.[58] Dygai, who was now the USSR Minister of Construction, complained, "many architects understand architecture as an artistic activity, and not an activity in the realm of building."[59] Dygai saw standardized, mass construction as the most important field in Soviet architecture, but noted that "many architects see standardized design as a third-rate mode of work."[60] For some time, Dygai stated, "many architects have thought that a design without a tower or spire is no design at all."[61] As Minister of Construction, Dygai would see to it that this approach to urban development would change.

The delegates in attendance at the Builders' Conference returned home in December 1954 having witnessed the country's nascent leader intervening directly in the affairs of urban professionals. It surely came as no surprise to them, then, when the following year a series of reforms brought real, institutional change to Soviet architecture. From 1955 onward, the symbolic concerns of Stalinist monumentalism were swept aside in favor of a new mandate for urban development that was to be far less costly per square meter, though no less ambitious.

WHITHER MONUMENTALISM

The most tangible result of Khrushchev's intervention in Soviet architecture can be seen in the prefabricated mass housing districts that exist in cities across the former Soviet Union. In 1957, Khrushchev pledged to alleviate the Soviet Union's housing crisis within ten years when he unveiled his mass housing campaign. All Soviet families were to be provided a single-family apartment in new neighborhoods built mainly on the outskirts of cities throughout the country. And while the housing crisis was never fully alleviated, the results of Khrushchev's mass housing campaign were impressive. In the years between 1953 and 1970, over 38 million apartments and individually-built homes were constructed in both city and countryside and over 140 million residents moved into newly-built housing.[62] The mass housing campaign turned what had been an elite privilege during the Stalin era—the private, single-family apartment—into a more accessible dream.

Moscow would remain the epicenter of innovation as Khrushchev's mass housing campaign got underway in the late 1950s. The Cheremushki district that formerly housed skyscraper construction workers in the city's southwest was renamed "New (Novye) Cheremushki" as the area was redeveloped into a model "microdistrict"—the basic building block of the mass housing campaign. With its centralized amenities, communal parks, and small but comfortable apartments, the Novye Cheremushki microdistrict would be replicated for years to come in cities across the Soviet Union. As this prefabricated district went up in Moscow, it stood in sharp contrast with the MGU skyscraper that loomed on the horizon not far away. Moscow's skyscrapers became, at the very moment of their completion, negative models of urban design.

The popular and specialized press highlighted the contrast between Stalin's skyscrapers and Khrushchev's apartment blocks. In images published in architectural journals of the period, the skyscrapers were displaced to the background, where they served as foils against which Moscow's new housing districts were assessed. In an image from 1958, MGU is shown standing in the distance, its silhouette framed by tower cranes and partially obscured by the prefabricated apartment complex that might soon grow tall enough to block the university skyscraper entirely from view (fig. 8.2). In fact, in the late 1950s the most common form of mass housing was the shorter, five-story apartment block, nicknamed the "khrushchevka"; these shorter, squatter buildings were never intended to compete in height or monumentality with Moscow's skyscrapers. Mass housing blocks engaged the skyscrapers on different

Figure 8.2: "The Construction of Residential Buildings in the Southwest Region," Moscow.
Arkhitektura SSSR, February 1958.

terms, sending a message that the broader needs of the masses would now be elevated above symbolic or aesthetic concerns.

But before the Soviet Union's new apartment blocks appeared on the horizon, a series of institutional changes had to be introduced. Not long after the Builders' Conference, in the summer of 1955, the USSR Academy of Architecture was liquidated and replaced by the Academy of Construction and Architecture. A few months later, on November 4, 1955, the USSR Council of Ministers and the Communist Party Central Committee jointly issued a decree titled "On the Elimination of Excesses in Design and Construction."[63] The decree, which Gradov helped pen, codified many of the criticisms voiced at the Builders' Conference and set the path for the revolution in Soviet urban planning.[64] Architects and builders were officially called upon in 1955 to turn away from neoclassical and monumental design and to move toward a

Figure 8.3: "In the Family of an Architect," drawing by N. Lisogorskii. *Krokodil*, October 30, 1955.

Caption reads:

—Mommy, look at the cake that daddy bought!

—What are you talking about, that's the design for his new building.

pared-down prefabricated modernism. Some architects would view this shift as a return to the spirit of the avant-garde movements of the 1920s.[65] Gradov certainly favored this view and he would later credit Khrushchev with having rehabilitated Constructivism.[66]

The shift in Soviet architecture in the mid-1950s left Stalin's skyscrapers in the lurch. These buildings, designed to stand as proud symbols of Moscow's and the Soviet Union's greatness, were now prime examples of Stalinist "excess." The campaign against "excess" threatened to diminish the status of Stalin's skyscrapers not just in architectural circles but in the Soviet popular imagination as well. By 1955 the cartoonists at *Krokodil* had joined the campaign against architectural "excess." Once champions of Moscow's skyscraper project, *Krokodil*'s artists now created images that mocked the scorned approach to urban design (fig. 8.3). Ornate architectural models, like the one resembling an elaborately decorated cake in Lisogorskii's cartoon, were now objects of ridicule rather than veneration.

In the following years, Moscow's architects would reevaluate their work of the Stalin era through the new language of architectural "excess." In an article published in 1959, Moscow's former Chief Architect Aleksandr Vlasov looked back on the Builders' Conference as "a milestone marking the beginning of a decisive reform in architecture."[67] In the five years since that important event, Soviet architects like Vlasov had learned to conform with the new direction in architecture. "The basic element in any architectural style," Vlasov wrote, "is its attitude toward man and his needs. Soviet architects have not always been faithful to this principle." Evidence of this unfaithfulness, Vlasov wrote, could be seen most clearly in Moscow. It was in the Soviet capital in particular that "there have been crude distortions and extravagances, which are especially evident in the construction of tall buildings in Moscow," Vlasov argued. "What, for example, does the architecture of the Ukraine Hotel or the apartment building on the Kotelnicheskaya Embankment express?" Vlasov asked. "These buildings," he continued,

> are characterized by a contrived plan, an elaborate structure with many super-structures that have no rational function, irrational construction and, as a result, fabulously high cost of apartments. Only a few years have passed, but we are right in saying that the architecture of these tall buildings has not stood the test of time.[68]

While Vlasov was not himself the architect of any of Moscow's skyscrapers, he had participated in the evaluation of the designs proposed for these buildings in 1947.[69] This architect's assessment of Stalin's tall buildings twelve years later showed the rapidity with which the profession had shifted under the strain of new political pressures.

Vlasov, once one of the country's preeminent proponents in Stalinist "excess," had swiftly found himself pursuing the new path in architecture. In the autumn of 1955, he and ten other urban specialists were dispatched on a trip to the US to study the latest advances in American housing construction. Nearing the end of this trip abroad, Vlasov had found himself at the center of an international scandal. Before Vlasov's visit, news of the dramatic changes brought about by the Builders' Conference had travelled well beyond Soviet borders and American newspapers began to speculate wildly about what was going on in the Moscow architectural scene. In March 1955, the *New York Times* reported that there had been a "ban on skyscrapers" in the Soviet Union.[70] In September, the paper claimed that "standardization is ordered for nearly all construction within two years."[71] Then, that November when Vlasov was in America, the newspaper erroneously reported that Vlasov had been sacked from his job back in Moscow. As the *New York Times* stated, the architect was unable to comment on his dismissal, since he was "not acquainted with it."[72] Vlasov and his Soviet delegation were taken completely by surprise.

The American press knew that Khrushchev had targeted Vlasov and others at the Builders' Conference in 1954.[73] The report on Vlasov's dismissal was likely the result of the confusion that foreign observers faced when trying to make heads or tails of the rapidly changing currents in Soviet architecture in those years. Despite the report about Vlasov not being true, the *New York Times* story set in motion a series of events that would prove hard to rein in. Vlasov made his way back quickly to Moscow via Paris the day after the report of his dismissal came out in the *Times*. And to his great surprise, Vlasov was greeted in Paris by, as the *New York Times* itself reported, "a small group of anti-Communist Russian exiles and French students [who] attempted to wrest Alexander V. Vlasov away from his Soviet colleagues . . ."[74] Under the impression that Vlasov was keen to defect, this group of Parisians had sought to rescue him. In the end, Vlasov made his way safely back to Moscow. The Cold War had changed the dynamic of Soviet-American relations in the field of architecture. Moscow's turn toward prefabrication and mass construction led to the renewal of ties between the Soviet and American building professions. But Soviet architects would not experience in the 1950s the comparatively relaxed foreign ties enjoyed by their colleagues in the 1930s. The Vlasov episode demonstrated the potential for dangerous forms of misunderstanding and mistranslation in this newly tense global atmosphere.

Soviet architects adapted to changes in their profession in a variety of ways. Figures like Vlasov and Mordvinov were agile enough to swim in new currents. The new era in Soviet architecture also, of course, made room for individuals like Georgii Gradov. He rose through the ranks in the late 1950s at the new Academy of Construction and Architecture and at the Union of Architects, quickly becoming Director of the Soviet Research Institute for Public Building (NIIOZ). In 1955, Gradov was sent to The Hague, where he represented the Soviet architectural profession at the fourth congress of the International Union of Architects (UIA). This organization, founded in 1946 in Lausanne, Switzerland, had a strong Soviet presence, and its members watched Moscow closely as the climate in the country shifted under Khrushchev. As Catherine Cooke notes, the Builders' Conference was an important moment for Soviet internationalism in that it paved the way toward the "parallel development" of Soviet architecture and architectural practice abroad.[75] The UIA was one forum facilitating this parallel development and the renewed internationalism that accompanied it. In 1958, three years after Gradov attended the UIA conference at The Hague, this organization would hold its fifth international congress in Moscow. But while Soviet and foreign architects found themselves in agreement on questions of design, Cold War rivalries limited the potential for real engagement. In the years after 1953, the Soviet Union would continue to use architecture as a tool in its competition with the West.

"WHY FLY TO THE SKY? WHAT'S WRONG WITH THE GROUND?"

In 1956, Khrushchev took his criticism of Soviet architectural monumentalism on the road. At a speech to Polish officials at the Central Committee plenum of the Polish United Workers' Party, Khrushchev spoke at length about the waste of state resources under his predecessor in all manner of projects, from dams to Moscow State University. "We built the university," Khrushchev stated, "it is a very beautiful university; very beautiful, but very unwisely built. Why should a student or professor go all the way up to the 36th floor? What for?" Denying that a university should serve any purpose beyond the education of students, Khrushchev questioned the wish to build in excess of practical need. "Why fly to the sky," Khrushchev asked, "what's wrong with the ground?"[76]

Khrushchev's criticism of MGU rested principally on the issue of wasted funds, but the new Soviet leader also articulated a clear, functionalist position that stripped the built environment of its symbolic potential. "If someone took a pencil and started to count," Khrushchev told his Polish audience, "we, by using the same money we wasted on this university, could have built three or four universities of the same capacity." And beyond the funds used to build the structure, Khrushchev lamented, were those devoted to operating it into the future: "almost an entire factory" was needed to keep the university up and running. "Who needed it?" Khrushchev asked,

> It was silliness. Stupidity. In America, the buildings are tall. There, Americans do it smartly and wisely. All of America is one story high. But Americans build only in the big cities; in centers, where the land is more expensive than the construction of the high-rise. It's economically justified under capitalistic conditions; but we are located in the fields . . . where, you understand, parks could be formed . . . When our people will become richer and smarter, they will refuse to use high buildings and build a building of two, three, four floors in height. And use the money from the operating cost and use it for something more useful.[77]

Khrushchev need not have used the example of Moscow State University to make his point in this speech delivered in Poland in 1956. Stalinist monumentalism had travelled westward in the late Stalin era.[78] In 1951 and 1952, the Soviet government gave skyscrapers as "brotherly gifts" to the Eastern Bloc capital cities of Warsaw, Prague, and Bucharest and to the Soviet capital cities of Kiev and Riga. Poland's Stalinist skyscraper was completed in 1955, less than one year before Khrushchev delivered his address at the plenum. But pointing to Warsaw's new skyscraper as an example of wasted state resources may have been too undiplomatic, even for Khrushchev.

While Khrushchev had paved the way for the new direction in Soviet architecture in Moscow, cities on the periphery of the Soviet sphere were sent mixed signals in the mid 1950s. At the very moment that the Stalinist skyscraper was being unceremoniously discarded from the pantheon of Soviet architectural achievements in Moscow, identical buildings were under construction in Eastern Europe. After 1953, the distinctive Soviet skyscraper would continue to serve as a useful tool in helping to forge ties in the expanding socialist sphere.[79] While Warsaw's Stalinist skyscraper opened its doors in 1955, Riga's skyscraper, a structure serving as the new headquarters of this city's Academy of Sciences, was completed only in 1961. That building would stand as a testament to the slow unravelling of Stalinist aesthetics on the periphery of the empire.

When duplicated abroad, Moscow's Stalin-era skyscrapers served a dual purpose: they stood as examples of socialist realism and as iconic and instantly recognizable symbols of membership in the socialist sphere. And so, while its progenitors back in Moscow were facing increasing hostility, Warsaw's new Palace of Culture and Science, for example, was being hailed in official circles as a "beautiful gift." The links that skyscraper construction forged went well beyond the aesthetic. According to the agreements drawn up for the transfer of these "gifts," the Soviet state provided funding, supplies, labor, and expertise, while each receiving nation agreed to have the silhouette of its capital city permanently altered to reflect its ties to Moscow.

In the Warsaw case, an agreement had been drawn up on April 5, 1952, between the Soviet and Polish governments. The Soviet Union pledge to fund the construction of a 28–30-story Palace of Culture and Science (PKiN). This building would serve as the headquarters for the Polish Academy of Sciences, and as an important public building housing youth and cultural organizations, exhibitions, congress and concert halls, and a movie theater. Assigning responsibility for the construction of this skyscraper to the USSR Ministry of Construction of Heavy Industry, the Soviet government agreed to send design teams, engineers, and workers to Warsaw to build the Palace. The Polish government in turn would, according to the initial agreement, supply an additional 4,000–5,000 Polish workers for the project, as well as logistical support on the ground.[80]

Warsaw's Palace of Culture and Science was presented in 1952 as a Soviet contribution to the postwar reconstruction of this city. Following the announcement that the skyscraper would be built, various groups wrote to Polish newspapers expressing their thanks in the gracious and obsequious manner that the situation demanded. Participants at the Fourth Polish Assembly of Builders, for example, wrote a letter addressed to the Soviet state and published in the newspaper *Żołnierz Wolności* (*Soldiers of Freedom*). "We builders," they wrote, "are especially happy to receive the news today that our Soviet comrades are coming to visit us, not only to lend a hand and to give more materials towards the reconstruction of Warsaw, but, as we especially value, to teach us through concrete construction applications all [their] wonderful achievements"—the pinnacle of which were, of course, Moscow's tall buildings, "the most vanguard construction in the world."[81]

Back in Moscow, planning on the new skyscraper for Warsaw had been in the works since early 1951. A Council of Ministers decree of October 1951 made the project official by establishing requirements for height and other elements of the new structure.[82] And by February 1952, before the agreement between the Polish and Soviet governments had been reached, the team of architects working on Warsaw's Palace had already drawn up plans for the building. This team was led by Lev Rudnev, head architect of Moscow State University. Rudnev approached the Warsaw skyscraper as a structure that should, like its Moscow forerunners, combine the latest technological advances in steel-frame construction with design elements that reflected national—in this case Polish—culture.

Just as Moscow's skyscrapers were understood to be rooted in Russian national heritage, so too was Warsaw's new Palace to reflect Polish national form in its ornate façade and throughout the building's interior. Rudnev toured Poland for inspiration in 1951. Admiring the heritage restoration work underway in cities like Krakow and in Warsaw's Old Town, Rudnev was especially impressed by the Polish tradition of metalworking, which he incorporated into the detailing of Warsaw's new Palace.[83] Stalinist monumentalism proved to be a convenient vehicle through which to make the Soviet skyscraper more palatable to a variety of local audiences. Classical architectural vocabularies, in particular, offered architects the flexibility to present an imperialistic urban vision as the product of local, vernacular traditions.

Warsaw's new skyscraper, known initially as the "Palace of Culture and Science in honor of Joseph Stalin," officially opened its doors in July 1955 (fig. 8.4). Further solidifying the link between skyscrapers and communism, the opening ceremony of

Figure 8.4: Palace of Culture and Science in Warsaw, 1955. Collection of the State Central Museum of Contemporary Russian History.

the building was held on the occasion of the anniversary of the Polish People's Republic.[84] The Palace—with its congress hall equipped with seating for 3,500, its scientific institute, movie theater, and concert hall, and its swimming pool, basketball, and volleyball courts—was transferred to the Polish state on July 21, 1955. Along with the Palace, the Soviet state also gave Poland "Friendship" ("*Druzhba*")—a workers' village that had been built nearby and included 83 dormitories and 83 single-family cottages formerly occupied by Soviet construction workers.[85] In his speech at the opening ceremony, the Chairman of the Polish Council of Ministers thanked the builders of the Palace of Culture and Science for their "beautiful and noble gift" to the Polish people.[86]

The city of Warsaw was thus caught in the same puzzle as Moscow: structures that had only just appeared on the cityscape and that were, in actuality, quite useful were all of a sudden deemed immediately after their arrival to have "not stood the test of time." In Warsaw as in Moscow, now that they had arrived on the skylines of their respective cities the Stalinist skyscrapers proved to be more than just monuments. The Warsaw Palace for its part was a flexible, multi-use complex that successfully and continuously served the population of the city. As Michał Murawski shows in his study of the building, the Palace of Culture and Science complex has served as the "center of gravity" in Warsaw well into the post-socialist period.[87] In 1958, three years after opening, Warsaw's Palace had already received twenty million visitors. The popularity of the structure was in part the result of its scale and multiple purposes: as Murawski notes, this building was the only venue in Warsaw able to host the Rolling Stones when they played their first and only concert in communist Eastern Europe in 1967.

Khrushchev could not have been more wrong in his prediction in 1956 that when "our people" got "richer and smarter" they would refuse to use skyscrapers entirely. As Karl Schlögel writes, "if the architects of these buildings had been wholly informed by ideology and not by their practical purpose of providing space and splendid interiors—in other words, had they not been designed to be useful—then by now they would be ruins, or simply, as someone said to me in the Hotel Leningradskaya, 'architectural monuments.' But they are not."[88] Stalinist monumentalism, as it turned out, was as enduring as it was excessive.

MOSCOW'S SKYSCRAPERS AND THE THAW

The Stalinist skyscraper may have been cast as the enemy in the battle against "excess," but in Moscow the structures nevertheless served as key sites of the Thaw. In the late 1950s, foreign guests were welcomed by their Soviet hosts in the marbled halls of Moscow State University and in the opulent interiors of the Hotel Ukraine and Hotel Leningrad. And so, as de-Stalinization got underway, Stalin's tall buildings were found to be more than mere monuments on the cityscape. As aesthetically suspect as they were after 1954, these towers became icons of the time. In July 1957, the Sixth World Festival of Youth and Students was held in Moscow, attracting 34,000 visitors to the Soviet capital. Many of them stayed in the skyscraper hotels, and they joined together to dance and sing at mass events held at Moscow State University on the Lenin Hills.[89]

It was not just foreign youth who were received in the opulent surroundings of MGU. In the summer of 1958, the Union of Soviet Architects hosted the Fifth Congress of the International Union of Architects (UIA) in Moscow. Foreign curiosity about the Soviet Union ensured that the Fifth Congress was especially well attended. Over 1,400 architects from 44 different countries arrived in Moscow in July 1958, with many of them staying at the Hotel Ukraine.[90] The theme of the congress was "The Construction and Reconstruction of Cities from 1945–1957," but Moscow's architects organizing the proceedings took the event as an opportunity to showcase the new Soviet achievements in mass housing construction—achievements that had only just begun. An exhibition of Soviet architectural plans and drawings was mounted at MGU for all to see. The focus of the show was the country's designs for prefabricated mass housing construction.

While this architectural exhibition of 1958 sought to highlight the new trends in Soviet construction, it was impossible to erase traces of the Stalinist approach to design. As the Union of Architects representative dutifully reported, "the exhibition commission took great care to omit from the display buildings and structures with excesses."[91] But Soviet architects' efforts to purge all exhibition photographs of columns, spires, decorative friezes, and other "excesses" was hopeless. From the Lenin Hills, visitors gazed out across a cityscape newly dominated by Moscow's ornate, neoclassical skyscrapers. Moreover, the exhibition was held inside Moscow State University—the most pronounced example of Stalinist excess. As Khrushchev put it years later, "approaching [MGU] from a distance, someone who doesn't know better might think it's a church. He sees huge spires, cupolas on the horizon, silhouetted against the sky. When you get closer, the whole complex looks like an ugly formless mass."[92] It was a strange setting, to be sure, for an exhibition of Soviet advances in mass housing construction.

Stalin's tall buildings were enormous, intractable masses on the cityscape, whether officials like Khrushchev liked them or not. Seven of these buildings had been completed, or nearly completed, by the time Khrushchev had ascended to power. The eighth unbuilt skyscraper in the Zariad'e would never be finished. (In its place, the Zariad'e skyscraper's architect, Dmitrii Chechulin, built his modernist Hotel Rossiia in the mid-1960s. The hotel would be demolished in 2006 and replaced in 2017 with the Zaryadye Park, designed by the New York-based firm Diller Scofidio + Renfro. The churches saved on the Zariad'e site in the late-Stalin period remain.) The only question remaining was what to do about the unbuilt Palace of Soviets.

A NEW PALACE OF SOVIETS

It did not take long after Stalin's death for doubts about the Palace of Soviets project to be raised openly by those in charge of Moscow's urban development. As early as August 1953 Khrushchev and Malenkov received a letter jointly written by the head of the Moscow Communist Party Committee, Nikolai A. Mikhailov, and the head of Mossovet, Mikhail A. Iasnov. These two municipal-level officials wished to express their concerns about the Palace. The new General Plan for Moscow of 1951–1960 stated that the Palace of Soviets would be constructed, at last, after Moscow's eight monumental skyscrapers were completed. In their letter, Mikhailov and Iasnov recalled that Iofan had reworked the design for the Palace of Soviets during the war: in the revised design, the structure was to be shorter and stouter—at 364 meters in all—than was originally planned. Still, the monumentality of the planned Palace would be impressive, with the dome of its grand amphitheater reaching a height of 103 meters.[93] For Mikhailov and Iasnov, it was precisely this monumentalism that presented a problem.

Mikhailov and Iasnov stressed in their letter that construction costs for the as-yet-unbuilt Palace of Soviets had already reached the incredible sum of 240 million rubles, with "120 million rubles spent on design, survey, and experimental work."[94] But beyond their financial concerns, there were more serious defects in the planned structure caused, they asserted, by "a desire for gigantomania." "For example," the two officials wrote, "nothing can justify the installation of a sculpture of V. I. Lenin at such a height, so that for much of the year it will be up in the clouds or the fog."[95] The amphitheater within the structure was also gargantuan. What would the acoustics be like in such an enormous space? How would maintenance work be carried out in such a building? These were questions, Mikhailov and Iasnov noted, that had no clear answers.

The letter of August 1953 from Mikhailov and Iasnov was no doubt received by at least one sympathetic reader in Nikita Khrushchev. Still, it would take a few more years before the Palace of Soviets project, as designed by Iofan, Gel'freikh, and Shchuko, would be abandoned once and for all. In February 1955, Iofan himself wrote to Khrushchev. Having spent many years writing to Stalin, Iofan now approached this new interlocutor with some caution. The architect opened his letter by recounting for Khrushchev the history of the project. He explained that construction of the Palace had been put on hold in 1941, but that design work had continued through the war and up to the present. Iofan stressed the role his building would play in commemorating Lenin. He also emphasized how swiftly Moscow's tallest tower could be built. "Resuming construction work on the Palace of Soviets has been seriously delayed," Iofan wrote.[96] The postwar period had nonetheless served to strengthen the Palace's construction workers, who now had the experience and technical knowledge needed to quickly bring the Palace of Soviets into reality.

When writing to Khrushchev in 1955, Iofan surely sensed, amidst the dramatic shifts underway that year in Soviet architecture, that his Palace of Soviets would never be built. Later that year, the Communist Party Central Committee issued an order calling for a new design competition for the structure.[97] Held between 1957 and 1959, the new competition revealed the enormous changes that had taken hold in architecture in the short time since Stalin's death. A new location was chosen for the Palace outside the city center, on a site situated just southwest of MGU. In a meeting of the Central Committee in November 1955, Khrushchev, Kaganovich, Iofan, and others discussed the new Palace project in broad outlines. Insisting that while the structure would maintain its original purpose as a monument to Lenin, Khrushchev was adamant that the new Palace "does not need to be 460 stories tall."[98]

Rather than emphasizing monumentalism and verticality, as the design by Iofan, Shchuko, and Gel'freikh had done in the 1930s, the new design submissions by and large emphasized horizontality.[99] Some proposals were reminiscent of Hector Hamilton's winning entry for the Palace competition of 1932. Others made extensive use of glass, steel, and mosaic-work, and still more were futuristic, drawing on the new aesthetic of the space age. By the time the competition advanced to the second round in 1959, all proposals for the Palace of Soviets were long, flat structures designed to work in concert with, but not overshadow, MGU. In the end, like the first Palace of Soviets, the second one would never be built to completion.

The unbuilt Palace of Soviets lives on in Moscow today in the seven Stalinist sky-scrapers that were built to completion in the 1950s. Yet the afterlife of the Palace of Soviets is not limited to these structures built during the Stalin era. The building's legacy stretches into the twenty-first century. When they traveled to America in 1934, Iofan and his team from the USDS could not have predicted that their work with Moran & Proctor would contribute to the construction of a highrise business district in post-Soviet Moscow. The sleek glass skyscrapers that make up the Moscow International Business Center, known as Moskva-City, bear little resemblance to the Palace of Soviets, but there are connections between the two projects all the same.

In the mid-2000s, Mueser Rutledge Consulting Engineers (formerly Moran & Proctor) was hired as the geotechnical consultant for Moskva-City's Mercury City Tower, completed in 2013. When they began work on this 75-story bronze-tinted glass structure, the engineers at Mueser Rutledge turned to their firm's work in Moscow seven decades earlier for guidance. They sifted through records in the company's past projects vault, looking for information collected in the 1930s on the Palace of Soviets site. Among the hundreds of pages documenting Moran & Proctor's work in Moscow, they found feasibility studies, settlement analyses, and site load tests. These subsurface investigations remained useful since, as the engineers put it recently, "conditions were not that different" on the site chosen for Mercury City Tower.[100] The careful measurements taken in the 1930s of the limestone and marl that lie beneath Moscow have not expired with the passage of time or with the passing of communism. Similarly, the impulse to build monumentally has survived from one era into the next.

EPILOGUE

Moscow's Stalinist skyscrapers continue to dominate the cityscape of the Russian capital today. These buildings serve, as they were intended to, as luxury hotels and residences. Moscow State University still looks out across the city from the Lenin (now Sparrow) Hills and the Ministry of Foreign Affairs still looms intimidatingly over Smolensk Square. Decades after their construction, the seven towers that were built to completion in the postwar years stand as icons on the Moscow cityscape. Stalinist architectural monumentalism served to make Moscow distinctive, while at the same time connecting the city to global discussions and trends. Building monumentally in Moscow after 1945 also led to broader consequences that this book has explored. From displaced residents, to construction workers, to those who received luxury apartments in these structures, the threads of so many individual lives are woven through the history of eight buildings—nine if we count the Palace of Soviets. And as long as they are standing, Moscow's skyscrapers will continue to shape daily life in the city.

The lasting symbolic power of Moscow's Stalinist skyscrapers can be seen in copycat structures built in recent years. In 2001, at the start of Vladimir Putin's first term as Russian President, construction began on a 57-story skyscraper—the so-called "Triumph Palace"—in the Sokol district in northwest Moscow (fig. E.1). When this building was completed in 2006, it was briefly the tallest skyscraper in Europe. The Triumph Palace contains around one thousand luxury apartments in nine separate wings of the structure. A boutique hotel is located on the upper floors and the underground parking lot below has space for 1,500 luxury cars. According to the skyscraper's own website, this structure is equipped with all modern amenities necessary for living a "comfortable life": a hair and nail salon, a world-class fitness center, a bakery and other shops on the first floor, fountains, well-manicured grounds, an apple orchard in the inner courtyard, and a covered walkway leading out to the street. As for the Triumph Palace's location, Sokol is billed as a "green oasis near central Moscow."[1]

The Triumph Palace's position at the apex of European skyscraper building was short-lived. By 2017, in the rankings of Europe's tallest buildings, it had fallen from first to eleventh place. For the most part, new construction within Moscow itself is to blame for this. The number of new skyscrapers built in the city in recent years is impressive, even by international standards. Still, the Triumph Palace holds a unique position on the Moscow cityscape. Its classical ornamentation separates it from Moscow's other new skyscrapers, like the cluster of buildings constructed since the early 2000s in Moskva-City (fig. E.2). Skyscrapers in Moscow today tend to feature sleek glass façades and asymmetrical masses—qualities that make them the same sort of building you might see under construction in Dubai, Frankfurt, or New York City. The Triumph Palace, by contrast, stands out with its tall spire, classical detailing,

Figure E.1: Triumph Palace, Moscow, photographed in 2019. Built 2001–2006.
Photography by Natalia Melikova.

Figure E.2: Moscow International Business District, known as "Moskva-City," photographed in 2011. The Mercury City Tower was still in construction in this image. Also visible in the image are the tall spires of the Hotel Ukraine (to the right of Moskva-City) and the Triumph Palace (to the left in the distance). Photography by Natalia Melikova.

and "wedding-cake"-like shape. These features are, of course, the characteristic markers of Moscow's Stalinist towers—a connection that the Triumph Palace's website, through which units are viewed and sold, openly references. At the heart of this building's design was "the idea of a revival of the style of the '50s and a continuation of the best traditions of the Stalinist skyscrapers."[2]

The Triumph Palace caters to the post-socialist tastes of Russia's post-Soviet elites, but the building's silhouette makes it the unmistakable progeny of Moscow's seven Stalin-era skyscrapers.[3] By placing new buildings like the Triumph Palace in conversation with the city's Stalin-era heritage, real estate developers and architects are banking on the power of Stalinism as a brand in post-Soviet Russia. This brand revives the Stalin-era values of luxury and high culture propagated from the 1930s to the 1950s. And in the same way that Moscow's Stalinist skyscrapers did sixty years ago, the Triumph Palace works to create spaces of elite culture and exclusivity on the Moscow skyline.

The Triumph Palace builds on the Stalinist foundation in other ways as well. The Putin-era turn to the Stalinist past carries on the Cold War-era tradition of distancing Russia from foreign influence. Stalinist monumentalism functions not just as a sign of luxury, but also as a symbol of Russian nationalism and Russia's unique cultural contribution to world architecture. In mimicking the Stalinist skyscraper, the Triumph Palace signals a turning away from the "global" architecture cropping up in commercial spaces like Moskva-City. It stands as a rejection of what Leslie Sklair calls the "icons of capitalist globalization"—the seemingly identical glass towers that have transformed and flattened out distinctions between cityscapes around the world in recent decades.[4]

Moscow's Triumph Palace is not alone in referencing Stalinism's unique architectural tradition. Other buildings in Moscow follow suit, and Stalinist architectural monumentalism can be found in new construction beyond Moscow as well. In 2006, for example, the Stalinist skyscraper made its way to Central Asia with the construction of the Triumph of Astana, a building that is both residential complex and shopping center. Boris Groys writes that "every artist in any area once under Communism still finds him- or herself under the shadow of the state art that has just gone under. It is not easy for an artist to compete today with Stalin, Ceausescu, Tito."[5] This is undoubtedly true. But not all artists, architects, and construction companies wish to compete. As Stalin-era architects themselves understood, returning to historic models can serve a legitimating purpose. So long as Stalinism is associated with power and national prestige, we will continue to see tiered monumental skyscrapers on the rise throughout the region.

Notes

INTRODUCTION

1. "Zamechaniia Tovarishcha Stalina I.V. pri obsuzhdenii voprosa o general'nom plane rekonstruktsii Moskvy na zasedanii Politbiuro TsK VKP(b) 17 iiunia 1949 goda," *Istochnik*, 4, (2001): 110.
2. Trigger, "Monumental Architecture," 119.
3. Lefebvre, *The Production of Space*, 220.
4. GARF f. R-5446, op. 86a, d. 11686, l. 1.
5. The classic text on Stalinist industrial-urban development during the First Five-Year Plan is Kotkin's *Magnetic Mountain*. More recent studies of Stalinist interwar urban planning include DeHaan, *Stalinist City Planning;* and Crawford, "The Socialist Settlement Experiment: Soviet Urban Praxis, 1917–1932."
6. Zubkova, *Russia after the War*.
7. Dunham, *In Stalin's Time*.
8. Brandenberger, *National Bolshevism*; Plamper, *The Stalin Cult*.
9. Barnes, *Death and Redemption*; Bell, *Stalin's Gulag at War*; Barenberg, *Gulag Town, Company Town*.
10. On postwar urban reconstruction in the Soviet Union, see Qualls, *From Ruins to Reconstruction*; Smith, *Property of Communists*; Dale, "Divided We Stand: Cities, Social Unity and Post-War Reconstruction in Soviet Russia, 1945–1953"; Maddox, *Saving Stalin's Imperial City*; Jones, *Everyday Life and the "Reconstruction" of Soviet Russia During and After the Great Patriotic War, 1943–1948*.
11. Fürst, "Late Stalinist society: history, policies and people," 2.
12. On youth culture and intellectuals see Fürst, *Stalin's Last Generation* and Tromly, *Making the Soviet Intelligentsia*; on continuities in architecture and housing construction see Smith, *Property of Communists*; on the late-Stalinist origins of bribery and corruption typically associated with later periods, see Heinzen, *The Art of the Bribe*.
13. The richest Russian-language study of Moscow's Stalinist skyscrapers is Kruzhkov, *Vysotnye zdaniia stalinskoi Moskvy*. Kruzhkov focuses on questions of design and construction technologies, drawing chiefly on published sources. The skyscrapers are also discussed, with the focus mainly on their formal characteristics, in Papernyi, *Architecture in the Age of Stalin: Culture Two*; Schlögel, *Moscow*; Khmel'nitskii, *Zodchii Stalin*; Colton, *Moscow: Governing a Socialist Metropolis*. The architectural designs of the skyscrapers have also been widely exhibited and published in exhibition catalogues and albums, including Sedov and Sarkisyan, *Les sept tours de Moscou, 1935–1950*; Vas'kin and Nazarenko, *Stalinskie neboskreby*.

CHAPTER 1: RED MOSCOW

1. Sidorow, *Moskau*, xi.
2. Kollmann, *By Honor Bound*, 196.
3. Martin, *Enlightened Metropolis*, 61; Martin, "Policing and the Creation of an Early Modern City," 116–129.
4. Bradley, *Muzhik and Muscovite*, 345. See also Colton, *Moscow*, 53–63.
5. These population numbers are from GARF f. R-5446, op. 86a, d. 11032, l. 128; and Colton, *Moscow*, 757–758.
6. Hoffmann, *Peasant Metropolis, 31*.
7. Sidorow, *Moskau*, xi.
8. Sidorow, *Moskau*, xiii.
9. Sidorow, *Moskau*, vii.
10. Cooke, "The Garden City Idea," 358.
11. Colton, *Moscow*, 106–107, 225–228; Kazus', *Sovetskaia arkhitektura 1920x godov*, 41; Khan-Magomedov, *Pioneers of Soviet Architecture*, 272–273.

12. This building now houses the Russian State Archive of Social-Political History (RGASPI).
13. Thomas R. Ybarra, "New Tombs for the Pilgrims to Visit," *New York Times*, September 1, 1929, 8.
14. Hilton, "Retailing the Revolution," 939–964.
15. Benjamin, *Moscow Diary*, 66. Benjamin also noted, "there are no trucks in Moscow, no delivery vans, etc. Whether it be a small purchase or a major shipment, everything has to go by tiny sled or *izvozchik* [coachman]" (19).
16. The Sukharevskii market was closed in November 1932 because of alleged profiteering. Hoffmann, *Peasant Metropolis*, 155.
17. Kozhin and Lebedev, *Aleksei Alekseevich Sidorov*, 3–4, 7–14.
18. Kozhin and Lebedev, *Aleksei Alekseevich Sidorov*, 9–10. In 1917, when the art historical profession tended more toward formal analysis, Sidorov's argument was reactionary. Sidorov was responding in particular to the art historical method advanced by German art historian Heinrich Wölfflin, with whom Sidorov had studied while in Munich in 1913 or 1914. Wölfflin, one of the foundational thinkers of formalism at the turn of the twentieth century, saw stylistic developments over time as the result of changes that were internal to art form itself. See Kozhin and Lebedev, *Aleksei Alekseevich Sidorov*, 7.
19. Sidorov, *Revoliutsiia i Iskusstvo,* 3.
20. This museum was given its current name—the Pushkin Museum of Fine Arts—only in 1937, on the occasion of the centenary of the poet's death.
21. The exhibition was held in honor of the 400th anniversary of Dürer's death.
22. On Grinberg, see Shneer, *Through Soviet Jewish Eyes,* 31–34. See also Stolarski, "The Rise of Photojournalism in Russia and the Soviet Union, 1900–1931," 283–284.
23. On the return of documentary photography in the post-Stalin period, see Reid, "Photography in the Thaw," 33–39.
24. Castillo, "Gorky Street and the Design of the Stalin Revolution," 57–70.
25. Oksana Bulgakowa notes that the real Moscow made for a unruly backdrop for Soviet films of the 1930s: "on every big square, monasteries and warehouses blocked the view and bore little correspondence to the new city's ideal vision." Bulgakowa, "Spatial Figures in Soviet Cinema of the 1930s," 64.
26. This building, located at 16 Vozdvizhenka, belonged to Arsenii Abramovich Morozov. A relation of merchant patron Savva Morozov, Arsenii was the younger brother of Ivan Morozov, whose art collection famously included paintings by Picasso and Matisse. After 1917, Proletkul't maintained its offices and studios in the building.
27. As Albert Schmidt writes, this well-known building with its Hall of Columns "more than any other symbolized the 'golden age of the Russian nobility.'" Schmidt, *The Architecture and Planning of Classical Moscow*, 74.
28. Merridale, *Red Fortress*, 282–283.
29. Stites, *Revolutionary Dreams*, 91–92.
30. von Geldern, "Putting the Masses in Mass Culture: Bolshevik Festivals, 1918–1920," 123–144.
31. Stites, *Revolutionary Dreams*, 92.
32. On experiments with urban communes by architects and others in the 1920s, see Andy Willimott, *Living the Revolution*.
33. Ikonnikov, *Arkhitektura Moskvy XX vek*, 48–49.
34. Moscow party committee statement of December 28, 1930 quoted in Rees, *Iron Lazar*, 152–153; Also quoted in Colton, *Moscow*, 252.
35. "O Moskovskom gorodskom khoziaistve i o razvitii gorodskogo khoziaistva SSSR. Doklad tov. Kaganovicha L.M. na iunskom plenume TsK VKP(b)," *Pravda*, July 4, 1931, 6; Kaganovich, *Socialist Reconstruction of Moscow and Other Cities in the USSR*.
36. While ambitious, this planned development could not keep pace with the rapidly growing city. As David L. Hoffmann notes, in 1931 and 1932 alone, Moscow gained an additional 1 million residents. Hoffmann, *Peasant Metropolis*, 7.
37. Kaganovich, *Socialist Reconstruction*, 29, 34, 47.
38. Kaganovich, *Socialist Reconstruction*, 47.
39. On the Moscow Metro, see Jenks, "A Metro on the Mount"; O'Mahony, "Archaeological Fantasies." On the Moscow-Volga Canal, see Ruder, *Building Stalinism*.
40. "Dvorets sovetov—Proletarskaia vyshka," *Sovetskoe isskustvo*, July 23, 1931, 2.
41. GARF f. R-3316, op. 64, d. 562, ll. 1–2. The project was first proposed in 1922 on the occasion of the First Congress of Unions. Planning began when Avel' Enukidze, Kliment Voroshi-

lov, and Konstantin Ukhanov met in January 1928 to discuss the earlier idea. They envisioned a building with a large hall for congresses and meetings of up to 20,000 people, two smaller halls for 5,000 and 1,500 people each, four rooms for smaller gatherings of a few hundred people, a dining hall with the capacity to feed 10,000 people per day, and hotel rooms for 5,000. The building would be completed, by their estimate, in five years.

42. On the Cathedral and its fate, see Kirichenko, *Khram khrista spasitelia v Moskve.*

43. GARF f. R-3316, op. 64, d. 563, l. 188.

44. The other locations proposed in 1928 were the Arbat market and the "swamp" on the Sophia embankment across from the Kremlin. A third location was explored from 1928 to 1931: an already densely built-up plot adjacent to the House of Unions, between Okhonyi riad, Tverskaia, Georgievskii proezd, and Bol'shaia Dmitrovka. By 1930, studies were being drawn up for this nearly 28,000 square meter plot. A report of May 1930 confirmed that this third site would require the displacement of 1,500 residents, along with the destruction of various nonresidential buildings located on the site, including a hotel, all of which brought in an annual revenue of 550,000 rubles. This report estimated that the total value of the existing structures on this third plot was 3,054,240 rubles. The final decision to build the Palace on the site of the Cathedral of Christ the Savior was made in June 1931. See GARF f. R-3316, op. 64, d. 562, ll. 1–3, 23, 51.

45. GARF f. R-3316, op. 25, d. 625, l. 5. Until at least 2015, these sculptural elements were stored on the grounds of Moscow's Donskoi Monastery, formerly the USSR Academy of Architecture's museum.

46. Vzryvprom is the acronym for the All-Union State Trust for Boring and Explosive Work (*Vsesoiuznyi gosudarstvennyi trest Buro-Vzryvnykh Rabot*).

47. GARF f. R-3316, op. 64, d. 564, l. 148.

48. Quoted in L. Levin, "Tema odinokoi sud'by. O tvorchestve Iuriia Oleshi," *Literaturnaia gazeta*, June 17, 1933, 3.

49. Hoffmann, "Moving to Moscow," 847–848.

50. "Sotsialisticheskaia Moskva," *Arkhitektura SSSR*, October-November 1935, 11.

51. Clark, "The 'New Moscow' and the New 'Happiness'," 189–200. Karen Petrone discusses the cultivation of happiness through carnivals held in the 1930s in public urban spaces. Petrone, *Life Has Become More Joyous, Comrades*, 100–102.

52. *O general'nom plane rekonstruktsii gor. Moskvy*, 7.

53. *O general'nom plane*, 7.

54. On the General Plan, see Papernyi, *Architecture in the Age of Stalin*, 56–59; Bodenschatz and Post, *Städtebau im Schatten Stalins*, 153–155; Cohen, "When Stalin Meets Haussmann."

55. On the academy's early years, see *10 let Akademii arkhitektury SSSR (1934–1944)*.

56. Siegelbaum, "The Shaping of Soviet Workers' Leisure," 78–92.

57. Cooke, "The Garden City Idea," 353–363; Cohen, *Scenes of the World to Come*, 28.

58. Clark, *The Soviet Novel.*

59. Cohen, "When Stalin Meets Haussmann," 247.

60. *Otvety na voprosy rabochikh i kolkhoznikov*, 13.

61. *Otvety na voprosy*, 13.

62. "Kalendar' stroitel'stva," *Sovetskoe iskusstvo*, September 28, 1931, 1.

CHAPTER 2: THE PALACE

1. "Postanovlenie Soveta stroitel'stva dvortsa sovetov pri presidiume TsIK Soiuz SSR 19 fevralia 1934 goda," *Pravda*, February 20, 1934, 2.

2. Accounts of the design competitions include Hoisington, "'Ever Higher': The Evolution of the Project for the Palace of Soviets"; Suzuki, "Konkurs na dvorets sovetov 1930-x gg. v Moskve i mezhdunarodnyi arkhitekturnyi kontekst"; Hudson, *Blueprints and Blood: The Stalinization of Soviet Architecutre, 1917–1937*, 140–141; Adkins et al, *Naum Gabo and the Competition for the Palace of Soviets, Moscow, 1931–1933*; Kostyuk, *Boris Iofan*, 32–52, 239–264; Lizon, *The Palace of the Soviets*; Cunliffe, "The Competition for the Palace of the Soviets, 1931–33"; Vronskaya, "Urbanist Landscape," 68–71.

3. "Dvorets sovetov. Monumental'nost', tsel'nost', prostota," *Sovetskoe iskusstvo*, March 3, 1932, 3.

4. Architectural historian Spiro Kostof worked to counter this taxonomy by juxtaposing American architecture of the New Deal era (the Department of Commerce building in Washington,

D.C., and the San Francisco Mint, built in 1932 and 1937, respectively) with Albert Speer's *Zeppelinfeld* in Nuremberg. As Kostof writes, "this public architecture of America, uneasy as the thought might be for those who believe that what we build is what we are, looks very much like the public architecture of the Thirties in Hitler's Germany, Mussolini's Italy, and Stalin's Russia" (719). Kostof, *A History of Architecture*, 717–720.

5. The preliminary competition was held in spring 1931. The Open Competition in fall 1931. The third (closed) competition was held from March-June 1932. And the fourth (also closed) competition was held from August 1932-February 1933. Confirmation of the final design was reached only in February 1934. See Hoisington, "'Ever Higher': The Evolution of the Project for the Palace of Soviets," 57–60. On the entries submitted to the first competition, see A. Mikhailov, "O vystavke proektov dvortsa sovetov," *Za proletarskoe iskusstvo*, no. 9, (1931): 14–19.

6. Hoisington, 43–45.

7. Cohen, *Le Corbusier and the Mystique of the USSR*, 195–196.

8. Le Corbusier, "The Atmosphere of Moscow," 260–261. See also Mumford, *The CIAM Discourse on Urbanism*, 71–72. On the effects of this severing of relations between CIAM and Moscow, see Anderson, "The Future of History," 1–7.

9. TsGA Moskvy f. R-694, op. 1, d. 43, l. 70.

10. TsGA Moskvy f. R-694, op. 1, d. 43, l. 70.

11. On the continued influence of modernism and modernists into the 1930s, see Udovički-Selb, "Between Modernism and Socialist Realism."

12. Cooke, "Beauty as Route to the Radiant Future"; Clark, "The 'New Moscow' and the New 'Happiness'."

13. L. M. Kaganovich, speech at Communist Party Plenum, 29 October 1933. In L. Perchik, "Gorod sotsializma i ego arkhitektura," *Arkhitektura SSSR*, no. 1 (1934): 3.

14. *Raboty arkhitekturno-proektirovochnykh masterskikh za 1934 god*, 14.

15. In her article on the Palace of Soviets competitions, Sona Hoisington argues against the persistent 'myth' that the Open Competition signaled "a conscious repudiation of modernism and a deliberate return to classical models," showing instead that the shift from modern architecture toward the eclectic and monumental took place gradually and haphazardly.

16. TsGA Moskvy f. R-694, op. 1, d. 2, l. 41.

17. Aleksei Tolstoi, "Poiski monumental'nosti," *Izvestiia*, 27 February 1932, 2.

18. Tolstoi, "Poiski monumental'nosti," 3.

19. Tolstoi, "Poiski monumental'nosti," 3.

20. Tolstoi, "Poiski monumental'nosti," 3.

21. TsGA Moskvy, f. R-694, op. 1, d. 2, l. 92.

22. Although Tatlin was unsuccessful in his bid to enter the competition for the Palace of Soviets, Mikhailov ensured that a handful of other modernists were included in the third round. Moisei Ginzburg, Nikolai Ladovskii, and Il'ia Golosov were invited to participate. Hoisington, 53.

23. "Soviet Palace Competition," *The Architectural Forum* LVI, no. 3 (March 1932): A.

24. "Soviet Palace Competition," *The Architectural Forum*, C.

25. "Soviet Palace Competition," *The Architectural Forum*, C.

26. GARF f. R-3316, op. 64, d. 563, l. 138.

27. GARF f. R-3316, op. 64, d. 563, l. 151.

28. "Red Palace to Fill Site 7 Blocks Long," *New York Times*, April 13, 1932, 40. This article was picked up by the Soviet press and an excerpt of it was printed in *Izvestiia* on April 28, 1932. The *Izvestiia* version referred to Hamilton as a "main consultant (*glavnyi konsul'tant*)" who had been invited by the Soviet government to Moscow, noting that Hamilton was already on his way to the Soviet capital. The bulk of the Russian article consisted of a quote from Hamilton's farewell reception, in which the architect compared the future Palace of Soviets to great American buildings: while the volume of the Empire State building was 24.5 million cubic feet, the Palace of Soviets would be 51.8 million cubic feet, and so on. "Arkhitektor Gektor Gamil'ton o dvortse sovetov," *Izvestiia*, April 28, 1932, 1.

29. Twenty architects participated in the third round of the competition. Hoisington, 50–53.

30. "Red Palace," *New York Times*, 40.

31. Hamilton encountered a chilly reception in Moscow. He was so put out by the confusion over the fate of his design that the following year he tried to file a claim against the Soviet state (via Amtorg) "for designs previously accepted for the Palace" in the amount of $297,000. Ham-

ilton claimed that "his refusal to join the Communist Party in Russia had a bearing on the award." See "High Lenin Statue on Palace Planned," *New York Times*, May 31, 1933, 19. While still in Moscow in July 1932, Hamilton had sent a letter to Mikhailov pleading that he be allowed to continue working on his design. GARF f. R-3316, op. 64, d. 563, ll. 152–153.

32. "Stalin to Voroshilov, Kaganovich, and Molotov, August 7, 1932," in *The Stalin-Kaganovich Correspondence, 1931–36*, 177.

33. "Stalin to Voroshilov, Kaganovich, and Molotov, August 7, 1932," 177.

34. "Stalin to Voroshilov, Kaganovich, and Molotov, August 7, 1932," 177–178.

35. TsGA Moskvy f. R-694, op. 1, d. 3, ll. 65–66; GARF f. R-3316, op. 64, d. 562, l. 15. Before 1931, Iofan had already been working as Chief Resident Engineer and Deputy Head of Construction (*Nachal'nik rabot i zamestitel' nachal'nika stroitel'stva*) for the Palace project.

36. In October 1931, Kriukov wrote a letter to Molotov accusing Iofan of insubordination and asking that either he (Kriukov) be relieved of his duties at the USDS, or Iofan and engineer G. B. Krasin be fired. Kriukov would go on to be the first rector of the USSR Academy of Architecture when it was created in 1933. In 1938 Kriukov was arrested and sent to the Gulag camp at Vorkuta, where he died in 1944. GARF f. R-3316, op. 64, d. 564, ll. 103–103ob.

37. On Mikhailov, Iofan, and their apartments in the House of Government, see Slezkine, *The House of Government*, 408–409, 488–492.

38. TsGA Moskvy, f. R-694, op. 1, d. 1, ll. 1–2.

39. They advised that three rounds of competitions, closed-open-closed, would be best, all of which should be completed over the course of nine months. TsGA Moskvy f. R-694, op. 1, d. 4, l. 4.

40. TsGA Moskvy f. R-694, op. 1, d. 3, ll. 46, 65; TsGA Moskvy f. R-694, op. 1, d. 4, l. 6.

41. TsGA Moskvy f. R-694, op. 1, d. 1, l. 8ob.

42. "Postanovlenie soveta stroitel'stva dvortsa sovetov pri prezidiume TsIK Soiuza SSR," *Pravda*, February 20, 1934, 2.

43. The visitors' comments were typed up by USDS staff and categorized according the following types of responses: positive comments, negative comments, suggestions relating to design, suggestions relating to planning, comments about the Lenin statue, comments about the organization of the exhibition. TsGA Moskvy f. R-694, op. 1, d. 44, ll. 62–83.

44. TsGA Moskvy f. R-694, op. 1, d. 44, l. 65.

45. TsGA Moskvy f. R-694, op. 1, d. 44, l. 12.

46. TsGA Moskvy f. R-694, op. 1, d. 44, l. 65.

47. TsGA Moskvy f. R-694, op. 1, d. 44, ll. 66, 67.

48. TsGA Moskvy f. R-694, op. 1, d. 44, l. 66.

49. TsGA Moskvy f. R-694, op. 1, d. 44, l. 83.

50. TsGA Moskvy f. R-694, op. 1, d. 44, l. 83.

51. TsGA Moskvy f. R-694, op. 1, d. 44, l. 83.

52. TsGA Moskvy f. R-694, op. 1, d. 44, l. 62.

53. TsGA Moskvy f. R-694, op. 1, d. 44, l. 63.

54. TsGA Moskvy f. R-694, op. 1, d. 44, l. 63. For other comments not mentioned here, see Hoisington, 62.

55. On the phenomenon of the mass circulation of icons like the Palace of Soviets in the Stalinist 1930s, see Rolf, "A Hall of Mirrors."

56. *Oktiabr'skaia 3ia Vystavka planirovki i arkhitektury na ul. Gor'kogo*, 19–20.

57. Gronow, *Caviar with Champagne*, 46.

58. *Izvestiia*, November 26, 1940, 4.

59. Nikolai Kolli, "Arkhitekturnaia praktika v Moskve," in *Arkhitektura SSSR*, no. 7 (1935): 10.

60. Kolli, "Arkhitekturnaia praktika," 10.

61. Archive of Mueser Rutledge Consulting Engineers (formerly Moran & Proctor), Project 647, unnumbered files. The USDS signed a further five contracts with the firm in 1935. According to Moran & Proctor's documentation, this was "because of the [Soviet] government restrictions applying to sizable contracts and because funds for different services by [the firm] will come out of different budget accounts." The second delegation was made up of Palace of Soviets engineers B. P. Popov, A. T. Gridunov, and A. L. Rubinshtein. See GARF f. R-5446, op. 16a, d. 560, ll. 14–16.

62. See Clark's study of Moscow's internationally-engaged artists and intellectuals of the 1930s in *Moscow, The Fourth Rome*; and Sanchez-Sibony's examination of the Soviet Union's

economic relationship with the West through the Stalin and into the Khrushchev periods in *Red Globalization.*

63. Sutton, *Western Technology and Soviet Economic Development,* 346–347.

64. Sutton, *Western Technology,* 8.

65. "'Sovetskoe pravitel'stvo sovershaet chudesa v promyshlennosti' Amerikanskii arkhitektor o SSSR," *Izvestiia,* July 15, 1930, 1.

66. On Kahn Associates' work in the USSR, see Zimmerman, "Building the World Capitalist System"; Kopp, "Foreign Architects in the Soviet Union during the First Two Five-Year Plans," 38–44. The disagreement over terms between Kahn and the Soviet government had to do with a new policy of 1932 that had the USSR pay foreign firms partly in rubles, due to the foreign currency shortage in the country.

67. GARF f. R-3316, op. 64, d. 564, l. 65.

68. Soviet engineers from the Stalingrad tractor plant travelled to the US in 1929, for example. Other examples can be found in Sutton's three-volume history *Western Technology and Soviet Economic Development.*

69. Davis and Trani, *Distorted Mirrors,* 42.

70. Felix Cole to U.S. Department of State, Dispatch no. 8175, 30 October 1931, file 861.78/12, T1249, Records of the Department of State Relating to Internal Affairs of the Soviet Union, 1930–1939, National Archives and Records Administration (NARA), 1.

71. Felix Cole to U.S. Department of State, 2.

72. American Consul General G. C. Hanson to U.S. Department of State, Memorandum no. 46, 21 May 1934, file 861.157/2, T1249, Records of the Department of State Relating to Internal Affairs of the Soviet Union, 1930–1939, NARA, 1.

73. Hanson to U.S. Department of State, 1.

74. Hanson to U.S. Department of State, 2.

75. Bailes, "The American Connection."

76. On Amtorg in the interwar period, see Ropes, "American-Soviet Trade Relations," 89–94. Ropes was writing prior to Amtorg's Cold War fate: the company briefly coordinated Soviet-American lend-lease agreements before this program was terminated. In October 1949, the entire staff in Amtorg's New York office was arrested, accused, according to a 1938 US law, of being unregistered "foreign agents" (Amtorg had, until this time, avoided having to register as a "foreign agent"). See RGASPI f. 82, op. 2, d. 729, ll. 52–53, 129.

77. Ad on imported lines in *Crockery & Glass Journal* 97, (December 1, 1935): 6; ad for Bokharan rugs in *The Spur* 55 (April 1, 1935): 4. On recognition, see Budish and Shipman, *Soviet Foreign Trade.*

78. Ropes, "American-Soviet Trade Relations," 91.

79. "As Others See Us: A Russian on American Efficiency," *The Living Age,* (September 1935): 88.

80. "As Others See Us," 88.

81. Starrett Brothers and Eken, "Notes on Construction of Empire State Building," in *Building the Empire State,* 47–184.

82. GARF f. R-5446, op. 15a, d. 997, l. 1. On Bogdanov, see G. P. Bogdanov and A. P. Bogdanov, *Dolg pamiati.* Following his post working for Amtorg in New York, Bogdanov worked as Deputy of the People's Commissariat of Local Industry of the RSFSR. He was arrested on November 22, 1937. On March 15, 1938 he was charged with participating in a "counter-revolutionary terrorist organization" and executed. See the Memorial Society, Moscow's database of victims of political terror in the USSR: lists.memo.ru.

83. TsGA Moskvy f. R-694, op. 1, d. 39, l. 2; GARF R-5446, op. 15a, d. 997, l. 5.

84. TsGA Moskvy f. R-694, op. 1, d. 39, l. 20.

85. TsGA Moskvy f. R-694, op. 1, d. 39, l. 1.

86. TsGA Moskvy f. R-694, op. 1, d. 39, ll. 20–24.

87. GARF f. R-5446, op. 15a, d. 997, l. 4ob. Corrected for inflation, this was $459,000 in 2015. Molotov, who was still the Chairman of the Council for the Palace of Soviets, approved the budgets. Enukidze suggested that all four men on the commission be given new suits for their journey.

88. TsGA Moskvy f. R-694, op. 1, d. 39, l. 22.

89. Prokofiev, *The Palace of Soviets,* 22.

90. Prokofiev, *The Palace of Soviets,* 22.

91. TsGA Moskvy f. R-694, op. 1, d. 39, l. 1.

92. Archive of Mueser Rutledge Consulting Engineers (formerly Moran & Proctor), Project 647, unnumbered files.

93. "Otchet ob inzhenerno-geologicheskom issledovanii stroitel'noi ploshchadki Dvortsa Sovetov" in Archive of Mueser Rutledge Consulting Engineers (formerly Moran & Proctor), Project 647, unnumbered files.

94. Archive of Mueser Rutledge Consulting Engineers (formerly Moran & Proctor), Project 647, unnumbered files.

95. Later they would work on the United Nations building and Yankee Stadium. In the 2000s, Mueser Rutledge worked on the Mercury City Tower in Moskva-City, Moscow.

96. Cross, *75 Years of Foundation Engineering*, 172–189.

97. GARF f. R-5446, op. 16a, d. 1186, l. 1. Payment to a second firm, the American Asphalt Grouting Company, that Moran & Proctor had secured on behalf of the USDS, was included in this amount.

98. Archive of Mueser Rutledge Consulting Engineers (formerly Moran & Proctor), Project 647, unnumbered files.

99. Archive of Mueser Rutledge Consulting Engineers (formerly Moran & Proctor), Project 647, unnumbered files.

100. "Proctor Back, Praises Soviet for Palace Plans," *New York Herald Tribune*, July 5, 1935, 13.

101. Cermak and Tamaro, "Foundations of High-Rise Structures in Moscow and New York City," 359–364.

102. Ralph W. Barnes, "Soviet Changes Palace Designs after Look at Skyscrapers Here," *New York Herald Tribune*, May 31, 1935, 13.

103. *Princeton Alumni Weekly* 35, (July 1, 1935): 797.

104. "Carleton S. Proctor, 76, Is Dead; Engineer on Major Structures," *New York Times*, August 27, 1970, 35.

105. "Carleton S. Proctor," *New York Times*, 35.

106. "Soviet Architects Hailed: New York League Entertains at Tea for Iofan and Aides," *New York Times*, October 26, 1934, 13.

107. "Huge Palace Held Feasible in Moscow: Bedrock 90 Feet Below Surface," *New York Times*, May 30, 1935, 2.

108. Buck-Morss, *Dreamworld and Catastrophe*, 176.

109. GARF f. R-3316, op. 64, d. 563, l. 173–174. The letter, sent in March 1934, was received by the Central Committee and translated in Russian.

110. TsGA Moskvy, f. 649, op. 1, d. 39, l. 3.

111. TsGA Moskvy f. R-694, op. 1, d. 50, l. 42.

112. TsGA Moskvy f. R-694, op. 1, d. 50, l. 34. Kahn replied with more information on May 7 (l. 54).

113. TsGA Moskvy f. R-694, op. 1, d. 50, l. 48.

114. TsGA Moskvy f. R-694, op. 1, d. 50, l. 76.

115. TsGA Moskvy f. R-694, op. 1, d. 50, l. 77.

116. TsGA Moskvy f. R-694, op. 1, d. 50, ll. 80–80ob. Sona Hoisington discusses the stylistic influence of the Rockefeller Center on a number of Iofan's other design projects of the 1930s in "Soviet Schizophrenia and the American Skyscraper," 162–164.

117. Biographical file of V. K. Oltarzhevskii, A. V. Shchusev State Museum of Architecture (GNIMA). In 1933, Oltarzhevskii published *Contemporary Babylon,* a book of drawings of New York's skyscrapers, with an introduction by Harvey Wiley Corbett. Oltarzhevskii returned to Moscow in 1934, worked on the VDNKh, was arrested during the Great Terror in 1938, and became the head of construction and main architect at one of the largest Gulag camps at Vorkuta. He was released from the Gulag in 1943 and worked on one of Moscow's postwar skyscrapers starting in 1947.

118. Clark, *Moscow, The Fourth Rome*, 8.

119. Boris Iofan, "Na ulitsakh gorodov Evropy i Ameriki," *Pravda*, March 13 1935, 2. Translation in Clark, 8.

120. Vladimir Shchuko, "Tvorcheskii otchet," *Arkhitektura SSSR,* no. 6 (1935): 19–20.

121. On Iofan's connections to Italy, see Patti, "Boris Iofan in Rome." On Soviet-Italian architectural ties in the 1930s, see Vyazemtseva, "The Transformation of Rome and the Masterplan to Reconstruct Moscow."

122. TsGA Moskvy f. R-694, op.1, d. 39, l. 2; GARF f. R-3316, op. 64, d. 563, l. 186.

123. Shchuko, "Tvorcheskii otchet," 20.

124. Iofan, "Na ulitsakh," 2.

125. As Rósa Magnúsdóttir notes, during the interwar years the Soviet image of "America" was strongly shaped by Russian and Soviet writers' descriptions of life in American cities. Magnúsdóttir, *Enemy Number One*, 6.

126. Cohen, "L'Oncle Sam au Pays des Soviets," 403–436.

127. Gorky, *The City of the Yellow Devil*, 8–9.

128. Il'f and Petrov, "Single-Storey America," in *Ilf and Petrov's American Road Trip*, 128.

129. Il'f and Petrov, 127.

130. The claim that American and Western European architectures had reached a dead end, but that they nonetheless offered useful traditions to be mined for socialist urbanism, would continue into the postwar years. Greg Castillo shows how these claims dovetailed with Cold War competition as the socialist sphere expanded into Eastern Europe in "East as True West: Redeeming Bourgeois Culture, from Socialist Realism to *Ostalgie*."

131. Jean-Louis Cohen notes that Frank Lloyd Wright replaced Le Corbusier in the 1930s as the "architect friend" of the Soviet Union. Cohen, "Constructing Wright in Soviet Russia and France," 106.

132. The title of the book in Russian is *From Log Cabin to Skyscraper (Ot brevenchatogo doma do neboskreba)*. The book was translated into Russian from an earlier German edition: Lewis Mumford, *Vom Blockhaus sum Wolkenkratzer: Eine Studie uber amerikanische Architectur und Zivilisation*, (Berlin: Bruno Cassirer Verlag, 1926). Mumford's influence on Soviet architecture in the 1930s is also evident in the fact that he is quoted in the introductory address of the Moscow General Plan of 1935.

133. Arkin, "Amerikanskaia arkhitektura i kniga Mumforda," in *Ot brevenchatogo doma do neboskreba*, 12–13. On Arkin's engagement with Mumford, see Cohen, *Scenes of the World to Come*, 153–154.

134. Iofan, "Materialy o sovremennoi arkhitekture SShA i Italiii," *Akademiia Arkhitektury*, 1936, 13. On Iofan's experience in Italy, also see Eigel', *Boris Iofan*, 23–34.

135. English taken from Mumford's original. Mumford, *Sticks and Stones*, 175–176.

136. Iofan, "Materialy," 23.

137. TsGA Moskvy f. R-694, op. 1, d. 39, l. 2.

138. Danilo Udovički-Selb discusses the stylistic influence of the Rockefeller Center on Iofan's Palace of Soviets and on this architect's design for the Soviet Pavilion at the 1937 World's Fair in Paris. Udovički-Selb, "Between Modernism and Socialist Realism," 481–485.

139. Linsley, "Utopia Will Not Be Televised," 59.

140. Iofan's statements about New York in *Pravda* were reprinted in "Moscow Architect Finds New York Is Depressing," *New York Times*, February 12, 1939, 33.

141. GARF f. R-5283, op. 14, d. 203, l. 170.

142. Trapeznikov, *Problema ansamblia v sovetskoi arkhitekture*, 3.

143. RGASPI f. 82, op. 2, d. 505, ll. 6–7; RGASPI f. 82, op. 2, d. 504, ll. 86, 103.

144. RGASPI, f. 82, op. 2, d. 505, l. 134.

145. In addition to Mikhailov, other victims of the Terror at the USDS include Nikolai Fedorovich Raznitsin, an administrator; Mairam Sadulaevich Tsakhilov, a chauffeur; Ian Davydovich Lentsman who worked in the personnel department; Aleksandr Pavlovich Bubnov, employed in the material supplies department; and Ivan Eduardovich Salomon, a translator-consultant. See the Memorial Society, Moscow's database of victims of political terror in the USSR: lists.memo.ru.

146. Mikhailov was arrested on June 11, 1937 and sentenced on September 26, 1937. He was executed the same day of his sentencing. Slezkine, *The House of Government*, 863.

147. Born in 1886 to a family of workers, Prokof'ev joined the Bolshevik party in February 1917. He participated in the October Revolution in Leningrad and was a member of the Red Army during the Civil War. Prokof'ev worked in the Cheka from 1919 to 1926, before starting a career in the construction industry. See the obituary for Prokof'ev in *Pravda*, October 21, 1949, 4. Also considered as potential successors to Mikhailov were G. N. Teplov, Chief Engineer at ZIS; and Illarion D. Gotseridze, then head of construction of the Mayakovskaya metro station. RGASPI f. 82, op. 2, d. 504, l. 141.

148. These denunciations against Prokof'ev were sent in by a former USDS employee who had been sacked some months earlier and, more damningly, by B. M. Gol'denberg, a Komsomol member who worked in the editorial bureau of the *Palace of Soviets* construction site newspaper. RGASPI, f. 82, op. 2, d. 505, ll. 69–71, 139–142.

149. Molotov instructed Z. Belen'kii to investigate Prokof'ev ("*proshu proverit', ne ustraivaia shuma*") on September 20, 1938. RGASPI, f. 82, op. 2, d. 505, l. 69.

150. Prokof'ev had served as head of the "Builder" construction trust since 1926. See the obituary for Prokof'ev in *Pravda,* October 21, 1949, 4.

151. RGASPI, f. 82, op. 2, d. 504, l. 123.

152. The pavilion was co-designed by Iofan and Karo Alabian. "USSR," in *The Architecture Forum* 70, no. 6 (June 1939): 459.

153. On Democracity see Conn, *Americans Against the City*, 111. On the Soviet pavilion and exhibitions in 1939 see Swift, "The Soviet World of Tomorrow at the New York World's Fair, 1939."

154. Iofan's assistant Isaak Iu. Eigel' discusses this approach in his biography of Iofan. Eigel', *Boris Iofan*, 125–147. Sona Hoisington discusses Iofan's return to New York in 1939 in "Soviet Schizophrenia and the American Skyscraper," 164–166.

155. RGASPI, f. 82, op. 2, d. 504, l. 123.

156. RGASPI, f. 82, op. 2, d. 504, l. 123.

157. Goldman, *Inventing the Enemy*, 118.

158. TsGA Moskvy, f. R-694, op. 1, d. 261, l. 121.

159. TsGA Moskvy, f. R-694, op. 1, d. 261, l. 124

160. TsGA Moskvy, f. R-694, op. 1, d. 272, l. 7.

161. By January 1, 1942, over 1.5 million evacuees had been sent to the Urals, and a similar number would arrive again by the start of 1943. M. N. Potemkina estimates the figure at 1,620,243 for the entire Urals region as of January 1, 1942, and 1,281,257 by January 1, 1943. Potemkina, *Evakonaselenie v Ural'skom tylu*, 256.

162. Diary of K. Loriston (pseudonym, real name unknown), entry from May 3, 1942. *Ia pomniu,* http://iremember.ru/grazhdanskie/k-loriston.html, accessed December 1, 2014.

CHAPTER 3: THE WAR

1. "Vystuplenie po radio V. M. Molotova," *Pravda*, June 23, 1941, 1.

2. The notable exception was the Moscow Metro, which served a defensive purpose.

3. Gorinov, "Muscovites' Moods, 1941–42," 110–111.

4. Stahel, *Operation Typhoon*, 222.

5. Timofeev, "Memuary, arkhivy, svidetel'stva." 165–168. November 7, 1941 entry. Timofeev was a philologist, literary scholar, and editor at the journal *Znamia*. He held a professorship at the A. M. Gorky Literature Institute.

6. The team working on this was led by Boris Iofan and included Karo Alabian. "Postanovlenie komissii o maskirovke Kremlia, prilegaiushchikh k nemu territorii i zdanii," in *Lubianka v dni bitvy za Moskvu*, 44–45.

7. Stahel, *Operation Typhoon*, 224.

8. The most damaging attacks were suffered on that first night, July 21–22, as well as on the nights of August 11–12 and October 29, 1941, and on January 6 and March 28–29, 1942. "Akt o razrusheniiakh zdanii i sooruzhenii Moskovskogo Kremlia v rezul'tate naletov nemetskoi aviatsii," in *Lubianka v dni bitvy za Moskvu*, 136–140.

9. Werth, *Moscow '41*, 104. Werth was born in Russia. He had left Petrograd for England with his industrialist father in the wake of the February Revolution of 1917.

10. Werth, *Moscow '41*, 9, 17, 104.

11. Werth, *Moscow '41*, 120.

12. Two industrial facilities were destroyed by air attacks, and 112 others were damaged; 226 residential buildings were destroyed; the Bolshoi and Vakhtangov theaters were hit, as were the university and the Manege. Iu. I. Sevast'ianov, "Moskovskie stroiteli v velikoi otechestvennoi voine," *Voprosy istorii,* no. 11 (1970): 37.

13. Stahel, *Operation Typhoon*, 215–216.

14. Ustinov, *Voina v ob'ektive*, 30.

15. Gorinov, "Muscovites' Moods, 1941–42," 122.

16. "Raport zamestitelia nachal'nika 1 otdela NKVD SSSR D.N. Shadrina o rezul'tatakh osmotra zdaniia TsK VKP(b) posle evakuatsii personala," October 20, 1941, *Lubianka v dni bitvy za Moskvu*, 90–91. This document is also in *Moskva prifrontovaia 1941–1942,* 272.

17. *Moskva prifrontovaia 1941–1942,* 264–265.

18. On the panic and popular resentment that arose as a result of the chaotic October evacuation of Moscow, see Manley, *To the Tashkent Station*, 107–111.

19. Werth, *Russia at War*, 240.

20. Georgii Popov, "Vospominaniia," in *"Partiinyi gubernator" Moskvy*, 178–179.

21. *Lubianka v dni bitvy za Moskvu,* 97, 108–113.

22. Stahel, *Operation Typhoon,* 213–216; Gorinov, 115–116. Gorinov writes that by December 1, 3,528 cases had been heard in the tribunal, resulting in 3,338 convictions.

23. Werth, *Russia at War,* 240–241; Timofeev, "Memuary, arkhivy, svidetel'stva," 160.

24. Colton, *Moscow,* 250–51. Gorinov gives the following population figures for Moscow in 1941: from just over 4.2 million at the start of the war, the population rose slightly as refugees arrived from the west (they did not stay; their arrival and subsequent departure from the capital was monitored). The population decreased in October to 3.1 million, due to mobilization from Moscow into the Red Army (850,000 Muscovites joined up), and evacuation of others to the east. By January 1942, there were just over 2 million people living in Moscow. Gorinov, "Muscovites' Moods, 1941–42," 108–137.

25. Manley, *To the Tashkent Station,* 58.

26. Timofeev, "Memuary, arkhivy, svidetel'stva," 168.

27. Timofeev, "Memuary, arkhivy, svidetel'stva," 139.

28. Timofeev, "Memuary, arkhivy, svidetel'stva," 167. A number of diarists write that Hitler vowed to be in Moscow to march across Red Square himself on November 7. Timofeev wrote in his diary entry of October 29 that the Germans had been dropping leaflets into Moscow, one of which announced, "in the name of Hitler," that the Fuhrer would enter Moscow on the 1st, and "he hopes that Stalin will not prosecute him if he is 15 or so minutes late" (165).

29. Gorinov, "Muscovites' Moods, 1941–42," 126.

30. Ustinov, *Voina v ob'ektive,* 41.

31. Weiner, *Making Sense of War,* 19.

32. I take this figure from Zubkova, *Russia After the War,* 20.

33. *Moskovskii Kreml' v gody Velikoi Otechestvennoi voiny,* 56–57.

34. Stalin stated that, in addition to the large amount of territory that had fallen into German hands, the first four months of the war had caused the deaths of 350,000 people and injured over 1 million. I. V. Stalin, "24ia godovshchina velikoi oktiab'skoi sotsialisticheskoi revoliutsii, 6 noiabria 1941," in *O velikoi otechestvennoi voine sovetskogo soiuza,* 20.

35. I. V. Stalin, "24ia godovshchina," 33. The same statement was made in 1940 by Nikolai A. Voznesenskii, Chairman of the Soviet State Planning Commission (Gosplan). See Overy, *Why the Allies Won,* 208.

36. Aleksandr Deineka's decorative program for the Mayakovskaya metro station made this an especially appropriate location for Stalin's speech of November 6, 1941. On the artist's aviation-themed mosaics, see Friedman, "Soviet Mastery of the Skies at the Mayakovsky Metro Station."

37. I. V. Stalin, "24ia godovshchina," 33. The organization that would facilitate this and subsequent aid agreements was Amtorg, which had served to connect American and Soviet finance and industrial expertise since the period of the First Five-Year Plan. RGASPI f. 82, op. 2, d. 729, ll. 52–53.

38. Both the November 6 and November 7 speeches were printed and distributed widely. In the days to come, the Communist Party and Red Army Command jointly decreed that this speech would be printed and distributed to soldiers along the front lines. It would also be dropped by air into the occupied territories and into Germany. The order called for 10 million copies to be printed in Russian, and millions more in German, Ukrainian, Belorussian, Polish, Finnish, Romanian, Hungarian, Italian, Latvian, Lithuanian, Estonia, Czech, and Spanish. *Moskva Prifrontovaia, 1941–1942,* 313.

39. "Vsia strana slushala doklad tovarishcha Stalina," *Izvestiia,* November 7, 1941, 3.

40. Ehrenburg and Simonov, *In One Newspaper,* 83.

41. The town of Ekaterinburg was renamed Sverdlovsk in 1924 after Bolshevik leader Iakov M. Sverdlov.

42. "Na Urale," *Izvestiia,* November 7, 1941, 3.

43. "Na Urale," *Izvestiia,* 3.

44. TsGA Moskvy f. R-694, op. 1, d. 261, l. 122.

45. Eigel', *Boris Iofan,* 108.

46. Sevast'ianov, "Moskovskie stroiteli," 35.

47. TsGA Moskvy f. R-694, op. 1, d. 272, l. 33; *Moskovskii Kreml',* 67–81; Cohen, *Architecture in Uniform,* 209.

48. RGASPI f. 82, op. 2, d. 506, l. 98.

49. RGASPI f. 82, op. 2, d. 506, l. 108. See also TsGA Moskvy f. R-694, op. 1, d. 272, l. 7. The Sovnarkom order requiring the USDS to work on the construction of the Urals Aluminum Factory dates to August 28, 1941.

50. RGASPI f. 82, op. 2, d. 506, l. 94.

51. RGAE f. 293, op. 1, d. 66, l. 22. The Academy of Architecture had special wartime groups in Novosibirsk, Sverdlovsk, Molotovsk, Kranoiarsk, and Bashkiriia, among other locations.

52. Dmitrii Chechulin likely supervised this work. Chechulin, *Zhizn' i zodchestvo*, 86.

53. "Interview with architect Brovchenko V. N.," conducted by E. Listova, 2006, 4. In the collection of GNIMA.

54. *Zadachi arkhitektorov v dni velikoi otechestvennoi voiny,* 28.

55. Soviet experts turned in particular to British experience and literature on camouflage. See for example, V. Grossman and B. Kogan, "Opyt stroitel'stva bomboubezhishch v Anglii," *Stroitel'stvo voennogo vremeni,* vol. 1, 1941, 28–46; "Iz perepiski Vserossiiskoi Akademii khudozhestv," *Iz istorii sovetskoi arkhitektury 1941–1945*, 11.

56. Voenproekt was established in 1930. Kazus', *Sovetskaia arkhitektura 1920kh godov,* 217.

57. "Interview with architect Brovchenko," 5.

58. "Interview with architect Brovchenko," 5.

59. "Interview with architect Brovchenko," 5.

60. RGASPI f. 82, op. 2, d. 506, l. 98.

61. RGASPI f. 82, op. 2, d. 506, l. 94. Emphasis Iofan's.

62. RGASPI f. 82, op. 2, d. 506, l. 94.

63. RGASPI f. 82, op. 2, d. 506, l. 94–95.

64. RGASPI f. 82, op. 2, d. 506, l. 115. Iofan carried out this work with co-author of the Palace, Vladimir Gel'freikh. Vladimir Shchuko had passed away in January 1939.

65. Eigel', *Boris Iofan*, 108.

66. RGASPI f. 558, op. 11, d. 737, l. 67; RGASPI f. 82, op. 2, d. 506, l. 113. According to Eigel', the new Sverdlovsk variant of the project was put on display in Moscow in 1944 in the Kremlin and in 1945 it was shown to the deputies of the Supreme Soviet. Eigel', 108.

67. "Boevye zadachi sovetskogo arkhitektora," *Stroitel'stvo voennogo vremeni,* 1941, v. 1, 2.

68. RGAE f. 293, op. 1, d. 49, ll. 4a-5.

69. RGAE f. 293, op. 1, d. 48, l. 1.

70. RGAE f. 293, op. 1, d. 48, l. 2.

71. Cohen, *Architecture in Uniform*, 395–397.

72. Reed, "Enlisting Modernism," 25.

73. Shanken, *194X*, 147.

74. Castillo, *Cold War on the Home Front,* 111–113.

75. Castillo, "Gorki Street and the Design of the Stalin Revolution," 63.

76. "Interview with architect Brovchenko," 5; Chechulin, *Zhizn' i zodchestvo*, 87.

77. Sevast'ianov, "Moskovskie stroiteli," 42.

78. Chechulin, *Zhizn' i zodchestvo*, 87.

79. The *Komitet po delam arkhitektury pri Sovnarkome SSSR* (the main body overseeing postwar reconstruction, general plans, and all subsequent urban planning in the USSR) has been translated differently across the English-language historiography. I have settled on USSR State Architecture Committee. Adding to the confusion, the organization was reconfigured at various times. At the all-union level (USSR), the Committee was renamed in 1949 and then liquidated in 1951 as its functions were passed to Gosstroi, which had been created in 1950. The organization went through the following metamorphosis: State Architecture Committee 1943–1949 (*Komitet po delam arkhitektury pri Sovnarkom/Sovmin SSSR*, RGAE f. 9432); 1949–1951 Ministry of Urban Construction of the USSR (*Ministerstvo gorodskogo stroitel'stva SSSR*, RGAE f. 9510); 1950–1991 State Construction Committee or Gosstroi (*Gosudarstvennyi komitet SSSR po delam stroitel'stva*, RGAE f. 339). At the republic level (RSFSR), similar changes took place, but at different times. The State Architecture Committee of the RSFSR (created in 1943) became Gosstroi RSFSR in 1955 (all files for these institutions from 1943–1957 are in GARF f. A-150). In May 1957, Gosstroi RSFSR was liquidated, its function passed to the Sovnarkhozy and the RSFSR Ministry of Public Services (*Ministerstvo kommunal'nogo khoziaistva RSFSR*). At the Moscow city level, the Chief Architect oversaw the affairs of the Moscow Architecture Committee. At the city level, the Committee structure was positioned beneath the broader office of the Main Architectural-Planning Administration of Moscow (*Glavnoe arkhitekturno-planirovochnoe upravlenie g. Moskvy Mosgorispolkoma*). TsGA Moskvy

f. R-534 holds the files for the following succession of institutions within this Main Administration: 1941–1944 Architectural-Planning Administration (*Arkhitekturno-planirovochnoe upravlenie*); 1944–1951 Administration for the Affairs of Architecture (*Upravlenie po delam arkhitektury*); 1951–1961 Architectural-Planning Administration (*Arkhitekturno-planirovochnoe upravlenie*).

80. Mordvinov was President of the Academy of Architecture from 1950–1955.

81. Day, "The Rise and Fall of Stalinist Architecture," 176–177.

82. "Vostanovitel'noe stroitel'stvo i zadachi arkhitektorov," *Arkhitektura SSSR*, 1944, v. 6, 1.

83. These five architects served regularly on the Architectural Council. They served together, for example, at the meeting of the Council held on December 24, 1947. During this period, the Council met 30–50 times per year, discussing 2–3 project proposals per meeting. TsGA Moskvy f. R-534, op. 1, d. 105, l. 3. Transcripts of these meetings are available in this fond.

84. Karl Qualls discusses the chaos that ensued in Sevastopol with the creation of the State Architecture Committees in *From Ruins to Reconstruction*, 83.

85. Shchusev, *Proekt vosstanovleniia goroda Istry*, 7.

86. "Iz otcheta Akademii arkhitektury SSSR po osnovnym temam nauchno-issledovatel'skoi i tvorcheskoi raboty za 1942 g. Moskva-Chimkent," December 1942, in *Iz istorii sovetskoi arkhitektury 1941–1945*, 58.

87. R. Podvol'skii, "Pamiatniki Russkogo zodchestva, razrushennye nemetskimi zakhvatchikami: Novyi Ierusalim na Istre," *Arkhitektura SSSR*, 1942, v. 1, 9.

88. On the Academy of Architecture's work in heritage conservation, see RGAE f. 293, op. 1, d. 49, l. 10. The USSR Union of Architects also had a Commission for the Conservation of Monuments active during the war.

89. *Architectural Chronicle,* July 1945, 4.

90. "Vystuplenie tovarishcha I.V. Stalina na prieme v Kremle v chest' komanduiushchikh voiskami Krasnoi armii," in *O velikoi otechestvennoi voine sovetskogo soiuza*, 196–197.

91. As David Brandenberger has shown, the use of Russian national heroes, imagery, and myths in party propaganda and mass culture dates to before the war, to the mid- to late-1930s. Yet, while official russocentrism had pre-war roots, in architecture the war played a central role in pushing the national heritage agenda to center stage. See Brandenberger, *National Bolshevism,* 43–45.

92. The archival collection of New York architect Simon Breines, for example, contains a 1944 edition of the journal, which included articles about "Restoration of the Cities in the Crimea," "The Architects of Democratic Poland and the Architects of the USSR," "The Architectural Section of the Ukrainian Society of Cultural Relations with Foreign Countries," and a New Books section. Simon Breines, Professional Papers, Box 20, Avery Architectural and Fine Arts Library Drawings and Archives, Columbia University. On the activities of VOKS in facilitating relations between the USSR and foreigners in the 1930s, see David-Fox, *Showcasing the Great Experiment.*

93. GARF f. R-5283, op. 14, d. 203, ll. 91.

94. GARF f. R-5283, op. 14, d. 203, ll. 3, 5.

95. GARF f. R-5283, op. 14, d. 203, l. 14.

96. "Lichnyi listok chlena soiuza," biographical file of V. K. Oltarzhevskii. GNIMA, l. 5ob. On the history of Vorkuta, see Barenberg, *Gulag Town, Company Town.*

97. RGALI f. 680, op. 2, d. 1696, ll. 15, 34. There are contradictory birth years for Oltarzhevskii across his various files. In this RGALI file of personal documents dating to the early 1900s, his birth year is 1884. In later Soviet files, such as in the collection of his personal documents held at GNIMA, his birth date is 1880. On his 1929 application for membership in the American Institute of Architects, Oltar-jevsky entered his birth year as 1880.

98. That Oltarzhevskii was released at the request of W. Averell Harriman is widely reported, but the exact source of this information is difficult to determine. See Cohen, "American Objects of Soviet Desire," 128.

99. GARF f. R-5283, op. 14, d. 203, l. 16.

100. GARF f. R-5283, op. 14, d. 265, l. 62.

101. GARF f. R-5283, op. 14, d. 265, l. 27.

102. GARF f. R-5283, op. 14, d. 265, l. 27.

103. Alice Barrows to Robert Lynd, February 16, 1943, American-Soviet Friendship Records, TAM 134, Box 5, Folder 1, Tamiment Archives, New York University.

104. American-Soviet Friendship Records, TAM 134, Box 5, Folder 1, Tamiment Archives, New York University.

105. American-Soviet Friendship Records, TAM 134, Box 5, Folder 2, Tamiment Archives, New York University.

106. In 1947, the NCASF was indicted for failing to register with the Subversive Activities Control Board.

107. GARF f. R-5283, op. 14, d. 203, l. 103.

108. The other officers and committee members mentioned in this letter are a Who's Who of American architecture during this period: Talbot Hamlin, John W. Root, Henry R. Shepley, Hugh Pomeroy, Vernon De Mars, William Wurster, Kenneth Reid, George Nelson, Kenneth K. Stowell, Joseph Hudnet, K. Lonberg Holm, and Jules Korchien.

109. GARF f. R-5283, op. 14, d. 203, ll. 103–106.

110. In fact, the language barrier did present a problem. The Architects Committee's report of its activities in 1945 made note of the fact that since most of the material sent to them was in Russian, it "presented quite a translation problem." Architects Committee, American-Soviet Friendship Records, TAM 134, Box 5, Folder 6, Tamiment Archives, New York University.

111. GARF f. R-5283, op. 14, d. 203, l. 104.

112. This exhibition was derived from an earlier show at the Museum of Modern Art on US Housing in War and Peace. Duplicates of the full MoMA exhibition were sent to Australia and South Africa, while the USSR received just the section about wartime building technologies. See Anderson, "USA/USSR," 89.

113. Architects Committee, American-Soviet Friendship Records, TAM 134, Box 5, Folder 6, Tamiment Archives, New York University.

114. Architects Committee, American-Soviet Friendship Records, TAM 134, Box 5, Folder 6, Tamiment Archives, New York University.

115. GARF f. R-5283, op. 14, d. 265, l. 28.

116. Anderson, "USA/USSR," 89; Architects Committee, American-Soviet Friendship Records, TAM 134, Box 5, Folder 6, Tamiment Archives, New York University.

117. GARF f. R-5283, op. 14, d. 265, l. 28.

118. Architects Committee, American-Soviet Friendship Records, TAM 134, Box 5, Folder 8, Tamiment Archives, New York University.

119. American-Soviet Friendship Records, TAM 134, Box 5, Folder 6, Tamiment Archives, New York University.

120. GARF f. R-5283, op. 14, d. 265, l. 96.

121. Purpose and Program Statement, Architects Committee, American-Soviet Friendship Records, TAM 134, Box 5, Folder 6, Tamiment Archives, New York University.

122. Purpose and Program Statement, Architects Committee, American-Soviet Friendship Records, TAM 134, Box 5, Folder 6, Tamiment Archives, New York University.

123. Lazar' K. Brontman, *Dnevnik*, September 11, 1945. Brontman's diary is available online at: http://prozhito.org/persons/18.

124. Tolstoi remembered that the shed was located near Obydenskii pereulok. V. P. Tolstoi, "O P. D. Korine," in *P. D. Korin ob iskusstve*, 170.

125. Tolstoi, "O P. D. Korine," 170.

126. Tolstoi, "O P. D. Korine," 170. Korin would later design mosaic panels for the interior of MGU. See Kruzhkov, *Vysotnye zdaniia stalinskoi Moskvy*, 83.

127. RGASPI f. 82, op. 2, d. 506, l. 124.

128. Voroshilov forwarded this request to Molotov. RGASPI f. 82, op. 2, d. 506, l. 126. Iofan was clearly hoping to use the Soviet Union's newfound access to Axis cities, from which entire architectural and planning workshops might be packed up and taken back to the Soviet Union as part of postwar reparations, to the USDS's advantage.

129. See TsGA Moskvy f. R-694, op. 1, d. 397 for projects the USDS was working on in 1946. The USDS continued to work on the Lenin Library until at least 1948.

130. TsGA Moskvy f. 88, op. 29, d. 136, ll. 24–25.

131. TsGA Moskvy f. 88, op. 29, d. 136, l. 25.

132. Stalin's remarks at this meeting of June 17, 1949 are in "Bez khoroshei stolitsy—net gosudarstva," *Istochnik* 52(4), 2001: 111. Dmitrii Khmel'nitskii interprets this document differently, writing that by 1949, Stalin and even Iofan himself had lost interest in the Palace of Soviets project. See Khmel'nitskii, *Zodchii Stalin*, 254–55.

CHAPTER 4: MOSCOW OF THE PLAN

1. The topic of "multistory buildings in Moscow" had been discussed in December 1946 at a meeting of the Bureau of the Presidium of the Council of Ministers. See *Politbiuro TsK VKP(b) i Sovet Ministrov SSSR, 1945–1953*, 485.
2. Ganson, *The Soviet Famine of 1946–47 in Global and Historical Perspective*, 57–64.
3. "Privetstvie tov. I. V. Stalina," *Pravda*, September 7, 1947, 1.
4. GARF f. R-5446, op. 1, d. 290, l. 68; TsGA Moskvy f. R-694, op. 1, d. 421, ll. 1–3. The GARF (Council of Ministers) copy contains hand-written edits on the text and has the signature of Iakov Chadaev, chief of administration at the Council of Ministers. Stalin's signature is absent. The edits were incorporated into the final version sent to all Ministries and organizations involved in the project.
5. Lazar' K. Brontman, *Dnevniki 1932–1947*, January 12, 1947. Brontman's diary is available online at: http://prozhito.org/persons/18.
6. Smith, *Mythmaking in the New Russia*, 57–61.
7. Specialized architectural journals began discussing the skyscraper decree in more detail at about the same time. See, for example, *Arkhitektura i stroitel'stvo*, issue of March 1947.
8. "Debate on the Report on the USSR State Budget for 1947: Speech of deputy T.A. Selivanov," *Pravda*, February 23, 1947, 3.
9. Earlier Stalin-era plans for development of the Lenin Hills included a Monument to the Stalin Constitution. Plamper, *The Stalin Cult*, 99–101.
10. The structure slated to be built near Dinamo stadium was quickly relocated to a spot near Kiev Station, on Dorogomilovo Embankment.
11. "Debate on the Report on the USSR State Budget for 1947: Speech of deputy T.A. Selivanov," *Pravda*, February 23, 1947, 3.
12. "Skyscrapers Gain Stalin's Approval," *New York Times*, March 2, 1947, 1.
13. "Skyscrapers Gain Stalin's Approval," *New York Times*, March 2, 1947, 1.
14. GARF R-5446, op. 1, d. 290, ll. 68–71.
15. The USDS was put in charge of building two of the structures (the Lenin Hills and the Zariad'e skyscrapers), the Ministry of Construction of Heavy Industry would build the structure on Smolensk Square and the building on Dorogomilovo embankment (initially to be located at Dinamo stadium), the Ministry of Construction of Army and Navy Industries would build the hotel on Komsomol Square, the Ministry of Aviation Industries was in charge of building the skyscraper on Uprising Square, the Ministry of Railways was in charge of the Red Gates building, and the Ministry of Internal Affairs would build the Kotel'nicheskaia building.
16. Gorlizki and Khlevniuk, *Cold Peace*, 31–38; Pollock, *Stalin and the Soviet Science Wars*.
17. On the anti-Americanism campaign, see Magnúsdóttir, *Enemy Number One*.
18. GARF f. R-5446, op. 1, d. 290, l. 70.
19. Crawford, "From Tractors to Territory," 61.
20. Honor courts were held in the late 1940s on the initiative of Stalin and Andrei Zhdanov in various intellectual and scientific fields, including architecture. These events functioned as a self-policing mechanism for all who participated and observed. An architect would be brought before a jury of his or her peers to be judged on designs or other intellectual work deemed to be in violation of the strict ideological orthodoxy of the postwar years. In Moscow's architectural scene, prominent figures rotated through the roles, playing a member of the jury one month and sitting on trial as the accused the next. On honor courts held by architects during this period, see Harris, "Two Lessons in Modernism." On honor courts in other fields, see Pollock, *Stalin and the Soviet Science Wars*, 46.
21. "Neboskreb" in *Bol'shaia sovetskaia entsiklopediia*, second edition, 1954, 332.
22. Aleksei Shchusev, "Arkhitektura," *Bol'shaia sovetskaia entsiklopediia*, first edition, 1927.
23. "Arkhitektura," *Bol'shaia sovetskaia entsiklopediia*, second edition, 1950, 220.
24. On the mobilization of socialist realist national architectural form in Cold War-era competition with the West, see Castillo, "East as True West." See also Brandenberger, *National Bolshevism*; David-Fox, "Conclusion: Transnational History and the East-West Divide," in *Imagining the West in Eastern Europe and the Soviet Union*, 260.
25. In the late 1940s, Soviet officials promoted narratives of Russian national greatness by celebrating Russian inventors like Popov and Lodygin. Brooks, *Thank You, Comrade Stalin!*, 214; Slezkine, *Arctic Mirrors*, 304.
26. RGAE f. 9432, op. 1, d. 404, l. 75.

27. See Arkadii Mordvinov's internal report of March 3, 1947, in which he discusses the "26-story skyscraper" that is planned for the Zariad'e. RGAE f. 9432, op. 1, d. 89, l. 23.
28. Zubovich, "'Debating 'Democracy': The International Union of Architects and the Cold War Politics of Expertise," 109–112.
29. Popov's official titles, putting him in charge of municipal affairs in Moscow in 1947, were Chairman of the Executive Committee of the Moscow Soviet and First Secretary of the Moscow City Party Committee/Moscow Oblast' Party Committee.
30. TsAOPIM f. P-3, op. 67, d. 12, l. 33.
31. TsAOPIM f. P-3, op. 67, d. 12, l. 34.
32. TsAOPIM f. P-3, op. 67, d. 12, l. 35.
33. *Moskovskaia vlast': istoricheskie portrety 1708–2012*, 555–556.
34. Colton, *Moscow*, 292.
35. TsAOPIM f. P-3, op. 67, d. 12, ll. 47–48. Popov dates this quote to a meeting in 1946 that Stalin held with Soviet architects. E. V. Taranov, "Stranitsy biografii Moskovskogo lidera G. M. Popova," in *'Partiinyi gubernator' Moskvy: Georgii Popov*, 68.
36. TsAOPIM f. P-3, op. 67, d. 12, l. 48.
37. The MVD representative at the meeting was Iuvel'ian D. Sumbatov. TsAOPIM f. P-3, op. 67, d. 12, ll. 35–36.
38. GARF f. R-5446, op. 1, d. 290, l. 70.
39. See Onufriev's (spelt Anufriev in transcript) comment in TsAOPIM f. P-3, op. 67, d. 12, l. 36.
40. TsAOPIM f. P-3, op. 67, d. 12, l. 37.
41. TsAOPIM f. P-3, op. 67, d. 12, l. 37.
42. Knight, *Beria: Stalin's First Lieutenant*; Gorlizki and Khlevniuk, *Cold Peace, 103–104*.
43. Beria's correspondence to Stalin about the skyscrapers is scant in the archival files consulted. But see, for example, the letter from Beria to Stalin of April 27, 1947 requesting the leader's approval on the number of rooms specified for each of the buildings in GARF f. R-5446, op. 113, d. 65, l. 192. See also Beria's letters to Stalin in 1947 and 1948 containing updates on the designs of the various buildings in GARF f. R-5446, op. 113, d. 66, ll. 203, 229 and GARF f. R-5446, op. 113, d. 91, ll. 40, 242, 336–337, 513–514. There is little to no evidence in the files of Stalin's impressions or responses.
44. This quote comes from notes, not a stenographic report, taken by Georgii Popov at the June 17, 1949 Politburo meeting about the new Moscow General Plan. "Zamechaniia Tovarishcha Stalina I.V. pri obsuzhdenii voprosa o general'nom plane rekonstruktsii Moskvy na zasedanii Politbiuro TsK VKP(b) 17 iiunia 1949 goda," *Istochnik*, 4, 2001: 110.
45. "Zamechaniia Tovarishcha Stalina," 110.
46. "Zamechaniia Tovarishcha Stalina," 110–111.
47. "Zamechaniia Tovarishcha Stalina," 111.
48. Popov, "Vospominaniia," in *"Partiinyi gubernator" Moskvy: Georgii Popov*, 229.
49. There is some debate about the origins of this statement. Kolson, *Big Plans*, 189.
50. TsGA Moskvy f. R-694, op. 1, d. 422, ll. 13, 24, 26.
51. GARF R-5446, op. 49a, d. 4608, ll. 67–68.
52. The drafted list was sent to Beria from Grigorii Simonov, head of the USSR State Architecture Committee. Simonov informed Beria that the list had been shown already to Popov. The list assigned architects as follows: Chechulin and Rudnev on the Zariad'e building; Shchusev, Zholtovskii, and Iofan on the Lenin Hills; the Vesnin Brothers, Mordvinov, and Kolli on the hotel near Dinamo Stadium; Dushkin, B. S. Mezentsev, and Alabian on the Red Gates building; V. Ia. Movchan, M. V. Posokhin, and Oltarzhevskii on the Uprising Square; L. M. Poliakov, A. F. Zhukov, and A. F. Khriakov on the hotel at Kalanchevskii Square; Gel'freikh, A. P. Velikanov, I. E. Rozhin on the office building on Smolensk Square; and Chechulin and Rostkovskii on the Kotel'nicheskaia embankment building. This draft order also contained a clause about holding an open competition for the Zariad'e and Lenin Hills buildings. RGAE f. 9432, op. 1, d. 89, ll. 135–136ob.
53. Two Council of Ministers decrees (No. 1331 and No. 1334) were issued on April 27, 1947, to set the parameters (heights, volumes, rooms, amenities required) for the Zariad'e and Lenin Hills structures and for the buildings at the Red Gates, on Smolensk Square, and on Komsomol (Kalanchevskii) Square. See TsGA Moskvy f. R-694, op. 1, d. 420, ll. 27–38, 41–55. Also see GARF f. R-5446, op. 49, dela 1220 and 1221. Earlier drafts of these decrees are in GARF f. R-5446, op. 1, d. 290.
54. RGAE f. 9432, op. 1, d. 89, ll. 44–47.

55. These individuals were among those who reviewed design proposals of the Kotel'nicheskaia building and the Uprising Square building. RGAE f. 9432, op. 1, d. 89, l. 139.

56. RGAE f. 9432, op. 1, d. 89, l. 140.

57. RGAE f. 9432, op. 1, d. 89, l. 139.

58. The three proposals came from P. I. Frolov; V. K. Oltarzhevskii and N. V. Kuznetsov; and M. V. Posokhin and A. A. Mndoiants. In the end, Posokhin and Mndoiants were selected as chief architects for the building. RGAE f. 9432, op. 1, d. 89, ll. 139–141.

59. The four designs were submitted by I. G. Taranov, A. N. Dushkin, G. I. Voloshinov, and S. M. Kravets. In the end Dushkin, along with B. S. Mezentsev, were selected as chief architects for the building. RGAE f. 9432, op. 1, d. 357, l. 39.

60. RGAE f. 9432, op. 1, d. 357, ll. 39–42.

61. RGAE f. 9432, op. 1, d. 375, l. 40. At this session in 1948, reviewers assessed both the architectural and technical elements of the building. Those serving as reviewers of the design's architectural features were Ia. A. Kornfel'd, D. S. Meerson, S. P. Turgenev, and S. F. Kibirev.

62. On May 30, 1947, the Council of Ministers issued a decree officially calling for the celebration of Moscow's 800th anniversary on September 7, 1947. *Moskva Poslevoennaia, 1945–1947*, 229. See also Popov's letter to Stalin of May 26, 1947, in Taranov, "Stranitsy biografii Moskovskogo lidera G. M. Popova," 77.

63. Steinbeck, *A Russian Journal*, 17–18.

64. Steinbeck, *A Russian Journal*, 17–18.

65. Steinbeck, *A Russian Journal*, 20.

66. The USSR did not fully demobilize until 1948. Between 1945 and 1948, 8.5 million men were demobilized in the Soviet Union. See Zubkova, *Russia After the War*, 22. On the experience of demobilization in the city of Leningrad, see Dale, *Demobilized Veterans in Late Stalinist Leningrad*.

67. Fitzpatrick, *On Stalin's Team*, 171. On postwar expectations, see also Zubkova, *Russia After the War*; Brooks, *Thank You, Comrade Stalin!*, 198–199.

68. Vavilov, *Sergei Vavilov: Dnevniki 1909–1951*, Book 2, 325. On Vavilov's involvement earlier that year in ideological debates in the field of philosophy, see Pollock, *Stalin and the Soviet Science Wars*, 22.

69. See also Brandenberger's discussion of the festivities in *National Bolshevism*, 216–217.

70. "Iz stenogrammy soveshchaniia sekretarei RK VKP(b) i predsedatelei Ispolkomov raionnykh sovetov g. Moskvy—O podgotovke k prazdnovaniiu 800-letiia Moskvy," in *Moskva Poslevoennaia, 1945–1947*, 222.

71. "Iz stenogrammy," 222. See also notes of meeting of August 23, 1947, in same document collection, p. 244.

72. "Informatsiia orginstruktorskogo otdela MGK VKP(b) G.M. Popovu," in *Moskva Poslevoennaia, 1945–1947*, 245.

73. "Informatsiia orginstruktorskogo otdela MGK VKP(b) G.M. Popovu," 240.

74. "Informatsiia orginstruktorskogo otdela MGK VKP(b) G.M. Popovu," 240.

75. "Nakanune 800-letiia Moskvy. Stalinskii plan rekonstruktsii Moskvy v deistvii," *Pravda*, August 19, 1947, 2.

76. "Programma peredach," *Pravda*, September 5, 1947, 4.

77. RGALI f. 674, op. 2, d. 237, l. 32; TsGA Moskvy f. R-534, op. 1, d. 102, l. 41.

78. TsGA Moskvy f. R-534, op. 1, d. 102, l. 34. The three churches were The Church of Our Lady of Joy of All Who Sorrow, The Church of St. Phillip Metropolitan, and The Church of St. Gregory Neo-Caesarea.

79. GARF f. R-5446, op. 1, d. 290, l. 70.

80. English-language guidebook writers and historians today routinely refer to these buildings as "wedding cakes." The reference dates back to the Palace of Soviets. In the 1930s, the Palace of Soviets was likened by one foreign correspondent to a "Gothic wedding cake with Lenin taken the place of the usual Cupid on the top." See "Architects in Moscow" *The Manchester Guardian*, July 10, 1937, 14. The "wedding cake" description was later applied to Moscow's eight skyscrapers. As a *Washington Post* correspondent wrote in 1954, "the nearest thing to a cathedral erected in the Soviet Union since the godless Bolshevik revolution is the new, 32-story Moscow University skyscraper. Fancy as a hundred-dollar wedding cake, it is the tallest building in Europe. Only six Manhattan skyscrapers are taller." Charles Klensch "New Moscow Skyscraper Is 'Cathedral' of Marxism," *The Washington Post*, September 26, 1954, B3.

81. GARF f. R-5446, op. 113, d. 92, l. 224.

82. The location initially chosen for this building was along Leningradskoe shosse between ul. Novaia Bashilovka and the Dinamo stadium. RGAE f. 9432, op. 1, d. 89, l. 104.
83. GARF f. R-5446, op. 113, d. 66, l. 229.
84. Although Kalanchevskii Square was renamed Komsomol Square in 1933, most Soviet documents having to do with skyscraper development on this plot use the pre-revolutionary name.
85. On the changing heights of the skyscrapers, see Kruzhkov, *Vysotnye zdaniia stalinskoi Moskvy*, 47.
86. The new plan for this structure in 1948 also altered the height of the building from the initial 32 stories down to 26. The Zariad'e building, which was never completed, similarly changed height over time, from the initial 26-story building called for in the first decree to a 32-story building in the final design.
87. Taranov, "Stranitsy biografii Moskovskogo lidera G. M. Popova," 63. Popov also claimed that it was on his own initiative that the university building was moved away from the edge of the Lenin Hills, where the initial design had placed it. The archival record shows that Popov requested that this and other changes be made to this building's design in a letter to Beria (also signed by Chechulin) of April 2, 1948. GARF f. R-5446, op. 113, d. 91, ll. 239–241.
88. Popov, "Vospominaniia," 230.
89. RGASPI f. 558, op. 11, d. 897, l. 52. Iofan was taken off the project officially with a Council of Ministers decree of July 3, 1948, which put Rudnev in charge, with the assistance of Chernyshev, Abrosimov, and Khriakov. GARF f. R-5446, op. 113, d. 92, l. 369.
90. TsGA Moskvy f. R-694, op. 1, d. 453, l. 1.
91. GARF f. R-5446, op. 1, d. 3950, ll. 28–29.
92. On the Leningrad Affair's impact on architecture, see Maddox, *Saving Stalin's Imperial City*, 28, 171–192.
93. See Gorlizki and Khlevniuk, *Cold Peace,* 79–89; Fitzpatrick, *On Stalin's Team*, 202–209.
94. Elena Zubkova refers to these events as the Moscow Affair. See Zubkova, *Russia After the War*, 133. The connection between the Leningrad and Moscow Affairs was a matter of political allegiances: Andrei Zhdanov and Nikolai Voznesenskii had together formed one faction (the so-called "Leningrad group") pitted against their rivals Malenkov and Beria in a war of succession. With both Zhdanov and Voznesenskii gone by 1949, a new balance of power was struck. Gorlizki and Khlevniuk see the Moscow Affair as "contrived from the very beginning with this end in mind." When Popov was replaced by Khrushchev, the latter's presence in Moscow provided a necessary counterweight to the power of Malenkov and Beria, two figures whose influence had increased following the Leningrad Affair. See Gorlizki and Khlevniuk, *Cold Peace*, 92; Tikhonov and Gregory, "Stalin's Last Plan," in *Behind the Facade of Stalin's Command Economy*, 164.
95. "Anonimnoe zaiavlenie v Politbiuro o zloupotrebleniiakh G.M. Popova," October 20, 1949, in *Politbiuro TsK VKP(b) i Sovet Ministrov SSSR, 1945–1953*, 319.
96. "Anonimnoe zaiavlenie," 319.
97. Translation in Gorlizki and Khlevniuk, *Cold Peace*, 90–91.
98. Popov served as Minister of Urban Construction from December 1949 to March 1951, and as Minister of Agricultural Machine Building from March to December 1951. From 1951 to 1953, he was Director of an airplane factory in Kuibyshev. He then served as Soviet ambassador to Poland from 1953–1954, followed by a position as Director of a factory in Vladimir until 1965, when he retired as a pensioner.
99. "Postanovlenie Politbiuro ob osvobozhdenii G.M. Popova ot obiazannostei sekretaria MK i MGK i sekretariia TsK VKP(b)," December 12, 1949, in *Politbiuro TsK VKP(b) i Sovet Ministrov SSSR, 1945–1953*, 323. Also see Gorlizki and Khlevniuk, *Cold Peace*, 90–91.
100. TsAOPIM f. P-88, op. 29, d. 136, l. 1.
101. GARF f. R-5446, op. 51, d. 4195, l. 82.
102. GARF f. R-5446, op. 51, d. 4195, l. 81. Emphasis in the original.
103. GARF f. R-5446, op. 51, d. 4195, l. 81. Emphasis in the original.
104. All main architects of each of the eight skyscrapers won Stalin prizes in 1948. Stalin prize recipients for that year are listed in *Literaturnaia gazeta*, April 10, 1949, 1–2.
105. GARF f. R-5446, op. 51, d. 4195, l. 78.
106. GARF f. R-5446, op. 51, d. 4195, l. 78.
107. Other Soviet architects and managers seem to have met with the same fate after having complained to higher-ups and party officials about Chechulin's behavior. N. Evstratov, the Secretary

of the party organization of the Mosgorispolkom Architecture Committee, claimed to have reported Chechulin to various party agencies, to no effect (see RGAE f. 9510, op. 1, d. 77, l. 54). Grigorii Simonov, head from 1947 to 1949 of the USSR State Architecture Committee, also met Chechulin's ire in 1949. At a party meeting, Simonov raised the issue to Popov of a possible conflict of interest resulting from Chechulin's simultaneous position as Chief Architect of Moscow and head architect on two of Moscow's skyscrapers. Having learned about this, Chechulin wrote to Simonov personally in April 1949, telling him that his claims were unsubstantiated (see GARF f. R-5446, op. 51, d. 4189, ll. 15–16).

108. GARF f. R-5446, op. 51, d. 4195, l. 77. Emphasis in the original.
109. GARF f. R-5446, op. 51, d. 4195, l. 77.
110. RGAE f. 9510, op. 1, d. 77, l. 49. On the 1-million-ruble cost of this change to the design, see the draft decree "On the work of architects Chechulin and Rostkovskii" in RGAE f. 9510, op. 1, d. 77, l. 112.
111. Rostkovskii, in turn, was overseeing eight construction projects in 1949 that included the Kotel'nicheskaia building, an ambassador's mansion, the Central School of the Komsomol, and the Moscow Energy Institute.
112. GARF f. R-5446, op. 51, d. 4195, ll. 83–84. On Chechulin's monthly income, see also RGAE f. 9510, op. 1, d. 77, l. 109. Rostkovskii, for his part, was making nearly ten thousand rubles a month in 1949.
113. This is the average wage for September 1950. Filtzer, *Soviet Workers and Late Stalinism*, 235.
114. GARF f. R-5446, op. 51, d. 4195, ll. 86, 92–94.
115. RGAE f. 9510, op. 1, d. 77, l. 72.
116. Each region of Moscow was assigned its own architect (in some cases a pair of architects) to oversee construction and planning at the local level.
117. RGAE f. 9510, op. 1, d. 77, l. 72.
118. Smith, *Property of Communists*, 34.
119. RGAE f. 9510, op. 1, d. 77, l. 73.
120. RGAE f. 9510, op. 1, d. 77, ll. 89–95.
121. GARF f. R-5446, op. 51, d. 4195, l. 92.
122. GARF f. R-5446, op. 86a, d. 11687, ll. 203–204. Prior to receiving this new housing, Gokhman had been living with his family of four in a communal apartment on Begovaia ulitsa. The family shared one room of 18 square meters. In justifying his entitlement to an apartment in the Kotel'nicheskaia building, Gokhman made the case that as the engineer of the structure, he would be useful in the building's upkeep if he lived on the premises. See letter from Gokhman to Beria of March 22, 1952 in GARF f. R-5446, op. 86a, d. 11686, l. 7. Rostkovskii had also been living with his family of 6 in a communal apartment (they had 45 square meters between them) prior to being granted a family apartment in the Kotel'nicheskaia building. See letter from Rostkovskii to Beria of March 22, 1952 in GARF f. R-5446, op. 86a, d. 11686, l. 10.
123. TsAOPIM f. P-88, op. 29, d. 136, l. 23.
124. TsAOPIM f. P-88, op. 29, d. 136, l. 23.
125. "Postanovlenie plenuma Moskovskogo oblastnogo i gorodskogo komitetov VKP(b)," in *"Partiinyi gubernator" Moskvy Georgii Popov*, 361.
126. Khrushchev, *Khrushchev Remembers*, 249. On Khrushchev's impressions of the Moscow Affair, see also Taubman, *Khrushchev*, 210.
127. On Vlasov's work with Khrushchev in Kiev, see Yekelchyk, *Stalin's Citizens*, 127, 174.
128. RGAE f. 9510, op 3, d. 94, l. 113.
129. "O razrabotke novogo general'nogo plana rekonstruktsii Moskvy," *Pravda*, February 1, 1949, 1.
130. GARF f. R-5446, op. 86a, d. 11032, l. 117.
131. GARF f. R-5446, op. 86a, d. 11032, ll. 2–9ob.
132. GARF f. R-5446, op. 86a, d. 11032, l. 130ob.
133. GARF f. R-5446, op. 86a, d. 11032, ll. 116–117ob.
134. As Mark B. Smith discusses in *Property of Communists* (61–62), the Soviet state was well aware in 1950 of the countrywide housing crisis, as a result of letters that flowed in from residents and data gathered by the USSR Ministry of Construction.
135. "Speech of Comrade N. S. Khrushchev," *Pravda*, March 8, 1950, 4.
136. See *Pravda*, October 10, 1952, 1; *Pravda*, October 12, 1952, 4.
137. Colton, *Moscow*, 353–354.
138. RGALI f. 2466, op. 1, d. 190, l. 6.

CHAPTER 5: MOSCOW OF THE SHADOWS

1. Posokhin, *Dorogi zhizni iz zapisok arkhitektora*, 26.
2. Posokhin, *Dorogi zhizni iz zapisok arkhitektora*, 31.
3. RGAE f. 293, op. 1, d. 212, l. 15.
4. Karo Alabian, "Tvorcheskie zadachi sovetskikh arkhitektorov v piatiletnem plane vosstanov- leniia i razvitiia narodnogo khoziaistva," *Materialy XII plenuma SSA SSSR*, (Moscow: Izd. Akademii arkhitektury SSSR, 1948), 9.
5. GARF f. A-150, op. 2, d. 1025, l. 3. The building inspectorate, known as GASK (*Glavnaia ins- pektsiia gosudarstvennogo arkhitekturno-stroitel'nogo kontrolia*), was a branch of Gosstroi RSFSR.
6. DeHaan, *Stalinist City Planning*, 91. DeHaan draws on Evgeny Dobrenko's notion of the "de-realization" of Soviet life, developed in Dobrenko, *The Political Economy of Socialist Realism*.
7. TsGA Moskvy f. R-694, op. 1, d. 453, l. 4.
8. TsGA Moskvy f. R-694, op. 1, d. 453, l. 4.
9. TsGA Moskvy f. R-694, op. 1, d. 422, ll. 20–21.
10. GARF f. R-5446, op. 51, d. 4183, l. 249.
11. Kostof, "His Majesty the Pick."
12. On New York's postwar urban renewal projects see Zipp, *Manhattan Projects*; on Pittsburgh see Muller, "Downtown Pittsburgh: Renaissance and Renewal;" Neumann, *Remaking the Rust Belt*, 26–28.
13. Anthropologists Pavel Kupriyanov and Lyudmila Sadovnikova were struck by how little his- torical awareness or interest former Zariad'e residents displayed when interviewed in the 2000s. See Kupriyanov and Sadovnikova, "Historical Zaryadye as Remembered by Locals: Cultural Meanings of City Spaces," 220–253.
14. From 1826, the Zariad'e was the only place in Moscow where Jewish merchants were al- lowed to settle. By the 1870s, there were two synagogues in the neighborhood. See Maga- zanik, "'Moskovskoe getto' (po materialam vystavki 'Zariad'e—iz proshlogo v budushchee' v Muzee Moskvy."
15. Sytin, *Iz istorii Moskovskikh ulits,* 34.
16. Leonov, *The Badgers*, 20. See also Martin, "Sewage and the City," 273.
17. Leonov, *The Badgers*, 20.
18. Leonov, "Padenie Zariad'ia," in *Slovo o Moskve*, 101.
19. *General'nyi plan rekonstruktsii goroda Moskvy*, 12.
20. This project was the headquarters of the People's Commissariat of Construction and Heavy Industry. An architectural competition was held for the design of this building in 1934. Con- struction was abandoned in 1941.
21. See the Memorial Society, Moscow's databases of victims of political terror, searchable by address of residence. "Bazy dannykh zhertv politicheskogo terrora," base.memo.ru, lists. memo.ru, mos.memo.ru.
22. RGAE f. 9510, op. 1, d. 107, l. 162.
23. GARF f. R-5446, op. 80, d. 3813, l. 25.
24. TsGA Moskvy f. R-694, op. 1, d. 582, ll. 2–6.
25. The responsibility to rehouse residents continued during the mass housing construction of the Khrushchev era. Smith, *Property of Communists*, 162. For a comparative case, see Met Life's involvement in rehousing tenants from New York City's Gas House District in the 1940s prior to the insurance company's construction of Stuyvesant Town. Zipp, *Manhattan Projects*, 98.
26. On veterans and their families as an entitlement group, see Edele, "Soviet Veterans as an Entitlement Group."
27. RGAE f. 9510, op. 1, d. 107, l. 149. Legal precedent for financial compensation like this dated back to the 1930s. A law of 1936 permitted municipal soviets to evict residents from housing without providing alternative living space for urban planning purposes in Moscow, Lenin- grad, and Kiev. Instead, the municipalities were required to pay such residents a sum of 2,500 rubles per person in Moscow (2,000 for Leningrad and Kiev). Hazard, *Soviet Housing Law*, 75, 161.
28. RGAE f. 9510, op. 1, d. 107, l. 145.
29. RGAE f. 9510, op. 1, d. 107, l. 145.
30. TsGA Moskvy f. R-694, op. 1, d. 505, ll. 16–22.

31. Edele, "Soviet Veterans as an Entitlement Group," 111.
32. TsGA Moskvy f. R-694, op. 1, d. 582, ll. 2–6.
33. RGAE f. 9510, op. 1, d. 107, l. 1. 166.
34. GARF f. R-5446, op. 86, d. 3958, l. 169.
35. This was not untypical. As Donald Filtzer notes, in 1947 over half of all urban dwellings in Soviet Russia had no running water and no sewage. Filtzer, "Standard of Living Versus Quality of Life," 85.
36. These Zariad'evskii Lane neighbors may have been thinking, in part, of newcomers to their own neighborhood. In 1950, the USDS housed a few hundred of its workers in fifteen temporary dormitories in the Zariad'e. TsGA Moskvy f. R-694, op. 1, d. 649, ll. 52, 57–61.
37. GARF f. R-5446, op. 86, d. 3958, l. 169ob.
38. GARF f. R-5446, op. 86, d. 3958, l. 170.
39. GARF f. R-5446, op. 86, d. 3958, l. 172.
40. Lovell, *Summerfolk*, 92. On Kuntsevo's history during the 1930s, see Vatlin, *Agents of Terror.*
41. GARF f. R-5446, op. 87, d. 2145, ll. 6–8.
42. GARF f. R-5446, op. 87, d. 2145, l. 6.
43. GARF f. R-5446, op. 87, d. 2145, l. 5.
44. GARF f. R-5446, op. 87, d. 2145, l. 1.
45. GARF f. R-5446, op. 50, d. 3436, l. 40.
46. GARF f. R-5446, op. 80, d. 3813, l. 3.
47. GARF f. R-5446, op. 51, d. 4184, ll. 16–17.
48. TsGA Moskvy f. R-694, op. 1, d. 649, l. 18.
49. RGAE f. 9510, op. 1, d. 107, l. 142. Timothy J. Colton's term "disjointed monism" captures well the tension that characterized relations between central authorities—who intervened routinely in city affairs, as in the order of January 1947 to build skyscrapers—and municipal officials, who were left scrambling to build projects at odds with local goals. Colton, *Moscow,* 6.
50. Fitzpatrick, "Suppliants and Citizens: Public Letter-Writing in Soviet Russia in the 1930s," 82–86.
51. On Soviet letter-writing practices and letters of denunciation in the late-Stalinist period, see Fürst, "In Search of Soviet Salvation"; Kozlov, "Denunciation and Its Functions in Soviet Governance."
52. Two studies that use this source base as a lens for understanding popular Soviet conceptions of urban citizenship and home are Varga-Harris, "Green is the Colour of Hope?"; Ruscitti Harshman, "A Space Called Home: Housing and the Management of the Everyday in Russia, 1890–1935."
53. GARF f. R-5446, op. 81, d. 3967, ll. 28–29.
54. GARF f. R-5446, op. 81, d. 3967, l. 31.
55. GARF f. R-5446, op. 81, d. 3967, l. 179.
56. GARF f. R-5446, op. 81, d. 3967, ll. 178–179.
57. GARF f. R-5446, op. 81, d. 3967, ll. 178–179.
58. GARF f. R-5446, op. 81, d. 3967, l. 185.
59. As Baranov learned, the unsanctioned recipients of housing in Tekstil'shchiki included the staff members of the USDS and Glavpromstroi MVD who were involved in the construction of Moscow State University. GARF f. R-5446, op. 81, d. 3967, l. 182.
60. GARF f. R-5446, op. 86, d. 3958, l. 15.
61. GARF f. R-5446, op. 86, d. 3958, l. 15.
62. GARF f. R-5446, op. 86, d. 3958, l. 15.
63. GARF f. R-5446, op. 86, d. 3958, l. 15
64. GARF f. R-5446, op. 86, d. 3958, l. 12.
65. GARF f. R-5446, op. 86, d. 3958, l. 25.
66. GARF f. R-5446, op. 86, d. 3959, l. 22.
67. GARF f. R-5446, op. 86, d. 3959, l. 22.
68. Katherine Lebow writes about similar experiences of residents of Nowa Huta when they made their way into central Krakow. Lebow, *Unfinished Utopia,* 56–59.
69. GARF f. R-5446, op. 86, d. 3959, l. 21. In response to Rekin's appeal, Beria sent a message to S. P. Afanas'ev at the Moscow Oblast' Executive Committee asking him to take the appropriate measures to speed up the construction of a road between the new settlement in Kuntsevo and the railway platform. GARF f. R-5446, op. 86, d. 3959, l. 23.

70. A. N. Komarovskii became head of the USDS in 1948. When he took on this position, Komarovskii retained his previous post as head of the Department of Industrial Construction (Glavpromstroi) of the MVD USSR—the industrial construction wing of the Gulag. While the Zariad'e skyscraper would never be completed, Komarovskii did oversee the completion of Moscow State University.

71. GARF f. R-5446, op. 86, d. 3959, ll. 62–63.

72. GARF f. R-5446, op. 81, d. 3967, l. 170.

73. GARF f. R-5446, op. 81, d. 3967, l. 170. The original Russian is: "*Ne lovite zhuravliia v nebe, poimaite sinitsu.*"

74. The Russian expression: "*Luchshe sinitsa v rukakh, chem zhuravl' v nebe.*" A near-equivalent expression in English is "A bird in the hand is worth two in the bush."

75. Prokof'ev was officially relieved of his position as head of the USDS in the Council of Ministers decree of October 14, 1948, "On the strengthening of construction of Moscow State University and the 32-story administrative building on the Zariad'e." See TsGA Moskvy f. R-694, op. 1, d. 456, l. 1. Prokof'ev's obituary is printed in *Arkhitektura i stroitel'stvo,* October 1949, 24.

76. TsGA Moskvy f. R-694, op. 1, d. 456, ll. 1–2.

77. See A. I. Kokurin and Iu. N. Morukov, "Priniat' predlozhenie tovarishcha Stalina," in *Istoricheskii arkhiv* 1 (2004): 28–32. I am grateful to Richard Anderson for bringing this source to my attention.

78. Komarovskii, *Zapiski stroitelia*, 200.

79. Komarovskii, *Zapiski stroitelia*, 200.

80. Komarovskii, *Zapiski stroitelia*, 200.

81. TsGA Moskvy f. R-694, op. 1, d. 505, ll. 21–22.

82. "Ob usilenii stroitel'stva zdanii Moskovskogo gosudarstvennogo universiteta v 1951 godu," in *Istoricheskii arkhiv* 4, (2004): 121–128; TsGA Moskvy f. R-694, op. 1, d. 505, l. 22.

83. GARF f. R-5446, op. 81, d. 3967, ll. 9–13.

84. GARF f. R-5446, op. 81, d. 3967, ll. 11–11ob.

85. TsGA Moskvy f. R-694, op. 1, d. 505, l. 21.

86. Andrusz, *Housing and Urban Development in the USSR*, 99; Attwood, *Gender and Housing in Soviet Russia: Private Life in a Public Space*, 149.

87. The average wage for industrial workers in September 1950 was 687 rubles per month. Filtzer, *Soviet Workers and Late Stalinism*, 235.

88. TsGA Moskvy f. R-694, op. 1, d. 505, ll. 19–21.

89. The Vasil'evs' letter was received at Beria's office in June 1953, just two days before Beria was arrested.

90. GARF f. R-5446, op. 87, d. 2145, l. 88.

91. GARF f. R-5446, op. 87, d. 2145, l. 87. Dunham, *In Stalin's Time*.

92. McKellar, *Landscapes of London,* 206.

93. The Institute for the History of Material Culture was founded in April 1919 (under the name State Academy of the History of Material Culture).

94. During the war, Rabinovich took part in preservation and excavation work in Novgorod. In the post-Stalin period, he led excavation work within Moscow's Kremlin. On the Kremlin, see Merridale, *Red Fortress*, 342–343.

95. As Mikhail Miller observed, in the postwar period, "in archaeology patriotic themes were raised to first place: the study of the origins of the Russian people, the development of ancient Russian culture and handicrafts, the rise and development of ancient Russian towns." See Miller, *Archaeology in the USSR*, 135.

96. See L. A. Beliaev, O. V. Budnitskii, V. Ia. Petrukhin, "Moskva i Rabinovich," in M. G. Rabinovich, *Zapiski sovetskogo intellektuala*, 7. A notable exception is the archaeological work conducted during construction of the first line of the Moscow metro. See M. Rabinovich and G. Latysheva, *Iz zhizni drevnei Moskvy*, 17.

97. Rabinovich, *Zapiski sovetskogo intellektuala*, 241.

98. Rabinovich, *Zapiski sovetskogo intellektuala*, 248–249.

99. Rabinovich, *Zapiski sovetskogo intellektuala*, 250; Rabinovich, "Arkheologicheskie issledovaniia moskovskogo posada," *Voprosy istorii* no. 5 (1951): 65–71.

100. Rabinovich, *Zapiski sovetskogo intellektuala*, 251.

101. On postwar anti-Semitism in the Soviet Union, see Slezkine, *The Jewish Century*, 289–308.

102. "Berezhno otnosit'sia k pamiatnikam zodchestva," *Sovetskoe iskusstvo*, October 27, 1951, 4.

103. Bittner, *The Many Lives of Khrushchev's Thaw*, 143–144.
104. TsGA Moskvy f. R-694, op. 1, d. 582, l. 7.
105. On the preservation of ecclesiastical architecture during the Soviet period, see Kelly, *Socialist Churches*.

CHAPTER 6: THE *VYSOTNIKI*

1. E. Martynov, "Iskusstvo elektrosvarki," in *Dvorets nauki*, 73.
2. "Novoe v literature," *Krokodil*, August 20, 1952, 2.
3. "Novoe v literature," 2.
4. Ministry of Internal Affairs (MID) certificate (*spravka*) for Ismail Guseinovich Sadarov of August 25, 1950, in uncatalogued materials on Moscow State University, green folder, Memorial Society Archive, Moscow.
5. Martynov, "Iskusstvo elektrosvarki," 76.
6. McCannon, "To Storm the Arctic"; Bailes, "Technology and Legitimacy."
7. Morshed, *Impossible Heights*, 1.
8. Kingwell, *Nearest Thing to Heaven*, 8.
9. Fedor Lagutin, "Radostnyi trud," in *Dvorets nauki*, 56.
10. On the significance of the wounded male body in socialist realist texts, see Kaganovsky, *How the Soviet Man was Unmade*.
11. Martynov, "Iskusstvo elektrosvarki," 72.
12. Key examples of production novels are Fedor Gladkov's *Cement* (written 1922–24) and N. N. Lyashko's *The Blast Furnace* (1925). On the production novel, see Clark, *The Soviet Novel*, 256–260.
13. *Ogonek*, no. 52, December 1952, 1.
14. On women in the Soviet workforce during Stalinism, see Goldman, *Women at the Gates: Gender and Industry in Stalin's Russia*, 89–92. On postwar Stalinism, see Greta Bucher, "Struggling to Survive: Soviet Women in the Postwar Years"; Susanne Conze, "Women's Work and Emancipation in the Soviet Union, 1941–50."
15. TsGA Moskvy f. R-694, op. 1, d. 545, ll. 13, 14ob, 26ob.
16. TsAOPIM f. P-88, op. 29, d. 136, l. 21.
17. On these demands and women's reactions to them, see Bucher, "Struggling to Survive: Soviet Women in the Postwar Years."
18. M. Nakonechnaia, "My stroim—my uchimsia!" in *Dvorets nauki*, 98–100.
19. Benjamin Tromly discusses the appeal in the postwar years of higher education as a path to social mobility in *Making the Soviet Intelligentsia*, 55–56.
20. See Fitzpatrick, *Education and Social Mobility in the Soviet Union, 1921–1934*.
21. Dunham, *In Stalin's Time*, 16.
22. Absenteeism and job-changing were made criminal offences in June 1940. See Filtzer, *Soviet Workers and Late Stalinism*, 159–160. As David Shearer notes, the harsher labor laws enacted and enforced in the 1940s and 1950s served to counter the ineffectiveness of the residence laws (passportization) introduced in the 1930s. Shearer, "Elements Near and Alien: Passportization, Policing, and Identity in the Stalinist State, 1932–1952."
23. GARF f. R-5446, op. 113, d. 66, l. 122.
24. GARF f. R-5446, op. 113, d. 66, ll. 120–121.
25. Filtzer, *Soviet Workers and Late Stalinism*, 21.
26. GARF f. R-5446, op. 49a, d. 4608, ll. 67–68. Among this total, 5,000 workers would go to the Ministry of Construction of Heavy Industry; 3,000 to the Ministry of Construction of Army and Navy Industries; 4,000 to the Ministry of Aviation Industries; 4,000 to the Ministry of Railways; and 7,000 to the USDS.
27. These workers were to be recruited through the organized labor recruitment system (*orgnabor*). TsGA Moskvy f. R-694, op. 1, d. 453, ll. 10, 15. An order printed in April 1948 specified that the 2,000 workers going to the USDS would come from Saratov oblast' and Vladimir oblast'. See TsGA Moskvy f. R-694, op. 1, d. 457, l. 8.
28. TsGA Moskvy f. R-694, op. 1, d. 454, l. 5. The supply was extended into 1949, see GARF f. R-5446, op. 51, d. 4184, l. 91.
29. GARF f. R-5446, op. 51, d. 4190, l. 52.
30. TsGA Moskvy f. R-694, op. 1, d. 458, l. 49. Beria forwarded Prokof'ev's letter to the Minister of Labor Reserves, Vasilii Pronin, with the note: "urgent—must help."

31. TsGA Moskvy f. R-694, op. 1, d. 649, ll. 70, 75.
32. GARF f. R-5446, op. 51, d. 4182, ll. 193–194.
33. GARF f. R-5446, op. 51, d. 4183, ll. 246–250.
34. Iakov Tsytsarkin, "Etazhi podnialis' v nebo," in *Dvorets nauki*, 71.
35. Siegelbaum, *Stakhanovism and the Politics of Productivity in the USSR, 1935–1941*, 184–186.
36. TsAGM f. R-694, op. 1, d. 649, l. 103. The average monthly wage in the Soviet construction industry as a whole in September 1950 was 565 rubles. Filtzer, *Soviet Workers and Late Stalinism*, 235.
37. TsAOPIM f. P-88, op. 18, d. 69, l. 32.
38. TsAOPIM f. P-4, op. 72, d. 84, l. 48.
39. TsAOPIM f. P-4, op. 72, d. 85, l. 1.
40. TsAOPIM f. P-66, op. 1, d. 613, l. 236.
41. TsAOPIM f. P-66, op. 1, d. 613, l. 236.
42. TsAOPIM f. P-66, op. 1, d. 613, l. 240.
43. TsAOPIM f. P-66, op. 1, d. 613, l. 239.
44. TsAOPIM f. P-1419, op. 2, d. 121, l. 3.
45. TsAOPIM f. P-88, op. 22, d. 180, l. 82.
46. TsAOPIM f. P-88, op. 22, d. 180, l. 82.
47. TsAOPIM f. P-88, op. 29, d. 134, l. 45.
48. V. Grushkin, "Po Stalinskim prednachertaniiam," in *Dvorets nauki*, 18.
49. Grushkin, "Po Stalinskim prednachertaniiam," 18.
50. *Pravda* and *Izvestiia* featured regular coverage of the World Peace Council congresses and activities from late July through November 1950.
51. GARF f. R-5446, op. 51, d. 4187, l. 138.
52. GARF f. R-5446, op. 51, d. 4185, l. 165.
53. Filtzer, *Soviet Workers and Late Stalinism*, 235–36.
54. TsAOPIM f. P-88, op. 22, d. 180, l. 155.
55. *Ogonek*, no. 52, December 1952, 1.
56. TsAOPIM f. P-4, op. 72, d. 85, ll. 1, 4.
57. TsAOPIM f. P-66, op. 1, d. 613, ll. 94, 239.
58. TsAOPIM f. P-4, op. 72, d. 85, l. 44.
59. D. Beliaev and Iu. Dobriakov, "Domik v piatom poselke," *Sovetskaia kul'tura*, August 29, 1953, 3.
60. TsAOPIM f. P-4, op. 72, d. 85, l. 44.
61. Grushkin, "Po Stalinskim prednachertaniiam," 20.
62. TsAOPIM f. P-88, op. 29, d. 134, l. 53.
63. While the newspaper article and the investigation did not explicitly mention that both Goberman and Iofan were Jewish, it is possible that the accusations against them were anti-Semitic attacks motivated by the ongoing anti-cosmopolitan campaign.
64. M. Kriukov, B. Turovetskii, and Leonid Lench, "Na dolzhnuiu vysotu," *Krokodil*, November 10, 1951, 5.
65. Lench himself worked for *Krokodil*.
66. Kriukov, Turovetskii, and Lench, "Na dolzhnuiu vysotu," 5.
67. Kriukov, Turovetskii, and Lench, "Na dolzhnuiu vysotu," 5.
68. Kriukov, Turovetskii, and Lench, "Na dolzhnuiu vysotu," 5.
69. On Liublino: GARF f. R-5446, op. 51, d. 4186, l. 38; GARF f. R-5446, op. 51, d. 4182, l. 193. On Ismailovo: GARF f. R-5446, op. 113, d. 66, l. 84.
70. GARF f. R-5446, op. 51, d. 4182, ll. 174–175.
71. GARF f. R-5446, op. 113, d. 91, l. 230.
72. TsGA Moskvy f. R-694, op. 1, d. 454, l. 4; TsGA Moskvy f. R-694, op. 1, d. 466, l. 3; TsAOPIM f. P-88, op. 29, d. 134, l. 44.
73. For a list of facilities that USDS officials planned to build in Cheremushki, see TsAOPIM f. P-1419, op. 2, d. 122, ll. 95–96.
74. GARF f. R-5446, op. 86, d. 3958, l. 181.
75. GARF f. R-5446, op. 86, d. 3958, ll. 179–180.
76. GARF f. R-5446, op. 86, d. 3958, ll. 177–178.
77. GARF f. R-5446, op. 86, d. 3958, ll. 176, 181.
78. See Gotovskaia's letter to Beria in GARF f. R-5446, op. 86, d. 3959, l. 99. Some of this information is disputed in other documents in the file. For example, according to a letter from

Aleksei Voronkov to Beria, Gotovskaia's passport indicated that she had arrived in Moscow not in 1951, but in April 1952.

79. GARF f. R-5446, op. 86, d. 3959, l. 99.

80. GARF f. R-5446, op. 86, d. 3959, ll. 99–100. Indication of Komarovskii's initial decision to grant Gotovskaia work and housing is on l. 102.

81. On the large number of non-registered residents in Moscow in the postwar years, see Filtzer, *The Hazards of Urban Life in Late Stalinist Russia*, 53–54.

82. GARF f. R-5446, op. 86, d. 3959, ll. 101–102.

83. GARF f. R-5446, op. 86, d. 3959, l. 105ob.

84. GARF f. R-5446, op. 86, d. 3959, ll. 104–105.

85. GARF f. R-5446, op. 113, d. 66, l. 119.

86. A. N. Komarovskii (1906–1973) was Head of Glavpromstroi MVD SSSR from May 1944 to November 1951 and again from July 1952 to March 1955. *Istoriia stalinskogo gulaga: konets 1920x-pervaia polovina 1950x godov*, vol. 2, 655.

87. Ruder, *Building Stalinism,* 62.

88. In the postwar years, the number of inmates across Glavpromstroi grew from 100,000 in 1945 to over 200,000 in 1951. See Tsepkalova, "Glavpromstroi v sisteme Gulaga," 268, 277.

89. In internal documents of 1953, the Gulag administration listed the number of prisoners in Glavpromstroi construction office No. 560 at 11,422 and No. 565 at 57,927. While these construction offices would soon merge, they are named separately in the list. GARF R-9414, op. 1, d. 117, l. 270.

90. GARF f. R-5446, op. 86a, d. 11681, l. 5. See also *Sistema ispravitel'no-trudovykh lagerei v SSSR,* 409–410, 435–437.

91. Other branches of the MVD were also involved in skyscraper building. A May 30, 1949 order that sought to quicken the pace on construction of the Kotel'nicheskaia building ("O sokrashchenii sroka stroitel'stva mnogoetazhnogo zhilogo doma MVD SSSR na Kotel'nicheskoi naberezhnoi na odin god") required General-Lieutenant T. F. Filippov, head of the GUPVI (Main Administration for Affairs of Prisoners of War and Internees) to supply 700 prisoners of war for the building's construction. See Kokurin and Morukov, "Gulag: Struktura i kadry," 117.

92. See GARF f. R-5446, op. 51a, d. 7800; Kokurin and Morukov, 116.

93. GARF f. R-5446, op. 51a, d. 7800, l. 13. A. A. Tsepkalova writes that construction office No. 352 was also involved in building MGU. Tsepkalova, "Glavpromstroi v sisteme Gulaga," 289.

94. GARF f. R-5446, op. 51a, d. 7798, l. 40.

95. GARF f. R-5446, op. 51a, d. 7798, ll. 40–41.

96. GARF f. R-5446, op. 51a, d. 7800, l. 8.

97. "O meropriatiakh po stroitel'stvu novikh zdanii Moskovskogo gosudarstvennogo universiteta na 1950 god," in *Istoricheskii arkhiv* No. 2 (2004): 42.

98. GARF f. R-9414, op. 1a, d. 275, ll. 8–19.

99. GARF f. R-9414, op. 1a, d. 275, ll. 6–7.

100. GARF f. R-9414, op. 1, d. 1363, l. 5. Oleg Khlevniuk discusses other cases of the early release of Gulag prisoners in 1950 and 1951 in "The Economy of the OGPU, NKVD, and MVD of the USSR, 1930–1953," in *The Economics of Forced Labor: The Soviet Gulag*, 55–56.

101. GARF f. R-9414, op. 1, d. 1363, l. 5.

102. GARF f. R-9414, op. 1, d. 1363, l. 7.

103. There is some discrepancy in the numbers listed here as they appear across the two documents in GARF f. R-9414, op. 1, d. 1363, ll. 6–7.

104. For further details about who these men were and where they came from, see the collection of three folders of uncatalogued documents from the MGU construction site at Memorial Society Archive, Moscow. I am grateful to archive Director Alena Kozlova for bringing these and other documents to my attention.

105. See collection of documents of Aleksei Grigor'evich Maksimov in the green folder of uncatalogued documents from the MGU construction site at the Memorial Society Archive, Moscow. Included in these documents is a request from Maksimov for the temporary use of his passport so that he could go to the ZAGS to get married.

106. See the grey folders of uncatalogued documents from the MGU construction site at the Memorial Society Archive, Moscow.

107. Letter in materials of Ismail Guseinovich Sadarov, in uncatalogued materials on Moscow State University, green folder, Memorial Society Archive, Moscow.

108. Letter in materials of Sergei Ivanovich Tsarev, in uncatalogued materials on Moscow State University, grey folder, Memorial Society Archive, Moscow.

109. The metaphor of the "Gulag archipelago" serves poorly, as many scholars have noted, as a model for understanding the widespread use of forced labor in urban areas. As David Shearer writes, new metaphors have been deployed in recent scholarship that seeks to complicate this image of the Gulag and to emphasize "a more dynamic and interactive relationship between the Gulag and the rest of Soviet society" (711). Shearer, "The Soviet Gulag—an Archipelago?" See also Barenberg, *Gulag Town, Company Town*; Khlevniuk, "The Gulag and Non-Gulag as One Interrelated Whole"; Alexopoulos, "Amnesty 1945: The Revolving Door of Stalin's Gulag"; Wilson Bell, "Was the Gulag an Archipelago?"; Brown, "Out of Solitary Confinement: The History of the Gulag,"; Viola, "Historicising the Gulag,"; Bell, *Stalin's Gulag at War*.

110. *Sistema ispravitel'no-trudovykh lagerei v SSSR, 1923–1960, spravochnik*, 535.

111. Tsepkalova, "Glavpromstroi v sisteme Gulaga," 259.

112. Tsepkalova, "Glavpromstroi v sisteme Gulaga," 259.

113. "Upper panel from door jamb casing in the building on the Kotel'nicheskaia embankment, 1/15, Moscow, 1952," GULAG History Museum (GMIG) NV-460. Last name can also be read as Astarov, Assharov, or Astafov.

114. "Ukaz Prezidiuma Verkhovnogo Soveta SSSR ob amnistii," *Pravda*, March 28, 1953, 1.

115. Dobson, *Khrushchev's Cold Summer*, 25.

116. Shaginian, *Dnevnik pisatelia 1950–1952*, 456.

117. Shaginian, *Dnevnik pisatelia*, 458.

118. Nicholas, *Writers at Work*, 78.

119. "Pervenets vysotnykh stroek," *Sovetskoe iskusstvo*, August 16, 1952, 1.

120. "Pervenets vysotnykh stroek," 1.

CHAPTER 7: THE VIEW FROM THE TOP

1. Getty, *Practicing Stalinism*, 27–28.

2. Hoffmann, *Stalinist Values,* 57–58.

3. Fitzpatrick, "Becoming Cultured: Socialist Realism and the Representation of Privilege and Taste," 227.

4. Dunham, *In Stalin's Time,* 15.

5. GARF f. R-5446, op. 86a, d. 11687, l. 86. Emphasis in the original.

6. GARF f. R-5446, op. 86a, d. 11687, l. 87.

7. On elites in the postwar Stalin era, see Duskin, *Stalinist Reconstruction and the Confirmation of a New Elite, 1945–1953*.

8. I found no archival evidence of successful appeals made in person to Beria or to other top officials, but I expect that more informal, face-to-face channels were used as well by those in search of skyscraper apartments. In his denunciatory letter to Khrushchev and Malenkov of July 2, 1953, Mikhail T. Pomaznev claimed that Beria took full control over the distribution of skyscraper apartments, ultimately treating the skyscrapers as "his own pet project [*schital svoim detishchem*]." *Lavrentii Beriia. 1953: Stenogramma iiul'skogo plenuma TsK KPSS i drugie dokumenty*, 81.

9. GARF f. R-5446, op. 86a, d. 11686, ll. 32–33, 52, 370. The Academy of Sciences President was Aleksandr Nikolaevich Nesmeianov. The Procurator General of the USSR was Grigorii Nikolaevich Safonov. Most of his staff were living in hotels. The Minister of Cinematography of the USSR was Ivan Grigor'evich Bol'shakov.

10. These residents are included in long lists of names of residents chosen for the Kotel'nicheskaia and Red Gates skyscrapers that can be found in GARF f. R-5446, op. 86a, d. 11687.

11. Sytin, *Iz istorii Moskovskikh ulits,* 329–334.

12. GARF f. R-5446, op. 86a, d. 11687, ll. 178–177.

13. These lists are in GARF f. R-5446, op. 86a, d. 11687.

14. "Engineering-technical workers," or ITRs, were personnel working in scientific, technical, and managerial positions in areas of production. See Duskin, *Stalinist Reconstruction*.

15. GARF f. R-5446, op. 86a, d. 11687, l. 211.

16. Sheila Fitzpatrick describes socialist realism as a Stalinist *mentalité* in *The Cultural Front*, 217.

17. Clark, "The 'New Moscow' and the 'New Happiness'," 195.

18. Slezkine, *The House of Government*.

19. A number of those granted skyscraper apartments were coming from dorms or apartments in buildings run by the TsK KPSS, MGB, or Gosplan. There are numerous instances of institutions requesting apartments in the skyscrapers because their staff were being housed in hotels, at great expense to the institution.

20. Note that "living space," in the Soviet definition, referred to rooms not including "auxiliary spaces" (kitchens, bathrooms, entryways, and hallways). Andrusz, *Housing and Urban Development in the USSR*, 36; see also Fitzpatrick, *Everyday Stalinism*, 99.

21. By 1946, the basic sanitary norms set were between 6 and 9 square meters per person. There are contradictory numbers listed in various sources. 6–9 are the numbers stated in correspondence about reconstruction between Giprogor and the Committee on the Affairs of Architecture in 1946 (RGAE, f. 9432, op. 3, d. 9, l. 192). The Committee and Gosplan recommended that Giprogor aim in some areas being rebuilt for between 9–11 square meters per person. In reality in Moscow, the documents prepared for the new Moscow General Plan (marked secret) state that the "average norm of living space per person (of the population in Moscow of 4,150,000) is about 4.8 square meters" in 1950. This looks to have been calculated on the basis of available living space in 1949 in the capital (20,500,000 square meters). GARF R-5446, f. 86a, d. 11032, l. 118ob.

22. On Gorky Street's metamorphosis in the 1930s, see Castillo, "Gorki Street and the Design of the Stalin Revolution." On this street in the postwar years, see Rüthers, "The Moscow Gorky Street in late Stalinism."

23. GARF f. R-5446, op. 86a, d. 11032, ll. 117, 130ob.

24. Complaints about lack of hot water, dysfunctional elevators, and the small size of Gorky Street's apartments came from an administrator at the TsK VKP(b) in 1952 who was looking for apartments for foreign communists. GARF f. R-5446, op. 86a, d. 11687, l. 9.

25. GARF f. R-5446, op. 86a, d. 11687, 78.

26. Smith, *Property of Communists*, 32.

27. TsAOPIM f. P-77, op. 1, d. 954, l. 4.

28. Gronow, *The Sociology of Taste*, 63. See also Gronow, *Caviar with Champagne*.

29. GARF f. R-5446, op. 86a, d. 11686, l. 1.

30. GARF f. R-5446, op. 86a, d. 11686, l. 1.

31. TsGA Moskvy f. R-496, op. 1, d. 1, ll. 1–3.

32. TsGA Moskvy f. R-496, op. 1, d. 1, l. 64. The Office sent its Directors at the Kotel'nicheskaia and Red Gates buildings repeated instructions on the collection of rent, noting that there were to be no reductions given for any special classes of people. From the 1920s, Soviet law allowed for rental rates to be set above or below the standard municipal rate in accordance with a building's condition, physical properties, and amenities. Other factors taken into consideration include the monthly wage and number of dependents of the resident. Hazard, *Soviet Housing Law*, 38–43.

33. These policies and budgeting were established in the Office's second-ever order of June 8, 1952. TsGA Moskvy f. R-496, op. 1, d. 1, ll. 2–5.

34. TsGA Moskvy f. R-496, op. 1, d. 1, l. 62.

35. TsGA Moskvy f. R-496, op. 1, d. 13, l. 68.

36. TsGA Moskvy f. R-496, op. 1, d. 13, l. 68. In another case, an abundance of books was used to upgrade apartments. M. A. Minkus, one of the architects of the Ministry of Foreign Affairs building, asked to be moved from the apartment he had been assigned into another one that had one room that was at least 20–22 square meters (the minimum he felt was necessary to contain his library and studio). His request was successful. Minkus moved up one floor and gained an additional 10 square meters of space at the Red Gates. (l. 30).

37. GARF f. R-5446, op. 86a, d. 11687, ll. 166–178.

38. Blokhin had just recently delivered a lecture on "Apartment Types and Standardization in 8–14-story Buildings in Moscow" at a conference in 1951 on the lessons to be learned from Moscow's skyscraper construction. RGAE f. 293, op. 1, d. 336, ll. 67–117.

39. Six family members plus a nanny.

40. TsGA Moskvy f. R-496, op. 1, d. 13, l. 44.

41. Alla Sarukhanian defended her dissertation in 1953 and became an expert on Irish literature.

42. On the mass housing campaign, begun in 1957, see Harris, *Communism on Tomorrow Street*.

43. GARF f. R-5446, op. 86a, d. 11687, l. 138.

44. GARF f. R-5446, op. 86a, d. 11687, l. 37.

45. GARF f. R-5446, op. 86a, d. 11687, ll. 116–119.
46. Karo Alabian, "Vysotnye zdaniia stolitsy," *Ogonek*, September 1952, 6.
47. David Arkin, "Zavoevanie vysoty," *Literaturnaia gazeta*, February 12, 1953, 1.
48. Arkin, "Zavoevanie vysoty," 1.
49. "So vsemi udobstvami," *Krokodil*, October 30, 1951.
50. GARF f. R-5446, op. 86a, d. 11687, l. 126.
51. GARF f. R-5446, op. 86a, d. 11687, l. 86.
52. TsGA Moskvy f. R-496, op. 1, d. 13, l. 65.
53. GARF f. R-5446, op. 1, d. 290, l. 70.
54. TsGA Moskvy f. R-496, op. 1, d. 13, l. 33.
55. *Faina Ranevskaia: Sluchai, shutki, aforizmy*, 83–84. The Russian equivalent of the expression "Bread and Circuses" is "*khleba i zrelishch*" (Bread and Spectacles).
56. Khrushchev, "On Wide-Scale Introduction of Industrial Methods," 167.

CHAPTER 8: DE-STALINIZATION AND THE BATTLE AGAINST "EXCESS"

1. The skyscraper on Uprising Square would open its doors to residents in 1954. The two hotels were the last to be completed—the Hotel Leningrad in 1954 and the Hotel Ukraine in 1957. The eighth skyscraper on the Zariad'e was never built to completion.
2. Taubman, *Khrushchev,* 270–275.
3. Davies and Ilic, "From Khrushchev (1935–1936) to Khrushchev (1956–1964): Construction Policy Compared," 205–210.
4. The full name of the event was the All-Union Conference of Builders, Architects, and Workers in the Building Materials Industry, the Building and Transport Mechanical Engineering, and in Design and Research Organizations.
5. Smith, *Property of Communists*, 5.
6. RGAE f. 339, op. 1, d. 1038.
7. Lists of attendees can be found in RGAE f. 339, op. 1, d. 1036; RGAE f. 339, op. 1, d. 1037; RGAE f. 339, op. 1, d. 1038.
8. RGAE f. 339, op. 1, d. 1037, l. 260.
9. Natalya Solopova and Daria Bocharnikova have discussed in detail the important role that Gradov played in the 1950s in their excellent studies of modern architecture in the Soviet Union. See Solopova, "La Préfabrication en URSS: Concept Technique et Dispositifs Architecturaux"; Bocharnikova, "Inventing Socialist Modern: A History of the Architectural Profession in the USSR, 1954–1971."
10. Adopting the surname "Gradov" in 1940, he was previously known as Georgii Sutiagin.
11. Biographical information in this and the following paragraphs is taken in part from the introductory remarks to the G. A. Gradov papers held at TsMAMLS (fond 226), prepared by archivist E. O. Shevchenko.
12. TsMAMLS f. 226, op. 1, d. 81, l. 10.
13. TsMAMLS f. 226, op. 1, d. 81, l. 10.
14. DeHaan, *Stalinist City Planning*, 89.
15. On Ivanitskii's approach to urban planning, on his work in Nizhnii Novgorod, and on his replacement by a new generation of Stalinist planners, see DeHaan, *Stalinist City Planning*.
16. TsMAMLS f. 226, op. 1, d. 81, l. 10.
17. In his book *The City and Daily Life* (*Gorod i byt*), published in 1968 and translated and published in German in 1971, Gradov argued that greater attention should be paid to public, communal buildings in the development of communist forms that would organize daily life.
18. TsMAMLS f. 226, op. 1, d. 67.
19. Davies and Ilic, "From Khrushchev (1935–1936) to Khrushchev (1956–1964): Construction Policy Compared," 211–225.
20. These passages from Khrushchev's 1935 speech are from Gradov's personal files. TsMAMLS f. 226, op. 1, d. 67, l. 12.
21. TsGA PD KR f. 4626, op. 1, d. 45, l. 40.
22. In 1941, one month before the war between Germany and the Soviet Union began, Gradov defended his dissertation at the Academy of Architecture. It was written on the topic of the "Central Ensemble of the City of Frunze and Questions about Architecture of the Kirgiz SSR." TsMAMLS f. 226, op. 1, d. 65.

23. TsMAMLS f. 226, op. 1, d. 233, l. 2.
24. TsMAMLS f. 205, op. 1, d. 162, l. 49.
25. TsMAMLS f. 226, op. 1, d. 244, ll. 1–6.
26. TsMAMLS f. 226, op. 1, d. 244, l. 3.
27. TsMAMLS f. 226, op. 1, d. 244, l. 3ob.
28. TsMAMLS f. 226, op. 1, d. 244, l. 3ob.
29. TsMAMLS f. 226, op. 1, d. 318, l. 3; TsMAMLS f. 226, op. 1, d. 74, l. 59.
30. TsMAMLS f. 226, op. 1, d. 318, l. 2.
31. See, for example, the lively commentary in the margins of Gradov's copy of Modvinov's article on high-speed mass construction printed in *Pravda* on May 17, 1953 in TsMAMLS f. 226, op. 1, d. 317, l. 46.
32. TsMAMLS f. 226, op. 1, d. 317, l. 47–54.
33. TsMAMLS f. 226, op. 1, d. 317, l. 49.
34. Gradov's letter and report sent to Khrushchev on February 12, 1954 is in TsMAMLS f. 226, op. 1, d. 319, l. 1–120 and in RGANI f. 5, op. 41, d. 6, ll. 47–166.
35. TsMAMLS f. 226, op. 1, d. 319, l. 2.
36. TsMAMLS f. 226, op. 1, d. 319, l. 2.
37. TsMAMLS f. 226, op. 1, d. 319, l. 2. This is a reference to Aleksei Arakcheev, a violent and tyrannical minister in the late eighteenth and early nineteenth centuries under Paul I and Alexander I. In 1950, Stalin referred to the need to crush the "Arakcheev regime" in Soviet linguistics. The phrase was subsequently taken up in other branches of the sciences. See Pollock, *Stalin and the Soviet Science Wars*, 127–128, 153. Konstantin Ivanov used the phrase in his assessment of the Soviet architectural profession as early as 1951 (TsMAMLS f. 226, op. 1, d. 317, l. 37) and both Gradov and Ivanov spoke of "Arakcheevism" in the profession in their 1952 letter to Yuri Zhdanov (TsMAMLS f. 226, op. 1, d. 318, l. 3).
38. TsMAMLS f. 226, op. 1, d. 319, ll. 89–90.
39. RGAE f. 339, op. 1, d. 1033, l. 243.
40. See, for example, Khrushchev's interjections in the transcript of Mordvinov's speech, given on December 1, 1954, in RGAE f. 339, op. 1, d. 1041.
41. TsMAMLS f. 226, op. 1, d. 97, ll. 55–56.
42. TsMAMLS f. 226, op. 1, d. 97, ll. 55–56.
43. TsMAMLS f. 226, op. 1, d. 97, ll. 55–56. A second transcript of the session (without Khrushchev's interjections) is in RGAE f. 339, op. 1, d. 1104, ll. 135–135ob. See also Dmitrii Khmel'nitskii's discussion of this exchange in *Arkhitektura Stalina,* 322–324.
44. TsMAMLS f. 226, op. 1, d. 97, l. 57.
45. TsMAMLS f. 226, op. 1, d. 97, l. 57.
46. TsMAMLS f. 226, op. 1, d. 97, l. 57–58.
47. TsMAMLS f. 226, op. 1, d. 97, l. 58.
48. RGAE f. 339, op. 1, d. 1104, l. 135ob. See also Davies, "The Builders' Conference," 452.
49. The transcript of Khrushchev's speech was published in *Pravda* and other outlets. The English translation here is taken from Nikita Khrushchev, "On Wide-Scale Introduction of Industrial Methods," 170.
50. Khrushchev, "On Wide-Scale Introduction," 167.
51. Khrushchev, "On Wide-Scale Introduction," 167–168.
52. Khrushchev, "On Wide-Scale Introduction," 169.
53. Khrushchev, "On Wide-Scale Introduction," 173.
54. Khrushchev, "On Wide-Scale Introduction," 172.
55. Khrushchev, "On Wide-Scale Introduction," 168.
56. Khrushchev, "On Wide-Scale Introduction," 172.
57. Bocharnikova, "Inventing Socialist Modern: A History of the Architectural Profession in the USSR, 1954–1971," 66.
58. Dygai was the Minister of Construction of Army and Navy Industries from 1947–1949. Iudin was Minister of Construction of Heavy Industry from 1946–1950. David Raizer was Deputy Minister, under Iudin, of the Ministry of Construction of Heavy Industry until 1950, when he took over as Minister.
59. RGAE f. 339, op. 1, d. 1039, l. 32.
60. RGAE f. 339, op. 1, d. 1039, l. 32.
61. RGAE f. 339, op. 1, d. 1039, l. 33.
62. Harris, *Communism on Tomorrow Street*, 5.

63. "Ob ustranenii izlishestv v proektirovanii i stroitel'stve," *Postanovleniia TsK KPSS i Soveta Ministrov SSSR po voprosam stroitel'stva ot 23, 24 avgusta i 4 noiabria 1955 g.,* (Moscow: Gosudarstvennoe izdatel'stvo politicheskoi literatury, 1956), 163–173.

64. On Gradov's involvement, see TsMAMLS f. 226, op. 1, d. 320.

65. See Bittner, "Remembering the Avant-Garde." By contrast, Daria Bocharnikova argues against the tendency of viewing the Stalin era as a moment that saw the defeat of modernism, but rather "as a period of coexisting projects for Socialist Modern." The Khrushchev era, she writes, "should also not simply be described as a return to modernism. For the legitimate question here is, a return to what *modernism*, or rather to what project or reading of Socialist Modern?" Bocharnikova, "Inventing Socialist Modern: A History of the Architectural Profession in the USSR, 1954–1971," 64.

66. Bittner, *The Many Lives of Khrushchev's Thaw*, 136.

67. Aleksandr Vlasov, "The Style of Our Architecture," *Izvestiia*, November 25, 1959, 2. This translation is taken from the copy published in *The Current Digest of the Soviet Press* XI, no. 47 (December 23, 1959): 8–10.

68. Vlasov, "The Style of Our Architecture," 2.

69. See, for example, Vlasov's participation in 1947 in the evaluation of Iofan's proposed design for the skyscraper on the Lenin Hills in GARF f. R-5446, op. 113, d. 66, l. 30.

70. Clifton Daniels, "Moscow to Scrap 46-story Building," *New York Times*, March 10, 1955, 5.

71. Clifton Daniels, "Soviet Reforming Building Method," *New York Times*, September 8, 1955, 4.

72. "Soviet Dismisses Top Architects: Vlasov, One of Those Named in Decree, Visiting U.S. in Housing Delegation," *New York Times*, November 10, 1955, 3.

73. "Who is guilty of holding back the designing [of reinforced concrete parts]?" Khrushchev had said, "Many architects are to blame and particularly Comrade Vlasov, Chief Architect of the city of Moscow. He is a good architect, but sometimes he lacks the necessary persistence." Khrushchev, "On Wide-Scale Introduction," 170.

74. "Exiles in Paris Try to Seize Soviet Aide," *New York Times*, November 16, 1955, 3.

75. Cooke (with Reid), "Modernity and Realism," 172.

76. "Speech by Comrade Khrushchev at the 6th PUWP CC Plenum, Warsaw," March 20, 1956, History and Public Policy Program Digital Archive, AAN, (Archive of Modern Records) PZPR 2631 Materialy do stosunkow partjynych polsko-radzieckich z lat 1956–1958, "Przemowienie tow. Chruszczowa na VI Plenum K.C." k. 14–87. Translated from Russian and Polish by L. W. Gluchowski. http://digitalarchive.wilsoncenter.org/document/111920.

77. "Speech by Comrade Khrushchev at the 6th PUWP CC Plenum, Warsaw," March 20, 1956.

78. On monumental construction in Eastern Europe during the period of Stalinization, see Åman, *Architecture and Ideology in Eastern Europe during the Stalin Era*, 120–146.

79. When traveling to the Soviet Union in the late 1940s and 1950s, architects from communist Eastern Europe were invariably taken on tours of Moscow's skyscraper construction sites. On East German architects' reactions to these tours, see Castillo, "Constructing the Cold War," 207. In 1955, visiting architects from West Germany were also taken on a tour of MGU. See RGANI f. 5, op. 41, d. 28, l. 116.

80. "Agreement between the government of the Union of Soviet Socialist Republics and the Government of the Polish Republic on the construction of the tall building the Palace of Culture and Science in Warsaw," April 5, 1952, *Dokumenty i materialy po istorii sovetsko-pol'skikh otnoshenii, tom x,* 178–180. On the history of this agreement, see Murawski, *The Palace Complex*, 57–63.

81. *Dokumenty i materialy po istorii sovetsko-pol'skikh otnoshenii, tom x,* 180.

82. The USSR Council of Ministers decree on the PKiN was issued October 29, 1951. See RGAE f. 339, op. 4, d. 2104, l. 4.

83. Ass et al, *Arkhitektor Rudnev*, 92. On the use of vernacular design in socialist realist architecture in Eastern Europe, see Castillo, "Soviet Orientalism: Socialist Realism and Built Tradition."

84. Crowley, *Warsaw*, 37–47.

85. *Dokumenty i materialy po istorii sovetsko-pol'skikh otnoshenii, tom x,* 443.

86. *Dokumenty i materialy po istorii sovetsko-pol'skikh otnoshenii, tom x,* 180.

87. Murawski, *The Palace Complex,* 9.

88. Schlögel, *Moscow,* 30.

89. On the Youth Festival of 1957, and dancing on the Lenin Hills, see Gilburd, "The Revival of Soviet Internationalism," 388. On the Youth Festival and its impact on Soviet art and socialist

realism, see Reid, "Toward a New (Socialist) Realism: The Re-engagement with Western Modernism in the Khrushchev Thaw."

90. The congress proceedings are printed in *V Kongress Mezhdunarodnogo soiuza arkhitektorov*, published in 1959.

91. RGALI f. 674, op. 8, d. 399, ed. khr. 52.

92. Khrushchev, *Khrushchev Remembers*, 99.

93. RGANI f. 3, op. 31, d. 39, ll. 1–3.

94. RGANI f. 3, op. 31, d. 39, l. 2.

95. RGANI f. 3, op. 31, d. 39, l. 2.

96. RGANI f. 3, op. 31, d. 39, l. 8.

97. The Presidium issued this "top secret" decree, titled "On the construction of a monument to V. I. Lenin—the Palace of Soviets," on November 5, 1955. This short decree called on Iofan, Iasnov, Vlasov, and others to organize a discussion to initiate this project. See *Prezidium TsK KPSS, 1954–1964, Volume 2, Postanovleniia 1954–1958*, 101.

98. Also on the Presidium's agenda that day was the question of how to celebrate Stalin's birthday that year. Protocol No. 167, Proceedings from November 5, 1955 session, *Prezidium TsK KPSS, 1954–1964, Volume 1, Chernovye protokol'nye zapisi zasedanii, Stenogrammy*, 57.

99. Vladimir Paperny discusses the transition in the early Stalin period from an aesthetic favoring evenness and horizontality to designs emphasizing hierarchy and verticality in *Kul'tura Dva*, 72–142. The Khrushchev era saw a shift back toward horizontality in designs like the new Palace of Soviets submissions and also in the new neighborhoods emerging in this period as part of the mass housing campaign.

100. Cermak and Tamaro, "Foundations of High-Rise Structures in Moscow and New York City," 362.

EPILOGUE

1. "O Komplekse," *Triumph Palace* website, http://triumfpalas.ru/o-komplekse. Accessed September 10, 2017.

2. "O Komplekse," *Triumph Palace* website, http://triumfpalas.ru/o-komplekse. Accessed September 10, 2017.

3. The lead architect of the Triumph Palace, Andrei Trofimov, lamented that the design was not more modern, stating that "the idea of building the 'eighth *vysotka*' came from the client." Agronskii, *Arkhitektura Rossii*, 289.

4. Sklair, *The Icon Project*, 5.

5. Groys, *Art Power*, 167.

Bibliography

ARCHIVES IN THE FORMER SOVIET UNION

Citations of Russian archival materials are by *fond* (collection), *opis'* (inventory), *delo* (file), *list* (page) or *edinitsa khraneniia* (item). These are abbreviated as f., op., d., l./ed. khr..

Arkhiv mezhdunarodnogo obshchestva "Memorial"
(Memorial Society Archive, Moscow)
> f. 2: Memoirs of Political Repression in the USSR
> Uncatalogued materials in three folders pertaining to construction of MGU

Gosudarstvennyi arkhiv Rossiiskoi Federatsii (GARF)
(State Archive of the Russian Federation)
> f. A-150: State Architecture Committee of the RSFSR
> f. R-3316: Central Executive Committee of the USSR
> f. R-5283: All-Union Society for Cultural Ties Abroad, or VOKS
> f. R-5446: Council of Ministers, USSR
> f. R-9414: Main Administration of Places of Confinement of the MVD, USSR

Gosudarstvennyi muzei arkhitektury im. A.V. Shchuseva (GNIMA)
(A. V. Shchusev State Museum of Architecture)

Gosudarstvennyi muzei istorii GULAGa, g. Moskva (GMIG)
(State Museum of the History of the Gulag, Moscow)

Rossiiskii gosudarstvennyi arkhiv ekonomiki (RGAE)
(Russian State Archive of the Economy)
> f. 293: Akademiia arkhitektury SSSR (Academy of Architecture of the USSR)
> f. 339: Gosudarstvennyi komitet Soveta Ministrov SSSR po delam stroitel'stva (USSR State Construction Committee, or Gosstroi USSR)
> f. 9432: Komitet po delam arkhitektury pri Sovete Ministrov SSSR (State Architecture Committee of the USSR)
> f. 9510: Ministerstvo gorodskogo stroitel'stva SSSR (Ministry of Urban Construction of the USSR)

Rossiiskii gosudarstvennyi arkhiv literatury i iskusstva (RGALI)
(Russian State Archive of Literature and Art)
> f. 674: Soiuz arkhitektorov SSSR (Union of Architects of the USSR)
> f. 680: Uchilishche zhivopisi, vaianiia i zodchestva (School of Painting, Sculpture and Architecture)
> f. 2466: Moskovskoe otdelenie Soiuza arkhitektorov SSSR (Moscow branch of the Union of Architects of the USSR, MOSA)

Rossiiskii gosudarstvennyi arkhiv sotsial'no-politicheskoi istorii (RGASPI)
(Russian State Archive of Social-Political History)
> f. 82: Records of V.M. Molotov
> f. 558: Records of I.V. Stalin

Rossiiskii gosudarstvennyi arkhiv noveishei istorii (RGANI)
(Russian State Archive of Contemporary History)
> f. 3: Politbiuro TsK KPSS (1952–1990)
> f. 5: Apparat TsK KPSS (1935–1991)

Glavnoe arkhivnoe upravlenie goroda Moskvy
(Main Archival Administration of the City of Moscow)
> *Otdel khraneniia dokumentov posle 1917 goda / Fondy byvshego Tsentral'nogo arkhiva goroda Moskvy* (TsGA Moskvy)
> (Division for the Preservation of Records since 1917 / Holdings from the former Central Archive of the City of Moscow)

f. R-496: Upravlenie vysotnykh domov i gostinits Mosgorispolkoma (Administration of Tall Buildings and Hotels of the Moscow Executive Committee)

f. R-534: Glavnoe arkhitekturno-planirovochnoe upravlenie g. Moskvy Mosgorispolkoma (Main Architectural-Planning Office of the City of Moscow of the Moscow Executive Committee)

f. R-694: Upravlenie stroitel'stva dvortsa sovetov (Administration for the Construction of the Palace of Soviets, or USDS)

Otdel khraneniia dokumentov obshchestvenno-politicheskoi istorii Moskvy / Fondy byvshego Tsentral'nogo arkhiva obshchestvenno-politicheskoi istorii Moskvy (TsAOPIM)

(Division for the Presentation of Records of Social-Political History of Moscow / Holdings from the former Central Archive of Social-Political History of Moscow)

f. P-3: Moskovskii komitet VKP(b) (Moscow Committee of the Communist Party)

f. P-4: Moskovskii gorodskoi komitet VKP(b) (Moscow City Committee of the Communist Party)

f. P-66: Zheleznodorozhnyi raionnyi komitet VKP(b) (Communist Party Committee of Moscow's Railroad District)

f. P-77: Kievskii raionnyi komitet VKP(b) (Communist Party Committee of Moscow's Kiev District)

f. P-88: Frunzenskii raionnyi komitet VKP(b) (Communist Party Committee of Moscow's Frunze District)

f. P-1419: Pervichnaia partorganizatsii stroitel'stva dvortsa sovetov Frunzenskogo raiona (First Party Organization of the Construction of the Palace of Soviets in Moscow's Frunze District)

Otdel khraneniia dokumentov lichnykh sobranii Moskvy / Fondy byvshego Tsental'nogo moskovskogo arkhiva-muzeia lichnykh sobranii (TsMAMLS)

(Division for Preservation of Records of Personal Collection of Moscow / Holdings from the former Central Moscow Archive-Museum of Personal Collections)

f. 205: Personal Files of Aleksandr Vasil'evich Vlasov

f. 226: Personal Files of Georgii Aleksandrovich Gradov

Tsentral'nyi gosudarstvennyi arkhiv obshchestvenno-politicheskoi dokumentatsii Kyrgyzskoi Respubliki (TsGA PD KR)

(Central State Archive of Social-Political Documentation of the Kyrgyz Republic)

f. 4626: Union of Architects

ARCHIVES OUTSIDE THE FORMER SOVIET UNION

Avery Drawings & Archives Collection, Columbia University
Simon Breines Professional Papers
Wallace K. Harrison Professional Papers
Hoover Institution Library and Archives, Stanford University
National Archives and Records Administration
Records of Mueser Rutledge Consulting Engineers, New York City
Palace of Soviets Project Files
Tamiment Library & Robert F. Wagner Labor Archives, New York University
National Council of American-Soviet Friendship Records

SOVIET NEWSPAPERS AND MAGAZINES

Akademiia arkhitektury
Architectural Chronicle (an English-language publication put out by VOKS)
Arkhitektura i stroitel'stvo
Arkhitektura i stroitel'stvo Moskvy
Arkhitektura SSSR
Gorodskoe khoziaistvo moskvy
Izvestiia
Krokodil
Literaturnaia gazeta
Ogonek
Pravda

Sovetskoe iskusstvo
Sovetskaia kul'tura
SSSR na stroike
Stroitel'naia gazeta
Stroitel'stvo voennogo vremeni
Voprosy istorii
Za proletarskoe iskusstvo

NON-SOVIET NEWSPAPERS AND MAGAZINES

The Architectural Forum
The Living Age
The Manchester Guardian
Mechanix Illustrated
New York Herald Tribune
The New York Times
Princeton Alumni Weekly
The Washington Post

OTHER PRIMARY DOCUMENTS

10 let Akademii arkhitektury SSSR (1934–1944): materialy k VI sessii Akademii arkhitektury SSSR. Moscow: Academy of Architecture of the USSR, 1944.

V Kongress Mezhdunarodnogo soiuza arkhitektorov. Moscow: Gosudarstvennoe izdatel'stvo literatury po stroitel'stvu, arkhitekture i stroitel'nym materialam, 1959.

Bol'shaia sovetskaia entsiklopediia.

Dokumenty i materialy po istorii sovetsko-pol'skikh otnoshenii. Vol. 10. Moscow: Nauka, 1980.

Dvorets nauki: rasskazy stroitelei novogo zdaniia Moskovskogo gosudarstvennogo universiteta. Moscow: Profizdat, 1952.

Dvorets sovetov, materialy konkursa 1957–1959. Moscow: Gosudarstvennoe izdatel'stvo literatury po stroitel'stvu, arkhitekture i stroitel'noi tekhnike, 1961.

Iz istorii sovetskoi arkhitektury 1941–1945, Dokumenty i materialy. Moscow: Nauka, 1978.

Materialy XII plenuma SSA SSSR. Moscow: Izdatel'stvo akademii arkhitektury SSSR, 1948.

Moskva. Edited by L. Kovalev. Moscow: Rabochaia Moskva, 1935.

"Notes on Construction of Empire State Building." In *Building the Empire State*, edited by Carol Willis, 47–184. New York: W. W. Norton & Company, 1998.

O general'nom plane rekonstruktsii gor. Moskvy. Moscow: Partizdat TsK VKP(b), 1935.

"Ob ustranenii izlishestv v proektirovanii i stroitel'stve." In *Postanovleniia TsK KPSS i Soveta Ministrov SSSR po voprosam stroitel'stva ot 23, 24 avgusta i 4 noiabria 1955 g.,* 163–173. Moscow: Gosudarstvennoe izdatel'stvo politicheskoi literatury, 1956.

Oktiabr'skaia 3ia vystavka planirovki i arkhitektury na ul. Gor'kogo. Moscow: Izdanie Mossoveta, 1934.

Otdelochnye materialy dlia dvortsa sovetov. Moscow: Izdatel'stvo akademii arkhitektury SSSR, 1945.

Otvety na voprosy rabochikh i kolkhoznikov. Moscow: Moskovskii rabochii, 1938.

Raboty arkhitekturno-proektirovochnykh masterskikh za 1934 god. Tom 1. Moscow: Otdel proektirovaniia Mosgorispolkoma i Mossoveta, 1936.

"Speech by Comrade Khrushchev at the 6th PUWP CC Plenum, Warsaw." March 20, 1956. History and Public Policy Program Digital Archive, AAN, (Archive of Modern Records) PZPR 2631 Materialy do stosunkow partyjnych polsko-radzieckich z lat 1956–1958. "Przemowienie tow. Chruszczowa na VI Plenum K.C." k. 14–87. Translated from Russian and Polish by L.W. Gluchowski. http://digitalarchive.wilsoncenter.org/document/111920

Vysotnye zdaniia v Moskve: proekty. Moscow: Gosudarstvennoe izdatel'stvo po stroitel'stvu i arkhitekture, 1951.

Zadachi arkhitektorov v dni velikoi otechestvennoi voiny, materialy X plenuma Soiuza sovetskikh arkhitektorov SSSR 22–25 aprelia 1942 g. Moscow: Gosudarstvennoe arkhitekturnoe izdatel'stvo akademii arkhitektury SSSR, 1942.

"Zamechaniia Tovarishcha Stalina I.V. pri obsuzhdenii voprosa o general'nom plane rekonstruktsii Moskvy na zasedanii Politbiuro TsK VKP(b) 17 iiunia 1949 goda." *Istochnik.* Vol. 4 (2001): 110–112.

Atarov, Nikolai. *Dvorets sovetov.* Moscow: Moskovskii rabochii, 1940.

Bogdanov, G. P. and A. P. Bogdanov. *Dolg pamiati: povest' ob ottse.* Moscow: Izdatel'stvo politicheskoi literatury, 1990.

Bunin, Andrei, Lev Il'in, Nikolai Poliakov, and Viacheslav Shkvarikov. *Gradostroitel'stvo.* Moscow:
Academy of Architecture Press, 1945.

Currie, Leonard J. *Russian Architecture through Western Eyes.* Blacksburg, Virginia, 1959.

Gradov, Georgii. *Gorod i byt: Perspektivy razvitiia sistemy i tipov obshchestvennykh zdanii.* Moscow:
Izdatel'stvo literatury po stroitel'stvu, 1968.

Kaganovich, Lazar. *Socialist Reconstruction of Moscow and Other Cities in the USSR.* New York: International Publishers, 1931.

Khrushchev, Nikita. "On Wide-Scale Introduction of Industrial Methods, Improving the Quality
and Reducing the Cost of Construction." In *Khrushchev Speaks: Selected Speeches, Articles, and
Press Conferences, 1949–1961,* edited by Thomas P. Whitney, 153–192. Ann Arbor: University of
Michigan Press, 1963.

Mumford, Lewis. *Ot brevenchatogo doma do neboskreba: ocherk istorii Amerikanskoi arkhitektury.*
Moscow: USSR Academy of Architecture Press, 1936.

Mumford, Lewis. *Sticks and Stones: A Study of American Architecture and Civilization.* New York:
Boni and Liveright Publishers, 1924.

Oltar-Jevsky, W. K. *Contemporary Babylon in pencil drawings.* New York: Architectural Book Pub.
Co., 1933.

Oltarzhevskii, V. K. *Stroitel'stvo vysotnykh zdanii v Moskve.* Moscow: Gosudarstvennoe izdatel'stvo
literatury po stroitel'stvu i arkhitekture, 1953.

Prokofiev, Andrei. *The Palace of Soviets.* Moscow: Foreign Languages Publishing House, 1939.

Shchuko, Vladimir and M. V. Babenchikov. *Risunki i akvareli.* Moscow: Izdatel'stvo akademii arkhitektury SSSR, 1940.

Shchusev, Aleksei. *Proekt vosstanovleniia goroda Istry.* Moscow: Izdatel'stvo akademii arkhitektury,
1946.

Shkvarikov, Viacheslav. *Sovetskaia arkhitektura za XXX let RSFSR.* Moscow: Izdatel'stvo akademii
arkhitektury SSSR, 1950.

Sytin, P. V. *Iz istorii Moskovskikh ulits.* Moscow: Moskovskii rabochii, 1948, 1951, 1958.

Trapeznikov, K. *Problema ansamblia v sovetskoi arkhitekture.* Moscow: Gosudarstvennoe izdatel'stvo
literatury po stroitel'stvu i arkhitekture, 1952.

Tsapenko, M. P. *O realisticheskikh osnovakh sovetskoi arkhitektury.* Moscow: Gosudarstvennoe
izdatel'stvo literatury po stroitel'stvu i arkhitekture, 1952.

Vlasov, Aleksandr. *Moscow's Multi-storey Buildings.* Moscow: Foreign Languages Publishing House,
1954.

DIARIES, MEMOIRS, AND OTHER FIRST-HAND ACCOUNTS

Faina Ranevskaia: Sluchai, shutki, aforizmy. Moscow: Zakharov, 1998.

Ilf and Petrov's American Road Trip: The 1935 Travelogue of Two Soviet Writers. Edited by Erika Wolf.
New York: Princeton Architectural Press and Cabinet Books, 2007.

'Partiinyi gubernator' Moskvy: Georgii Popov. Edited by E. V. Taranov. Moscow: Izd. Glavarkhiva
Moskvy, 2004.

Benjamin, Walter. *Moscow Diary.* Edited by Gary Smith, translated by Richard Sieburth. Cambridge:
Harvard University Press, 1986 (1926).

Brontman, Lazar' Konstantinovich. *Dnevnik,* Available on Prozhito: http://prozhito.org/persons/18

Chechulin, Dmitrii. *Zhizn' i zodchestvo.* Moscow: Molodaia gvardiia, 1978.

Le Corbusier. "The Atmosphere of Moscow." Translated by Edith Schreiber Aujame. In *Precisions
on the Present State of Architecture and City Planning.* Cambridge: MIT Press, 1991.

Ehrenburg, Ilya and Konstantin Simonov. *In One Newspaper: A Chronicle of Unforgettable Years.* New
York: Sphinx Press, 1985.

Eigel', Isaak. *Boris Iofan.* Moscow: Stroiizdat, 1978.

Gorky, Maxim. *The City of the Yellow Devil.* Moscow: Progress Publishers, 1972.

Herzen, Alexander. *My Past and Thoughts: The Memoirs of Alexander Herzen,* translated by Dwight
Macdonald. Berkeley: University of California Press, 1973.

Khrushchev, Nikita. *Khrushchev Remembers.* Boston: Little, Brown and Company, 1970.

——— *Khrushchev Remembers: The Last Testament.* Boston: Little, Brown, and Company, 1974.

Komarovskii, Aleksandr. *Zapiski stroitelia.* Moscow: Voenizdat, 1972.

Leonov, Leonid. *The Badgers.* London: Hutchinson International, 1947.

———— "Padenie Zariad'ia." In *Slovo o Moskve*. Moscow: Gos. izd. khudozhestvennoi literatury, 1947.

Lorinston, K. Diary from Moscow, 1941, published on http://iremember.ru/grazhdanskie/k-loriston.html

Posokhin, Mikhail V. *Dorogi zhizni iz zapisok arkhitektora*. Moscow: Stroiizdat, 1995.

Rabinovich, Mikhail G. *Zapiski sovetskogo intellektuala*. Edited by L. A. Beliaev, O. V. Budnitskii, V. Ia. Petrukhin. Moscow: Novoe literaturnoe obozrenie/Mezhdunarodnaia issledovatel'skii tsentr rossiiskogo i vostochnoevropeiskogo evreistva, 2005.

Riis, Jacob A. *How the Other Half Lives: Studies Among the Tenements of New York*. New York: Penguin Books, 1997 (1890).

Shaginian, Marietta. *Dnevnik pisatelia 1950–1952*. Moscow: Sovetskii pisatel', 1953.

Sidorov, Aleksei Alekseevich. *Revoliutsiia i Iskusstvo*. Moscow: Tipo-litografiia I.I. Bykova, 1918.

Sidorow, Alexys A. *Moskau*. Berlin: Albertus-Verlag, 1928.

Steinbeck, John. *A Russian Journal*. New York: The Viking Press, 1948.

Timasheff, Nicholas. *The Great Retreat*. New York: E. P. Dutton & Company, Inc., 1946.

Timofeev, Leonid I. "Memuary, arkhivy, svidetel'stva. Dnevnik voennykh let." *Znamia*, no. 6 (2002): 139–185. This diary is also available in full on Prozhito: http://prozhito.org/persons/69

Tolstoi, V. P. "O P.D. Korine." In *P.D. Korin ob iskusstve: stat'i, pis'ma, vospominaniia o khudozhnike*. Moscow: Sovetskii khudozhnik, 1988.

Ustinov, Aleksandr. *Voina v ob'ektive: Velikaia Otechestvennaia voina v reportazhakh, vospominaniiakh i razmyshleniiakh voennogo fotokorrespondenta gazety "Pravda" Aleksandra Ustinova*. Moscow: Atlantida-XXI vek, 2005.

Vavilov, Sergei I. *Sergei Vavilov: Dnevniki 1909–1951*. Moscow: Nauka, 2012.

Werth, Alexander. *Moscow '41*. London: Hamish Hamilton, 1942.

PUBLISHED DOCUMENT COLLECTIONS

Lavrentii Beriia. 1953: Stenogramma iiul'skogo plenuma TsK KPSS i drugie dokumenty. Edited by V. Naumov and Iu. Sigachev. Moscow: Mezhdunarodnyi fond "demokratiia", 1999.

Lubianka v dni bitvy za Moskvu. Edited by V. S. Khristoforov, V. K. Vinogradov, et al. Moscow: Zvonnitsa, 2002.

Moskovskii Kreml' v gody Velikoi Otechestvennoi voiny. Edited by E. A. Murov. Moscow: Kuchkovo pole, 2010.

Moskovskaia vlast': istoricheskie portrety 1708–2012. Moscow: Izd. glavnogo arkhivnogo upravleniia goroda Moskvy, 2013.

Moskva poslevoennaia, 1945–1947. Moscow: Mosgorarkhiv, 2000.

Moskva prifrontovaia 1941–1942, arkhivnye dokumenty i materialy. Moscow: Mosgorarkhiv, 2001.

O velikoi otechestvennoi voine sovetskogo soiuza. Moscow: Gosudarstvennoe izdatel'stvo politicheskoi literatury, 1947.

Politbiuro TsK VKP(b) i Sovet Ministrov SSSR, 1945–1953. Edited by Oleg Khlevniuk, Yoram Gorlitzki, et al. Moscow: ROSSPEN, 2002.

Prezidium TsK KPSS, 1954–1964. Edited by A. A. Fursenko. Three volumes. Moscow: ROSSPEN, 2006.

Sistema ispravitel'no-trudovykh lagerei v SSSR, 1923–1960, Spravochnik. Edited by M. B. Smirnov. Moscow: Zven'ia, 1998.

The Stalin-Kaganovich Correspondence, 1931–36. Edited by R. W. Davies, O. V. Khlevniuk, et al. New Haven: Yale University Press, 2003.

SECONDARY SOURCES

Addis, Bill. *Building: 3000 Years of Design Engineering and Construction*. London: Phaidon, 2007.

Adkins, Helen, et al. *Naum Gabo and the Competition for the Palace of Soviets, Moscow, 1931–1933*. Berlin: Berlinische Galerie, 1993.

Agronskii, Valerii. *Arkhitektura Rossii*. Moscow: Izdatel'stvo E, 2017.

Alexopoulos, Golfo. "Amnesty 1945: The Revolving Door of Stalin's Gulag." *Slavic Review* 64, 2 (2005): 274–306.

Åman, Anders. *Architecture and Ideology in Eastern Europe during the Stalin Era: An Aspect of Cold War History*. Cambridge: The MIT Press, 1992.

Anderson, Richard. "The Future of History: Cultural Politics of Soviet Architecture, 1928–41." PhD dissertation, Columbia University, 2010.

——— *Russia: Modern Architectures in History*. London: Reaktion Books, 2015.

——— "USA/USSR: Architecture and War." *Grey Room,* no. 34 (Winter 2009): 80–103.

Andrusz, Gregory D. *Housing and Urban Development in the USSR*. Albany: State University of New York Press, 1984.

Ass, V. I. et al. *Arkhitektor Rudnev*. Moscow: Gos. izd. literatury po stroitel'stvu, arkhitekture i stroitel'nym materialam, 1963.

Attwood, Lynne. *Gender and Housing in Soviet Russia: Private Life in a Public Space*. Manchester: Manchester University Press, 2010.

Bailes, Kendall. "The American Connection: Ideology and the Transfer of American Technology to the Soviet Union, 1917–1941." *Comparative Studies in Society and History* 23, no. 3 (1981): 421–448.

——— "Technology and Legitimacy: Soviet Aviation and Stalinism in the 1930s." *Technology and Culture* 17, no. 1 (1976): 55–81.

Barenberg, Alan. *Gulag Town, Company Town: Forced Labor and Its Legacy in Vorkuta*. New Haven: Yale University Press, 2014.

Barnes, Steven A. *Death and Redemption: The Gulag and the Shaping of Soviet Society*. Princeton: Princeton University Press, 2011.

Bater, James. *The Soviet City: Ideal and Reality*. Beverly Hills: Sage, 1980.

——— "Transience, Residential Persistence, and Mobility in Moscow and St. Petersburg, 1900–1914." *Slavic Review* 39, 2 (June 1980): 239–254.

Bell, Wilson. *Stalin's Gulag at War: Forced Labour, Mass Death, and Soviet Victory in the Second World War*. Toronto: University of Toronto Press, 2018.

——— "Was the Gulag an Archipelago? De-Convoyed Prisoners and Porous Borders in the Camps of Western Siberia." *Russian Review* 72, 1 (2013): 116–141.

Bittner, Stephen V. *The Many Lives of Khrushchev's Thaw: Experience and Memory in Moscow's Arbat*. Ithaca: Cornell University Press, 2008.

——— "Remembering the Avant-Garde: Moscow Architects and the 'Rehabilitation' of Constructivism, 1961–64." *Kritika* 2, no. 3 (2001): 553–576.

Bocharnikova, Daria. "Inventing Socialist Modern: A History of the Architectural Profession in the USSR, 1954–1971." PhD dissertation, European University Institute Florence, 2014.

Bodenschatz, Harald and Christiane Post. *Städtebau im Schatten Stalins: Die internationale Suche nach der sozialistischen Stadt in der Sowjetunion 1929–1935*. Berlin: Braun, 2003.

Bodenschatz, Harald and Thomas Flierl, Editors. *Von Adenauer zu Stalin: Der Einfluss des traditionally deutschen Städtebaus in der Sowjetunion um 1935*. Berlin: Theater der Zeit, 2016.

Bradley, Joseph. *Muzhik and Muscovite: Urbanization in Late-Imperial Russia*. Berkeley: University of California Press, 1985.

Brandenberger, David. *National Bolshevism: Stalinist Mass Culture and the Formation of Modern Russian National Identity, 1931–1956*. Cambridge: Harvard University Press, 2002.

Brooks, Jeffrey. *Thank You, Comrade Stalin!: Soviet Public Culture from Revolution to Cold War*. Princeton: Princeton University Press, 2000.

Brown, Kate. "Out of Solitary Confinement: The History of the Gulag." *Kritika* 8, 1 (2007): 67–103.

Bucher, Greta. "Struggling to Survive: Soviet Women in the Postwar Years." *Journal of Women's History* 12, no. 1 (Spring 2000) 137–159.

Buck-Morss, Susan. *Dreamworld and Catastrophe: The Passing of Mass Utopia in East and West*. Cambridge: MIT Press, 2000.

Bulgakowa, Oksana. "Spatial Figures in Soviet Cinema of the 1930s." In *The Landscape of Stalinism: The Art and Ideology of Soviet Space*. Edited by Evgeny Dobrenko and Eric Naiman, 51–76. Seattle: University of Washington Press, 2003.

Castillo, Greg. *Cold War on the Home Front: The Soft Power of Midcentury Design*. Minneapolis: University of Minnesota Press, 2009.

——— "Constructing the Cold War: Architecture, Urbanism and the Cultural Division of Germany, 1945–1957." PhD dissertation, University of California, Berkeley, 2000.

——— "East as True West: Redeeming Bourgeois Culture, from Socialist Realism to Ostalgie." *Kritika: Explorations in Russian and Eurasian History* 9, no. 4, (Fall 2008): 747–768.

——— "Gorky Street and the Design of the Stalin Revolution." In *Streets: Critical Perspectives on Public Space*, edited by Zenep Celik, Diane Favro, and Richard Ingersoll, 57–70. Berkeley: University of California Press, 1994.

——— "Soviet Orientalism: Socialist Realism and Built Tradition." *Traditional Dwellings and Settlements Review* 8, no. 2 (1997): 33–47.

Cermak, Jan and G. J. Tamaro. "Foundations of High-Rise Structures in Moscow and New York City." In *Geotechnical Challenges in Megacities: Proceedings of the International Geotechnical Conference.* Moscow (2010): 359–364.

Clark, Katerina. *Moscow, The Fourth Rome: Stalinism, Cosmopolitanism, and the Evolution of Soviet Culture, 1931–1941.* Cambridge: Harvard University Press, 2011.

———— "The 'New Moscow' and the New 'Happiness': Architecture as a Nodal Point in the Stalinist System of Value." *Petrified Utopia: Happiness Soviet Style,* edited by Marina Balina and Evgeny Dobrenko, 189–200. London: Anthem Press, 2009.

———— *The Soviet Novel: History as Ritual.* Bloomington: Indiana University Press, 1981.

Cohen, Jean-Louis. *Architecture in Uniform: Designing and Building for the Second World War.* Montreal: Canadian Centre for Architecture, 2011.

———— "American Objects of Soviet Desire." In *Forty Ways to Think About Architecture: Architectural History and Theory Today,* edited by Iain Borden et al, 127–133. Sussex: John Wiley and Sons, 2014.

———— *Building a new New World: Amerikanizm in Russian Architecture.* New Haven: Yale University Press, 2020.

———— *Le Corbusier and the Mystique of the USSR: Theories and Projects for Moscow, 1928–1936.* Princeton: Princeton University Press, 1992.

———— "L'Oncle Sam au Pays des Soviets: Le temps des avant-gardes." In *Americanisme et modernite: l'ideal americain dans l'architecture,* edited by Cohen and Hubert Damisch, 403–436. Paris: Flammarion, 1993.

———— *Scenes of the World to Come: European Architecture and the American Challenge, 1893–1960.* Paris/Montreal: Flammarion/Canadian Center for Architecture, 1995.

———— "Useful Hostage: Constructing Wright in Soviet Russia and France." In *Frank Lloyd Wright: Europe and Beyond,* edited by Anthony Alofsin, 100–120. Berkeley: University of California Press, 1999.

———— "When Stalin Meets Haussmann: The Moscow Plan of 1935." *Art and Power: Europe under the Dictators, 1930–45,* edited by Dawn Ades et al, 246–256. London: Thames and Hudson, 1996.

Colton, Timothy J. *Moscow: Governing the Socialist Metropolis.* Cambridge: Harvard University Press, 1995.

Conn, Steven. *Americans Against the City: Anti-Urbanism in the Twentieth Century.* Oxford: Oxford University Press, 2014.

Conze, Susanne. "Women's Work and Emancipation in the Soviet Union, 1941–50." In *Women in the Stalin Era,* edited by Melanie Ilic, 216–234. London: Palgrave Macmillan, 2001.

Cooke, Catherine. "Beauty as Route to 'the Radiant Future': Responses of Soviet Architecture." *Journal of Design History* 10, no. 2, (1997): 137–160.

———— "The Garden City Idea: The Russians." *Architectural Review* 163, no. 976 (June 1978): 353–363.

Cooke, Catherine (with Susan E. Reid). "Modernity and Realism." In *Russian Art and the West: A Century of Dialogue in Painting, Architecture, and the Decorative Arts,* edited by Rosalind P. Blakesley and Susan E. Reid, 172–194. DeKalb: Northern Illinois University Press, 2007.

Crawford, Christina. "From Tractors to Territory: Socialist Urbanization through Standardization." *Journal of Urban History* 44, no. 1, (2018): 54–77.

———— "The Socialist Settlement Experiment: Soviet Urban Praxis, 1917–1932." PhD dissertation, Harvard University, 2016.

Cross, Wilbur. *75 Years of Foundation Engineering: Mueser Rutledge Consulting Engineers, A History of the Firm.* New York: Benjamin Co Inc., 1985.

Crowley, David. *Warsaw.* London: Reaktion Books, 2003.

Cunliffe, Antonia. "The Competition for the Palace of the Soviets, 1931–33." *Architectural Association Quarterly* 11, no. 2 (1979): 36–48.

Dale, Robert. *Demobilized Veterans in Late Stalinist Leningrad: Soldiers to Civilians.* London: Bloomsbury Academic, 2015.

———— "Divided We Stand: Cities, Social Unity and Post-War Reconstruction in Soviet Russia, 1945–1953." *Contemporary European History* 24, no. 4 (2015): 493–516.

David-Fox, Michael. *Showcasing the Great Experiment: Cultural Diplomacy and Western Visitors to the Soviet Union, 1921–1941.* New York: Oxford University Press, 2012.

———— "Transnational History and the East-West Divide." In *Imagining the West in Eastern Europe and the Soviet Union,* edited by Gyorgy Peteri, 258–268. Pittsburgh: University of Pittsburgh Press, 2010.

Davies, R. W. "The Builders' Conference." in *Soviet Studies* 6, no. 4 (1955): 443–457.

Davies, R. W. and Melanie Ilic. "From Khrushchev (1935–1936) to Khrushchev (1956–1964): Construction Policy Compared." In *Khrushchev in the Kremlin: Policy and Government in the Soviet Union, 1953–1964*. Edited by Jeremy Smith and Melanie Ilic. London: Routledge, 2011. 202–231.

Davis, Donald E. and Eugene P. Trani. *Distorted Mirrors: Americans and Their Relations with Russia and China in the Twentieth Century*. Columbia: University of Missouri Press, 2009.

Day, Andrew Elam. "Building Socialism: The Politics of the Soviet Cityscape in the Stalin Era." PhD dissertation, Columbia University, 1998.

——— "The Rise and Fall of Stalinist Architecture." In *Architectures of Russian Identity: 1500 to the Present*, edited by James Cracraft and Daniel Rowland, 172–190. Ithaca, NY: Cornell University Press, 2003.

DeHaan, Heather. *Stalinist City Planning: Professionals, Performance, and Power*. Toronto: University of Toronto Press, 2013.

Dobrenko, Evgeny. *The Political Economy of Socialist Realism*. New Haven: Yale University Press, 2007.

Dobson, Miriam. *Khrushchev's Cold Summer: Gulag Returnees, Crime, and the Fate of Reform after Stalin*. Ithaca: Cornell University Press, 2009.

Dunham, Vera S. *In Stalin's Time: Middleclass Values in Soviet Fiction*. Durham: Duke University Press, 1990.

Duskin, J. Eric. *Stalinist Reconstruction and the Confirmation of a New Elite, 1945–1953*. New York: Palgrave, 2001.

Edele, Mark. "Soviet Veterans as an Entitlement Group, 1945–1955." *Slavic Review* 65, no. 1 (Spring 2006): 111–137.

Filtzer, Donald A. *The Hazards of Urban Life in Late Stalinist Russia: Health, Hygiene, and Living Standards, 1943–1953*. Cambridge: Cambridge University Press, 2010.

——— *Soviet Workers and Late Stalinism: Labour and the Restoration of the Stalinist System after World War II*. Cambridge: Cambridge University Press, 2002.

——— "Standard of Living Versus Quality of Life: Struggling with the Urban Environment in Russia during the Early Years of Post-war Reconstruction." In *Late Stalinist Russia: Society between Reconstruction and Reinvention*, edited by Juliane Fürst, 81–102. London: Routledge, 2006.

Fitzpatrick, Sheila. *The Cultural Front: Power and Culture in Revolutionary Russia*. Ithaca: Cornell University Press, 1992.

——— *Education and Social Mobility in the Soviet Union, 1921–1934*. Cambridge: Cambridge University Press, 1979.

——— *Everyday Stalinism. Ordinary Life in Extraordinary Times: Soviet Russia in the 1930s*. Oxford: Oxford University Press, 1999.

——— *On Stalin's Team: The Years of Living Dangerously in Soviet Politics*. Princeton and Oxford: Princeton University Press, 2015.

——— "Supplicants and Citizens: Public Letter Writing in Soviet Russia in the 1930s." *Slavic Review* 55, no. 1 (1996): 78–105.

Friedman, Jane. "Soviet Mastery of the Skies at the Mayakovsky Metro Station." *Studies in the Decorative Arts* 7, no. 2 (2000): 48–64.

Fürst, Juliane. "In Search of Soviet Salvation: Young People Write to the Stalinist Authorities." *Contemporary European History* 15, 3 (2006): 327–345.

——— "Late Stalinist Society: History, Policies, and People." In *Late Stalinist Russia: Society between Reconstruction and Reinvention*, edited by Fürst, 1–20. London: Routledge, 2006.

——— *Stalin's Last Generation: Soviet Post-War Youth and the Emergence of Mature Socialism*. Oxford: Oxford University Press, 2010.

Ganson, Nicholas. *The Soviet Famine of 1946–47 in Global and Historical Perspective*. New York: Palgrave Macmillan, 2009.

Getty, J. Arch. *Practicing Stalinism: Bolsheviks, Boyars, and the Persistence of Tradition*. New Haven: Yale University Press, 2013.

Gilburd, Eleonory. "The Revival of Soviet Internationalism." In *The Thaw: Soviet Society and Culture during the 1950s and 1960s*, edited by Denis Kozlov and Eleonory Gilburd, 362–401. Toronto: University of Toronto Press, 2013.

Goldman, Wendy Z. *Inventing the Enemy: Denunciation and Terror in Stalin's Russia*. New York: Cambridge University Press, 2011.

——— *Women at the Gates: Gender and Industry in Stalin's Russia*. Cambridge: Cambridge University Press, 2002.

Gorinov, Mikhail M. "Muscovites' Moods, 1941–42." In *The People's War: Responses to World War II in the Soviet Union*, edited by Robert W. Thurston and Bernd Bonwetsch, 108–137. Urbana and Chicago: University of Illinois Press, 2002.

Gorlizki, Yoram and Oleg Khlevniuk. *Cold Peace: Stalin and the Soviet Ruling Circle, 1945–1953*. Oxford: Oxford University Press, 2004.

Gregory, Paul. "An Introduction to the Economics of the Gulag." In *The Economics of Forced Labor: The Soviet Gulag*, edited by Paul R. Gregory and V. V. Lazarev, 1–21. Stanford: Hoover Institution Press, 2003.

Gronow, Jukka. *Caviar with Champagne: Common Luxury and the Ideals of the Good Life in Stalin's Russia*. Oxford: Berg, 2003.

————— *The Sociology of Taste*. London: Routledge, 2003.

Groys, Boris. *Art Power*. Cambridge: MIT Press, 2008.

————— *The Total Art of Stalinism: Avant-Garde, Aesthetic Dictatorship, and Beyond*. London: Verso, 2011.

Harris, Steven E. *Communism on Tomorrow Street: Mass Housing and Everyday Life after Stalin*. Washington, DC: Woodrow Wilson Center Press/Johns Hopkins University Press, 2013.

————— "Two Lessons in Modernism: What the Architectural Review and America's Mass Media Taught Soviet Architects about the West." In *Trondheim Studies on East European Cultures and Societies*, no. 31, (August 2010): 1–93.

Hazard, John. *Soviet Housing Law*. New Haven: Yale University Press, 1939.

Heinzen, James. *The Art of the Bribe: Corruption Under Stalin, 1943–1953*. New Haven: Yale University Press, 2016.

Hilton, Marjorie L. "Retailing the Revolution: The State Department Store (GUM) and Soviet Society in the 1920s," *Journal of Social History* 37, no. 4 (2004): 939–964.

Hoffmann, David L. "Moving to Moscow: Patterns of Peasant In-Migration during the First Five-Year Plan," *Slavic Review* 50, no. 4 (1991): 847–857.

————— *Peasant Metropolis: Social Identities in Moscow, 1929–1941*. Ithaca: Cornell University Press, 1994.

Hoisington, Sona. "'Ever Higher': The Evolution of the Project for the Palace of Soviets." *Slavic Review* 62, no. 1 (Spring 2003): 41–68.

————— "Soviet Schizophrenia and the American Skyscraper." In *Russian Art and the West: A Century of Dialogue in Painting, Architecture, and the Decorative Arts*, edited by Rosalind P. Blakesley and Susan E. Reid, 156–171. DeKalb: Northern Illinois University Press, 2007.

Hudson, Hugh D. *Blueprints and Blood: The Stalinization of Soviet Architecture, 1917–1937*. Princeton: Princeton University Press, 1994.

Ikonnikov, Andrei. *Arkhitektura Moskvy XX vek*. Moscow: Moskovskii rabochii, 1984.

————— *Russian Architecture of the Soviet Period*. Moscow: Raduga Publishers, 1988.

Jenks, Andrew. "A Metro on the Mount: The Underground as a Church of Soviet Civilization." *Technology and Culture* 41, no. 4 (2000): 697–724.

Jones, Jeffrey W. *Everyday Life and the "Reconstruction" of Soviet Russian During and After the Great Patriotic War, 1943–1948*. Bloomington: Slavica, 2008.

Kaganovsky, Lilya. *How the Soviet Man was Unmade: Cultural Fantasy and Male Subjectivity Under Stalin*. Pittsburgh: University of Pittsburgh Press, 2008.

Kazus', Igor A. "The Great Illusion: Architecture." *Art and Power: Europe under the Dictators, 1930–45*. Edited by Dawn Ades et al. London: Thames and Hudson, 1996. 189–194.

————— *Sovetskaia arkhitektura 1920x godov: organizatsiia, proektirovaniia*. Moscow: Progress-Traditsiia, 2009.

Kelly, Catriona. *Socialist Churches: Radical Secularization and the Preservation of the Past in Petrograd and Leningrad, 1918–1988*. DeKalb: Northern Illinois University Press, 2016.

Khan-Magomedov, Selim. *Pioneers of Soviet Architecture*. New York: Rizzoli, 1987.

Khlevniuk, Oleg. "The Economy of the OGPU, NKVD, and MVD of the USSR, 1930–1953." In *The Economics of Forced Labor: The Soviet Gulag*, edited by Paul R. Gregory and V. V. Lazarev, 43–66. Palo Alto: Hoover Institution Press, 2003.

————— "The Gulag and Non-Gulag as One Interrelated Whole." *Kritika* 16, 3 (Summer 2015): 479–498.

Khmel'nitskii, Dmitrii. *Arkhitektura Stalina: psikhologiia i stil'*. Moscow: Progress-Traditsiia, 2007.

————— *Zodchii Stalin*. Moscow: Novoe literaturnoe obozrenie, 2007.

Kingwell, Mark. *Nearest Thing to Heaven: The Empire State Building and American Dreams*. New Haven: Yale University Press, 2006.

Kirichenko, Evgeniia I. *Khram Khrista Spasitelia v Moskve: Istoriia proektirovaniia i sozdaniia sobora. Stranitsy zhizni i gibeli, 1813–1931*. Moscow: Planeta, 1992.

Knight, Amy. *Beria: Stalin's First Lieutenant*. Princeton: Princeton University Press, 1993.

Kolson, Kenneth. *Big Plans: The Allure and Folly of Urban Design*. Baltimore: The Johns Hopkins University Press, 2001.

Kokurin, Aleksandr I. and Iurii N. Morukov. "Gulag: Struktura i kadry." *Svobodnaia mysl'* no. 3 (2001): 111–128.

——— "Priniat' predlozhenie tovarishcha Stalina. *Istoricheskii arkhiv* 1 (2004): 28–32.

Kopp, Anatole. "Foreign Architects in the Soviet Union during the First Two Five-Year Plans." In *Architecture and the New Urban Environment: Western Influences on Modernism in Russia and the USSR: A Special Report*. Washington, D.C.: Woodrow Wilson International Center for Scholars, 1988.

Kostof, Spiro. *The City Shaped: Urban Patterns and Meanings Through History*. London: Little, Brown and Company, 1991.

——— "His Majesty the Pick: The Aesthetics of Demolition." *Design Quarterly*, no. 118/119 (1982): 32–41.

Kostyuk, Maria. *Boris Iofan: Architect behind the Palace of the Soviets*. Moscow: Dom Publishers, 2019.

Kotkin, Stephen. *Magnetic Mountain: Stalinism as a Civilization*. Berkeley: University of California Press, 1995.

Kozhin, N.A. and A.P. Lebedev. *Aleksei Alekseevich Sidorov*. Moscow: Izdatel'stvo Nauka, 1964.

Kozlov, Vladimir. "Denunciation and Its Functions in Soviet Governance: A Study of Denunciations and Their Bureaucratic Handling from Soviet Police Archives, 1944–1953." *The Journal of Modern History* 68, 4 (1996): 867–898.

Kruzhkov, Nikolai. *Vysotnye zdaniia stalinskoi Moskvy: fakty iz istorii proektirovaniia i stroitel'stva*. Moscow: Vodolei, 2011.

Kupriyanov, Pavel and Lyudmila Sadovnikova. "Historical Zaryadye as Remembered by Locals: Cultural Meanings of City Spaces." In *Russian Cultural Anthropology After the Collapse of Communism*, edited by Albert Baiburin, Catriona Kelly, and Nikolai Vakhtin, 220–253. London: Routledge, 2012.

Lebow, Katherine. *Unfinished Utopia: Nowa Huta, Stalinism, and Polish Society*. Ithaca: Cornell University Press, 2013.

Lefebvre, Henri. *The Production of Space*. Oxford: Blackwell, 1991.

Le Normand, Brigitte. *Designing Tito's Capital: Urban Planning, Modernism, and Socialism in Belgrade*. Pittsburgh: University of Pittsburgh Press, 2014.

Levy, Nicholas. "Citizens Under Skyscrapers: Building Moscow's Stalin-era *Vysotki* and the Transformation of Soviet Urban Space." MA Thesis, University of Chicago, 2012.

Linsley, Robert. "Utopia Will Not Be Televised: Rivera at Rockefeller Center." *Oxford Art Journal* 17. no. 2 (1994): 48–62.

Lizon, Peter. *The Palace of the Soviets*. Colorado Springs: Three Continents Press, 1995.

Lovell, Stephen. *The Shadow of War. Russia and the USSR, 1941 to the Present*. Oxford: Wiley-Blackwell, 2010.

——— *Summerfolk: A History of the Dacha, 1710–2000*. Ithaca: Cornell University Press, 2003.

McCannon, John. "To Storm the Arctic: Soviet Polar Exploration and Public Visions of Nature in the USSR, 1932–1939." *Cultural Geographies* 2, no. 1 (1995): 15–31.

McKellar, Elizabeth. *Landscapes of London: The City, the Country and the Suburbs, 1660–1840*. New Haven: Yale University Press, 2013.

Maddox, Steven. *Saving Stalin's Imperial City: Historic Preservation in Leningrad, 1930–1950*. Bloomington: Indiana University Press, 2015.

Magnúsdóttir, Rósa. *Enemy Number One: The United States of America in Soviet Ideology and Propaganda, 1945–1959*. Oxford: Oxford University Press, 2019.

Magazanik, Marina. "'Moskovskoe getto' (po materialam vystavki 'Zariad'e—iz proshlogo v budushchee' v Muzee Moskvy." In *Studies in Jewish History and Culture: Proceedings of the Twenty-Second Annual International Conference on Jewish Studies*, no. 52 (2016): 327–345.

Manley, Rebecca. *To the Tashkent Station: Evacuation and Survival in the Soviet Union at War*. Ithaca and London: Cornell University Press, 2009.

——— "'Where should we settle the comrades next?" The adjudication of housing claims and the construction of the post-war order." In *Late Stalinist Russia: Society between Reconstruction and Reinvention*, edited by Juliane Fürst, 233–46. London: Routledge, 2006.

Markova, Elena V. *Vorkutinskie zametki katorzhanki "E-105."* Syktyvkar: Komi respublikanskii blagotvoritel'nyi obshchestvennyi fond zhertv politicheskikh repressii 'Pokaianie,' 2005.

Martin, Alexander M. *Enlightened Metropolis: Constructing Imperial Moscow, 1762–1855.* Oxford: Oxford University Press, 2013.

——— "Sewage and the City: Filth, Smell, and Representations of Urban Life in Moscow, 1770–1880." *The Russian Review* 67 (April 2008): 243–274.

Martin, Lindsey A. "Policing and the Creation of an Early Modern City: Moscow under Catherine the Great, 1762–1796." PhD dissertation, Stanford University, 2015.

Mazanik, Anna. "The City as a Transient Home: Residential Patterns of Moscow Workers Around the Turn of the Twentieth Century." *Urban History* 40, 1 (2013): 51–70.

Merridale, Catherine. *Red Fortress: History and Illusion in the Kremlin.* New York: Metropolitan Books, 2013.

Miller, Mikhail. *Archaeology in the USSR.* New York: Frederick A. Praeger Publishers, 1956.

Morshed, Adnan. *Impossible Heights: Skyscrapers, Flight, and the Master Builder.* Minneapolis: University of Minnesota Press, 2015.

Muller, Edward K. "Downtown Pittsburgh: Renaissance and Renewal." In *A Geographic Perspective of Pittsburgh and the Alleghenies,* edited by Kevin J. Patrick and Joseph L. Scarpaci, Jr., 7–20. Pittsburgh: University of Pittsburgh Press, 2006.

Mumford, Eric Paul. *The CIAM Discourse on Urbanism.* Cambridge: MIT Press, 2000.

Murawski, Michał. *The Palace Complex: A Stalinist Skyscraper, Capitalist Warsaw, and a City Transfixed.* Bloomington: Indiana University Press, 2019.

Neumann, Tracy. *Remaking the Rust Belt: The Postindustrial Transformation of North America.* Philadelphia: University of Pennsylvania Press, 2016.

Nicholas, Mary. *Writers at Work: Russian Production Novels and the Construction of Soviet Culture.* Lewisburg: Bucknell University Press, 2010.

Olson, Donald J. *The City as a Work of Art: London, Paris, Vienna.* New Haven: Yale University Press, 1986.

O'Mahony, Mike. "Archaeological Fantasies: Constructing History on the Moscow Metro." *The Modern Language Review* 98, no. 1 (2003): 138–150.

Overy, Richard J. *Why the Allies Won.* New York: W.W. Norton, 1995.

Papernyi, Vladimir. *Architecture in the Age of Stalin: Culture Two.* Cambridge: Cambridge University Press, 2011.

——— *Kul'tura Dva.* Moscow: Novoe literaturnoe obozrenie, 2011.

Patti, Federica. "Boris Iofan in Rome: professional training, contacts, designs, and realised buildings, between 1914 and 1924." In *Boris Iofan: Architect behind the Palace of the Soviets,* edited by Maria Kostyuk, 12–21. Moscow: Dom Publishers, 2019.

Petrone, Karen. *Life Has Become More Joyous, Comrades: Celebrations in the Time of Stalin.* Bloomington: Indiana University Press, 2000.

Plamper, Jan. *The Stalin Cult: A Study in the Alchemy of Power.* Stanford/New Haven: Stanford University/Yale University Press, 2012.

Pollock, Ethan. *Stalin and the Soviet Science Wars.* Princeton: Princeton University Press, 2006.

Potemkina, M. N. *Evakonaselenie v Ural'skom tylu (1941–1948 gg.).* Magnitogorsk: Magnitogorskii gosudarstvennyi universitet, 2006.

Qualls, Karl. *From Ruins to Reconstruction: Urban Identity in Soviet Sevastopol after World War II.* Ithaca: Cornell University Press, 2009.

Rabinovich, Mikhail and G. Latysheva. *Iz zhizni drevnei Moskvy.* Moscow: Moskovskii rabochii, 1961.

Reed, Peter S. "Enlisting Modernism," In *World War II and the American Dream: How Wartime Building Changed a Nation,* edited by Donald Albrecht, 2–41. Cambridge: MIT Press, 1995.

Rees, E. A. *Iron Lazar: A Political Biography of Lazar Kaganovich.* New York: Anthem Press, 2012.

Reid, Susan E. "Photography in the Thaw." *Art Journal* 53, no. 2 (1994): 33–39.

——— "Toward a New (Socialist) Realism: The Re-engagement with Western Modernism in the Khrushchev Thaw." In *Russian Art and the West: A Century of Dialogue in Painting, Architecture, and the Decorative Arts,* edited by Rosalind P. Blakesley and Susan E. Reid, 217–239. DeKalb: Northern Illinois University Press, 2007.

Rolf, Malte. "A Hall of Mirrors: Sovietizing Culture under Stalinism." *Slavic Review* 68, no. 3, (2009): 601–630.

Ropes, E. C. "American-Soviet Trade Relations." *Russian Review* 3, no. 1,(1943): 89–94.

Rosenberg, William G. "NEP Russia as a 'Transitional' Society." In *Russia in the Era of NEP: Explorations in Soviet Society and Culture*, edited by Sheila Fitzpatrick, Alexander Rabinowitch, and Richard Stites, 1–11. Bloomington: Indiana University Press, 1991.

Ruble, Blair A. *Second Metropolis: Pragmatic Pluralism in Gilded Age Chicago, Silver Age Moscow, and Meiji Osaka*. Cambridge, UK: Cambridge University Press, 2001.

Ruder, Cynthia. *Building Stalinism: The Moscow Canal and the Creation of Soviet Space*. London: Bloomsbury Publishing, 2018.

Ruscitti Harshman, Deirdre. "A Space Called Home: Housing and the Management of the Everyday in Russia, 1890–1935." PhD dissertation, University of Illinois at Urbana-Champaign, 2018.

Rüthers, Monica. "The Moscow Gorky Street in late Stalinism." In *Late Stalinist Russia: Society between Reconstruction and Reinvention*, edited by Juliane Fürst, 247–269. London: Routledge, 2006.

Sanchez-Sibony, Oscar. *Red Globalization: The Political Economy of the Soviet Cold War from Stalin to Khrushchev*. Cambridge: Cambridge University Press, 2014.

Schlögel, Karl. *Moscow*. London: Reaktion Books, 2005.

Sedov, Vladimir and Sarkisyan, David. *Les sept tours de Moscou, 1935–1950: les tours babyloniennes du communisme*. Bruxelles: Europalia International, 2005.

Schmidt, Albert J. *The Architecture and Planning of Classical Moscow: A Cultural History*. Philadelphia: American Philosophical Society, 1989.

Sevast'ianov, Iu. I. "Moskovskie stroiteli v velikoi otechestvennoi voine." *Voprosy istorii,* no. 11 (1970): 34–43.

Shanken, Andrew. *194X: Architecture, Planning, and Consumer Culture on the American Home Front*. Minneapolis: University of Minnesota Press, 2009.

Shearer, David. "Elements Near and Alien: Passportization, Policing, and Identity in the Stalinist State, 1932–1952." *The Journal of Modern History* 76, no. 4 (2004): 835–881.

———— "The Soviet Gulag—an Archipelago?" *Kritika* 16, 3 (Summer 2015): 711–724.

Shields Kollmann, Nancy. *By Honor Bound: State and Society in Early Modern Russia*. Ithaca: Cornell University Press, 1999.

Shneer, David. *Through Soviet Jewish Eyes: Photography, War, and the Holocaust*. New Brunswick, New Jersey, and London: Rutgers University Press, 2011.

Siegelbaum, Lewis. "The Shaping of Soviet Workers' Leisure: Workers' Clubs and Palaces of Culture in the 1930s." *International Labor and Working-Class History,* no. 56 (Fall 1999): 78–92.

———— *Stakhanovism and the Politics of Productivity in the USSR, 1935–1941*. Cambridge: Cambridge University Press, 1988.

Sklair, Leslie. *The Icon Project: Architecture, Cities, and Capitalist Globalization*. Oxford: Oxford University Press, 2017.

Slezkine, Yuri. *Arctic Mirrors: Russia and the Small Peoples of the North*. Ithaca: Cornell University Press, 1994.

———— *The House of Government: A Saga of the Russian Revolution*. Princeton: Princeton University Press, 2017.

———— *The Jewish Century*. Princeton: Princeton University Press, 2004.

Smith, Kathleen. *Mythmaking in the New Russia: Politics and Memory during the Yeltsin Era*. Ithaca: Cornell University Press, 2002.

Smith, Mark B. 'Individual Forms of Ownership in the Urban Housing Fund of the USSR, 1944–64'. *Slavonic and East European Review*, 86, 2 (2008), 283–305.

———— *Property of Communists: The Urban Housing Program from Stalin to Khrushchev*. DeKalb: Northern Illinois University Press, 2010.

Solopova, Natalya. "La Préfabrication en URSS: Concept Technique et Dispositifs Architecturaux." PhD dissertation, Université de Paris VIII, 2001.

Stahel, David. *Operation Typhoon: Hitler's March on Moscow, October 1941*. Cambridge: Cambridge University Press, 2013.

Stites, Richard. *Revolutionary Dreams: Utopian Vision and Experimental Life in the Russian Revolution*. Oxford: Oxford University Press, 1989.

Stolarski, Christopher. "The Rise of Photojournalism in Russia and the Soviet Union, 1900–1931." PhD Dissertation, Johns Hopkins University, 2013.

Sutton, Antony. *Western Technology and Soviet Economic Development, 1917–1930*. Stanford, CA: Stanford University Press, 1968.

Suzuki, Yuya. "Konkurs na dvorets sovetov 1930-x gg. v Moskve i mezhdunarodnyi arkhitekturnyi kontekst." PhD dissertation, State Institute for the Study of Art, Moscow, 2014.

Swift, Anthony. "The Soviet World of Tomorrow at the New York World's Fair, 1939." *The Russian Review* 57 (July 1998): 364–79.

Szelenyi, Ivan. *Urban Inequalities under State Socialism*. Oxford: Oxford University Press, 1983.

Taubman, William. *Khrushchev: The Man and His Era*. New York: W.W. Norton & Company, 2003.

Tikhonov, Aleksei and Paul R. Gregory. "Stalin's Last Plan." In *Behind the Facade of Stalin's Command Economy: Evidence from the Soviet State and Party Archives*, edited by Paul R. Gregory, 159–192. Stanford: Hoover Institution Press, 2001.

Trigger, Bruce. "Monumental Architecture: A Thermodynamic Explanation of Symbolic Behavior." *World Archaeology* 22 (1990): 119–132.

Tromly, Benjamin. *Making the Soviet Intelligentsia: Universities and Intellectual Life under Stalin and Khrushchev*. Cambridge: Cambridge University Press, 2013.

Tsepkalova, A. A. "Glavpromstroi v sisteme Gulaga: ekonomika prinuditel'nogo truda na 'Velikikh stroikakh kommunizma'." In *Ekonomicheskaia istoriia. Ezhegodnik 2008*. Moscow: Rosspen, 2009: 258–296.

Udovički-Selb, Danilo. "Between Modernism and Socialist Realism: Soviet Architectural Culture under Stalin's Revolution from Above, 1928–1938." *Journal of the Society of Architectural Historians* 68, no. 4 (2009): 467–495.

Varga-Harris, Christine. "Green is the Colour of Hope? The Crumbling Façade of Postwar *Byt* through the Public Eyes of *Vecherniaia Moskva*." *Canadian Journal of History* 34 (1999): 193–219.

——— *Stories of House and Home: Soviet Apartment Life during the Khrushchev Years*. Ithaca: Cornell University Press, 2015.

Vas'kin, A. A. and Nazarenko, Iu. I. *Stalinskie neboskreby: ot Dvortsa Sovetov k vysotnym zdaniiam*. Moscow: Sputnik+, 2011.

Viola, Lynne, "The Aesthetic of Stalinist Planning and the World of the Special Villages." *Kritika* 4, no. 1 (2003): 101–128.

——— "Historicising the Gulag." In *Global Convict Labour*, edited by Christian Giuseppe De Vito and Alex Lichtenstein, 361–379. Leiden: Brill, 2015.

von Geldern, James. "Putting the Masses in Mass Culture: Bolshevik Festivals, 1918–1920." *Journal of Popular Culture* 31, no. 4 (1998): 123–144.

Vronskaya, Alla G. "Urbanist Landscape: Militsa Prokhorova, Liubov' Zalesskaia, and the emergence of Soviet landscape architecture." In *Women, Modernity, and Landscape Architecture,* edited by Sonja Dümpelmann and John Beardsley, 60–80. London: Routledge, 2015.

Vyazemtseva, Anna G. "The Transformation of Rome and the Masterplan to Reconstruct Moscow: Historical Heritage between Modernity, Memory, and Ideology." In *Townscapes in Transition: Transformation and Reorganization of Italian Cities and Their Architecture in the Interwar Period*. Edited by Carmen M. Enss and Luigi Monzo, 113–126. New York: Columbia University Press, 2019.

Weiner, Amir. *Making Sense of War: The Second World War and the Fate of the Bolshevik Revolution*. Princeton: Princeton University Press, 2010.

Werth, Alexander. *Russia at War, 1941–1945*. New York: Carroll & Graf Publishers, Inc., 1964.

Willimott, Andy. *Living the Revolution: Urban Communes & Soviet Socialism, 1917–1932*. Oxford: Oxford University Press, 2019.

Wortman, Richard. *Scenarios of Power: Myth and Ceremony in Russian Monarchy from Peter the Great to the Abdication of Nicholas II*. Princeton: Princeton University Press, 2006.

Yekelchyk, Serhy. *Stalin's Citizens: Everyday Politics in the Wake of Total War*. Oxford: Oxford University Press, 2014.

Zelnik, Reginald E. *Labor and Society in Tsarist Russia*. Palo Alto: Stanford University Press, 1971.

Zimmerman, Claire. "Building the World Capitalist System: The 'Invisible Architecture' of Albert Kahn Associates of Detroit, 1900–1961." *Fabrications* 29, no. 2 (2019): 231–256.

Zipp, Samuel. *Manhattan Projects: The Rise and Fall of Urban Renewal in Cold War New York*. Oxford: Oxford University Press, 2010.

Zubkova, Elena. *Russia After the War: Hopes, Illusions, and Disappointments, 1945–1957*. Armonk, NY: M.E. Sharpe, 1998.

Zubovich, Katherine. "'Debating Democracy': The International Union of Architects and the Cold War Politics of Architectural Expertise." *Room One Thousand* 4 (2016): 103–116.

Index

Page numbers in *italics* indicate the presence of illustrations. Specific titles of works will be found under the author's name.